Shojo Beat

# Skip·Beat!

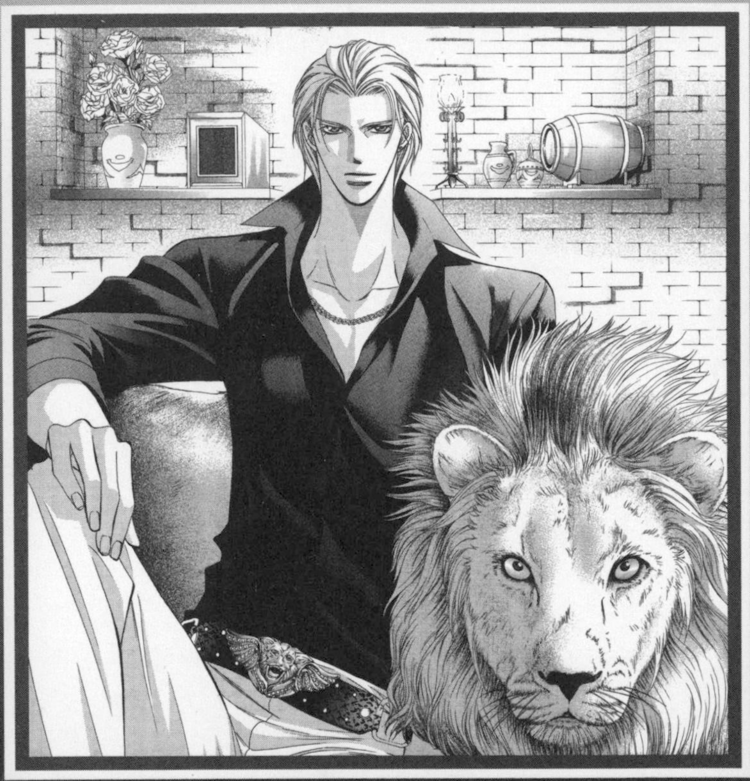

19

Story & Art by Yoshiki Nakamura

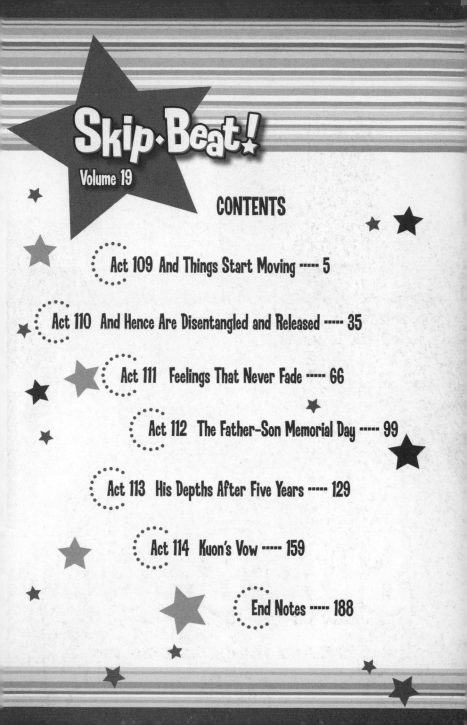

# Skip·Beat!
## Volume 19

## CONTENTS

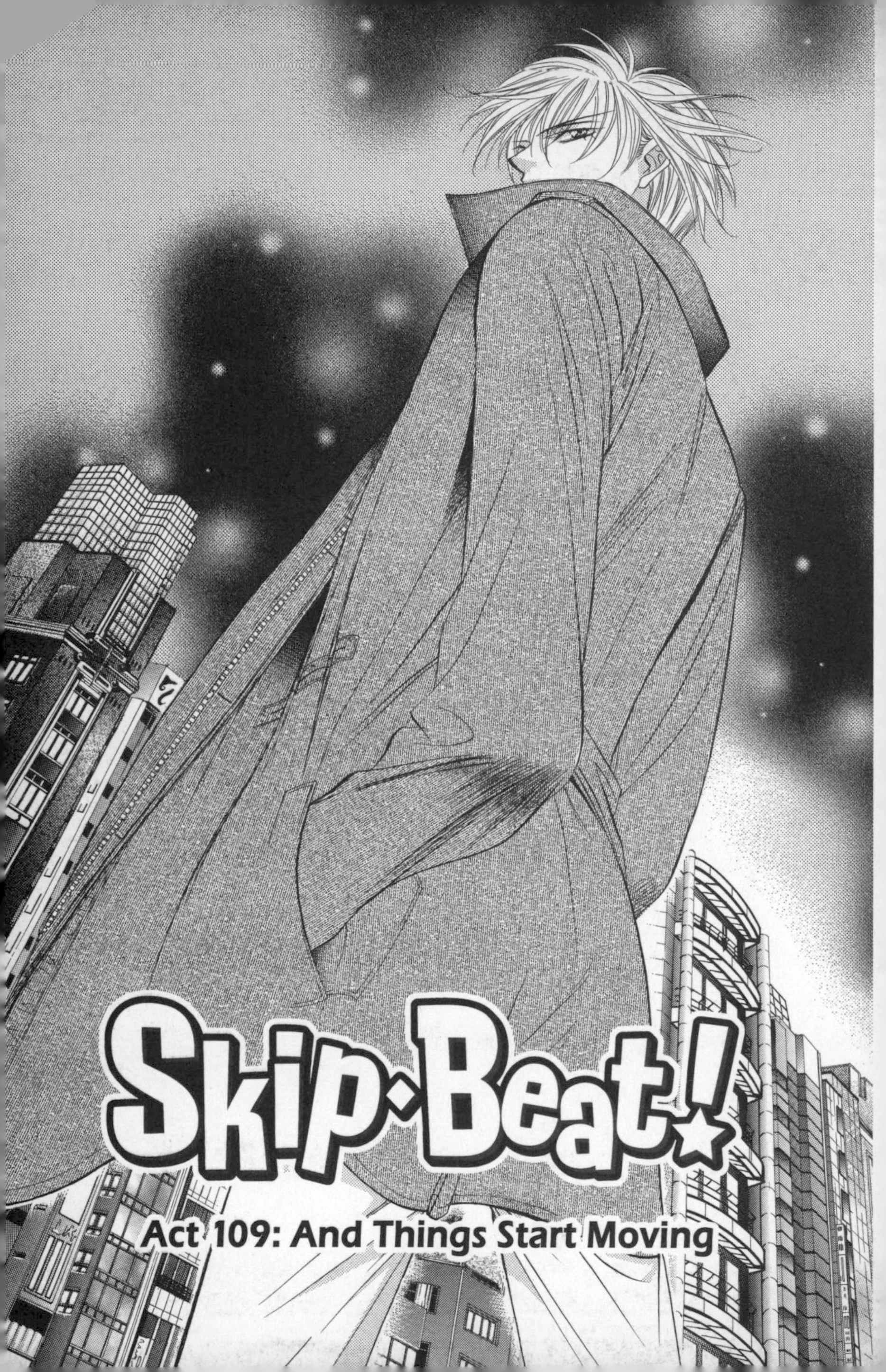
Skip·Beat!
Act 109: And Things Start Moving

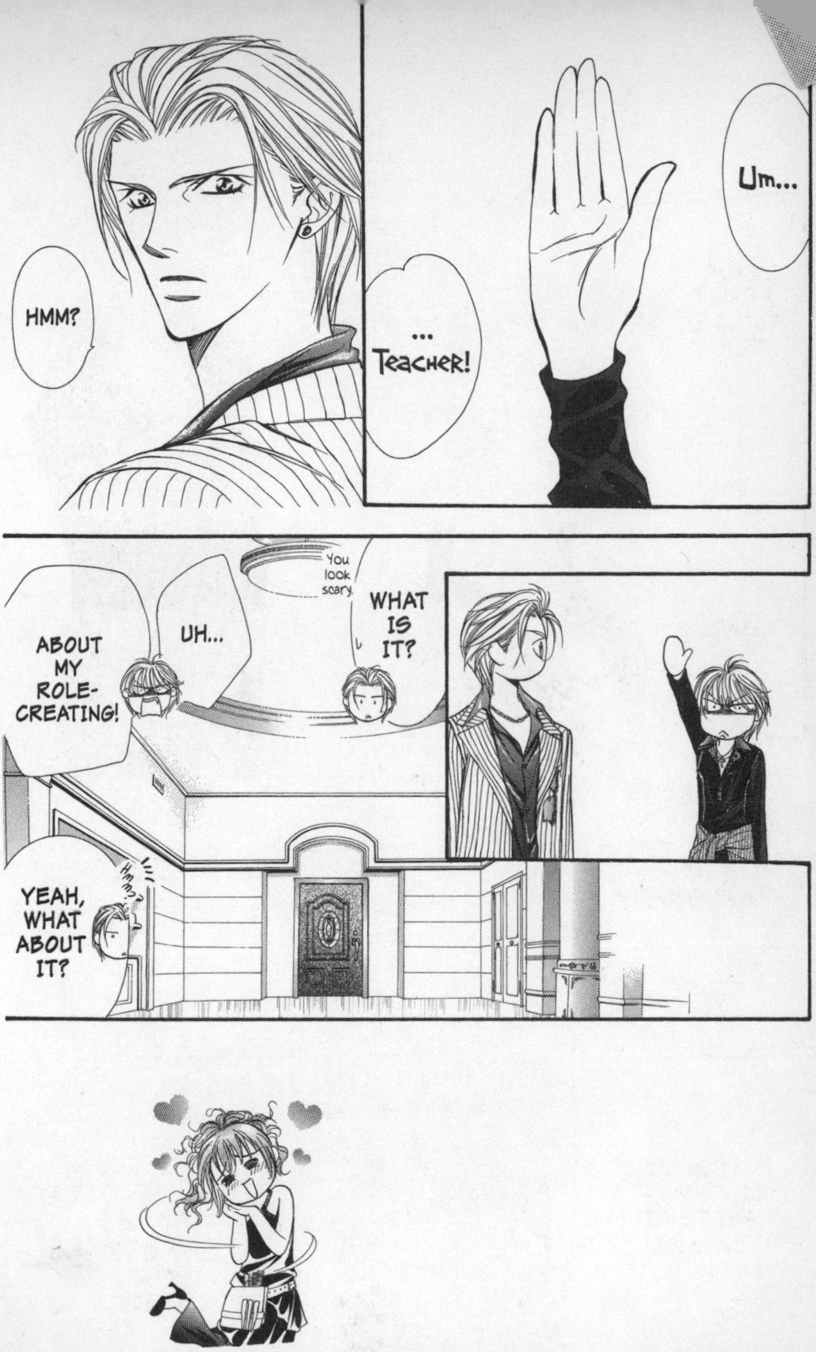
Um...
...Teacher!
HMM?
WHAT IS IT?
You look scary.
UH...
ABOUT MY ROLE-CREATING!
Hmm?
YEAH, WHAT ABOUT IT?

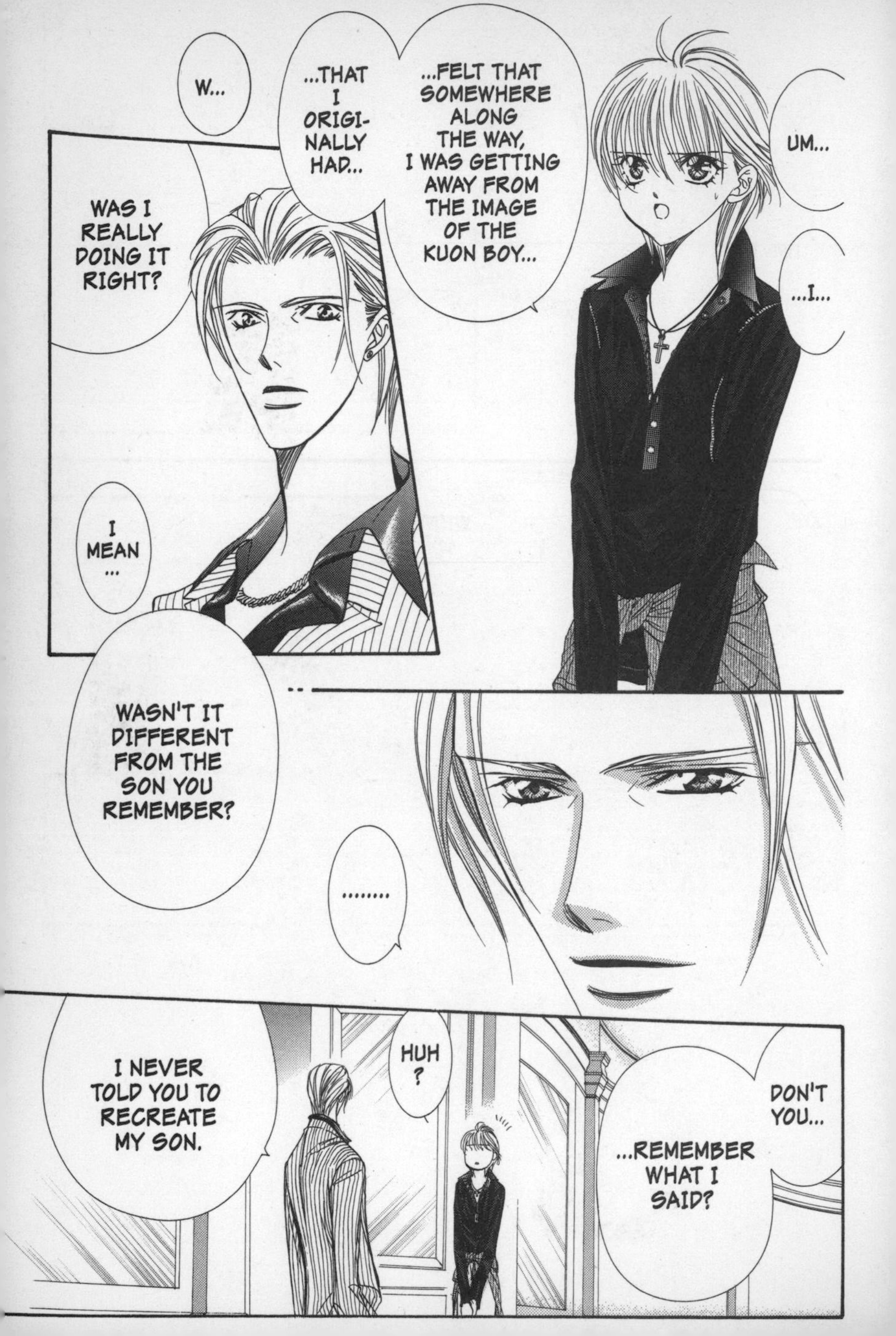
UM...
...I...
...FELT THAT SOMEWHERE ALONG THE WAY, I WAS GETTING AWAY FROM THE IMAGE OF THE KUON BOY...
...THAT I ORIGI-NALLY HAD...
W...
WAS I REALLY DOING IT RIGHT?
I MEAN ...
WASN'T IT DIFFERENT FROM THE SON YOU REMEMBER?
........
DON'T YOU...
...REMEMBER WHAT I SAID?
HUH?
I NEVER TOLD YOU TO RECREATE MY SON.

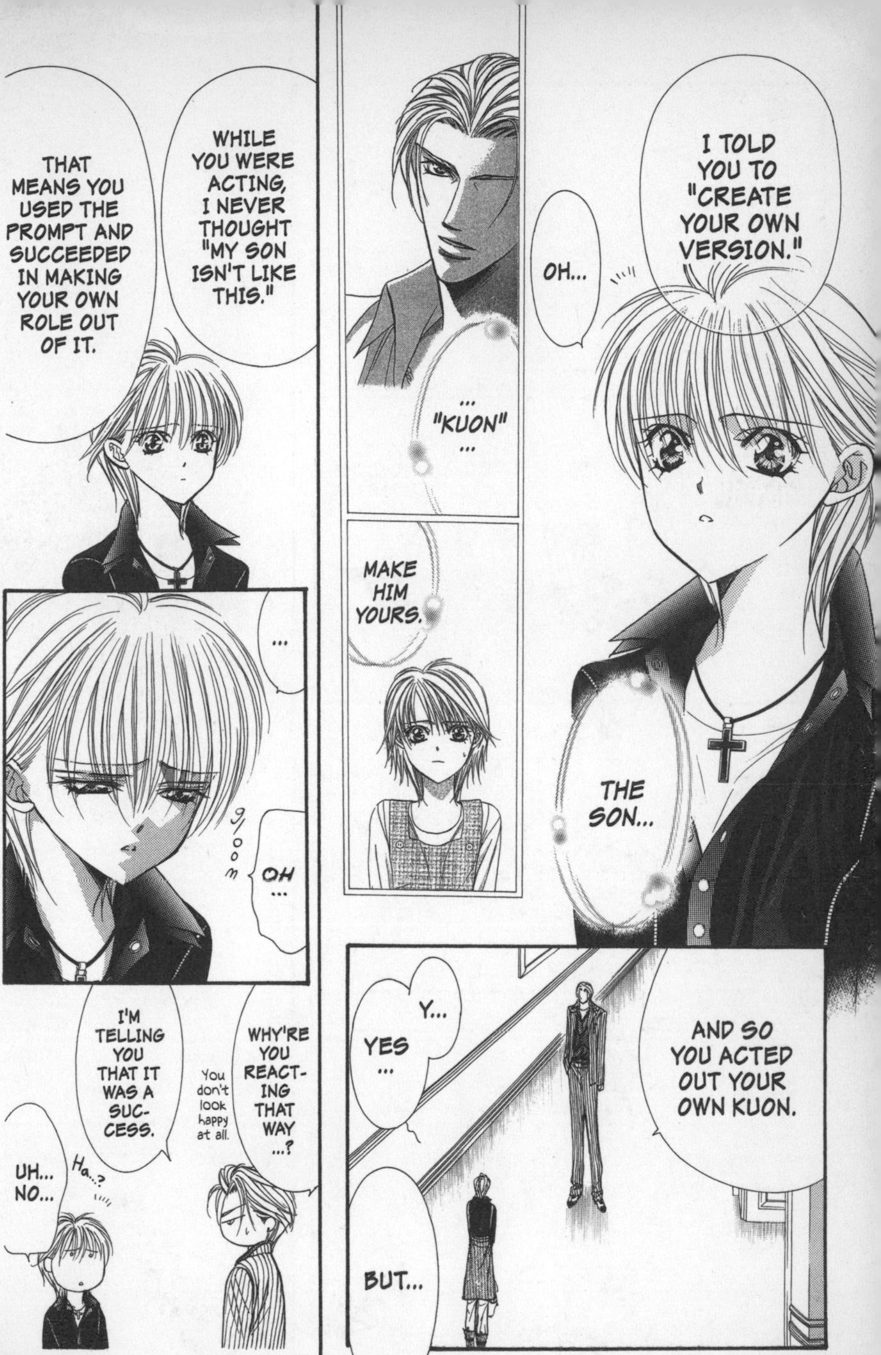
I TOLD YOU TO "CREATE YOUR OWN VERSION."
OH...
THE SON...
... "KUON" ...
MAKE HIM YOURS.
AND SO YOU ACTED OUT YOUR OWN KUON.
Y... YES...
BUT...
WHILE YOU WERE ACTING, I NEVER THOUGHT "MY SON ISN'T LIKE THIS."
THAT MEANS YOU USED THE PROMPT AND SUCCEEDED IN MAKING YOUR OWN ROLE OUT OF IT.
...
gloom
OH ...
WHY'RE YOU REACT-ING THAT WAY ...?
You don't look happy at all.
I'M TELLING YOU THAT IT WAS A SUC-CESS.
Ha..?
UH... NO...

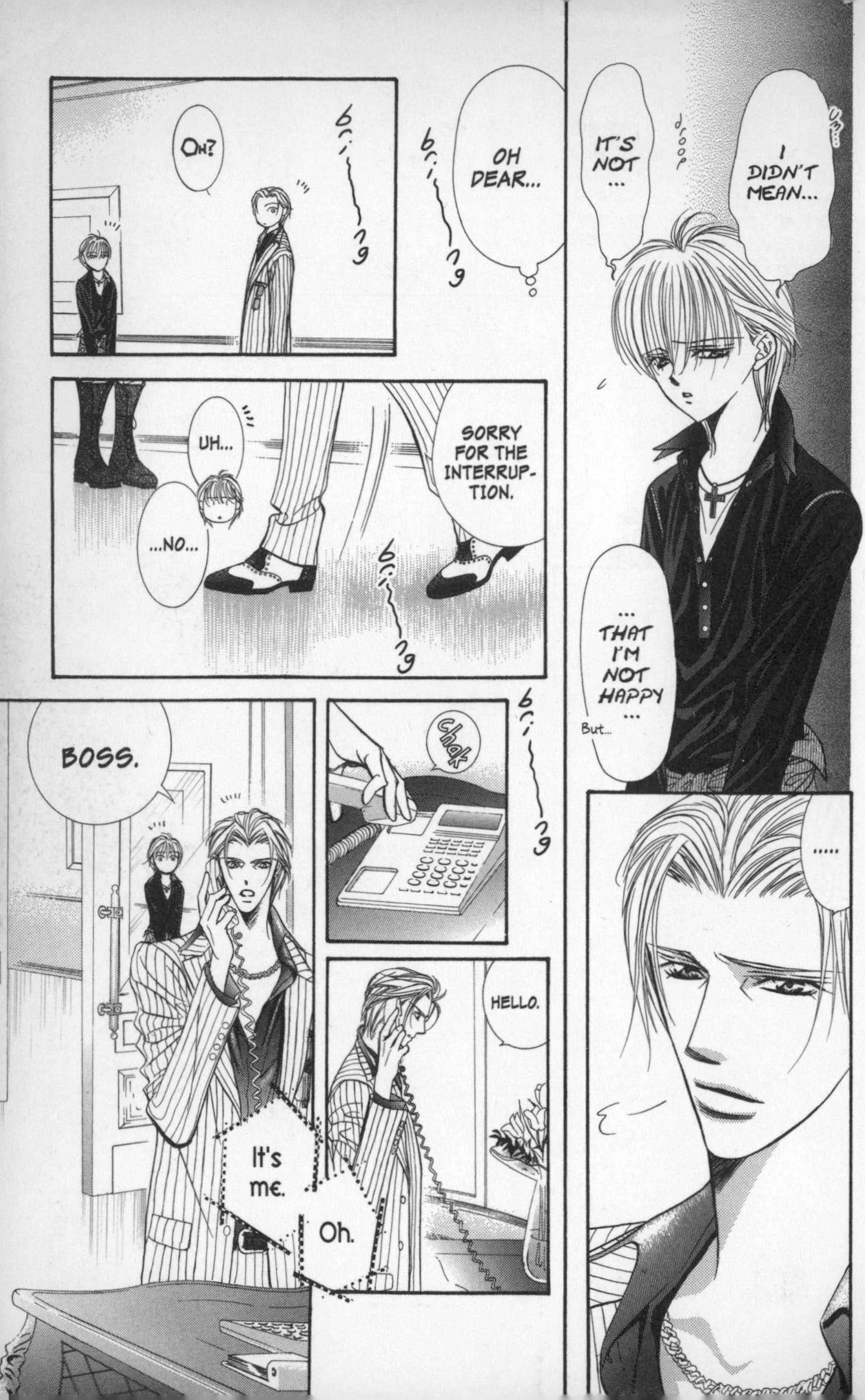
Um...
I DIDN'T MEAN...
droop
IT'S NOT ...
... THAT I'M NOT HAPPY ...
But...
.....
OH DEAR...
bri---ng
Oh?
bri---ng
SORRY FOR THE INTERRUP-TION.
bri---ng
UH...
...NO...
bri---ng
Chak
HELLO.
BOSS.
It's me.
Oh.

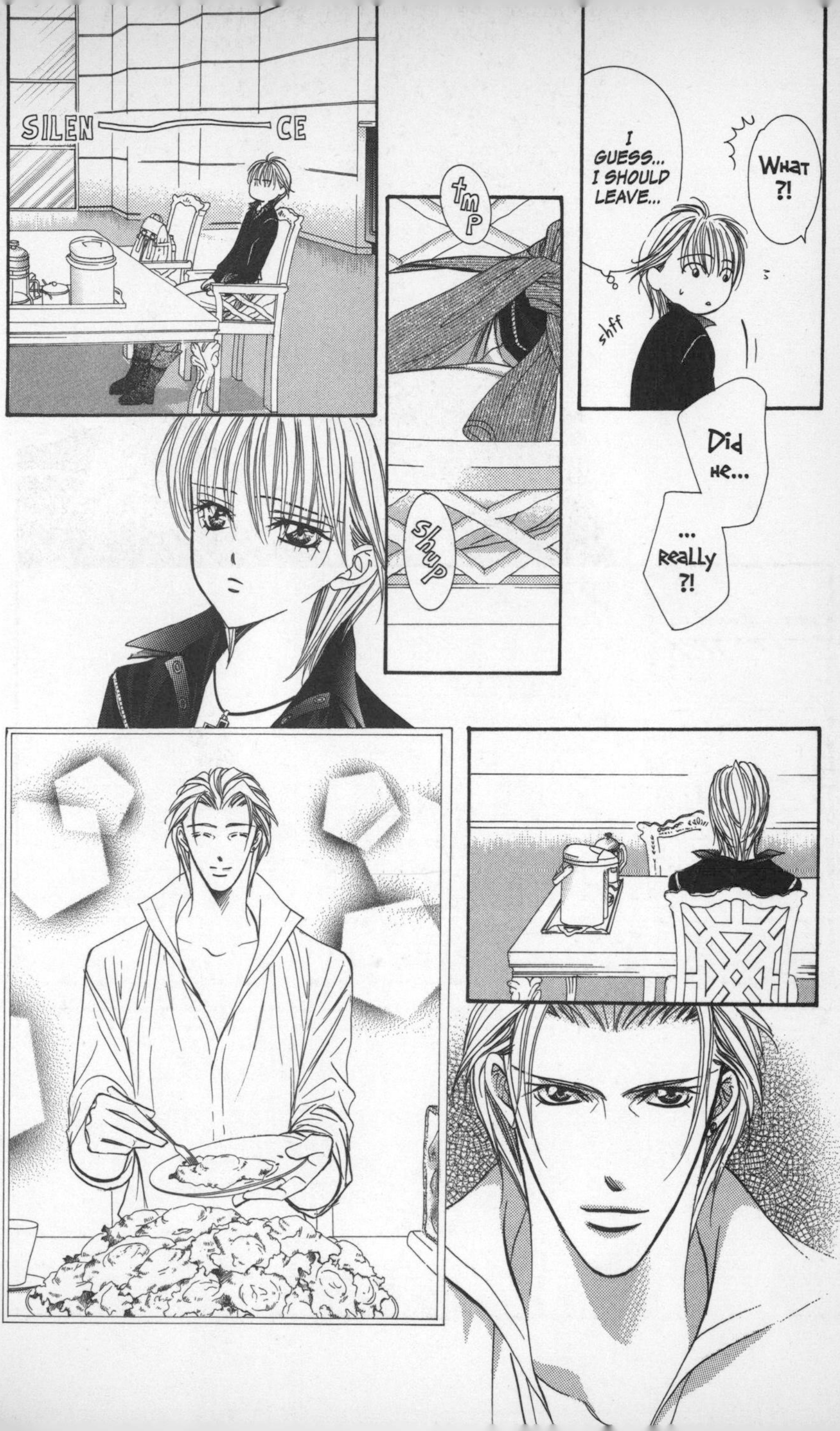
WHAT ?!
I GUESS... I SHOULD LEAVE...
shff
tmp
shup
Did he...
... really ?!
SILEN——CE

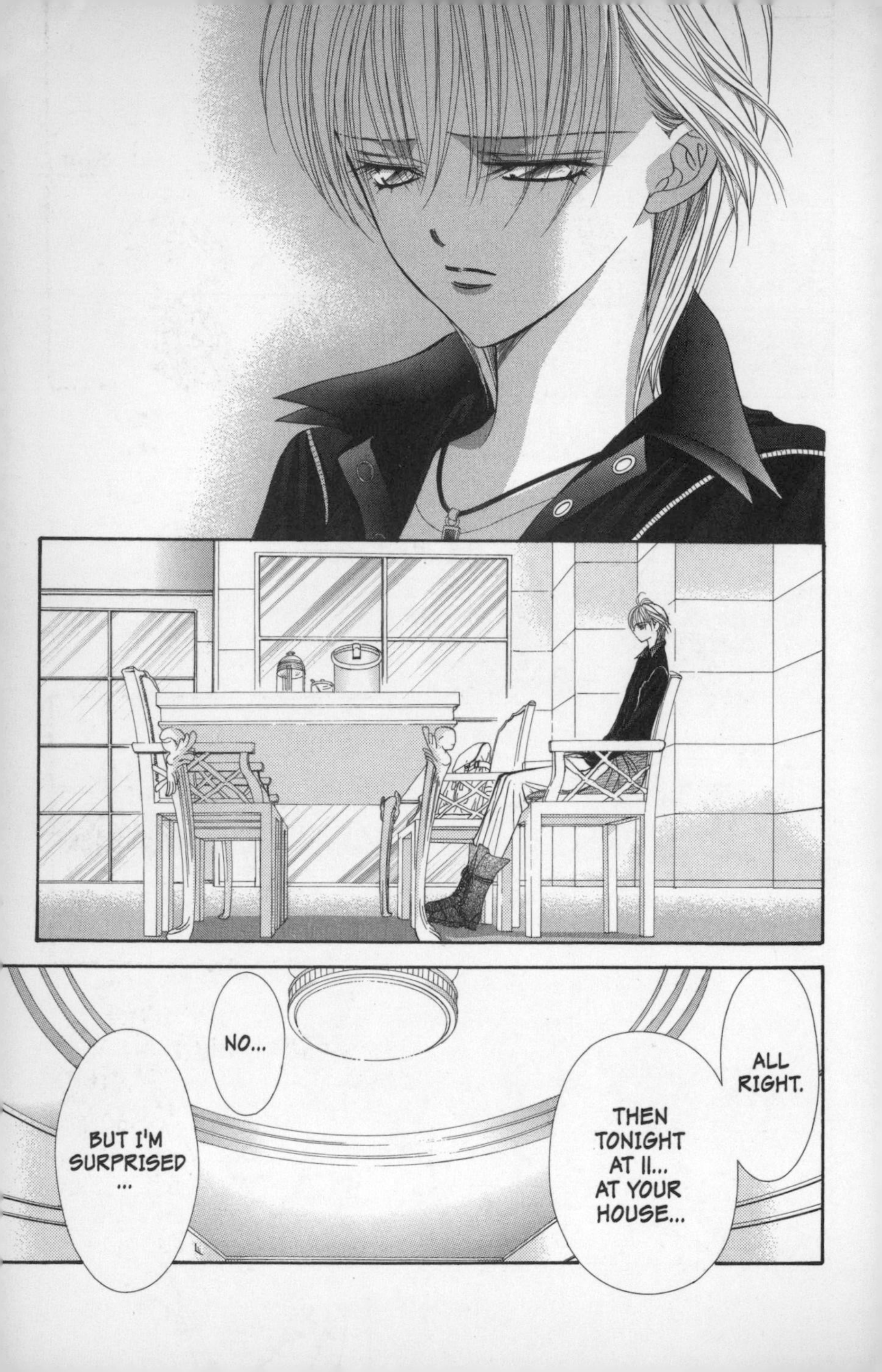
ALL RIGHT.
THEN TONIGHT AT 11... AT YOUR HOUSE...
NO...
BUT I'M SURPRISED ...

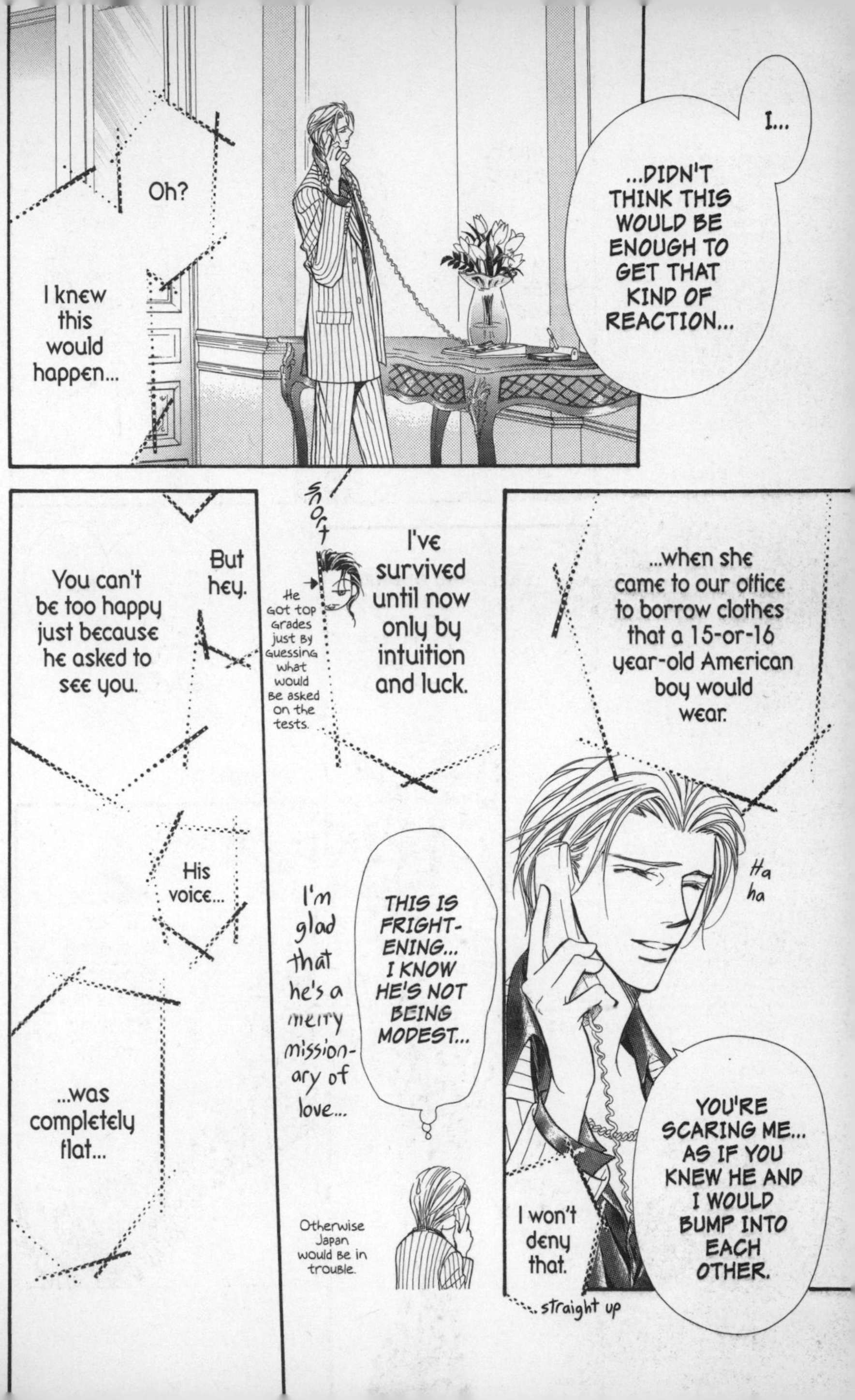
I...
...DIDN'T THINK THIS WOULD BE ENOUGH TO GET THAT KIND OF REACTION...
Oh?
I knew this would happen...
...when she came to our office to borrow clothes that a 15-or-16 year-old American boy would wear.
Ha ha
YOU'RE SCARING ME... AS IF YOU KNEW HE AND I WOULD BUMP INTO EACH OTHER.
I won't deny that.
straight up
snort
I've survived until now only by intuition and luck.
He got top grades just by guessing what would be asked on the tests.
THIS IS FRIGHTENING... I KNOW HE'S NOT BEING MODEST...
I'm glad that he's a merry missionary of love...
Otherwise Japan would be in trouble.
But hey.
You can't be too happy just because he asked to see you.
His voice...
...was completely flat...

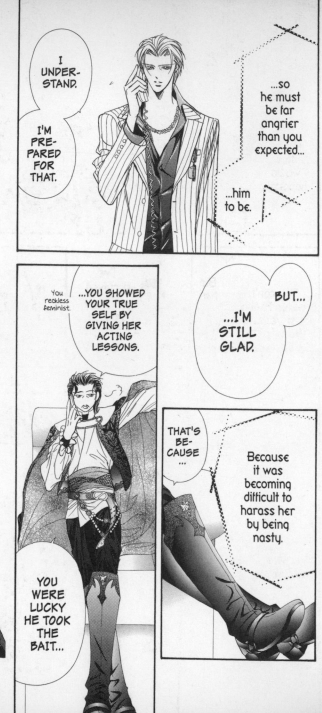

...so he must be far angrier than you expected...
...him to be.
I UNDER-STAND.
I'M PRE-PARED FOR THAT.
BUT...
...I'M STILL GLAD.
THAT'S BE-CAUSE ...
Because it was becoming difficult to harass her by being nasty.
...YOU SHOWED YOUR TRUE SELF BY GIVING HER ACTING LESSONS.
You reckless feminist.
YOU WERE LUCKY HE TOOK THE BAIT...

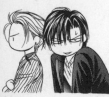

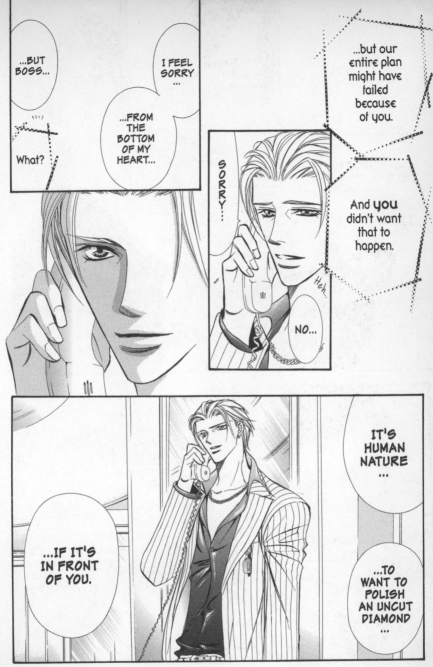

...but our entire plan might have failed because of you.
I FEEL SORRY ...
...FROM THE BOTTOM OF MY HEART...
...BUT BOSS...
What?
And you didn't want that to happen.
SORRY...
Heh...
NO...
IT'S HUMAN NATURE ...
...TO WANT TO POLISH AN UNCUT DIAMOND ...
...IF IT'S IN FRONT OF YOU.

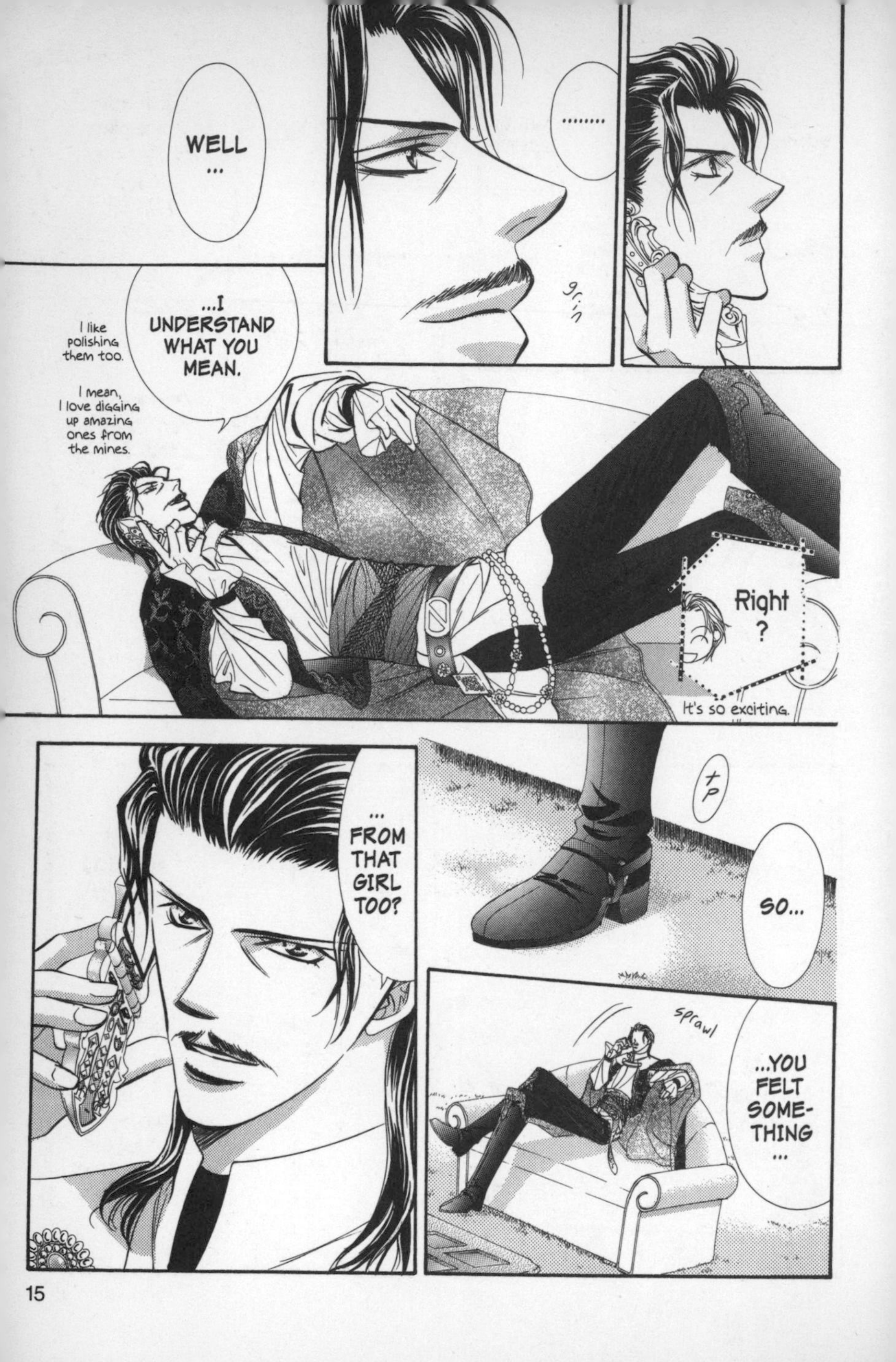

........
gr.in
WELL ...
Right ?
It's so exciting.
...I UNDERSTAND WHAT YOU MEAN.
I like polishing them too.
I mean, I love digging up amazing ones from the mines.
tp
SO...
sprawl
...YOU FELT SOMETHING ...
... FROM THAT GIRL TOO?

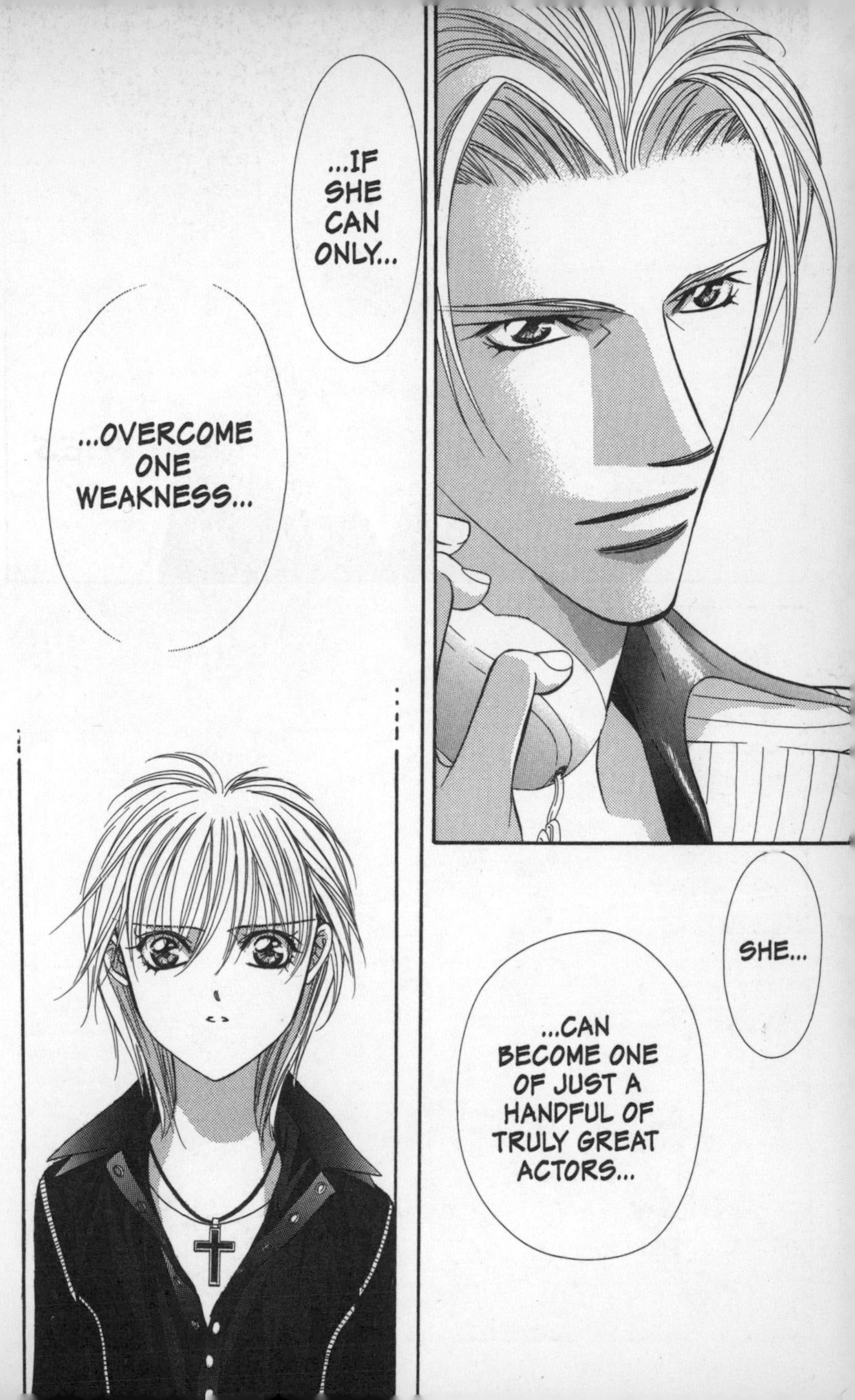
...IF SHE CAN ONLY...
...OVERCOME ONE WEAKNESS...
SHE...
...CAN BECOME ONE OF JUST A HANDFUL OF TRULY GREAT ACTORS...

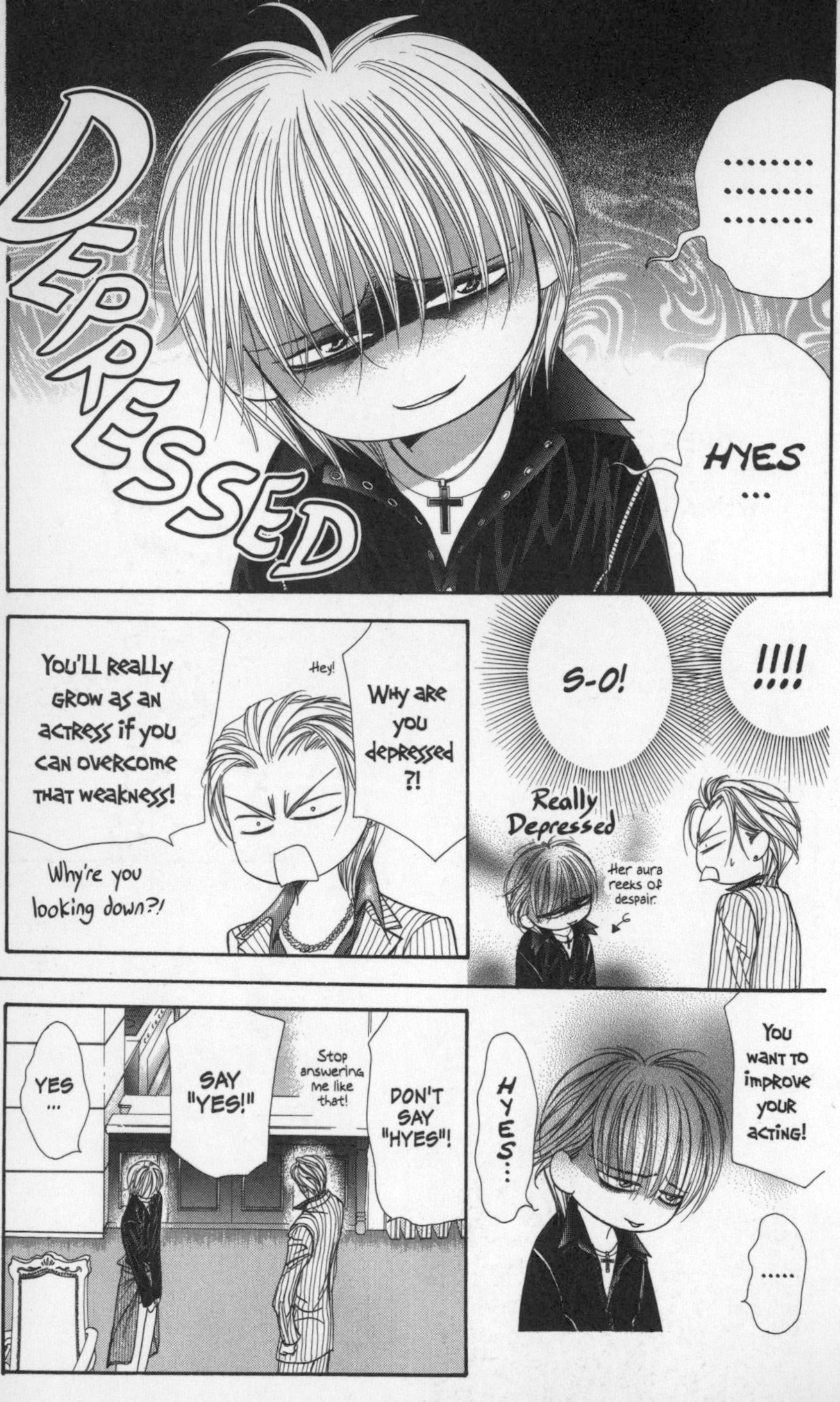

........ ........ ........
HYES ...
DEPRESSED
!!!!
S-O!
Really Depressed
Her aura reeks of despair.
Why are you depressed?!
Hey!
You'll really grow as an actress if you can overcome that weakness!
Why're you looking down?!
You want to improve your acting!
HYES...
.....
DON'T SAY "HYES"!
Stop answering me like that!
SAY "YES!"
YES ...

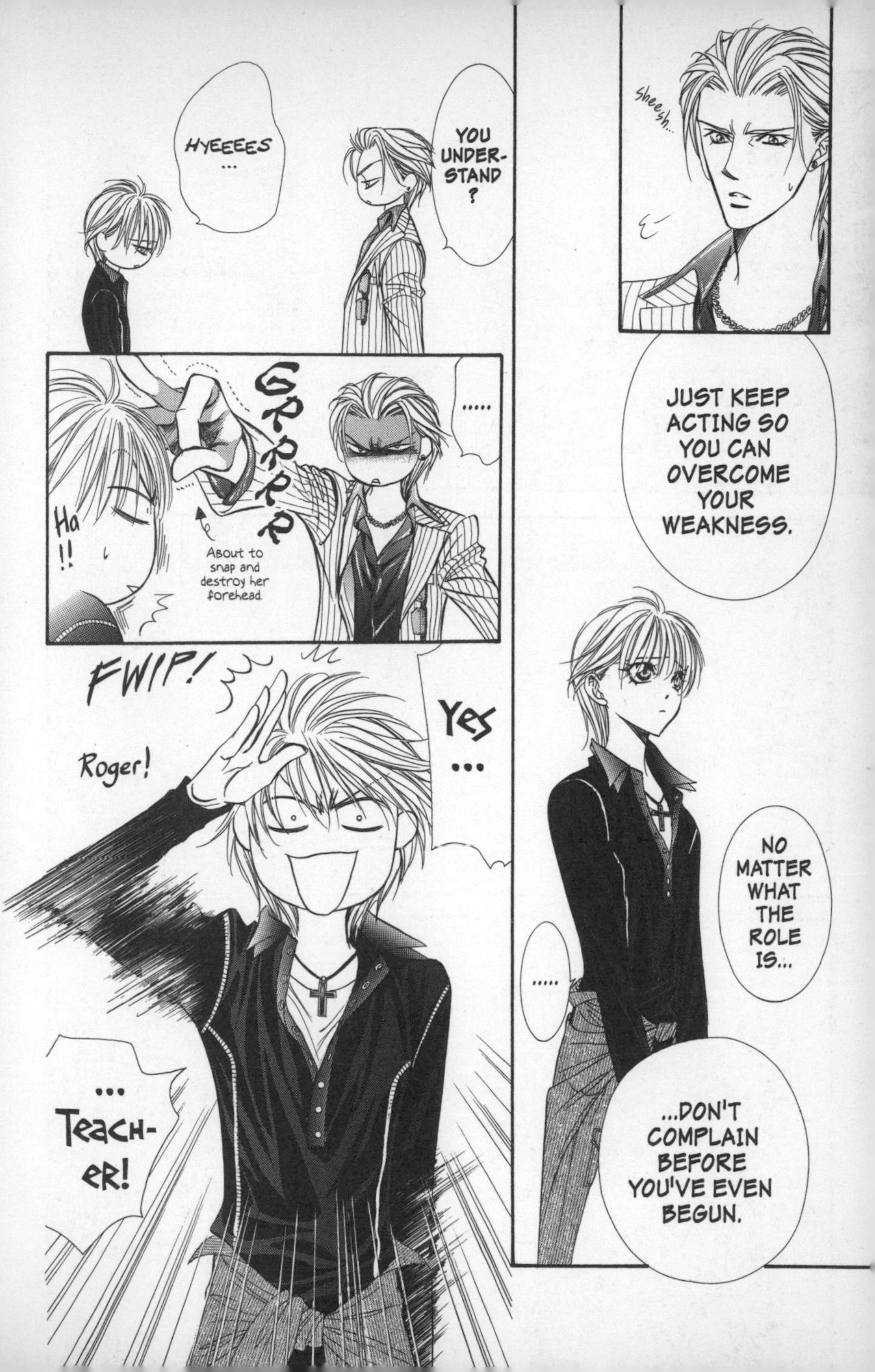
Sheesh...
JUST KEEP ACTING SO YOU CAN OVERCOME YOUR WEAKNESS.
NO MATTER WHAT THE ROLE IS...
.....
...DON'T COMPLAIN BEFORE YOU'VE EVEN BEGUN.
YOU UNDERSTAND?
HYEEEES...
.....
GRRRR
Ha!!
About to snap and destroy her forehead.
Yes...
FWIP!
Roger!
...Teacher!

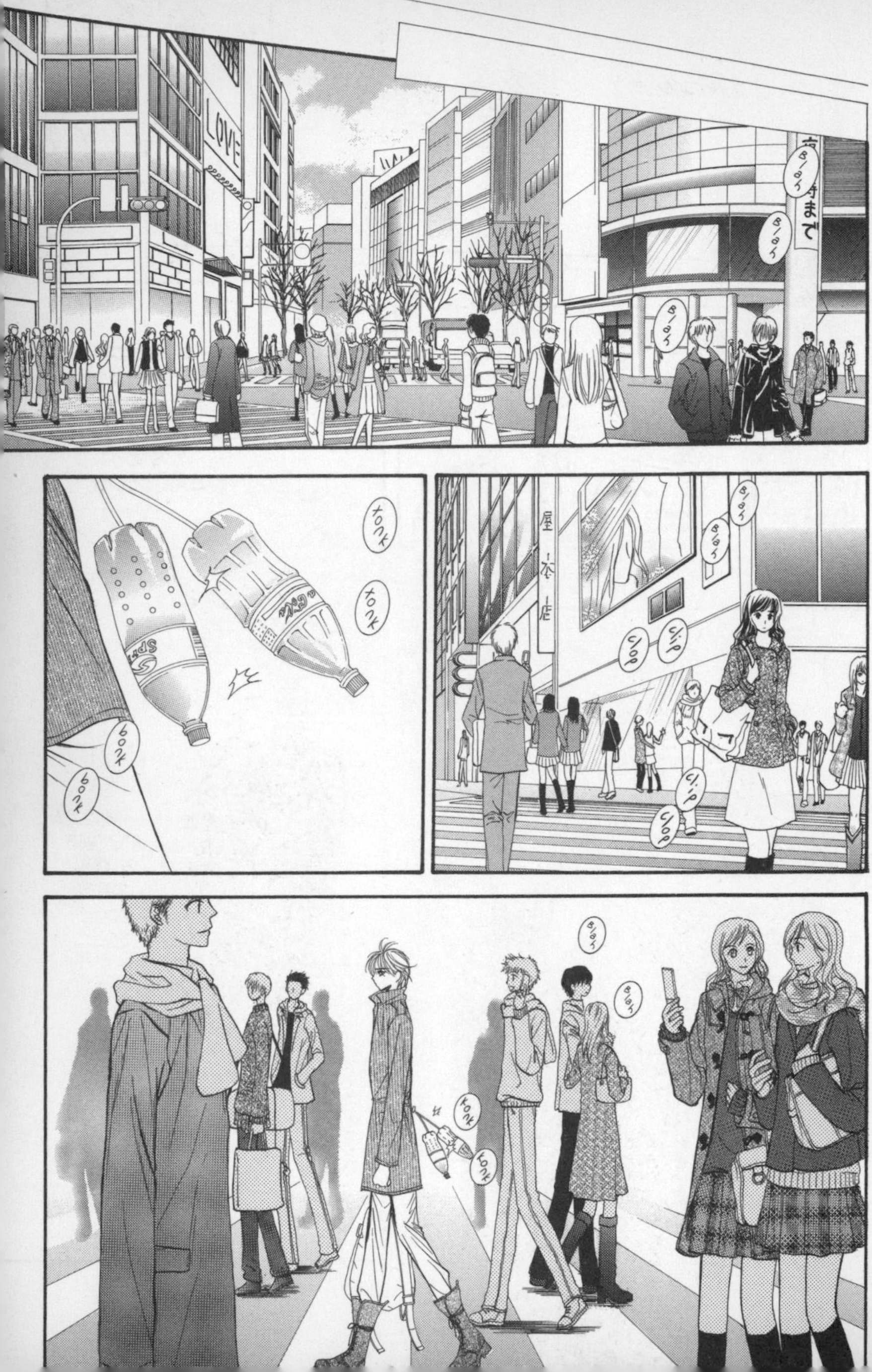
LOVE
Blah
Blah
Blah
Blah
Blah
Blah
clip
clop
clip
clop
klonk
klonk
bonk
bonk
Blah
Blah
klonk
klonk

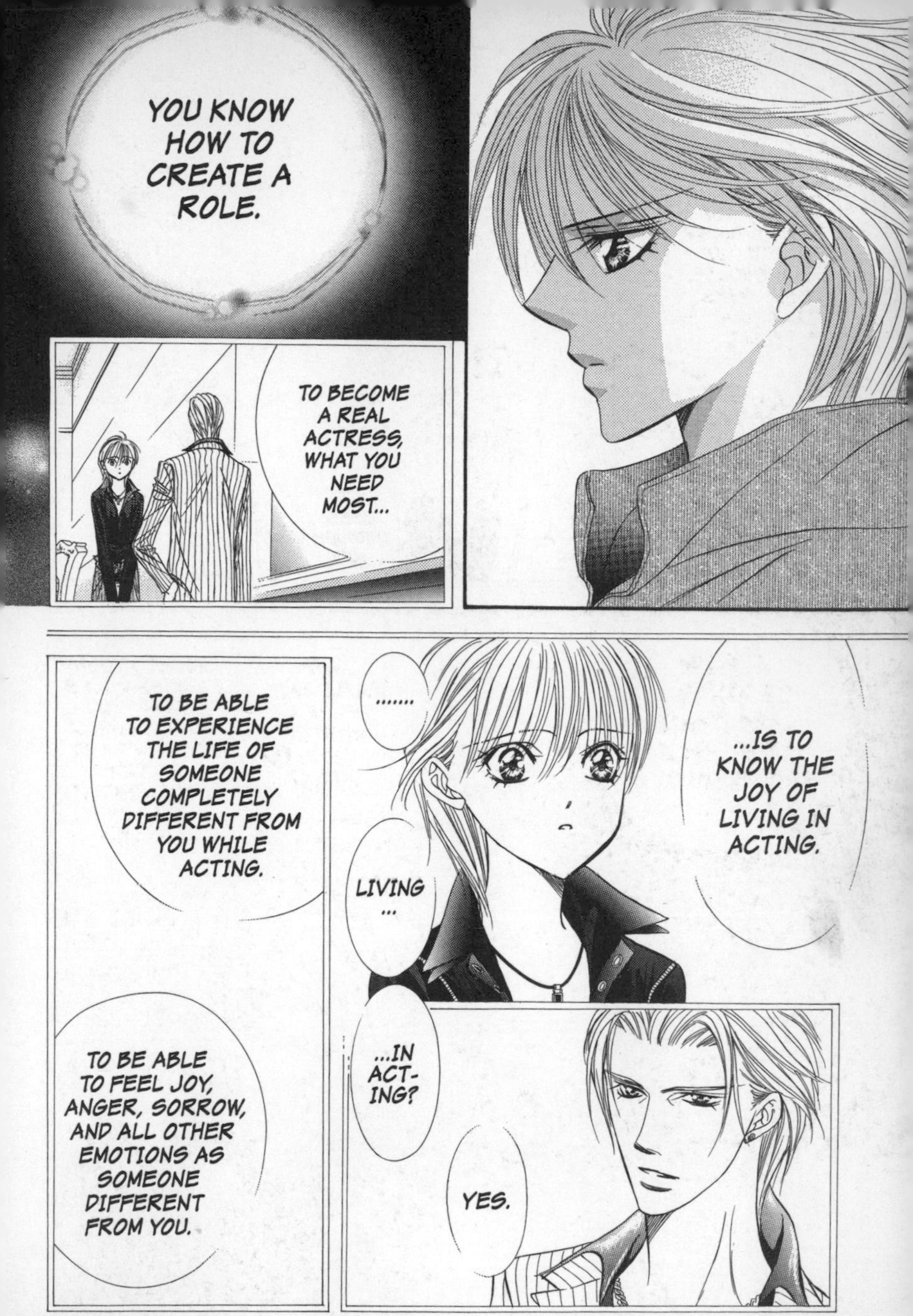
YOU KNOW HOW TO CREATE A ROLE.
TO BECOME A REAL ACTRESS, WHAT YOU NEED MOST...
...IS TO KNOW THE JOY OF LIVING IN ACTING.
.......
LIVING ...
...IN ACT-ING?
YES.
TO BE ABLE TO EXPERIENCE THE LIFE OF SOMEONE COMPLETELY DIFFERENT FROM YOU WHILE ACTING.
TO BE ABLE TO FEEL JOY, ANGER, SORROW, AND ALL OTHER EMOTIONS AS SOMEONE DIFFERENT FROM YOU.

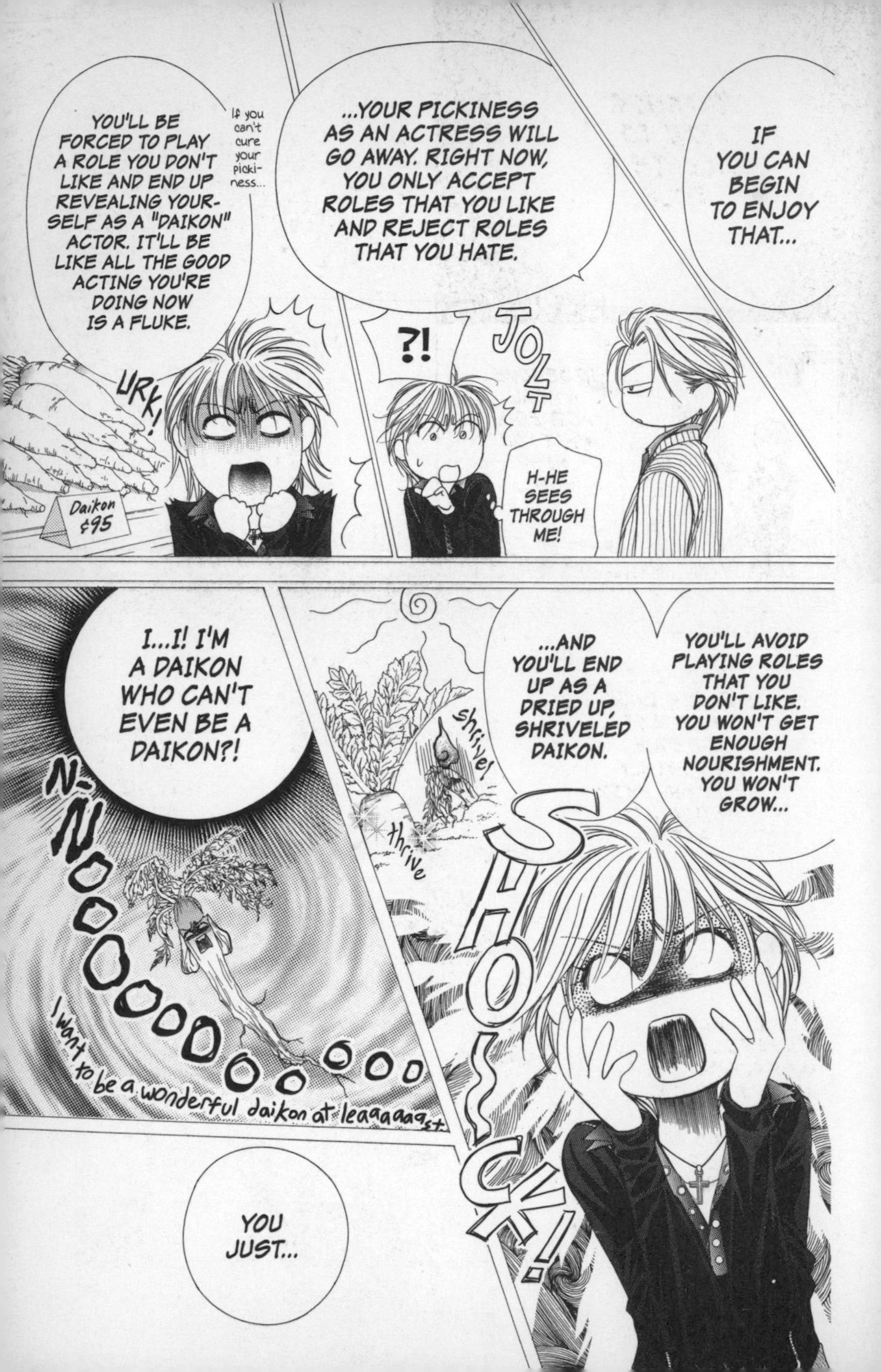
IF YOU CAN BEGIN TO ENJOY THAT...
...YOUR PICKINESS AS AN ACTRESS WILL GO AWAY. RIGHT NOW, YOU ONLY ACCEPT ROLES THAT YOU LIKE AND REJECT ROLES THAT YOU HATE.
JOLT
?!
H-HE SEES THROUGH ME!
If you can't cure your pickiness...
YOU'LL BE FORCED TO PLAY A ROLE YOU DON'T LIKE AND END UP REVEALING YOURSELF AS A "DAIKON" ACTOR. IT'LL BE LIKE ALL THE GOOD ACTING YOU'RE DOING NOW IS A FLUKE.
URK!
Daikon ¢95
YOU'LL AVOID PLAYING ROLES THAT YOU DON'T LIKE. YOU WON'T GET ENOUGH NOURISHMENT. YOU WON'T GROW...
...AND YOU'LL END UP AS A DRIED UP, SHRIVELED DAIKON.
shrivel
thrive
SHOCK!
I...I! I'M A DAIKON WHO CAN'T EVEN BE A DAIKON?!
N-NOOOOOOOOOO
I want to be a wonderful daikon at leaaaaaast.
YOU JUST...

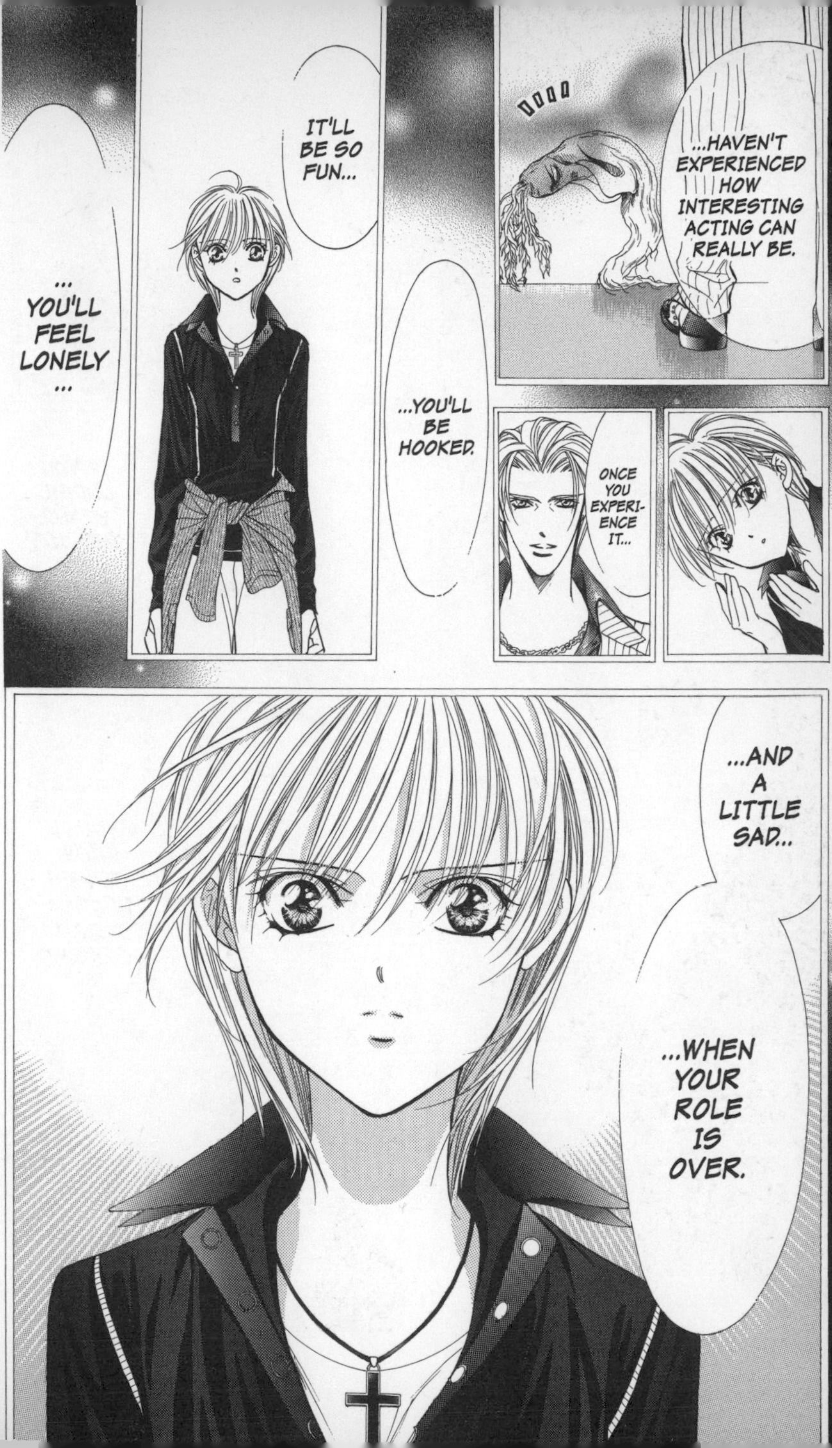
...HAVEN'T EXPERIENCED HOW INTERESTING ACTING CAN REALLY BE.
ONCE YOU EXPERIENCE IT...
...YOU'LL BE HOOKED.
IT'LL BE SO FUN...
...YOU'LL FEEL LONELY...
...AND A LITTLE SAD...
...WHEN YOUR ROLE IS OVER.

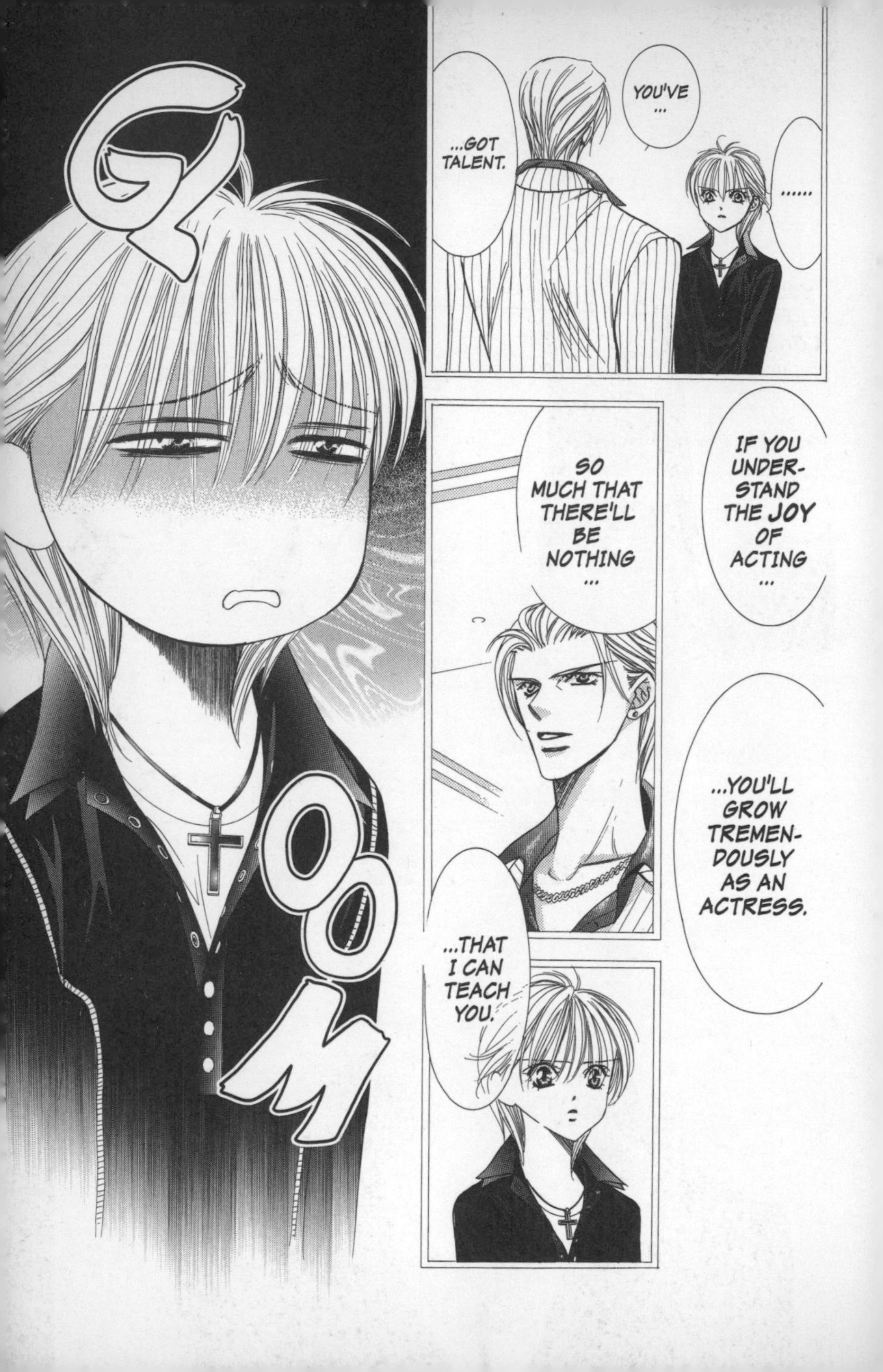
YOU'VE ...
...GOT TALENT.
......
IF YOU UNDER-STAND THE JOY OF ACTING ...
...YOU'LL GROW TREMEN-DOUSLY AS AN ACTRESS.
SO MUCH THAT THERE'LL BE NOTHING ...
...THAT I CAN TEACH YOU.
GLOOM

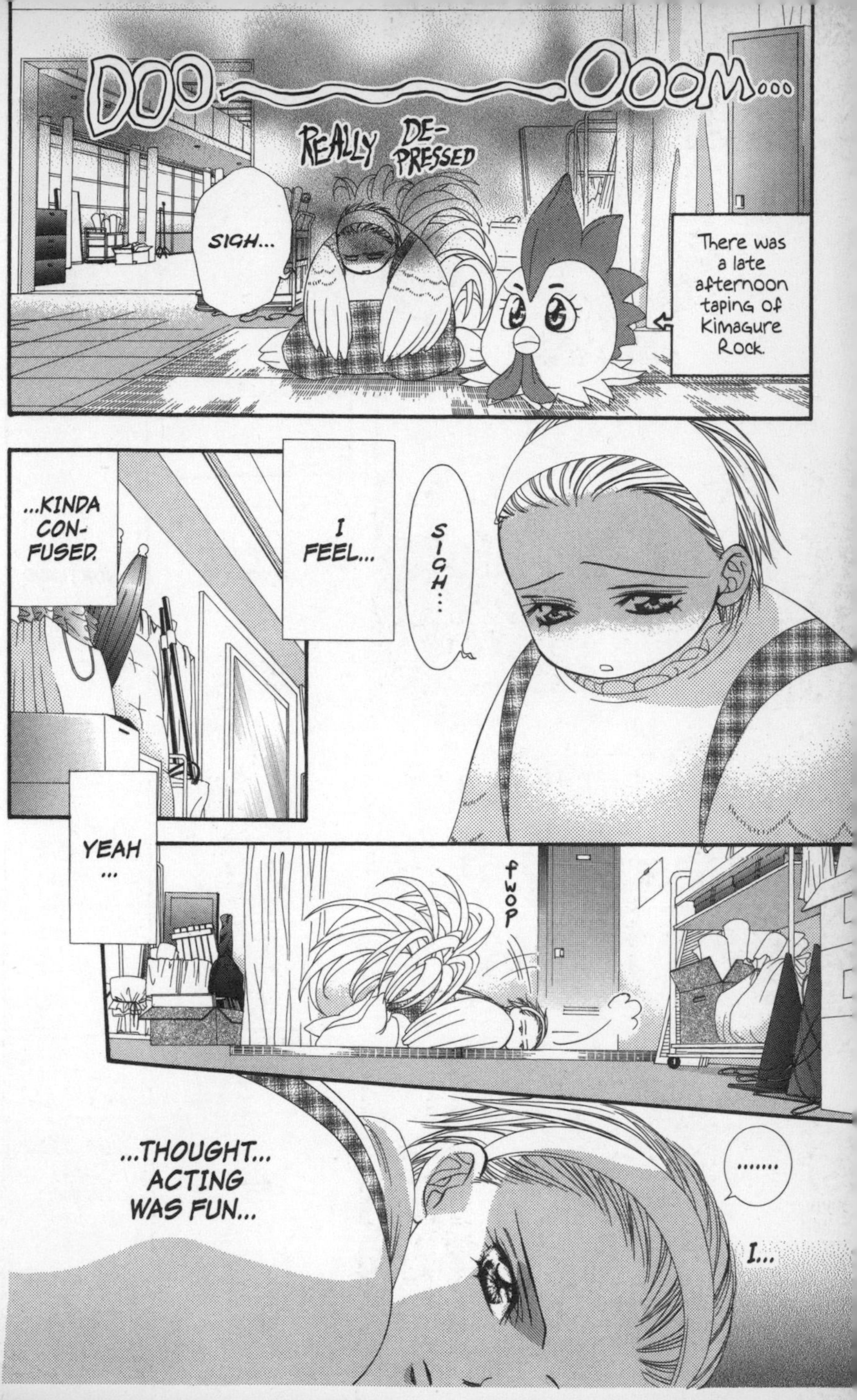
DOO————OOOM...
There was a late afternoon taping of Kimagure Rock.
REALLY DE-PRESSED
SIGH...
SIGH...
I FEEL...
...KINDA CON-FUSED.
fwop
YEAH ...
.......
I...
...THOUGHT... ACTING WAS FUN...

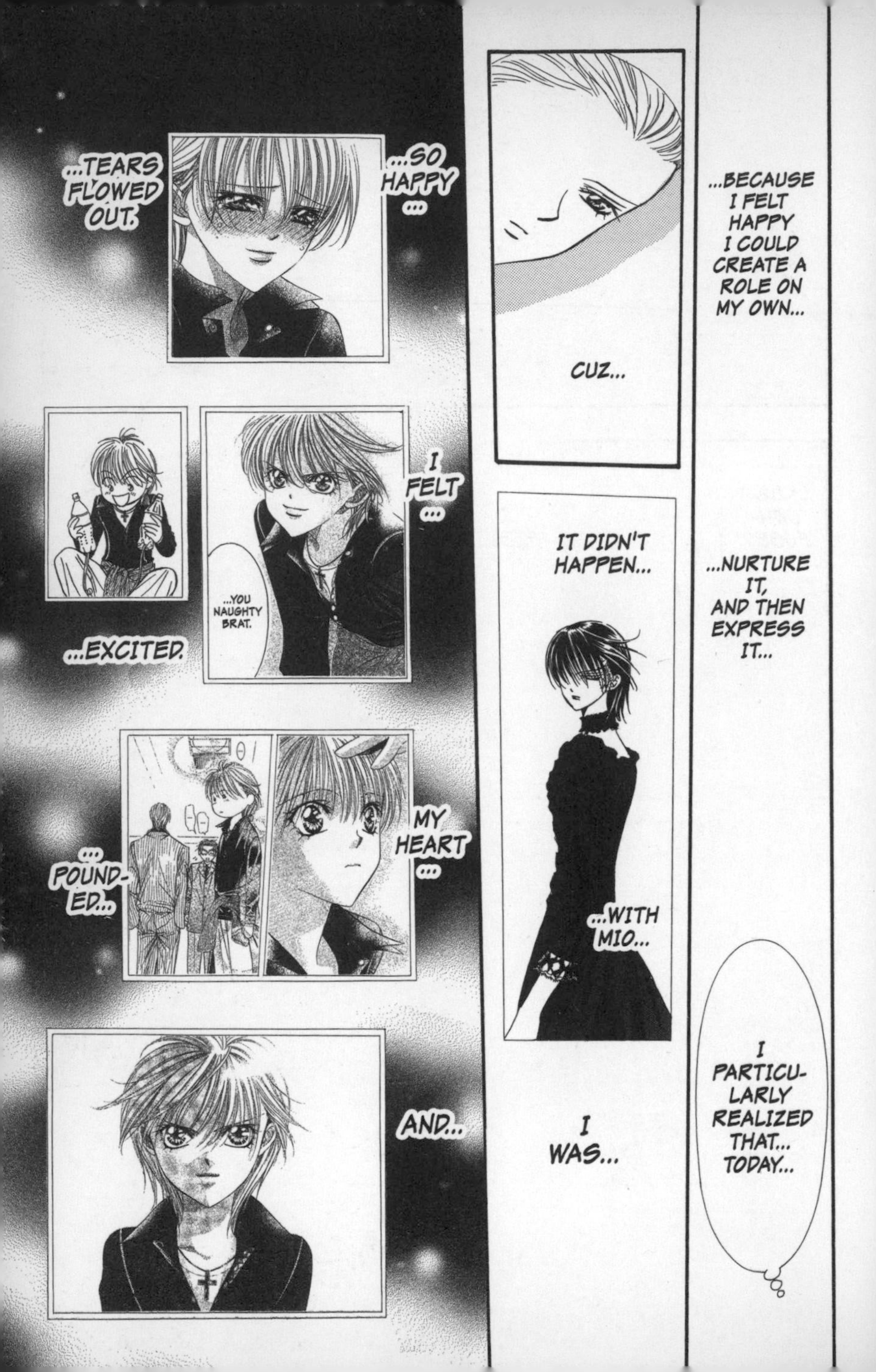
...BECAUSE I FELT HAPPY I COULD CREATE A ROLE ON MY OWN...
...NURTURE IT, AND THEN EXPRESS IT...
I PARTICU-LARLY REALIZED THAT... TODAY...
CUZ...
IT DIDN'T HAPPEN...
...WITH MIO...
I WAS...
...SO HAPPY...
...TEARS FLOWED OUT.
I FELT...
...YOU NAUGHTY BRAT.
...EXCITED.
MY HEART...
...POUND-ED...
AND...

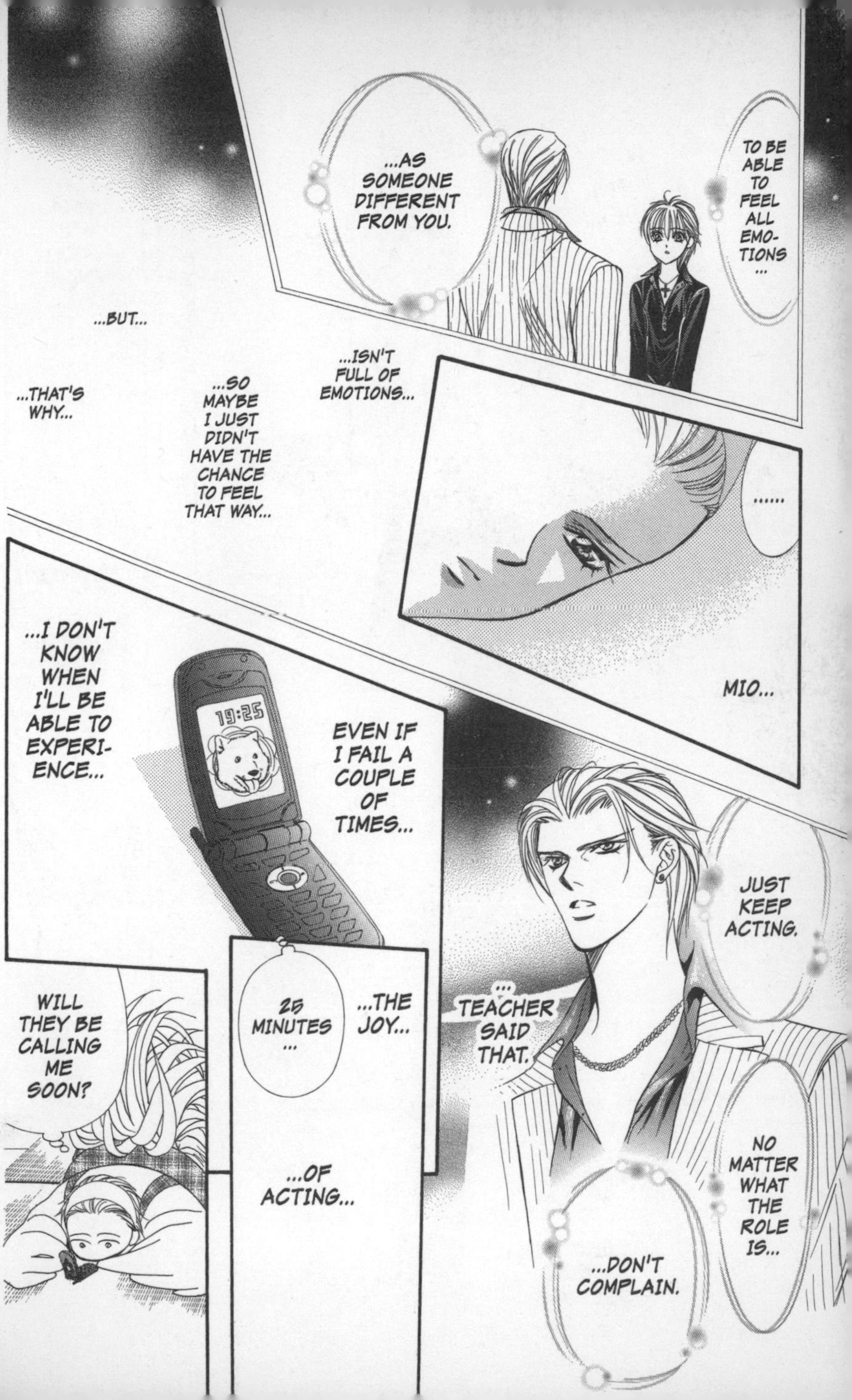
TO BE ABLE TO FEEL ALL EMOTIONS...
...AS SOMEONE DIFFERENT FROM YOU.
...BUT...
......
...ISN'T FULL OF EMOTIONS...
...SO MAYBE I JUST DIDN'T HAVE THE CHANCE TO FEEL THAT WAY...
...THAT'S WHY...
MIO...
JUST KEEP ACTING.
NO MATTER WHAT THE ROLE IS...
...DON'T COMPLAIN.
...TEACHER SAID THAT.
EVEN IF I FAIL A COUPLE OF TIMES...
19:25
...I DON'T KNOW WHEN I'LL BE ABLE TO EXPERIENCE...
...THE JOY...
25 MINUTES...
...OF ACTING...
WILL THEY BE CALLING ME SOON?

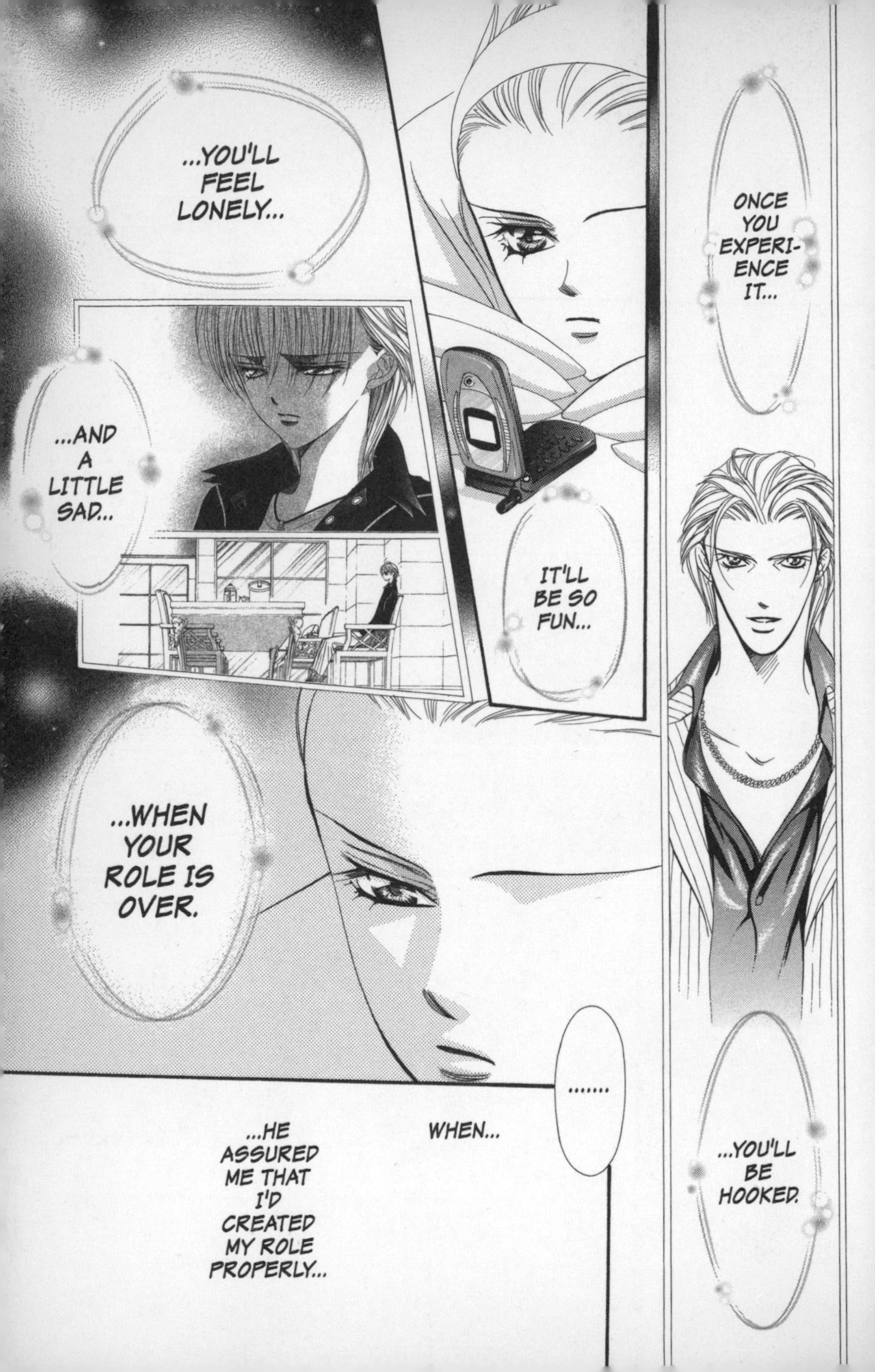
ONCE YOU EXPERIENCE IT...
...YOU'LL BE HOOKED.
IT'LL BE SO FUN...
...YOU'LL FEEL LONELY...
...AND A LITTLE SAD...
...WHEN YOUR ROLE IS OVER.
.......
WHEN...
...HE ASSURED ME THAT I'D CREATED MY ROLE PROPERLY...

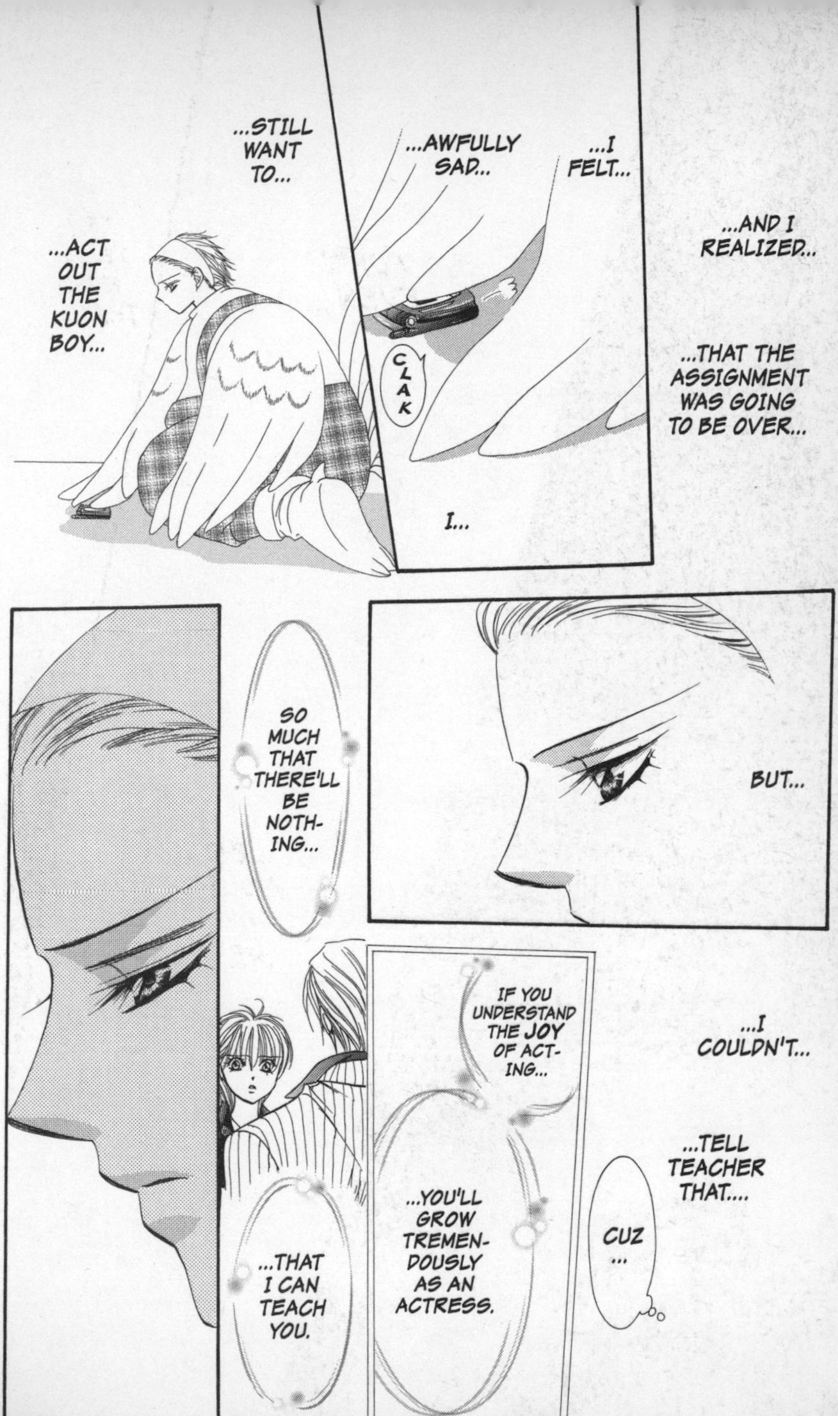
...AND I REALIZED...
...THAT THE ASSIGNMENT WAS GOING TO BE OVER...
...I FELT...
...AWFULLY SAD...
CLAK
I...
...STILL WANT TO...
...ACT OUT THE KUON BOY...
BUT...
...I COULDN'T...
...TELL TEACHER THAT....
CUZ ...
IF YOU UNDERSTAND THE JOY OF ACT-ING...
...YOU'LL GROW TREMEN-DOUSLY AS AN ACTRESS.
SO MUCH THAT THERE'LL BE NOTH-ING...
...THAT I CAN TEACH YOU.

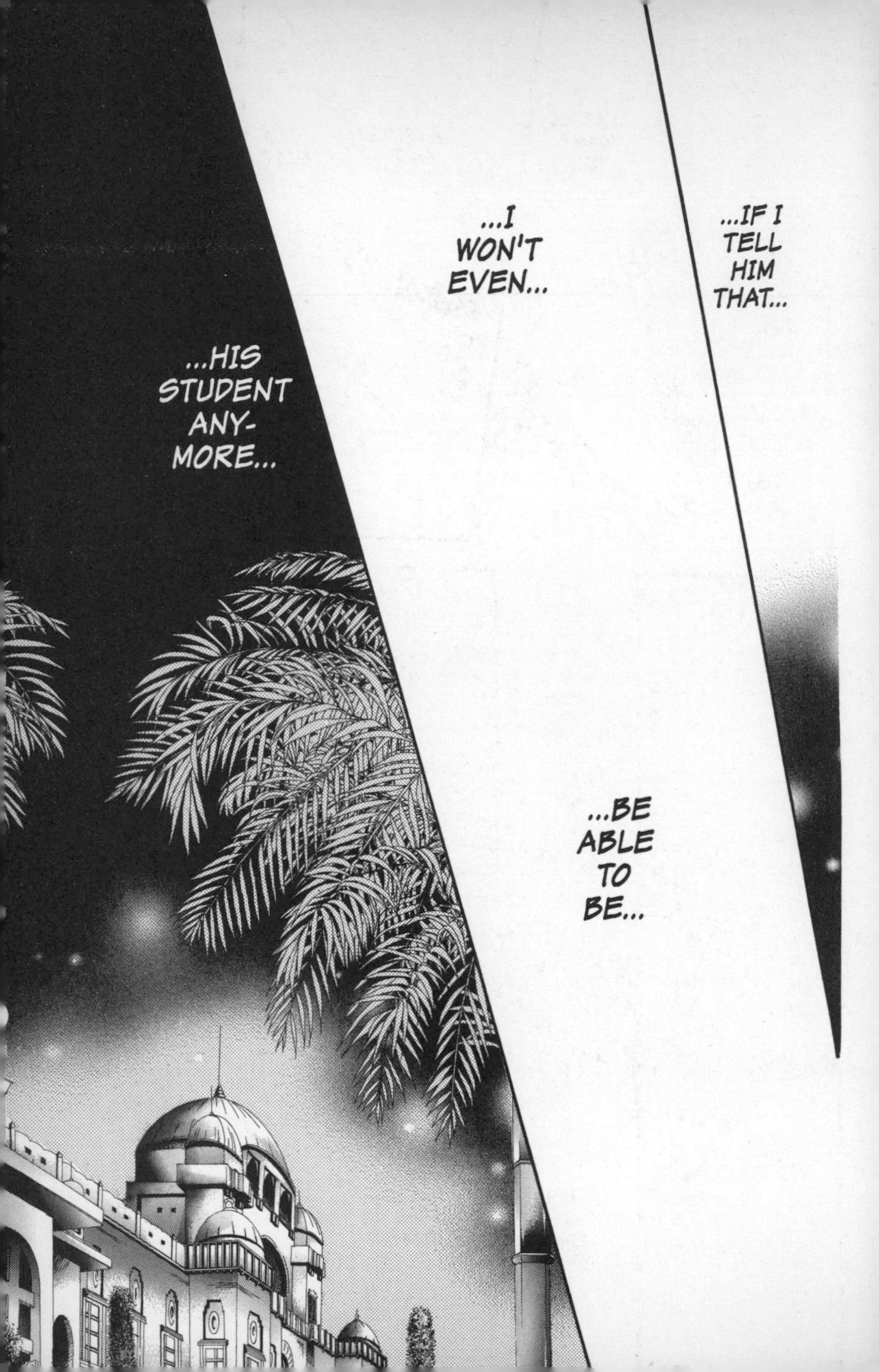
...IF I TELL HIM THAT...
...I WON'T EVEN...
...BE ABLE TO BE...
...HIS STUDENT ANY-MORE...

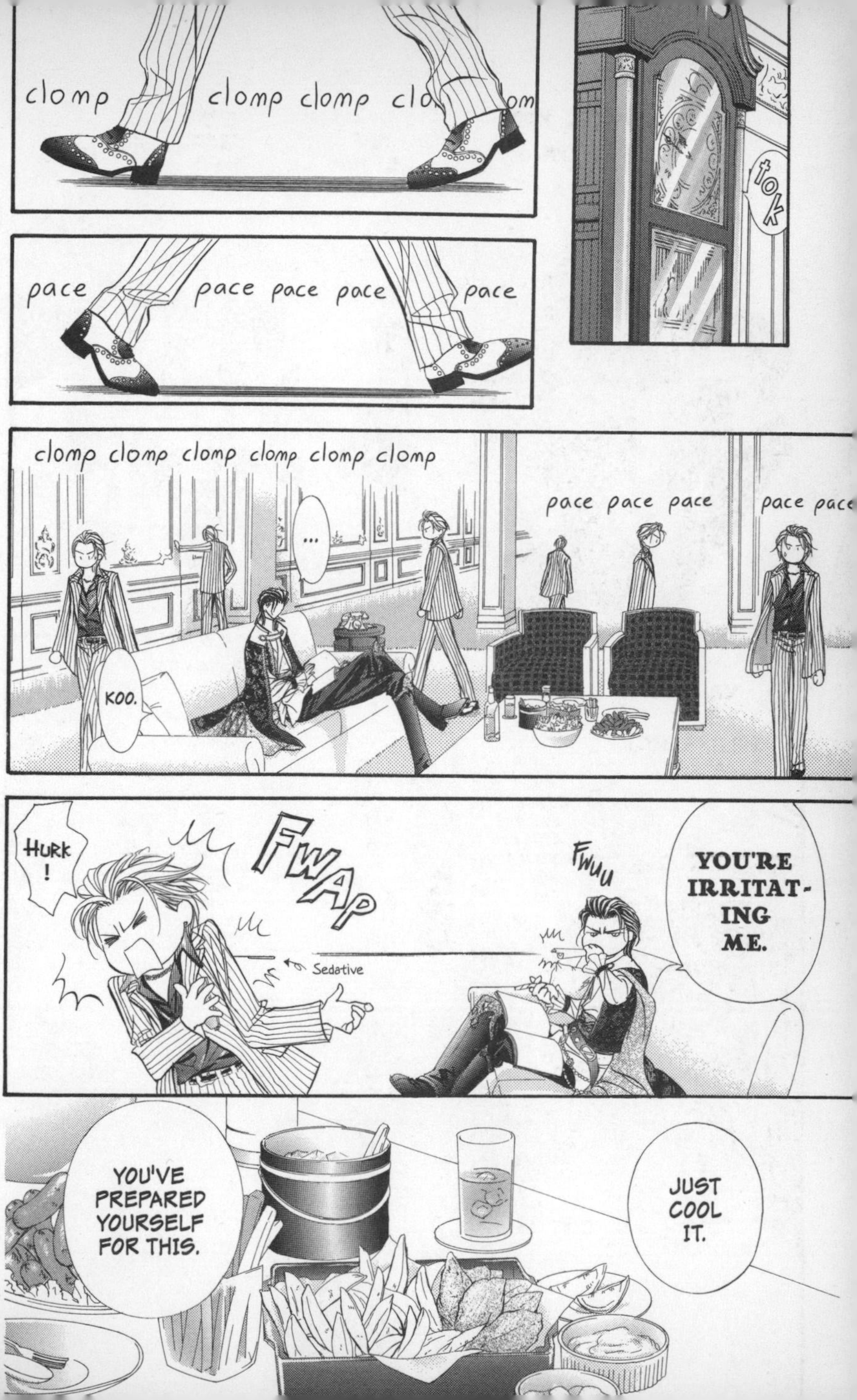
tok
clomp clomp clomp clo om
pace pace pace pace pace
pace pace pace pace pace
clomp clomp clomp clomp clomp clomp
...
KOO.
YOU'RE IRRITATING ME.
FWUU
FWAP
Sedative
HURK!
JUST COOL IT.
YOU'VE PREPARED YOURSELF FOR THIS.

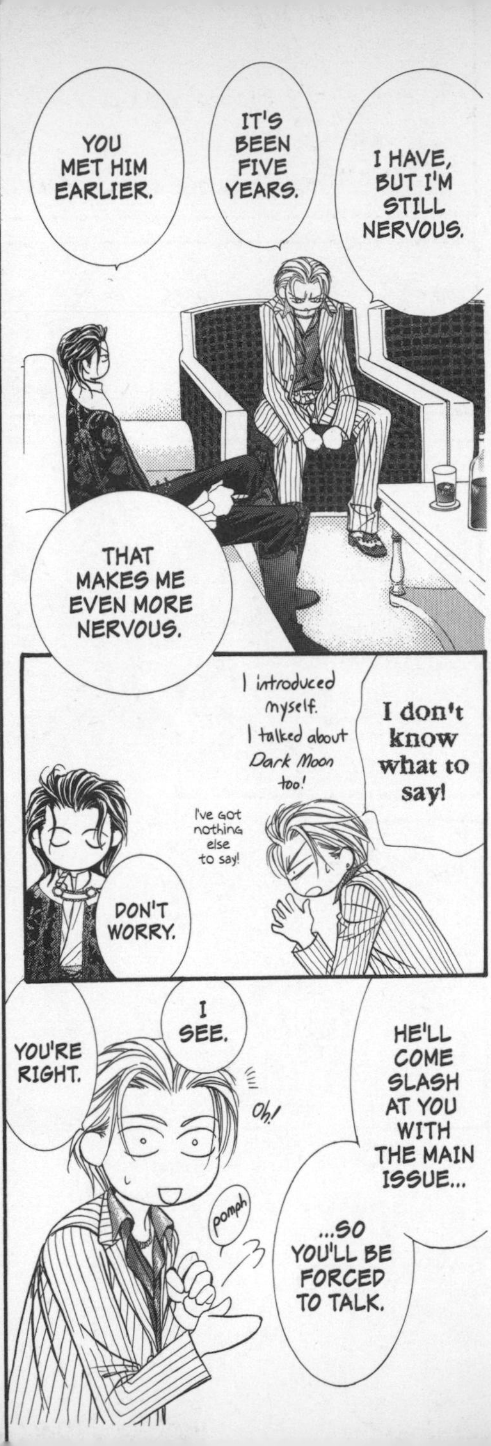
I HAVE, BUT I'M STILL NERVOUS.
IT'S BEEN FIVE YEARS.
YOU MET HIM EARLIER.
THAT MAKES ME EVEN MORE NERVOUS.
I don't know what to say!
I introduced myself. I talked about Dark Moon too!
I've got nothing else to say!
DON'T WORRY.
HE'LL COME SLASH AT YOU WITH THE MAIN ISSUE...
...SO YOU'LL BE FORCED TO TALK.
I SEE.
YOU'RE RIGHT.
Oh!
pomph

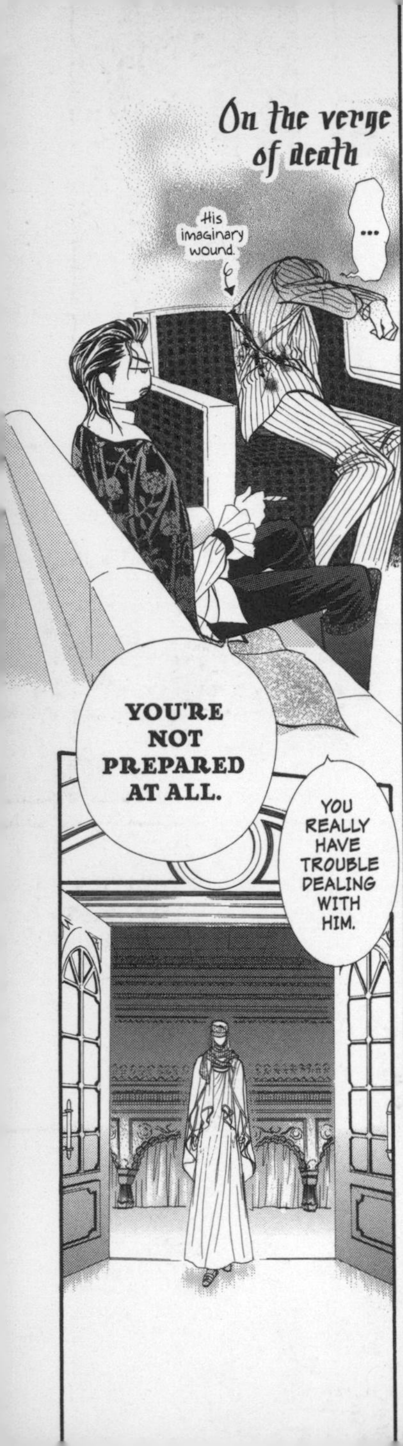
On the verge of death
...
His imaginary wound.
YOU'RE NOT PREPARED AT ALL.
YOU REALLY HAVE TROUBLE DEALING WITH HIM.

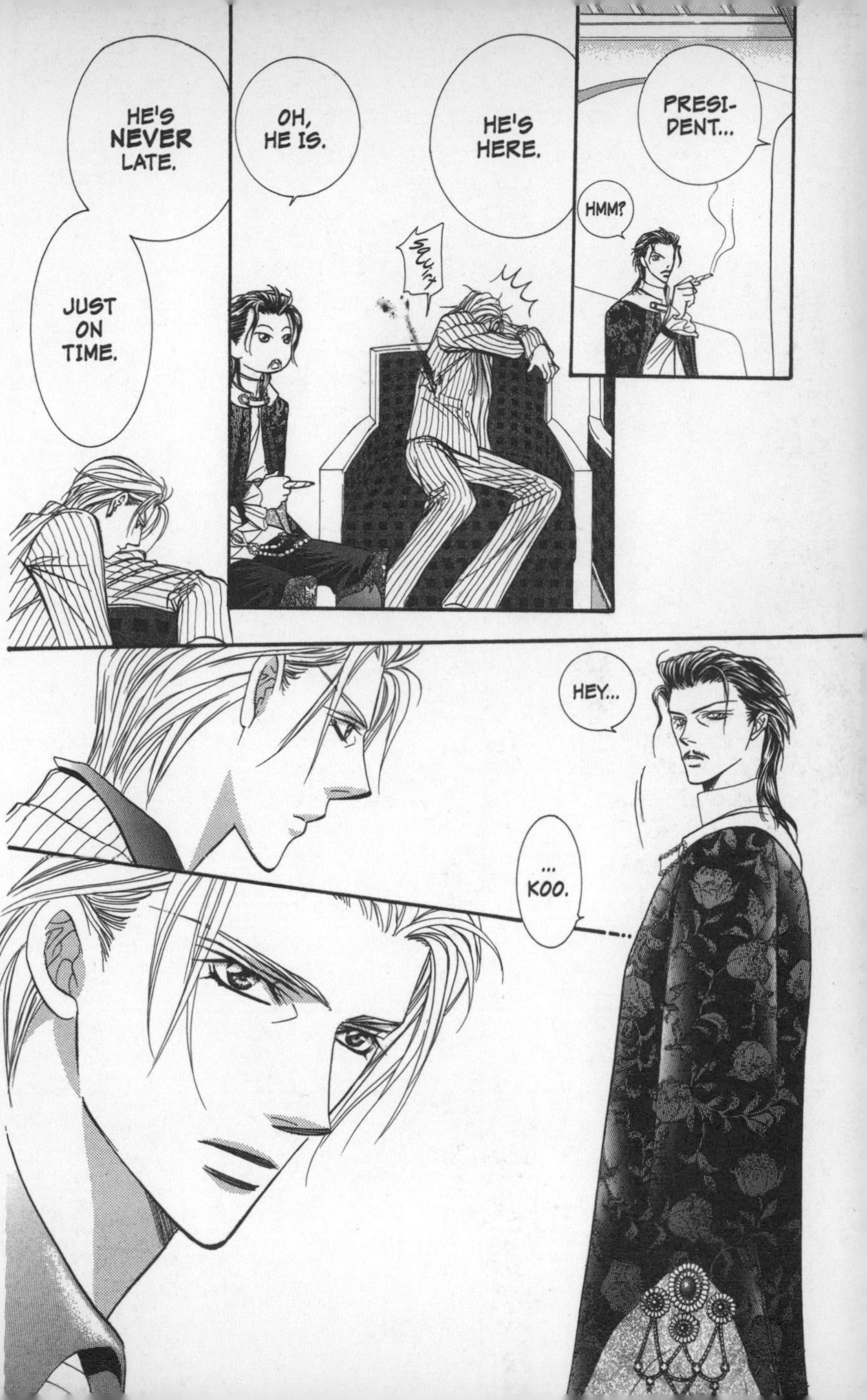
PRESI-DENT...
HMM?
HE'S HERE.
OH, HE IS.
HE'S NEVER LATE.
JUST ON TIME.
HEY...
...KOO.

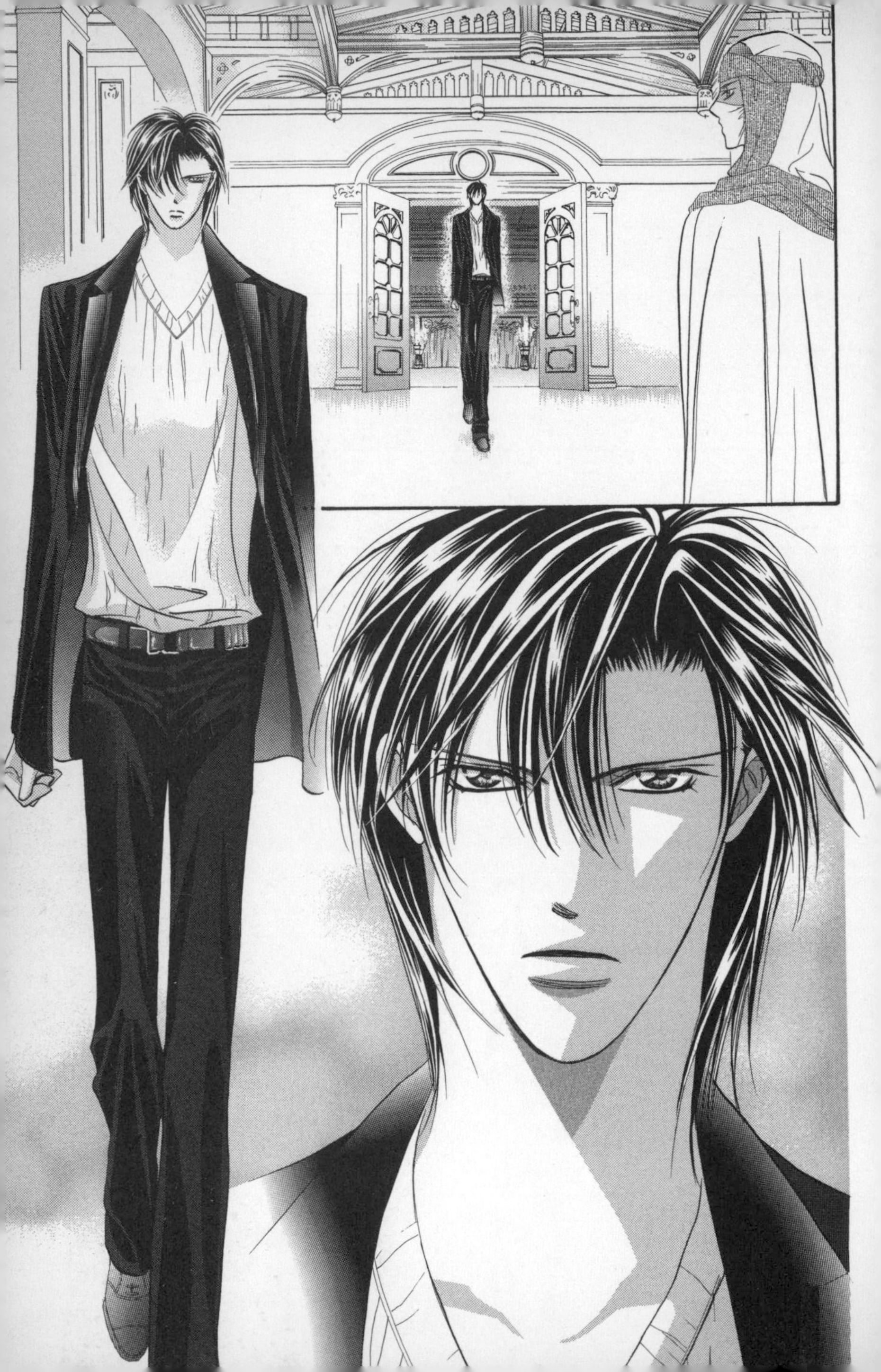

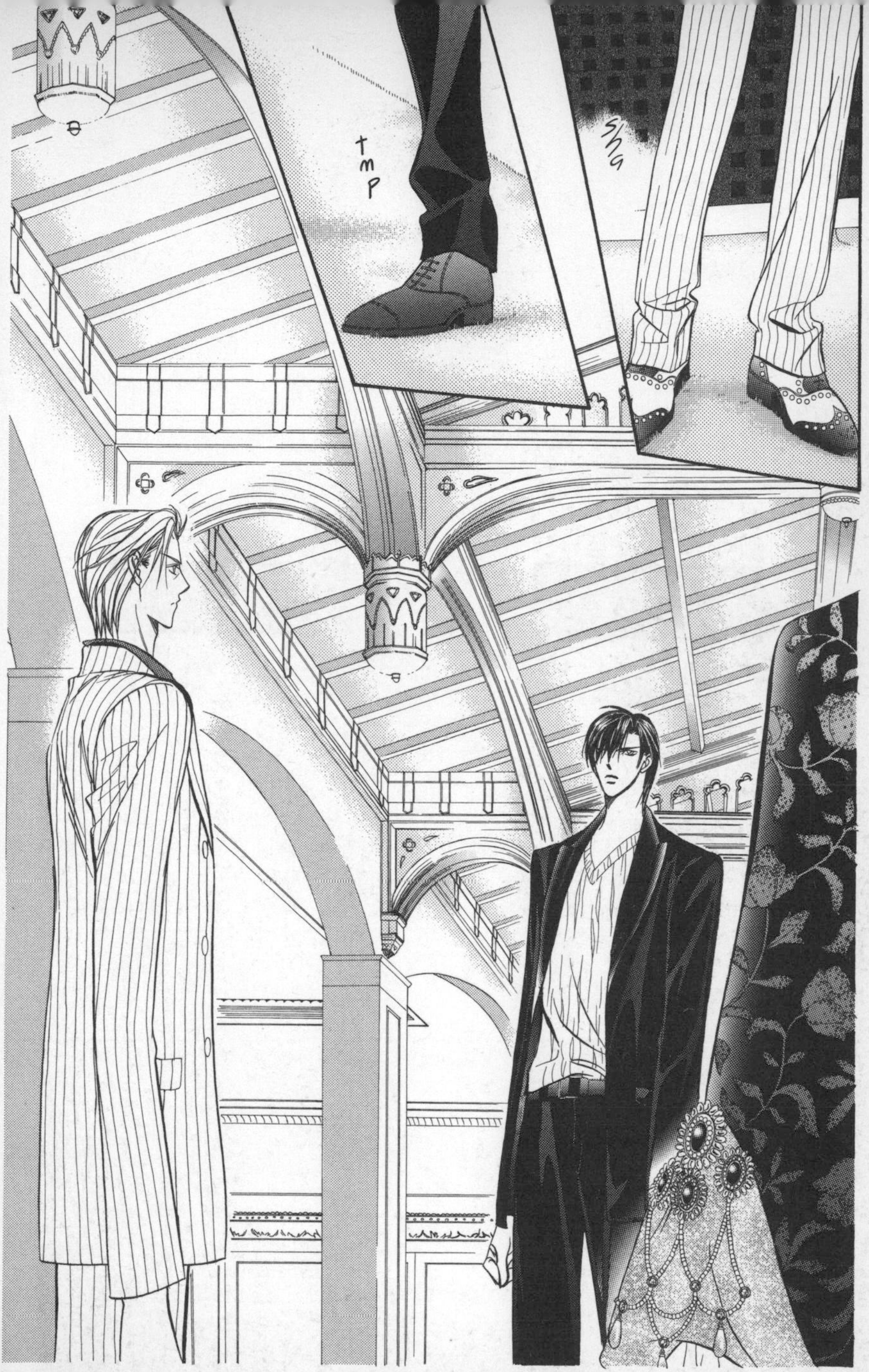
sng
tmp

**End of Act 109**

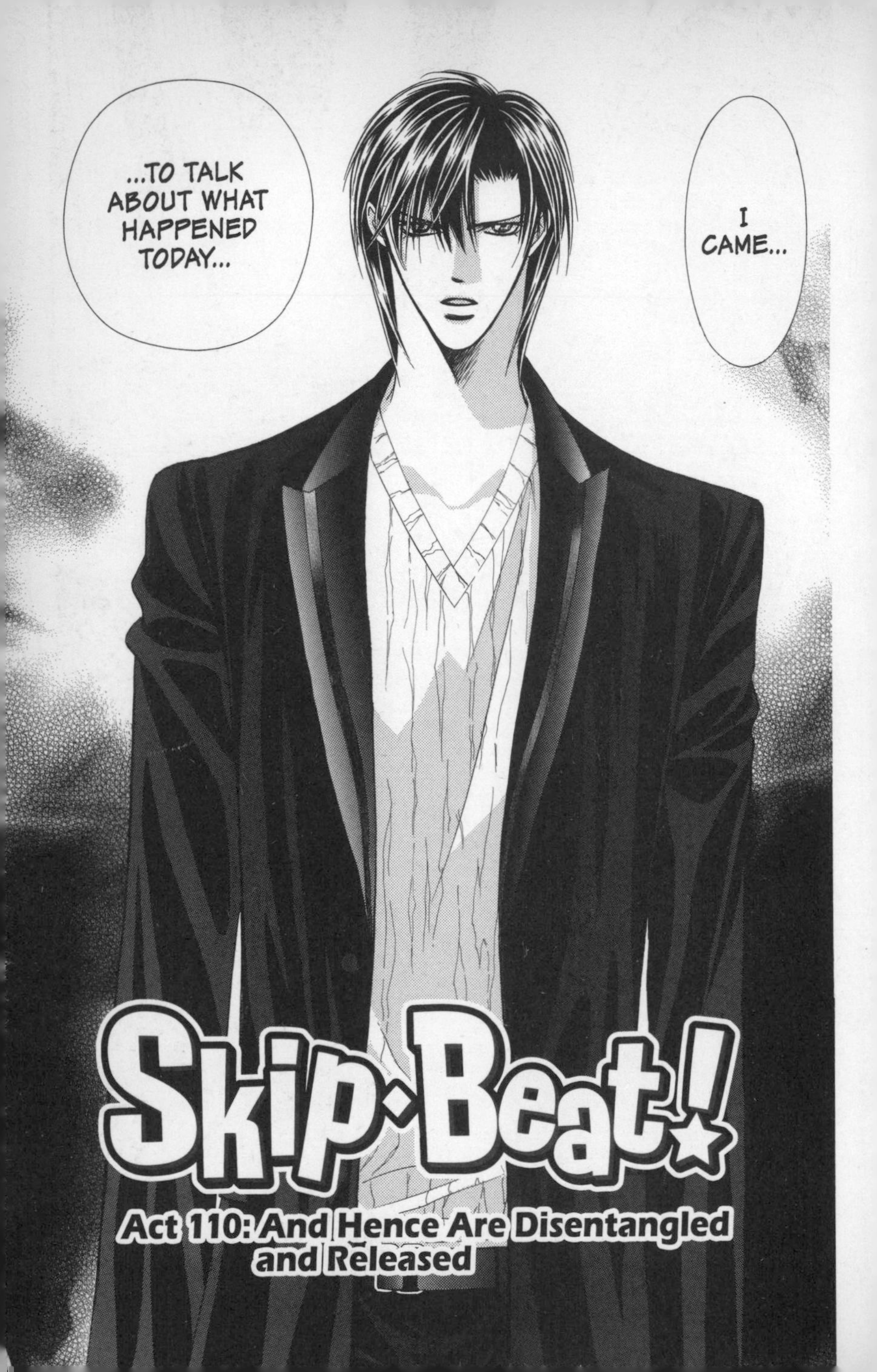
I CAME...
...TO TALK ABOUT WHAT HAPPENED TODAY...
Skip·Beat!
Act 110: And Hence Are Disentangled and Released

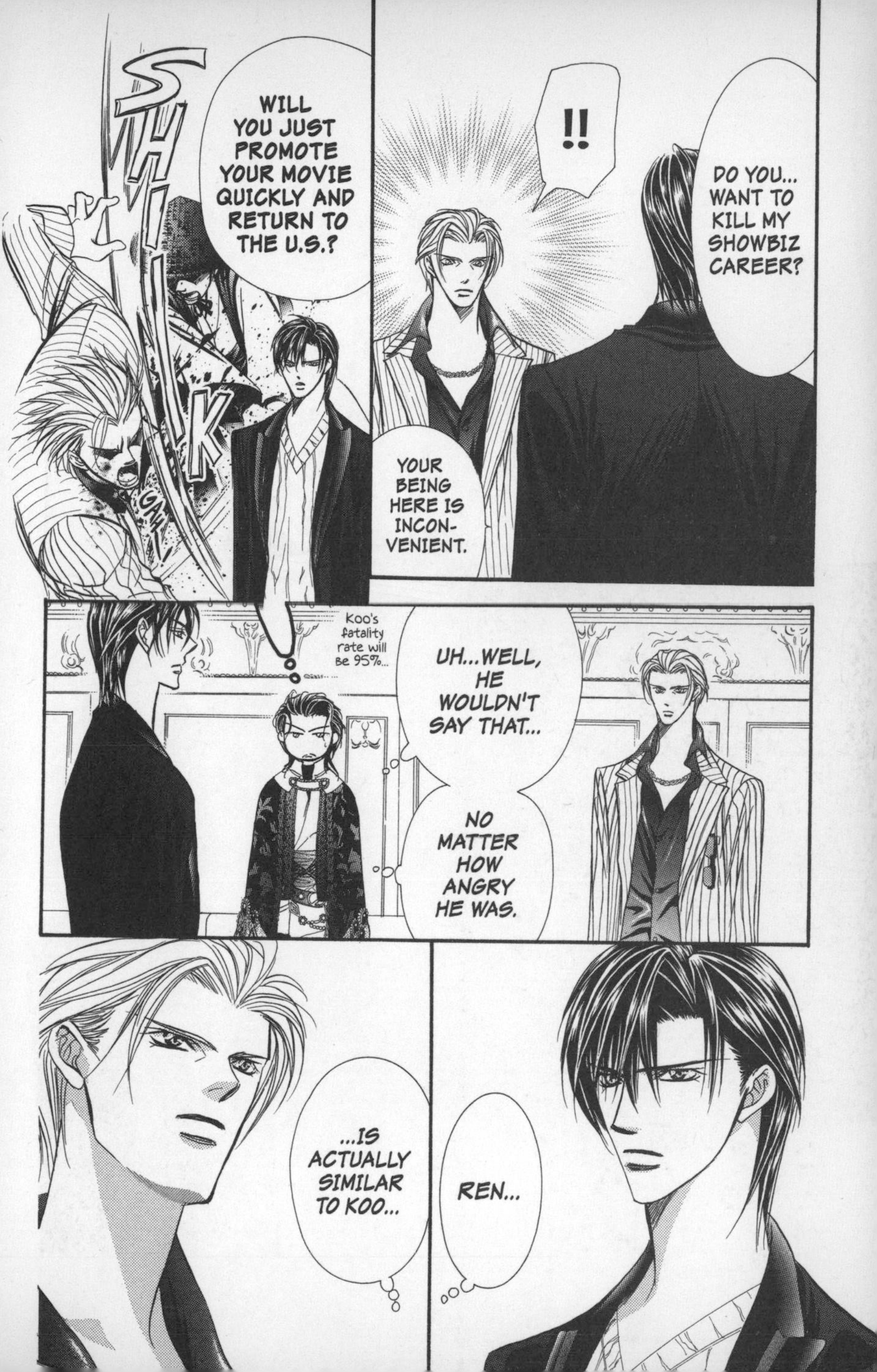
DO YOU... WANT TO KILL MY SHOWBIZ CAREER?
!!
YOUR BEING HERE IS INCONVENIENT.
WILL YOU JUST PROMOTE YOUR MOVIE QUICKLY AND RETURN TO THE U.S.?
SHHHK
GAH
UH...WELL, HE WOULDN'T SAY THAT...
NO MATTER HOW ANGRY HE WAS.
Koo's fatality rate will be 95%...
REN...
...IS ACTUALLY SIMILAR TO KOO...

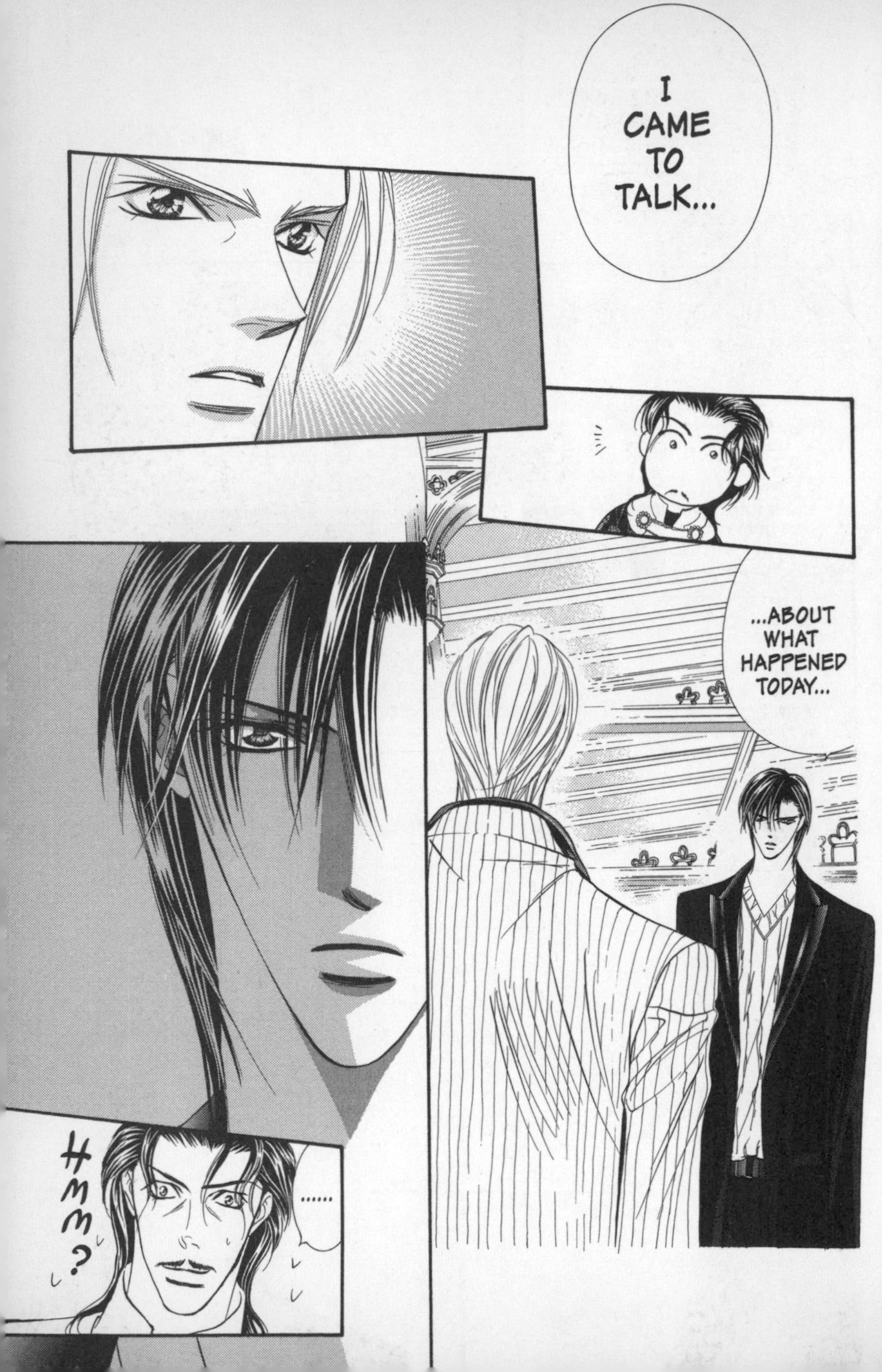
I CAME TO TALK...
...ABOUT WHAT HAPPENED TODAY...
......
HMM?

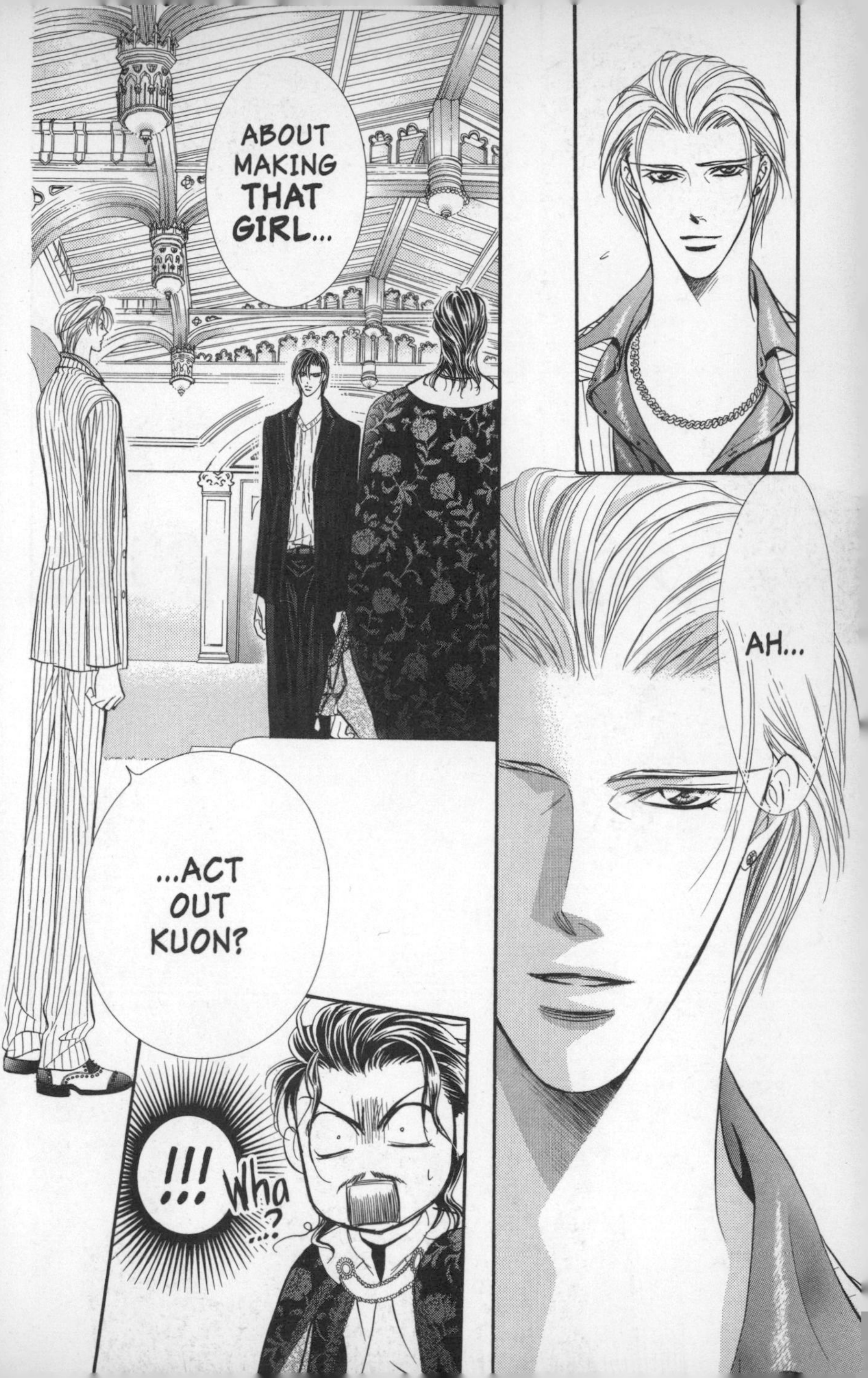
ABOUT MAKING THAT GIRL...
AH...
...ACT OUT KUON?
!!!
Wha...?

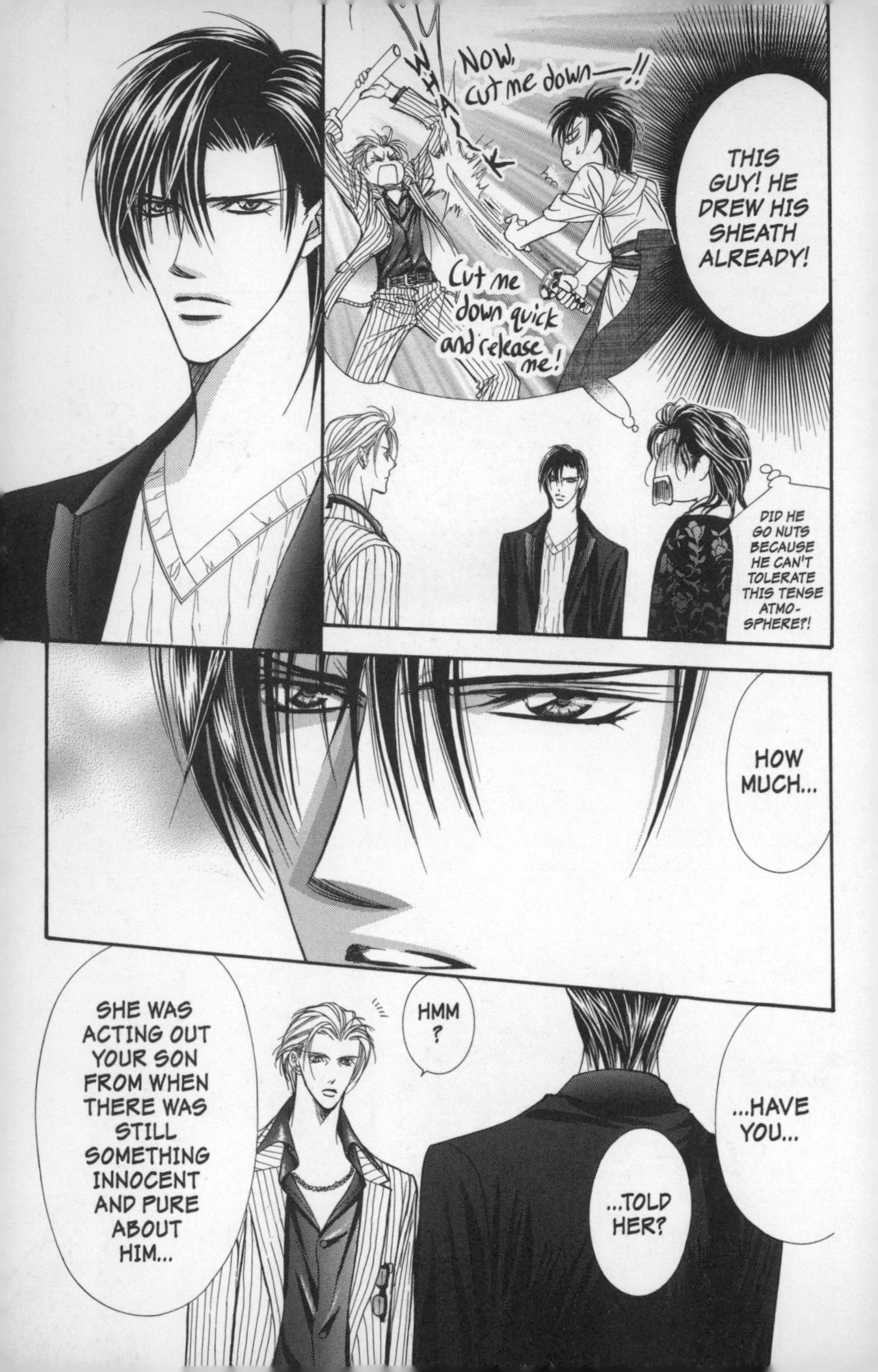
THIS GUY! HE DREW HIS SHEATH ALREADY!
Now, cut me down——!!
WHA~~K
Cut me down quick and release me!
DID HE GO NUTS BECAUSE HE CAN'T TOLERATE THIS TENSE ATMOSPHERE?!
HOW MUCH...
...HAVE YOU...
...TOLD HER?
HMM?
SHE WAS ACTING OUT YOUR SON FROM WHEN THERE WAS STILL SOMETHING INNOCENT AND PURE ABOUT HIM...

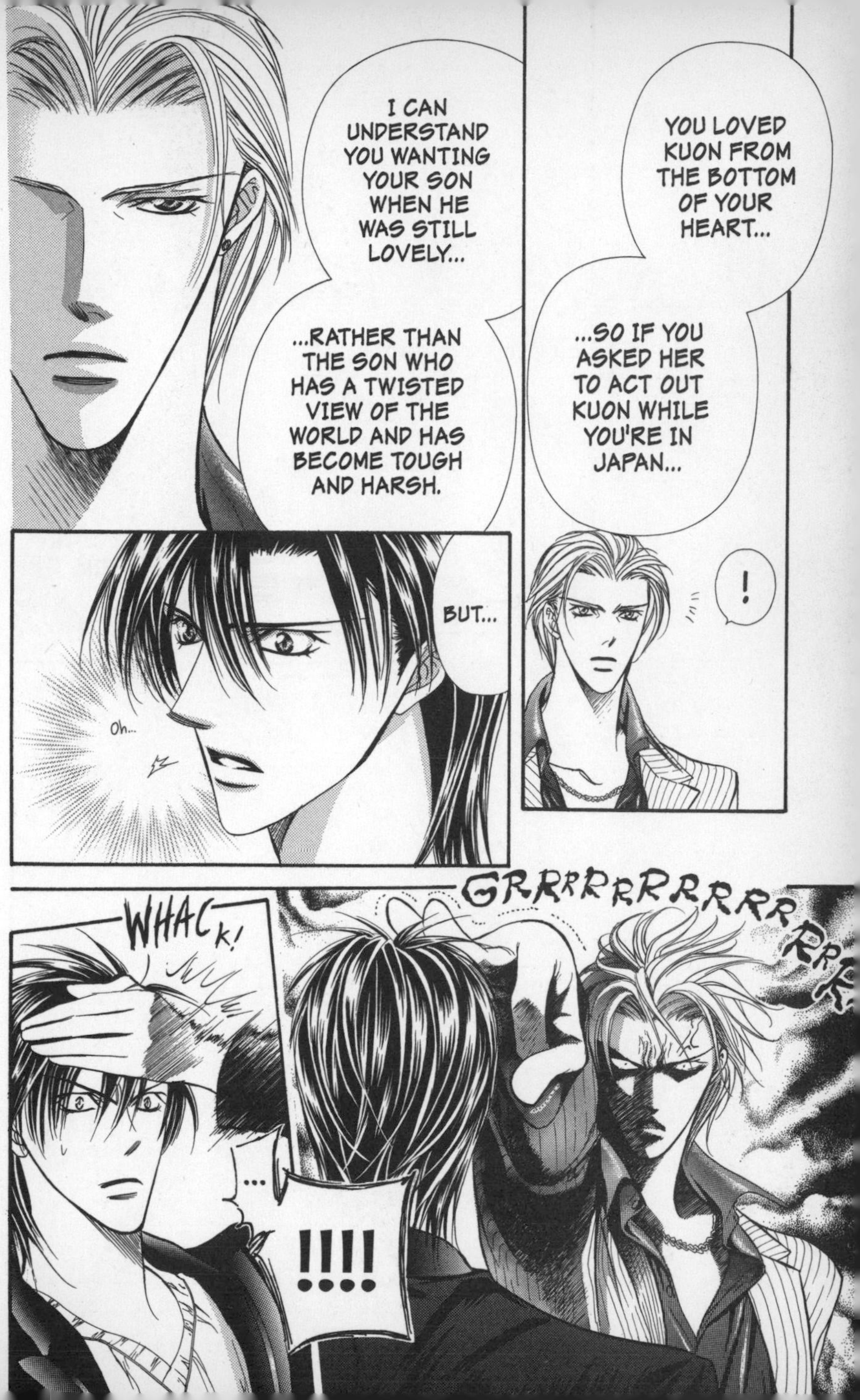
YOU LOVED KUON FROM THE BOTTOM OF YOUR HEART...
...SO IF YOU ASKED HER TO ACT OUT KUON WHILE YOU'RE IN JAPAN...
!
I CAN UNDERSTAND YOU WANTING YOUR SON WHEN HE WAS STILL LOVELY...
...RATHER THAN THE SON WHO HAS A TWISTED VIEW OF THE WORLD AND HAS BECOME TOUGH AND HARSH.
BUT...
Oh..
GRRRRRRRRRRRRRRRK
WHACk!
...
!!!!

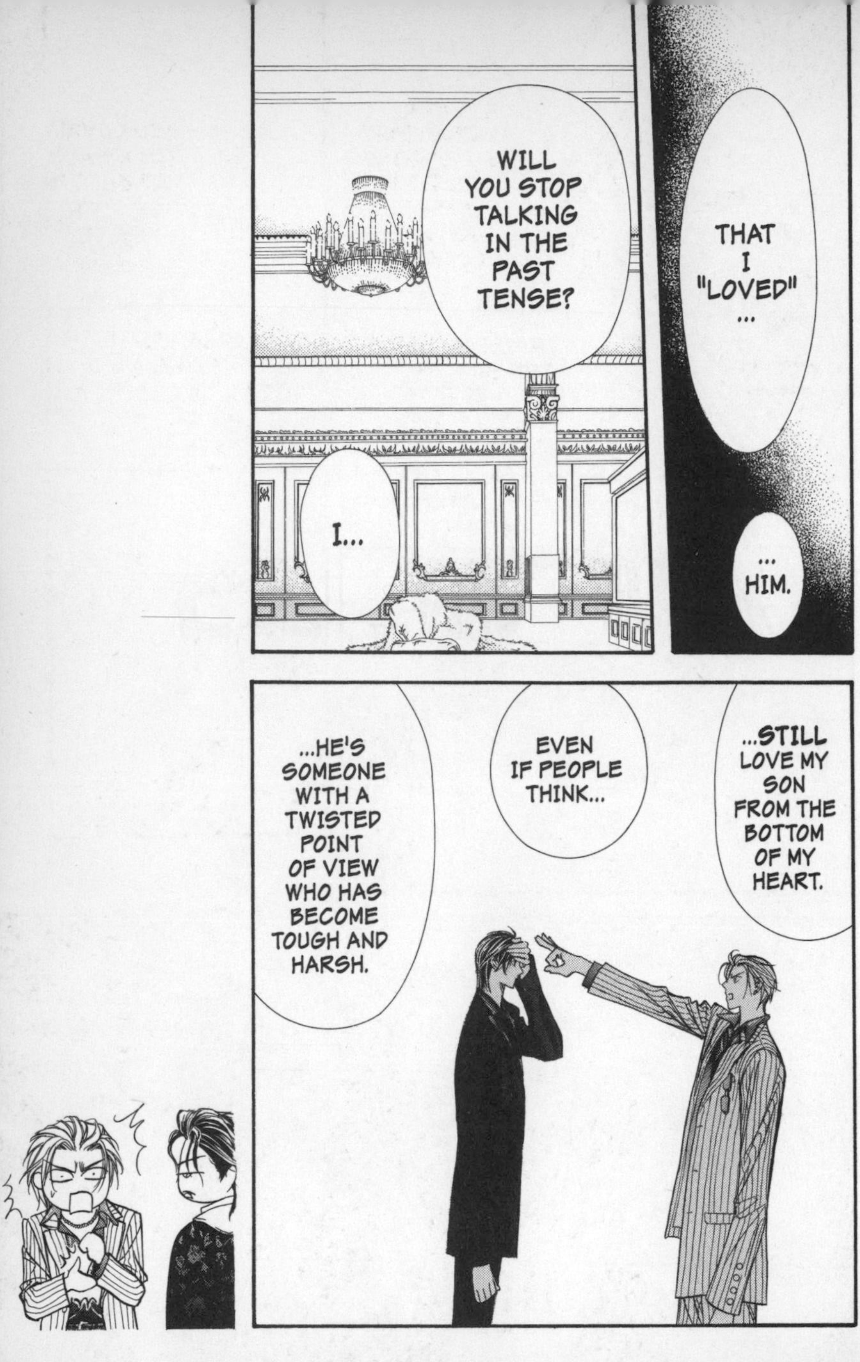
THAT I "LOVED"...
...HIM.
WILL YOU STOP TALKING IN THE PAST TENSE?
I...
...STILL LOVE MY SON FROM THE BOTTOM OF MY HEART.
EVEN IF PEOPLE THINK...
...HE'S SOMEONE WITH A TWISTED POINT OF VIEW WHO HAS BECOME TOUGH AND HARSH.

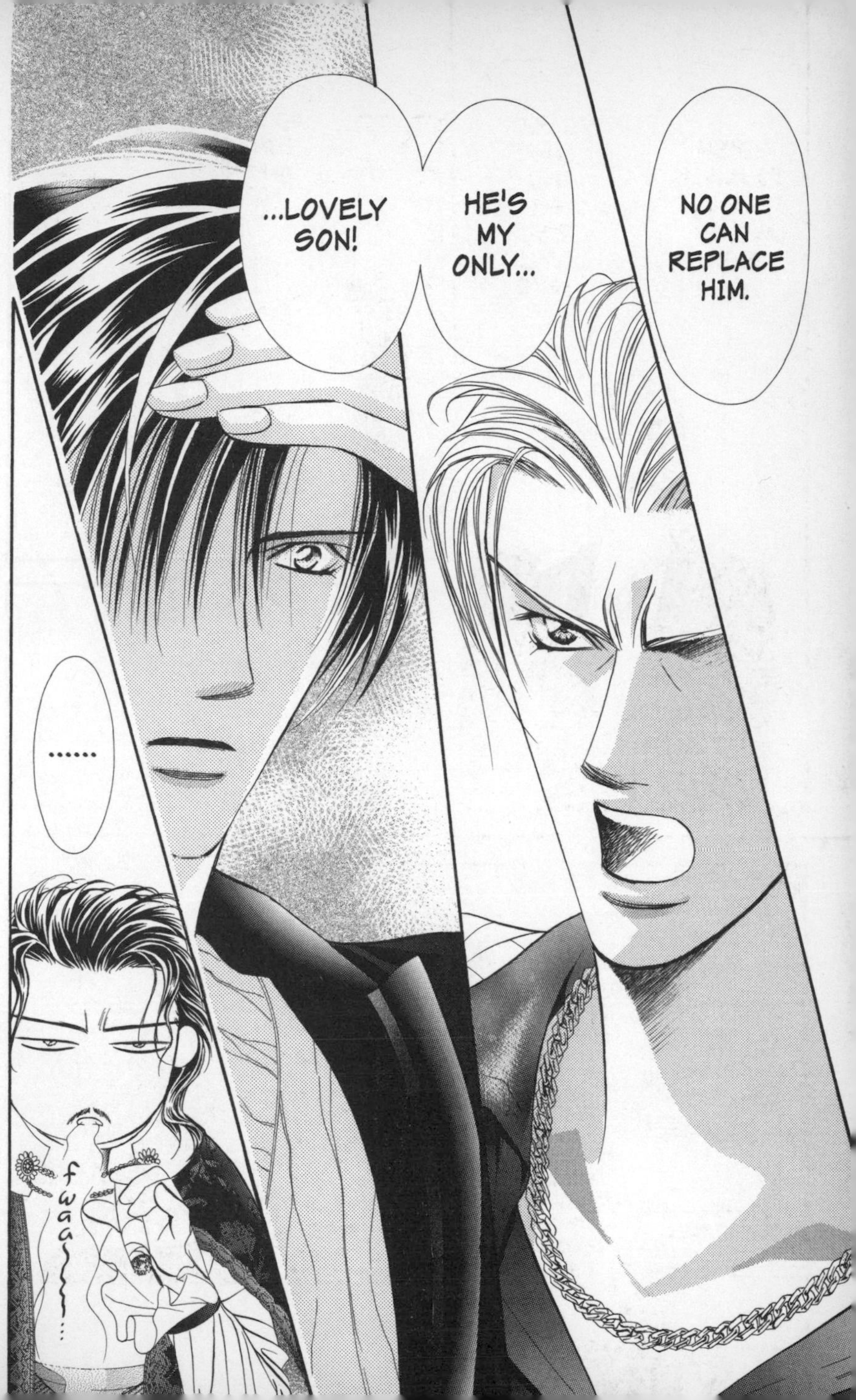
NO ONE CAN REPLACE HIM.
HE'S MY ONLY...
...LOVELY SON!
......
fwaa~~...

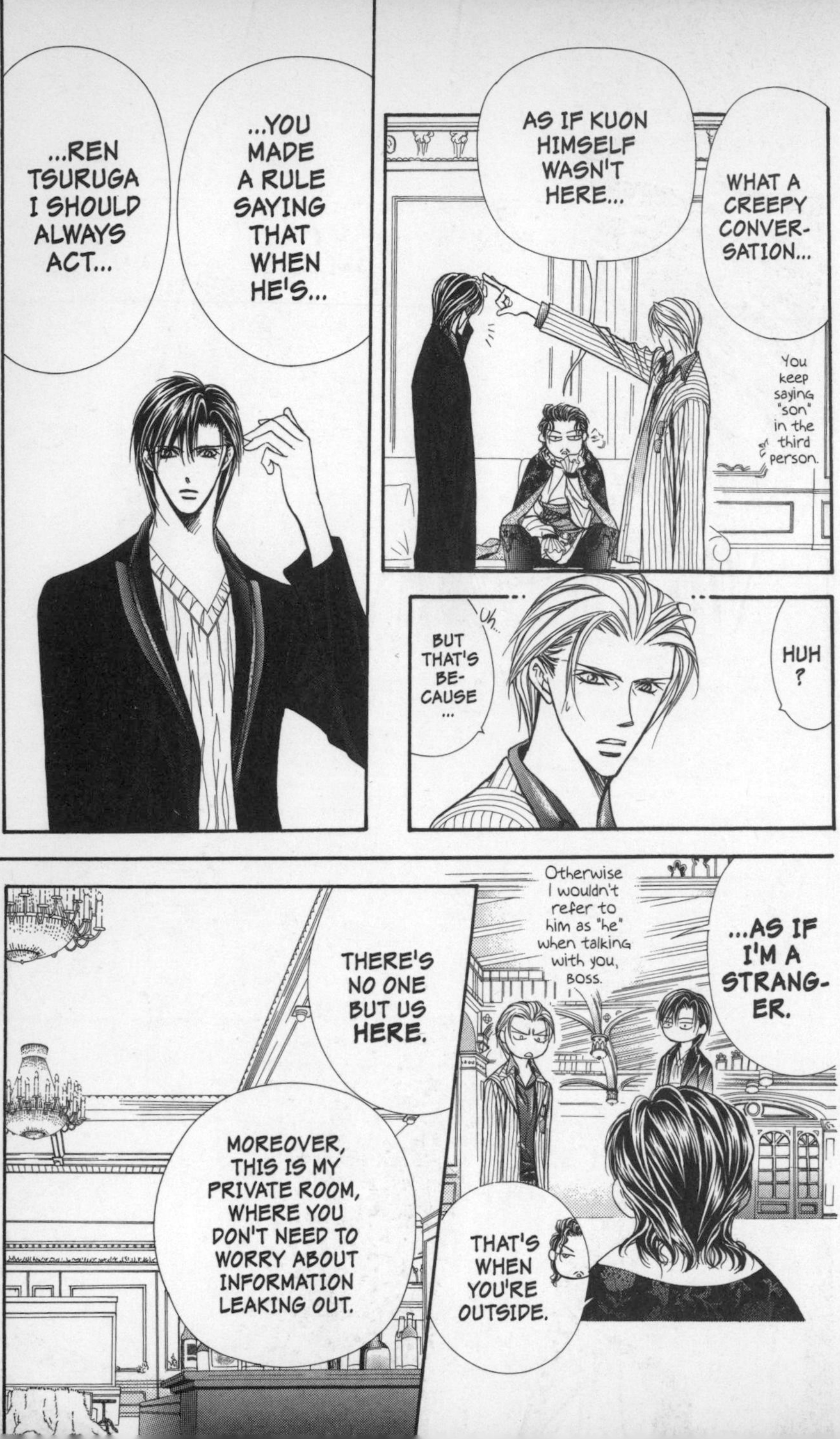
AS IF KUON HIMSELF WASN'T HERE...
WHAT A CREEPY CONVERSATION...
You keep saying "son" in the third person.
HUH?
Uh...
BUT THAT'S BECAUSE...
...YOU MADE A RULE SAYING THAT WHEN HE'S...
...REN TSURUGA I SHOULD ALWAYS ACT...
...AS IF I'M A STRANGER.
Otherwise I wouldn't refer to him as "he" when talking with you, BOSS.
THERE'S NO ONE BUT US HERE.
MOREOVER, THIS IS MY PRIVATE ROOM, WHERE YOU DON'T NEED TO WORRY ABOUT INFORMATION LEAKING OUT.
THAT'S WHEN YOU'RE OUTSIDE.

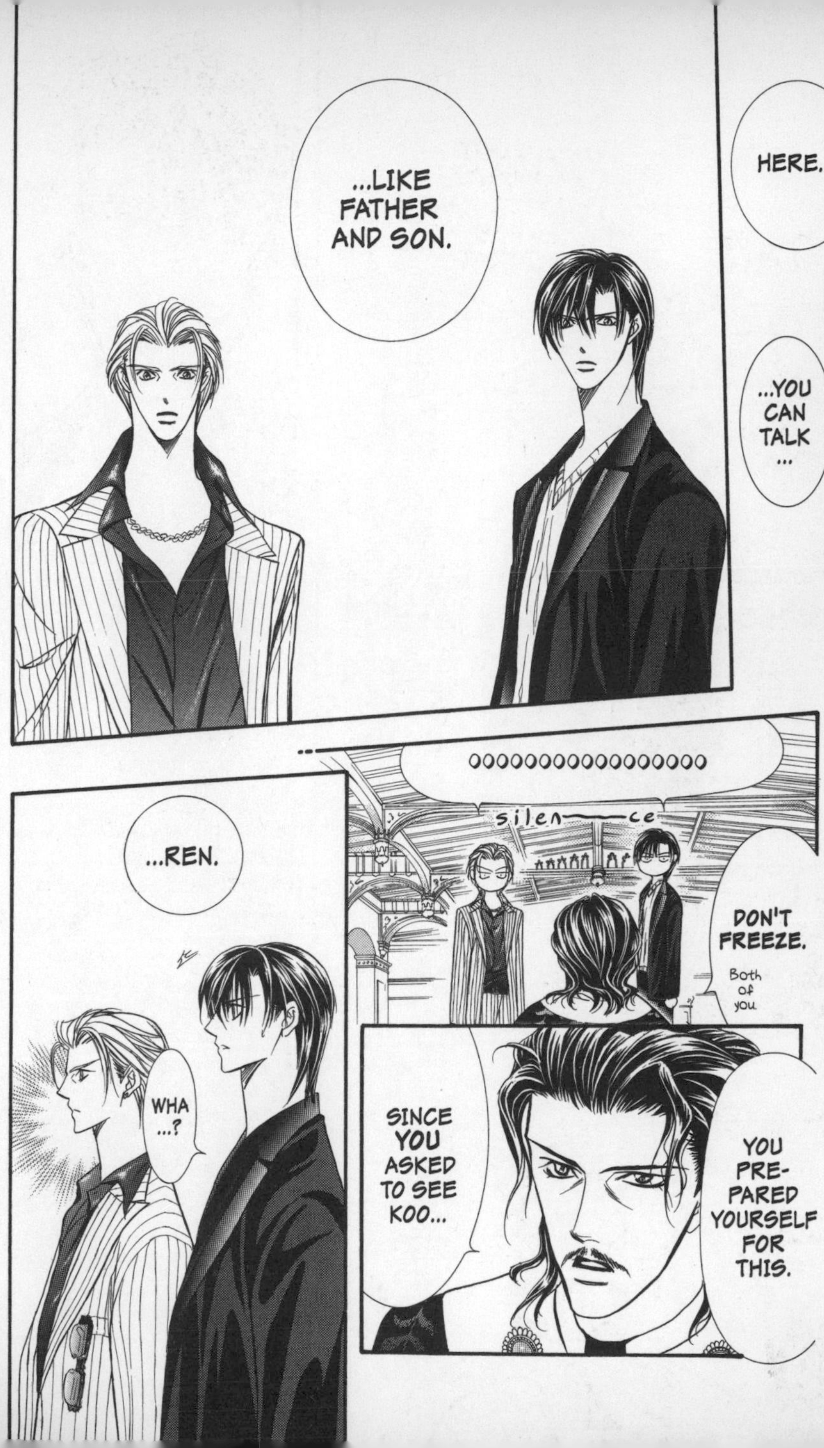
HERE...
...YOU CAN TALK ...
...LIKE FATHER AND SON.
OOOOOOOOOOOOOOOOOO
silen——ce
DON'T FREEZE.
Both of you
YOU PRE-PARED YOURSELF FOR THIS.
SINCE YOU ASKED TO SEE KOO...
...REN.
WHA ...?

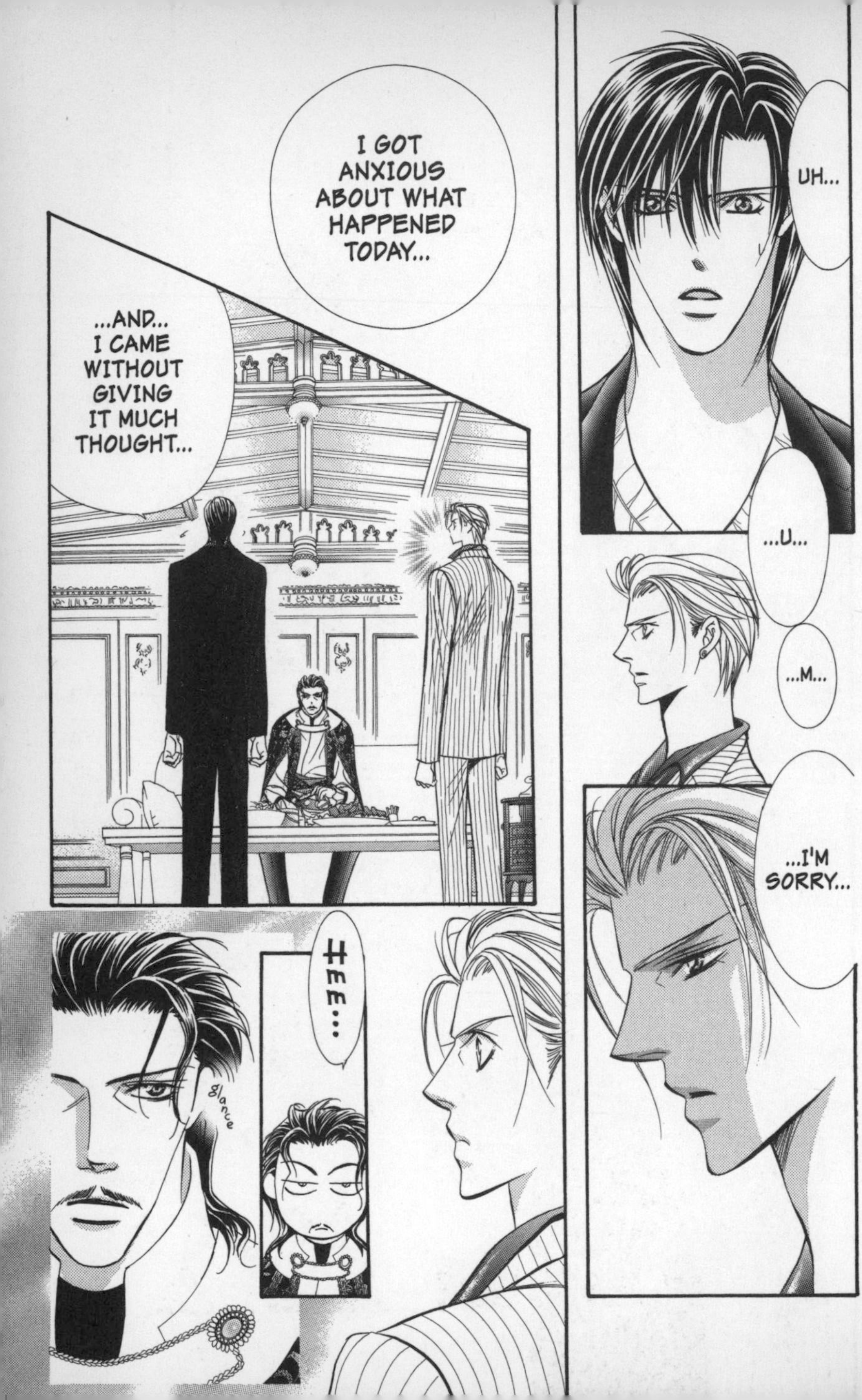
UH...
...U...
...M...
...I'M SORRY...
I GOT ANXIOUS ABOUT WHAT HAPPENED TODAY...
...AND... I CAME WITHOUT GIVING IT MUCH THOUGHT...
Hmm...
glance

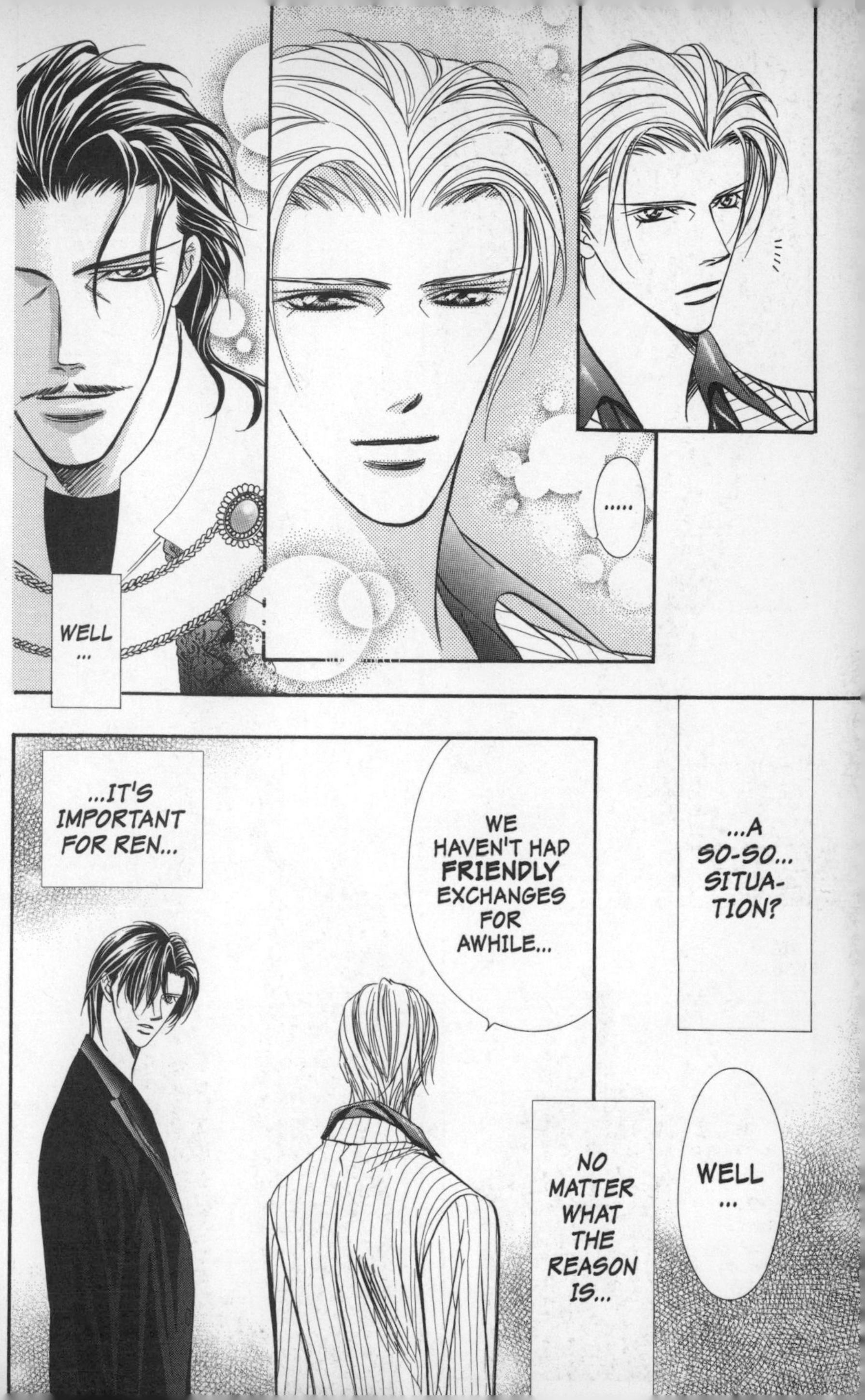
.....
WELL ...
...A SO-SO... SITUATION?
WELL ...
WE HAVEN'T HAD FRIENDLY EXCHANGES FOR AWHILE...
NO MATTER WHAT THE REASON IS...
...IT'S IMPORTANT FOR REN...

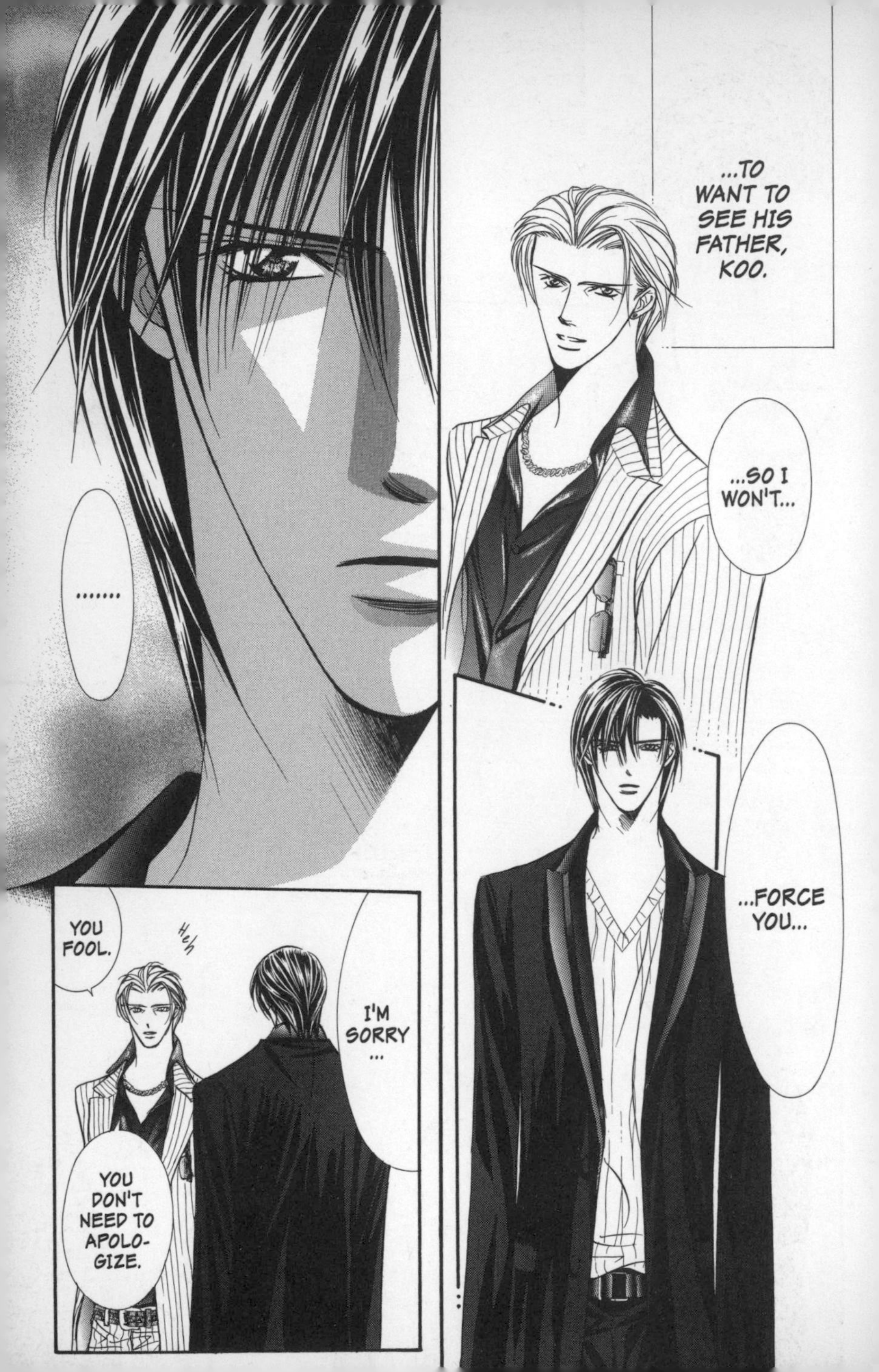
...TO WANT TO SEE HIS FATHER, KOO.
...SO I WON'T...
...FORCE YOU...
.......
I'M SORRY ...
YOU FOOL.
Heh
YOU DON'T NEED TO APOLOGIZE.

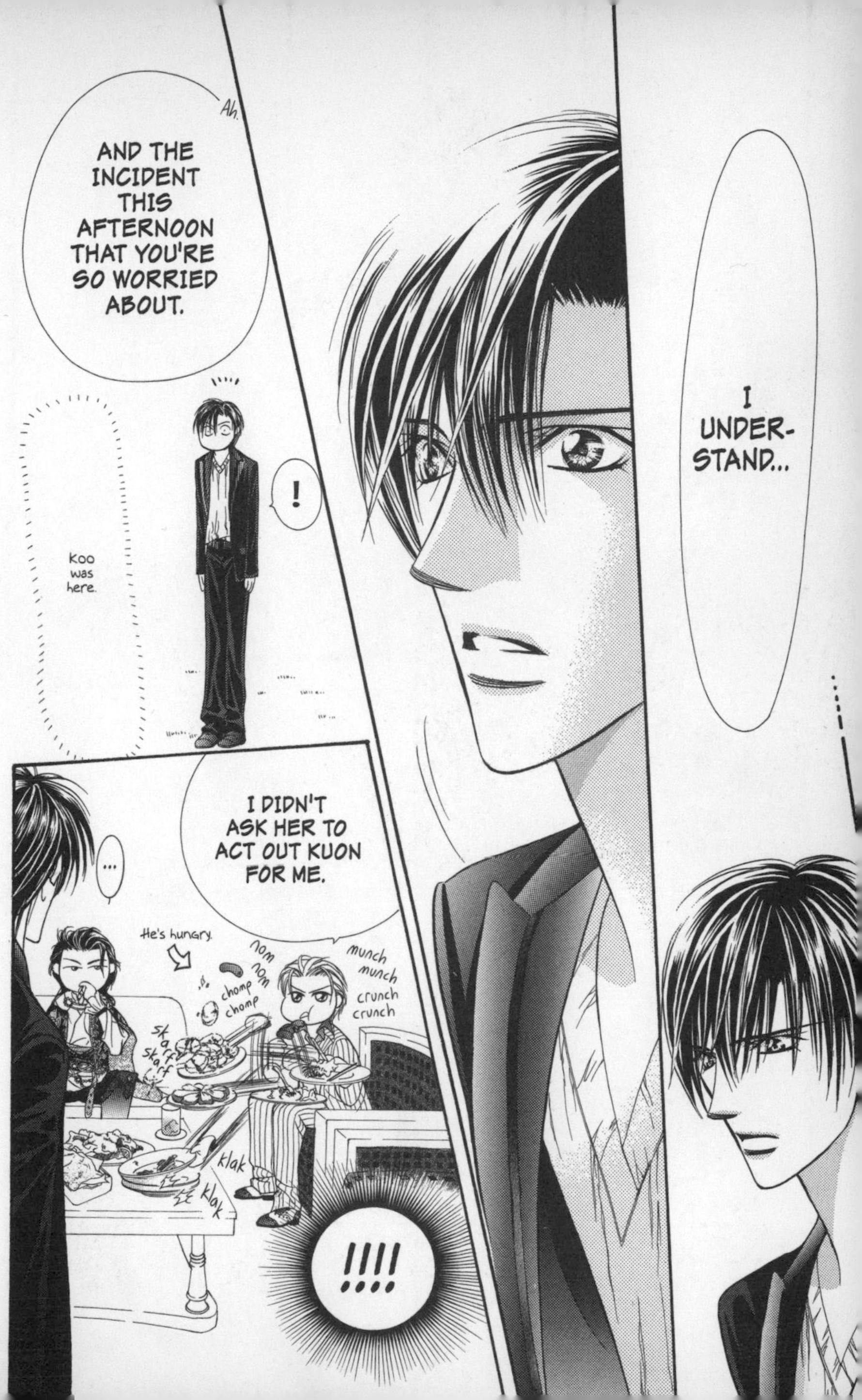
I UNDERSTAND...
Ah.
AND THE INCIDENT THIS AFTERNOON THAT YOU'RE SO WORRIED ABOUT.
!
Koo was here.
I DIDN'T ASK HER TO ACT OUT KUON FOR ME.
...
munch munch crunch crunch
nom nom
He's hungry.
chomp chomp
skarf skarf
klak klak
!!!!

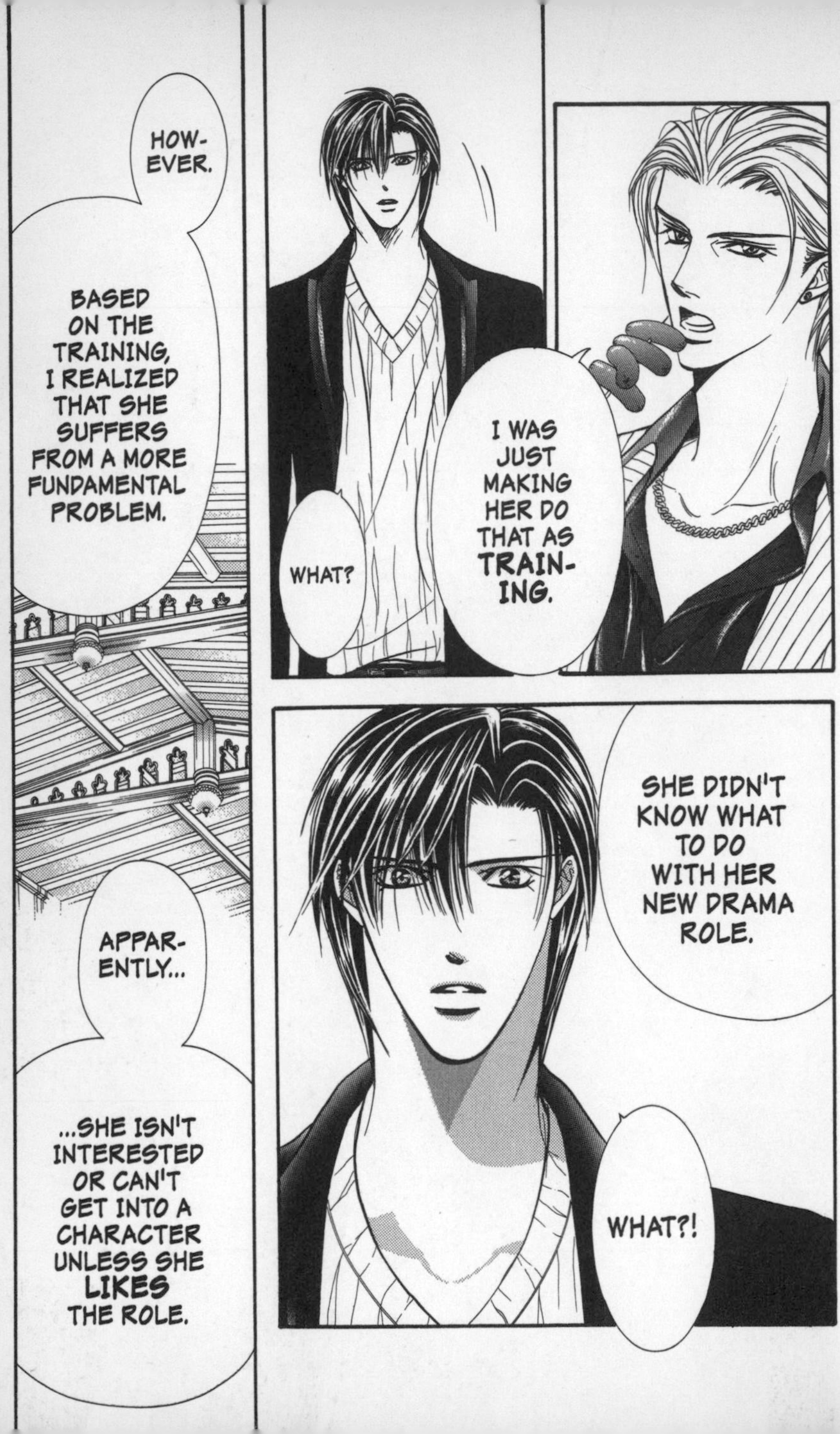
I WAS JUST MAKING HER DO THAT AS TRAINING.
WHAT?
SHE DIDN'T KNOW WHAT TO DO WITH HER NEW DRAMA ROLE.
WHAT?!
HOW-EVER.
BASED ON THE TRAINING, I REALIZED THAT SHE SUFFERS FROM A MORE FUNDAMENTAL PROBLEM.
APPAR-ENTLY...
...SHE ISN'T INTERESTED OR CAN'T GET INTO A CHARACTER UNLESS SHE LIKES THE ROLE.

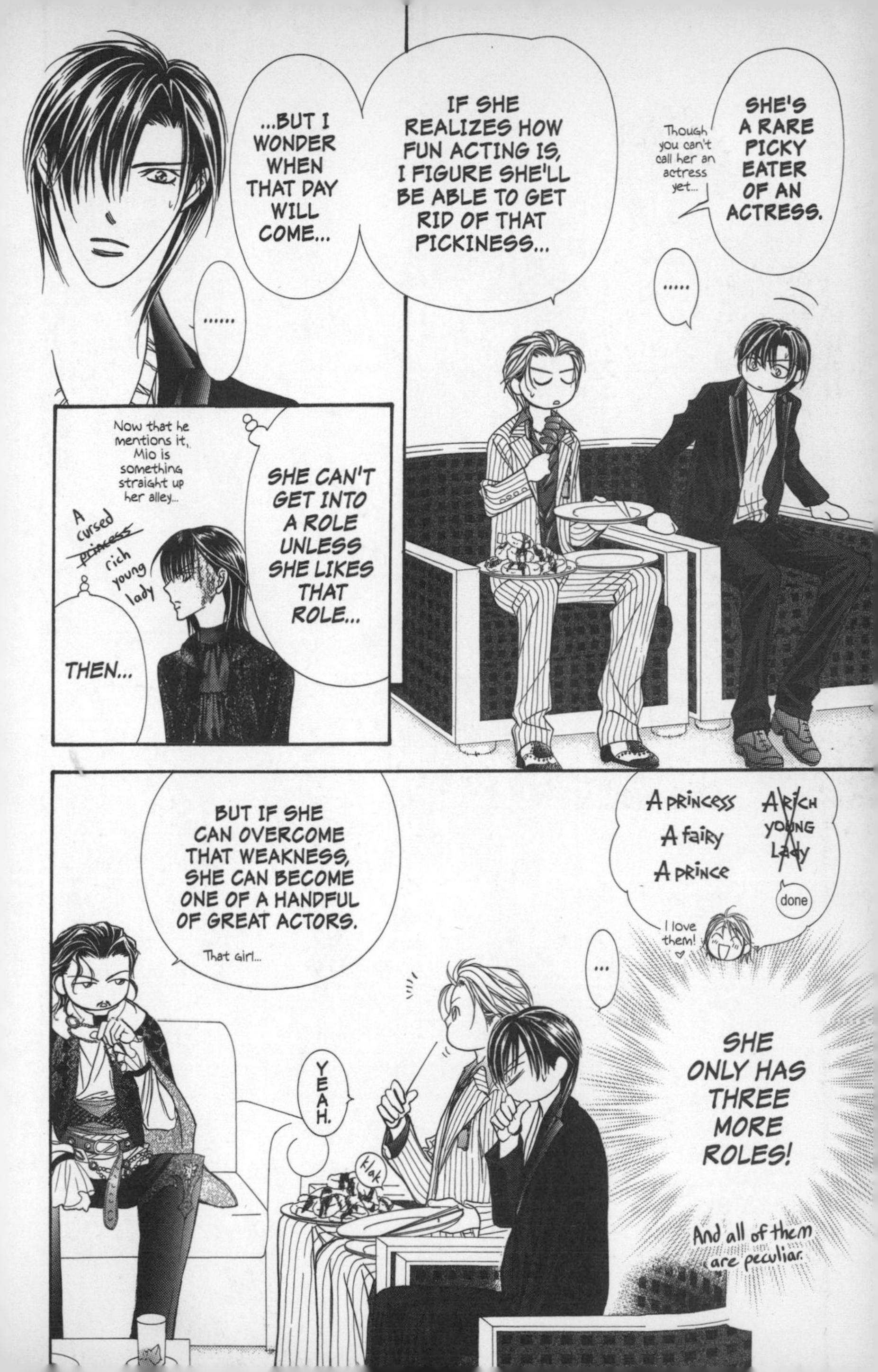
SHE'S A RARE PICKY EATER OF AN ACTRESS.
Though you can't call her an actress yet...
......
IF SHE REALIZES HOW FUN ACTING IS, I FIGURE SHE'LL BE ABLE TO GET RID OF THAT PICKINESS...
...BUT I WONDER WHEN THAT DAY WILL COME...
......
SHE CAN'T GET INTO A ROLE UNLESS SHE LIKES THAT ROLE...
Now that he mentions it, Mio is something straight up her alley...
A cursed princess rich young lady
THEN...
A princess
A fairy
A prince
A rich young lady
done
I love them!
SHE ONLY HAS THREE MORE ROLES!
And all of them are peculiar.
...
BUT IF SHE CAN OVERCOME THAT WEAKNESS, SHE CAN BECOME ONE OF A HANDFUL OF GREAT ACTORS.
That girl...
YEAH.
klak

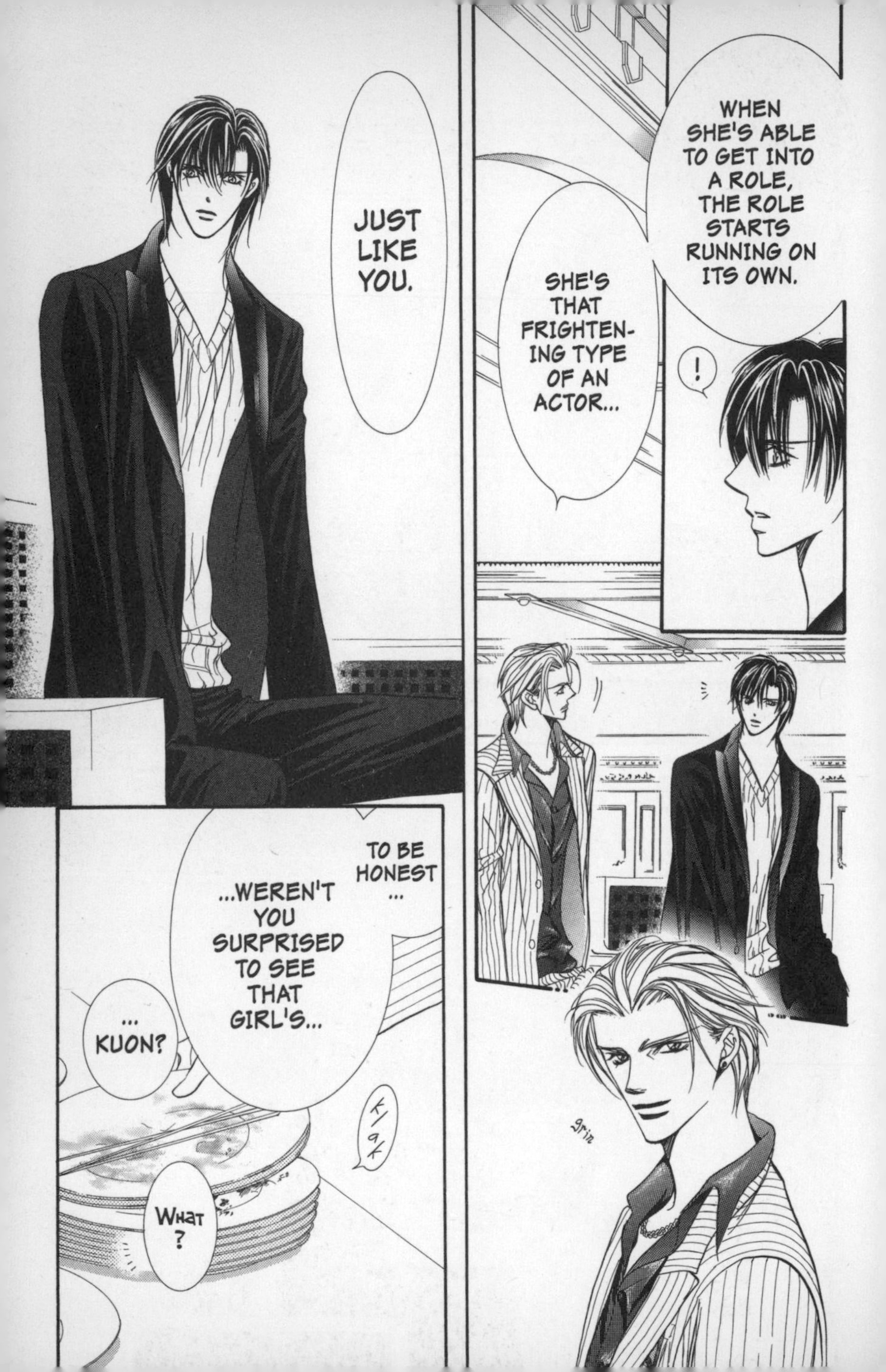
WHEN SHE'S ABLE TO GET INTO A ROLE, THE ROLE STARTS RUNNING ON ITS OWN.
SHE'S THAT FRIGHTEN-ING TYPE OF AN ACTOR...
!
grin
JUST LIKE YOU.
TO BE HONEST ...
...WEREN'T YOU SURPRISED TO SEE THAT GIRL'S...
... KUON?
WHAT ?

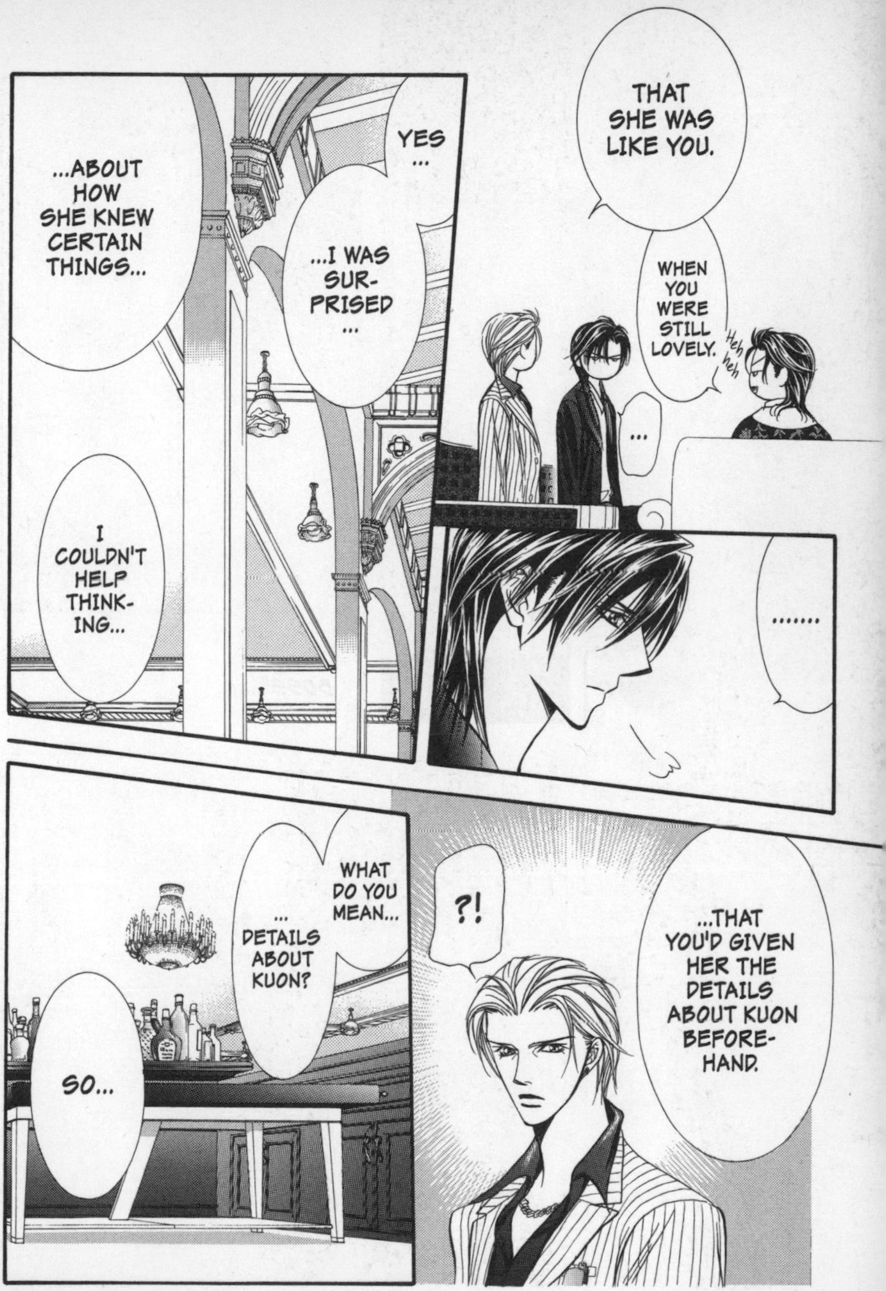
THAT SHE WAS LIKE YOU.
WHEN YOU WERE STILL LOVELY.
Heh heh
...
.......
YES ...
...I WAS SURPRISED ...
...ABOUT HOW SHE KNEW CERTAIN THINGS...
I COULDN'T HELP THINKING...
?!
...THAT YOU'D GIVEN HER THE DETAILS ABOUT KUON BEFOREHAND.
WHAT DO YOU MEAN...
... DETAILS ABOUT KUON?
SO...

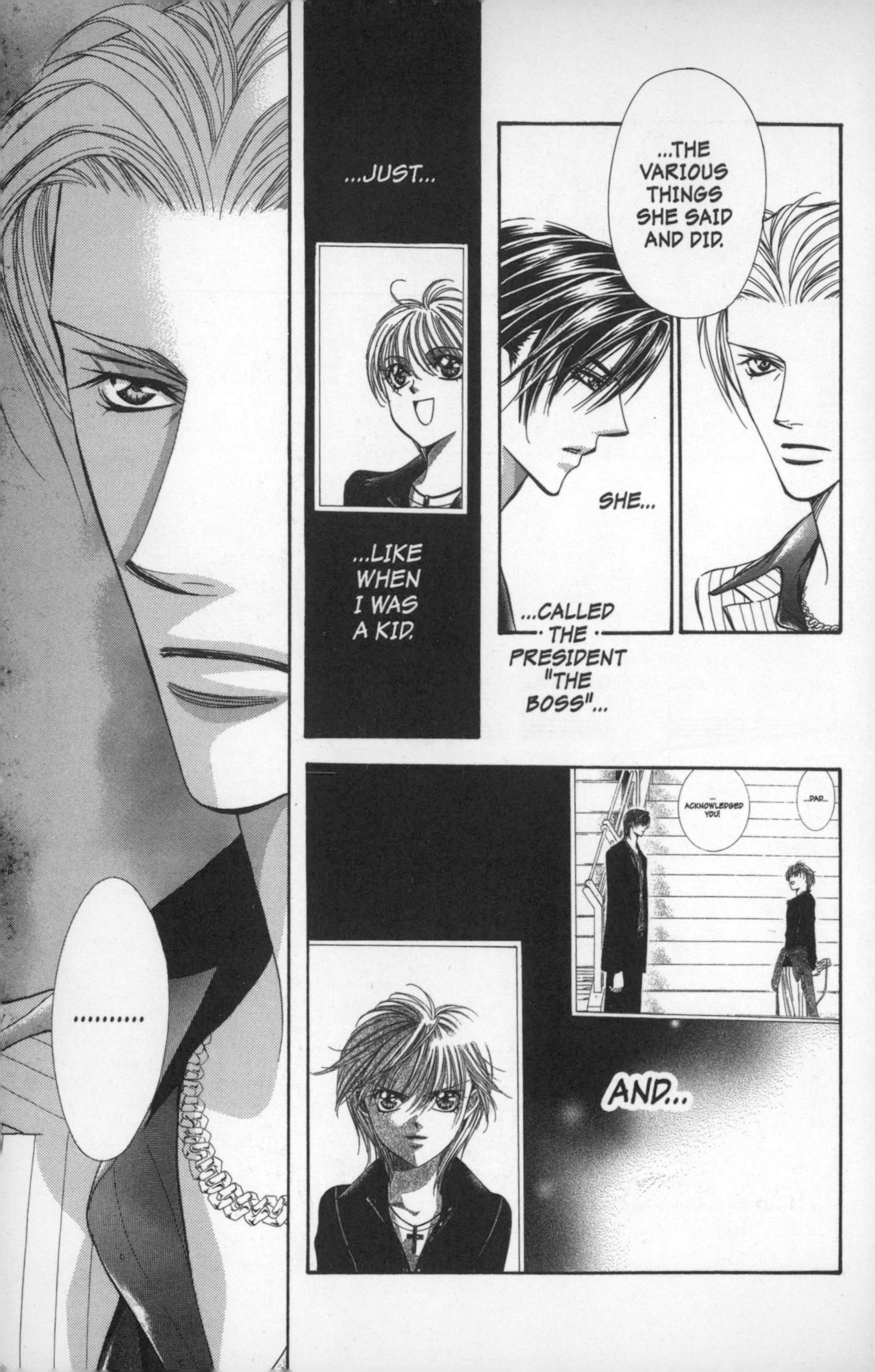
...THE VARIOUS THINGS SHE SAID AND DID.
SHE...
...CALLED THE PRESIDENT "THE BOSS"...
...JUST...
...LIKE WHEN I WAS A KID.
...DAD...
...ACKNOWLEDGED YOU!
AND...
..........

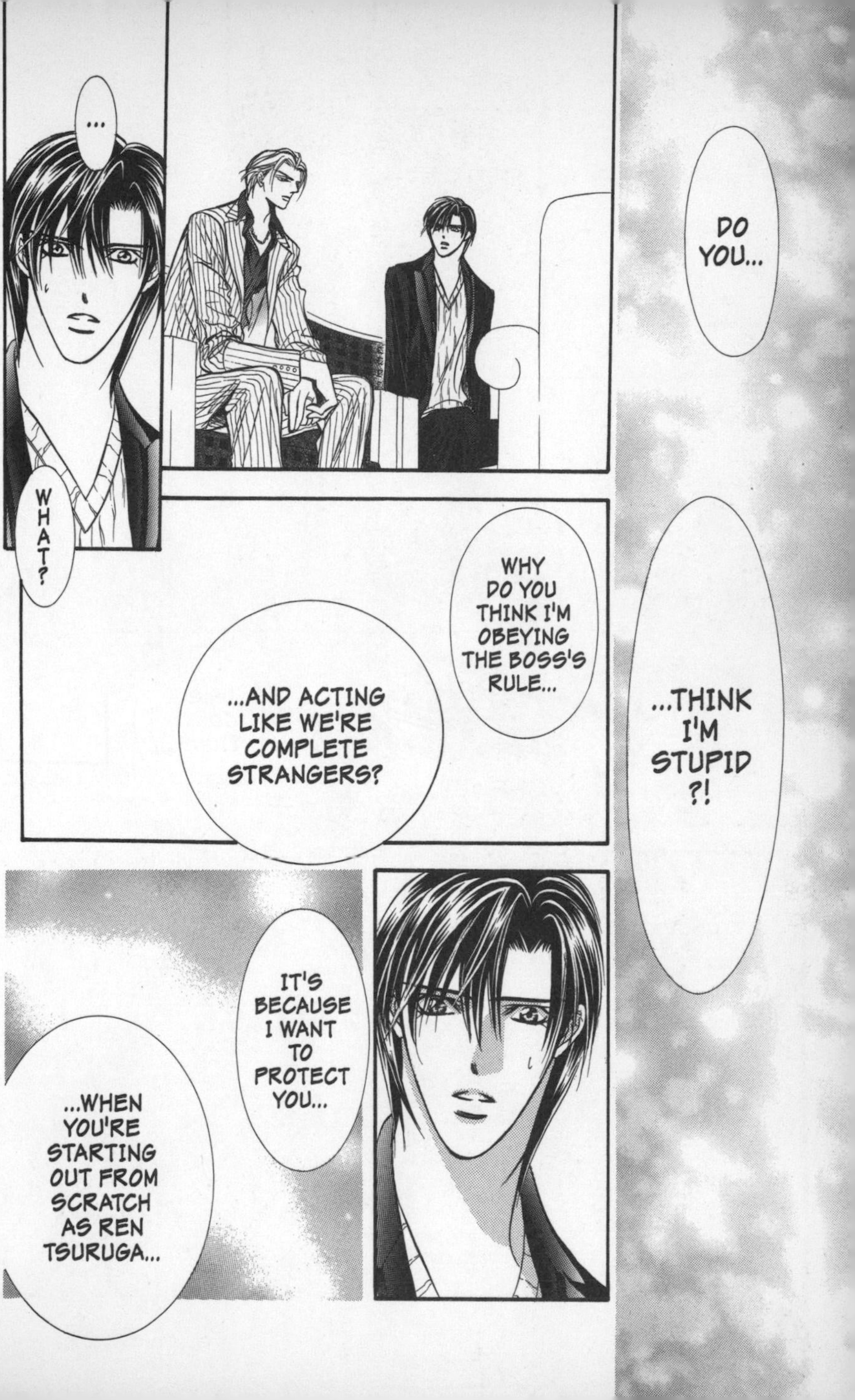
DO YOU...
...THINK I'M STUPID?!
...
WHAT?
WHY DO YOU THINK I'M OBEYING THE BOSS'S RULE...
...AND ACTING LIKE WE'RE COMPLETE STRANGERS?
IT'S BECAUSE I WANT TO PROTECT YOU...
...WHEN YOU'RE STARTING OUT FROM SCRATCH AS REN TSURUGA...

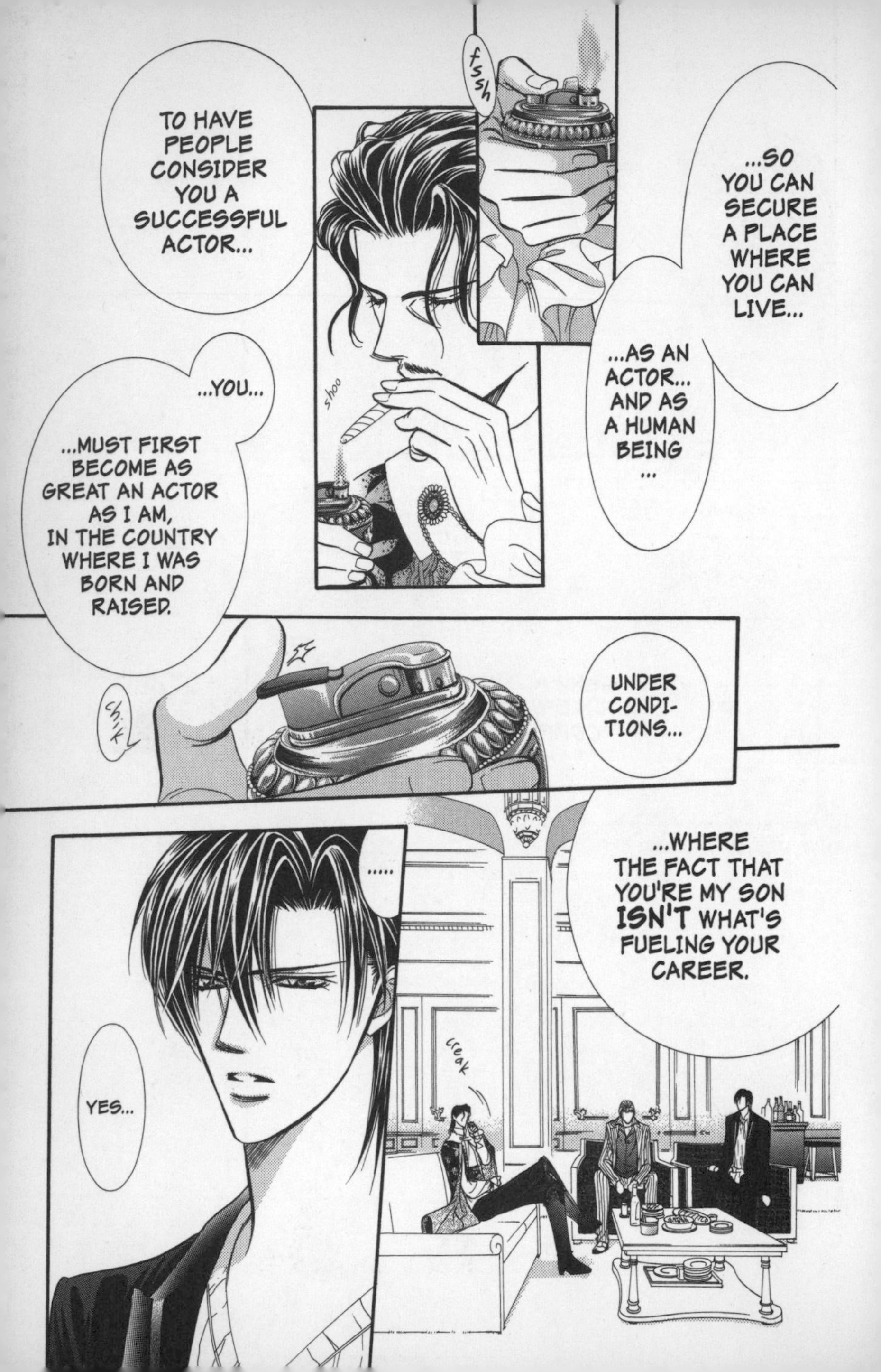
...SO YOU CAN SECURE A PLACE WHERE YOU CAN LIVE...
...AS AN ACTOR... AND AS A HUMAN BEING ...
fssh
shoo
TO HAVE PEOPLE CONSIDER YOU A SUCCESSFUL ACTOR...
...YOU...
...MUST FIRST BECOME AS GREAT AN ACTOR AS I AM, IN THE COUNTRY WHERE I WAS BORN AND RAISED.
UNDER CONDI-TIONS...
chik
...WHERE THE FACT THAT YOU'RE MY SON ISN'T WHAT'S FUELING YOUR CAREER.
creak
.....
YES...

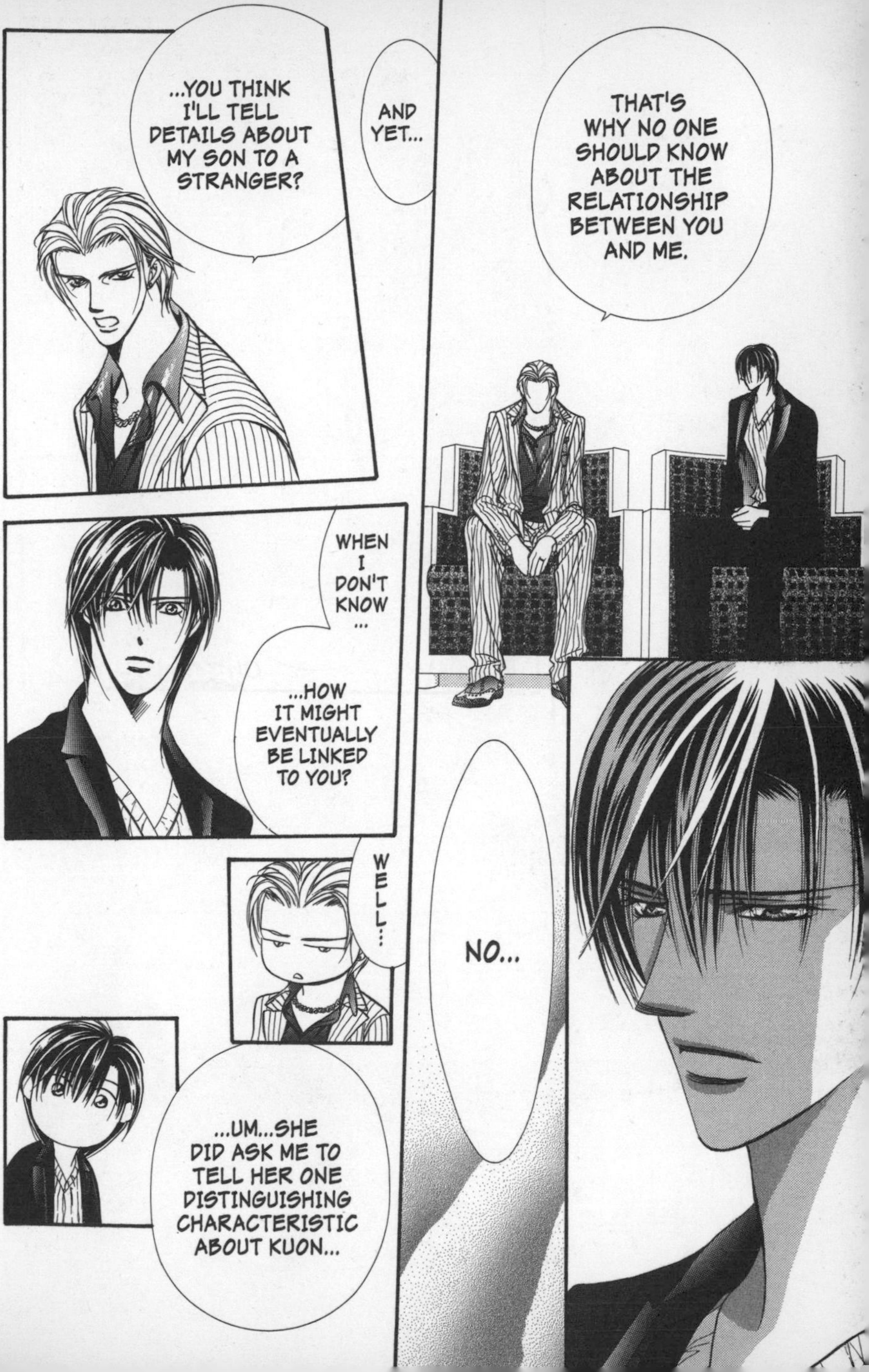
THAT'S WHY NO ONE SHOULD KNOW ABOUT THE RELATIONSHIP BETWEEN YOU AND ME.
NO...
AND YET...
...YOU THINK I'LL TELL DETAILS ABOUT MY SON TO A STRANGER?
WHEN I DON'T KNOW ...
...HOW IT MIGHT EVENTUALLY BE LINKED TO YOU?
WELL...
...UM...SHE DID ASK ME TO TELL HER ONE DISTINGUISHING CHARACTERISTIC ABOUT KUON...

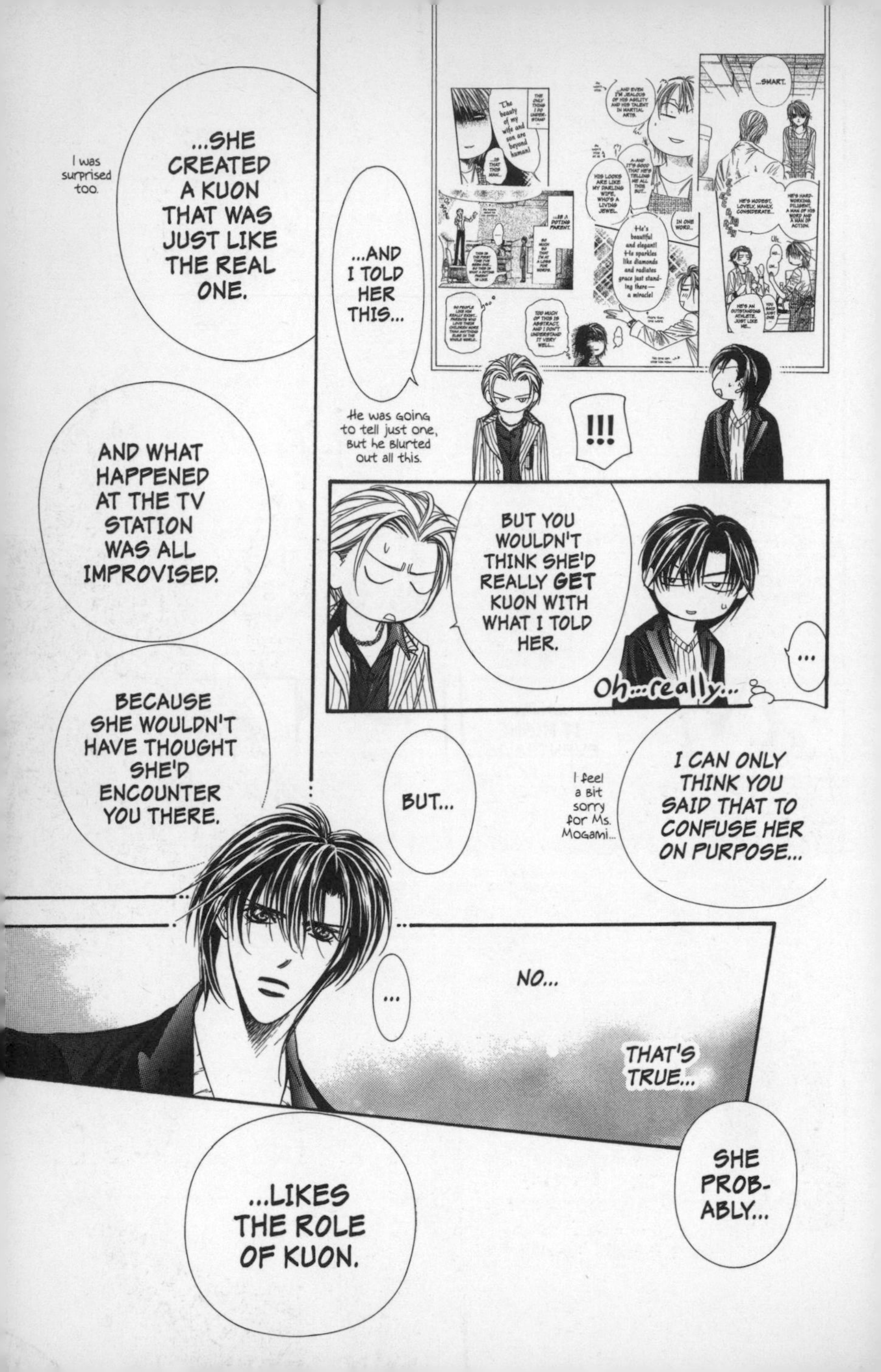
...AND I TOLD HER THIS...
The beauty of my wife and son are beyond human!
He's beautiful and elegant! He sparkles like diamonds and radiates grace just standing there— a miracle!
He was going to tell just one, but he blurted out all this.
!!!
BUT YOU WOULDN'T THINK SHE'D REALLY GET KUON WITH WHAT I TOLD HER.
...
Oh...really...
I CAN ONLY THINK YOU SAID THAT TO CONFUSE HER ON PURPOSE...
I feel a bit sorry for Ms. Mogami...
BUT...
...SHE CREATED A KUON THAT WAS JUST LIKE THE REAL ONE.
I was surprised too.
AND WHAT HAPPENED AT THE TV STATION WAS ALL IMPROVISED.
BECAUSE SHE WOULDN'T HAVE THOUGHT SHE'D ENCOUNTER YOU THERE.
NO...
...
THAT'S TRUE...
SHE PROBABLY...
...LIKES THE ROLE OF KUON.

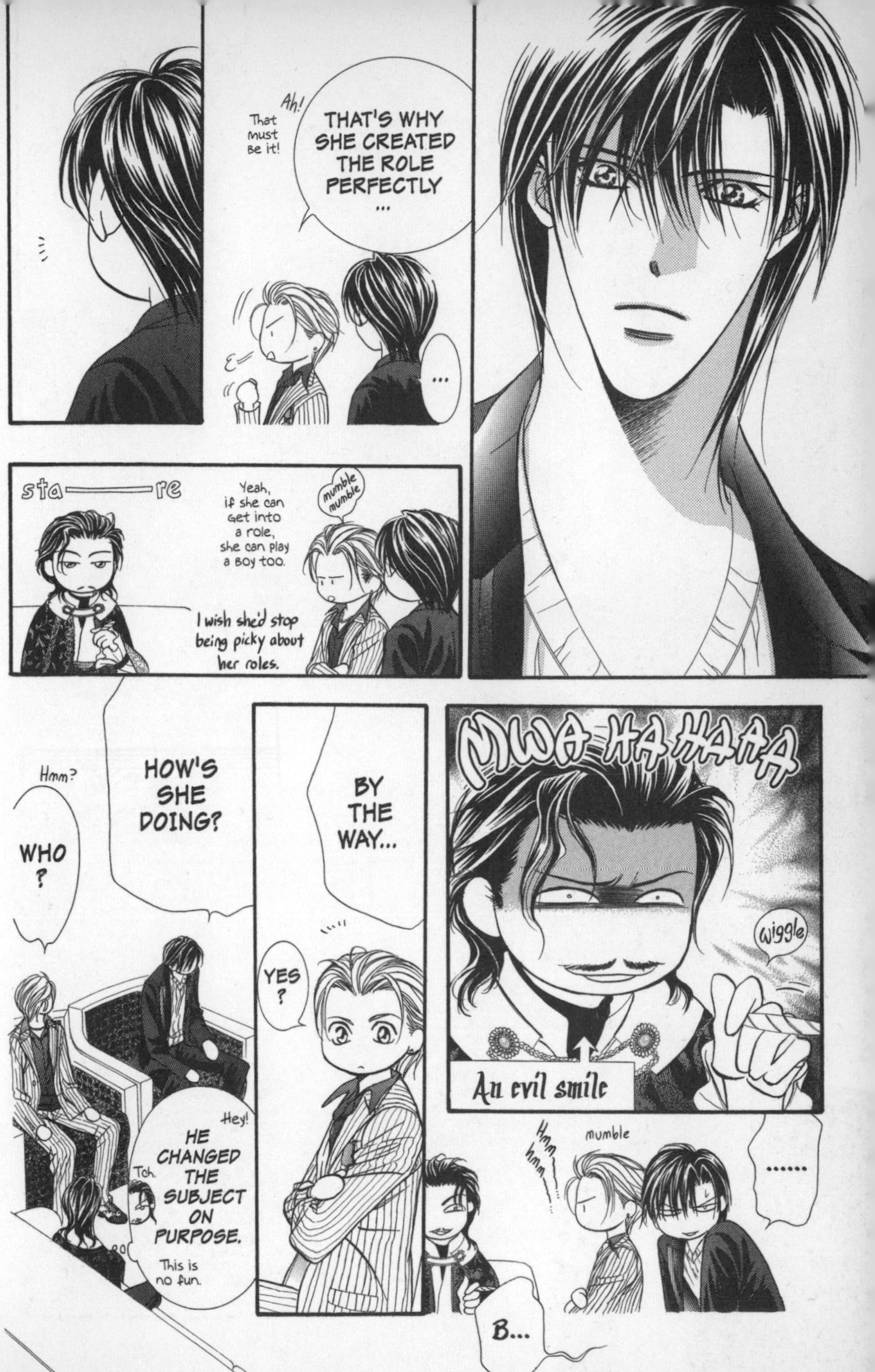
THAT'S WHY SHE CREATED THE ROLE PERFECTLY ...
Ah! That must be it!
...
mumble mumble
Yeah, if she can get into a role, she can play a boy too.
sta——re
I wish she'd stop being picky about her roles.
MWA HA HAAA
wiggle
An evil smile
......
mumble
Hmm hmm...
B...
BY THE WAY...
YES?
HOW'S SHE DOING?
Hmm?
WHO?
Hey!
HE CHANGED THE SUBJECT ON PURPOSE.
Tch.
This is no fun.

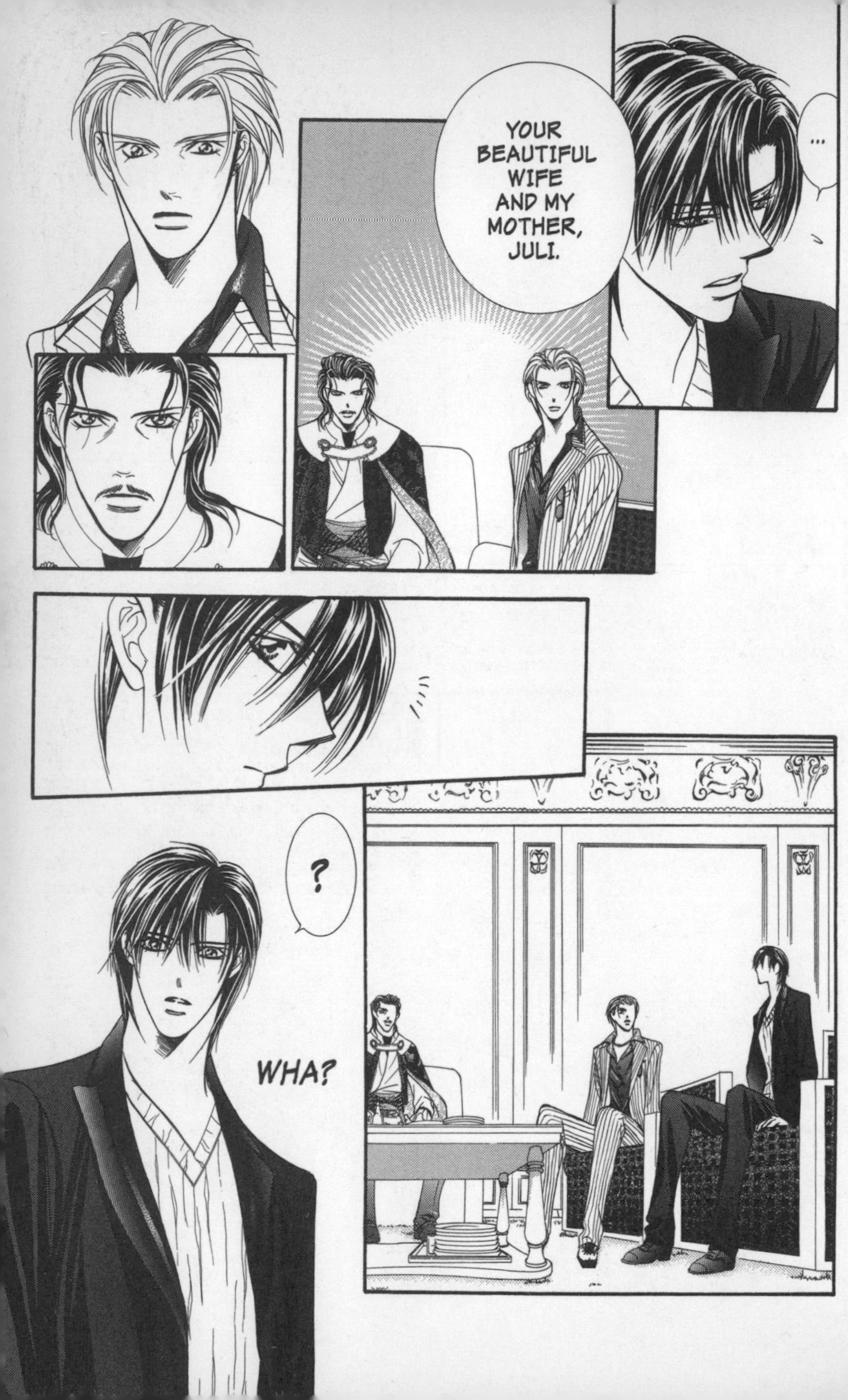
YOUR BEAUTIFUL WIFE AND MY MOTHER, JULI.
...
?
WHA?

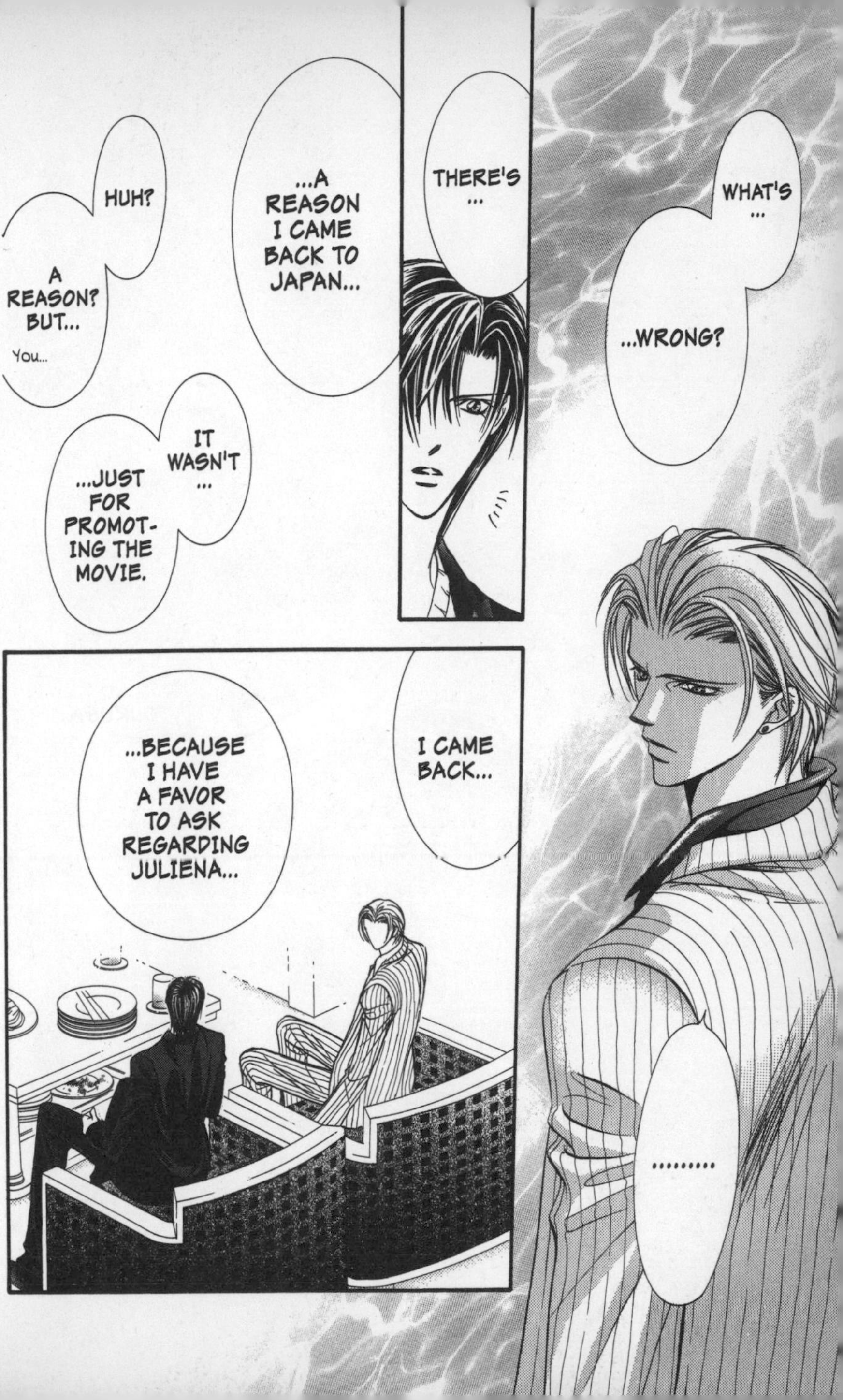
WHAT'S ... ...WRONG?
..........
THERE'S ...
...A REASON I CAME BACK TO JAPAN...
HUH?
A REASON? BUT...
You...
IT WASN'T ...
...JUST FOR PROMOT-ING THE MOVIE.
I CAME BACK...
...BECAUSE I HAVE A FAVOR TO ASK REGARDING JULIENA...

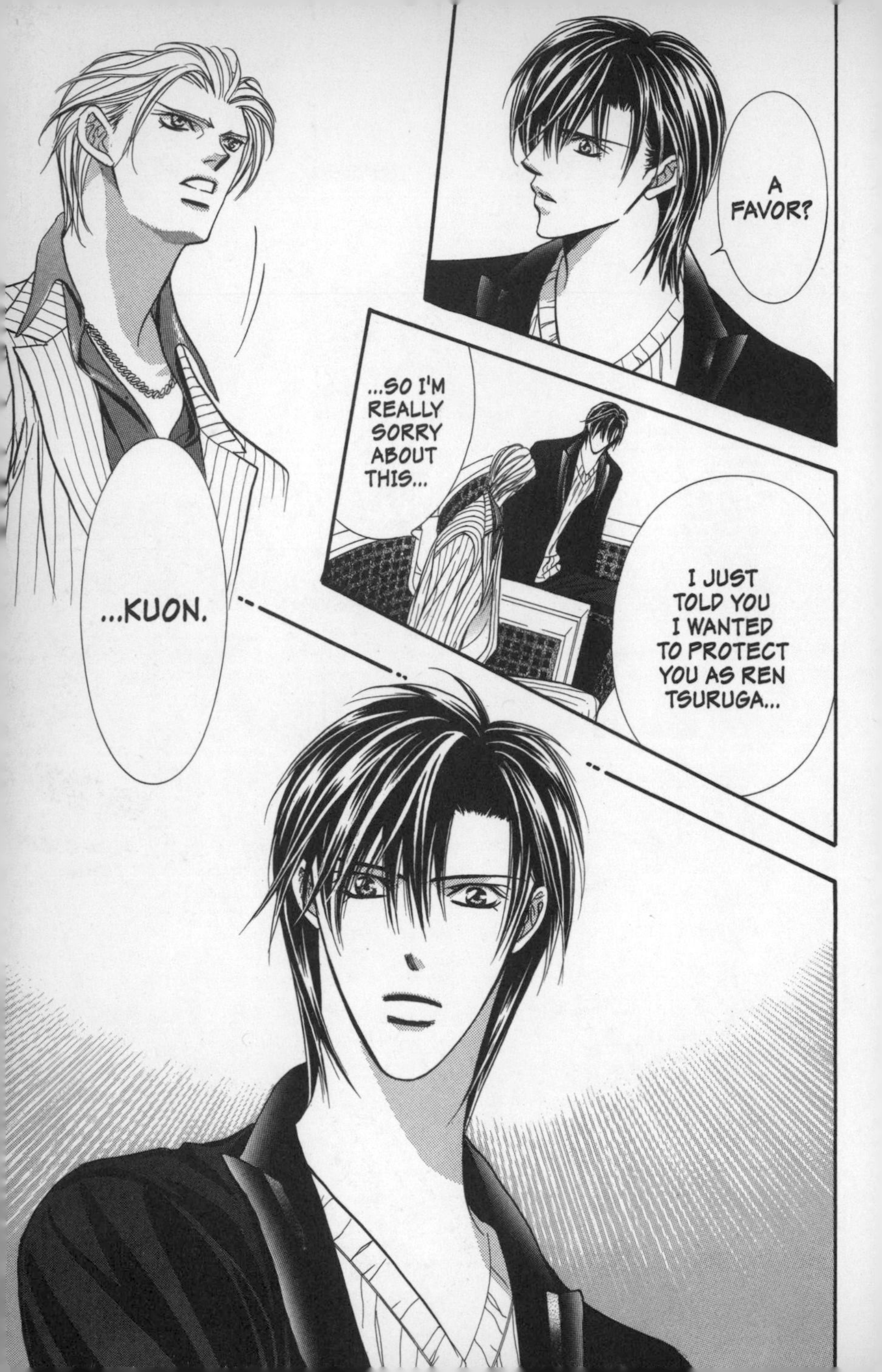
A FAVOR?
I JUST TOLD YOU I WANTED TO PROTECT YOU AS REN TSURUGA...
...SO I'M REALLY SORRY ABOUT THIS...
...KUON.

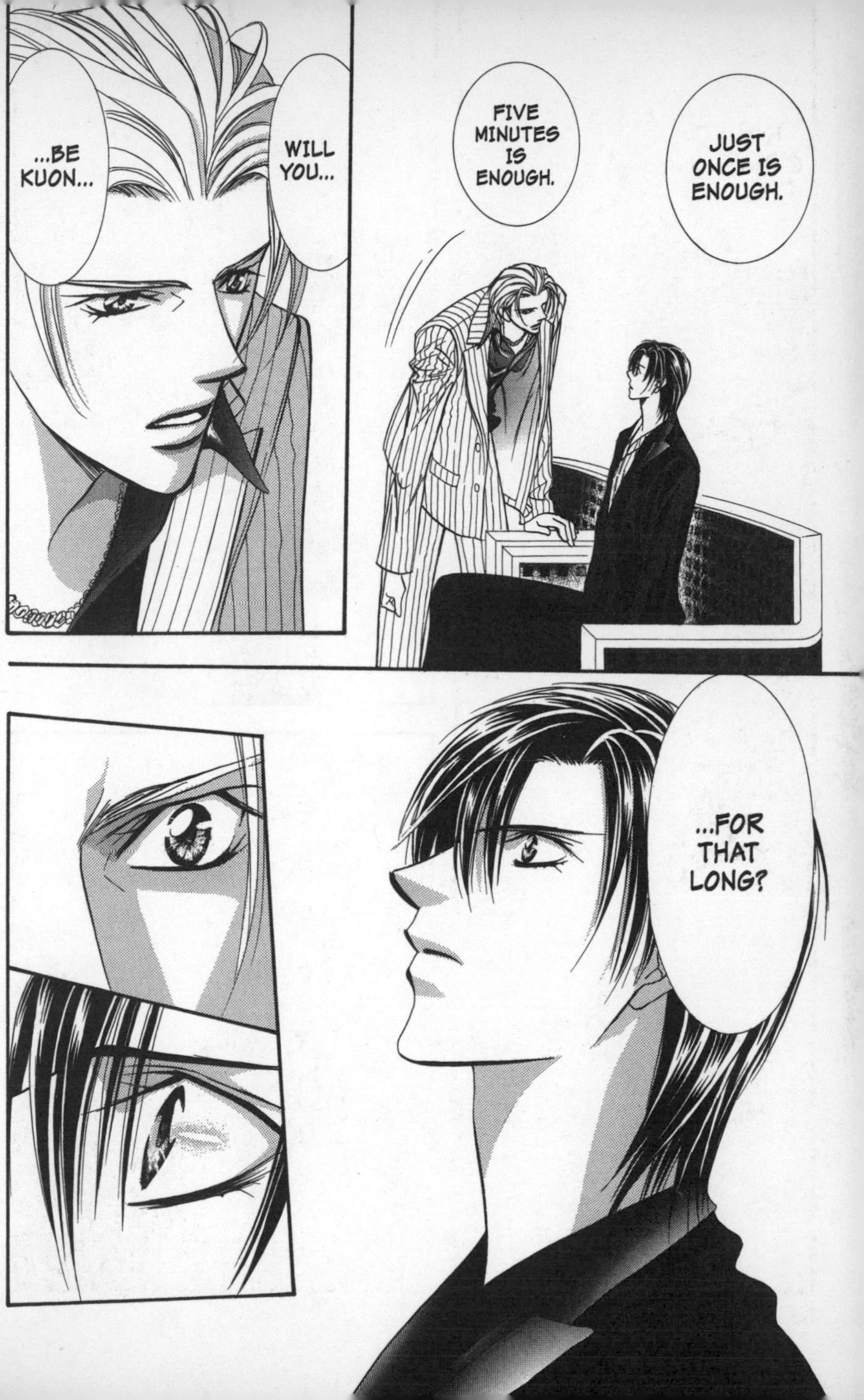
JUST ONCE IS ENOUGH.
FIVE MINUTES IS ENOUGH.
WILL YOU...
...BE KUON...
...FOR THAT LONG?

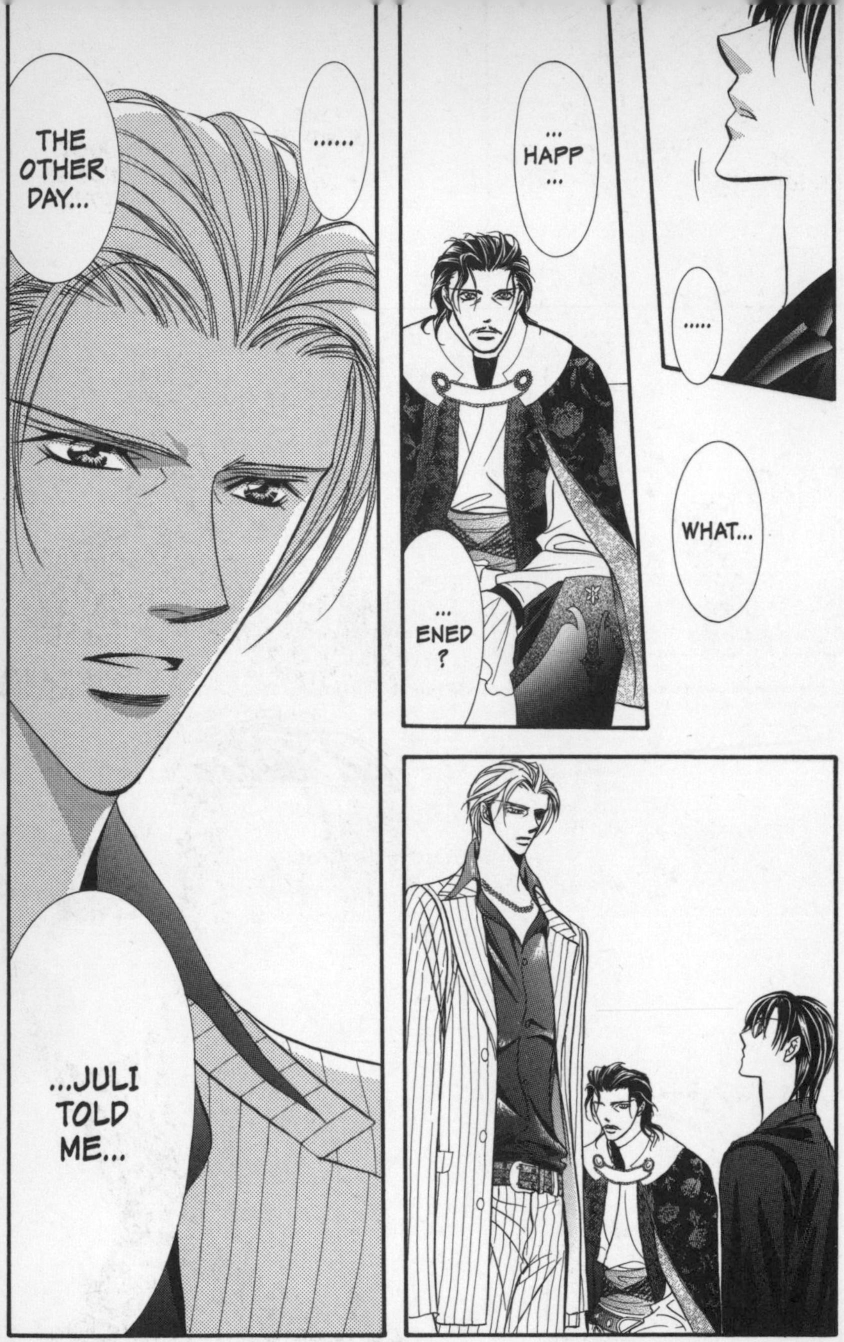
.....
WHAT...
...HAPP...
...ENED?
......
THE OTHER DAY...
...JULI TOLD ME...

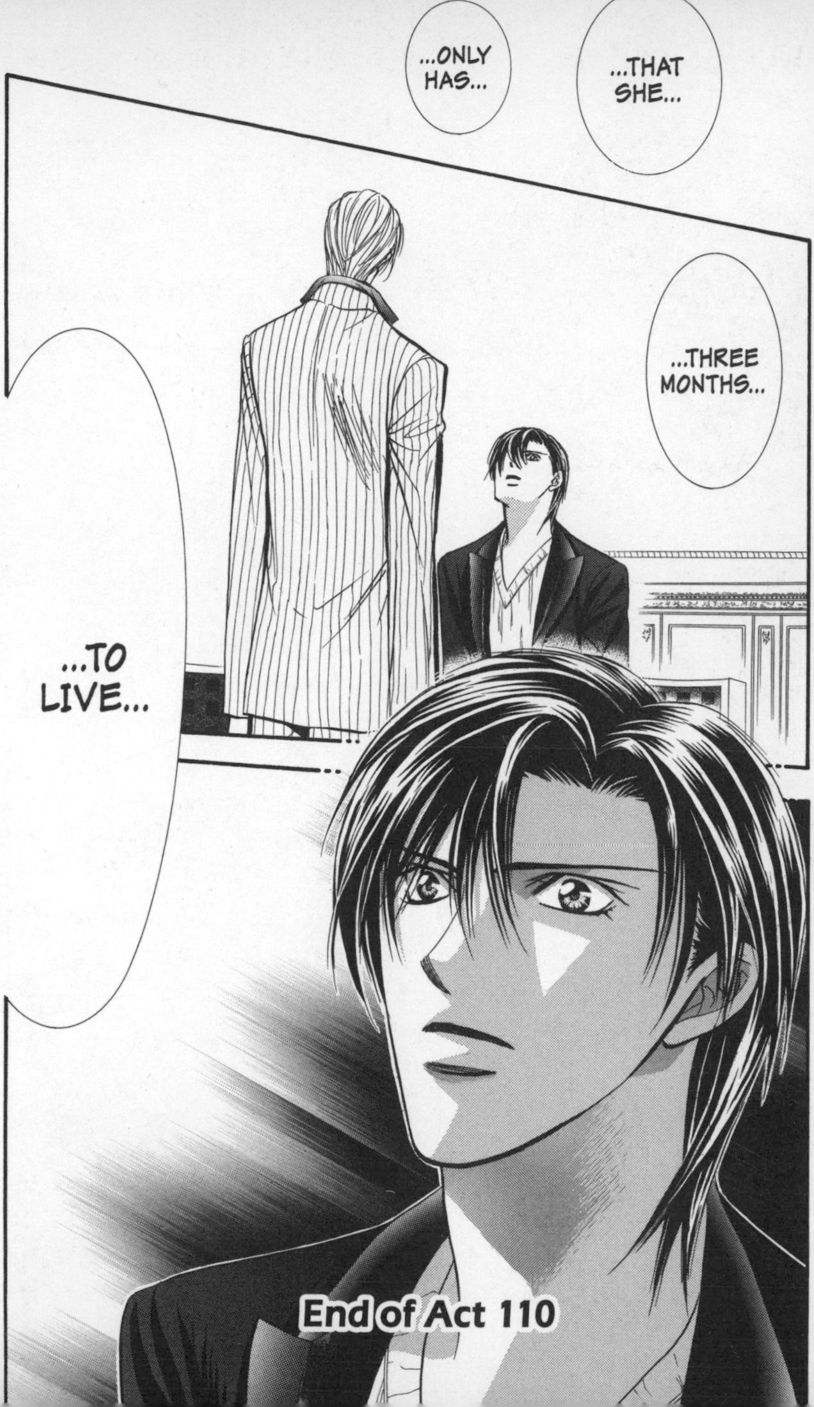
...THAT SHE...
...ONLY HAS...
...THREE MONTHS...
...TO LIVE...
End of Act 110

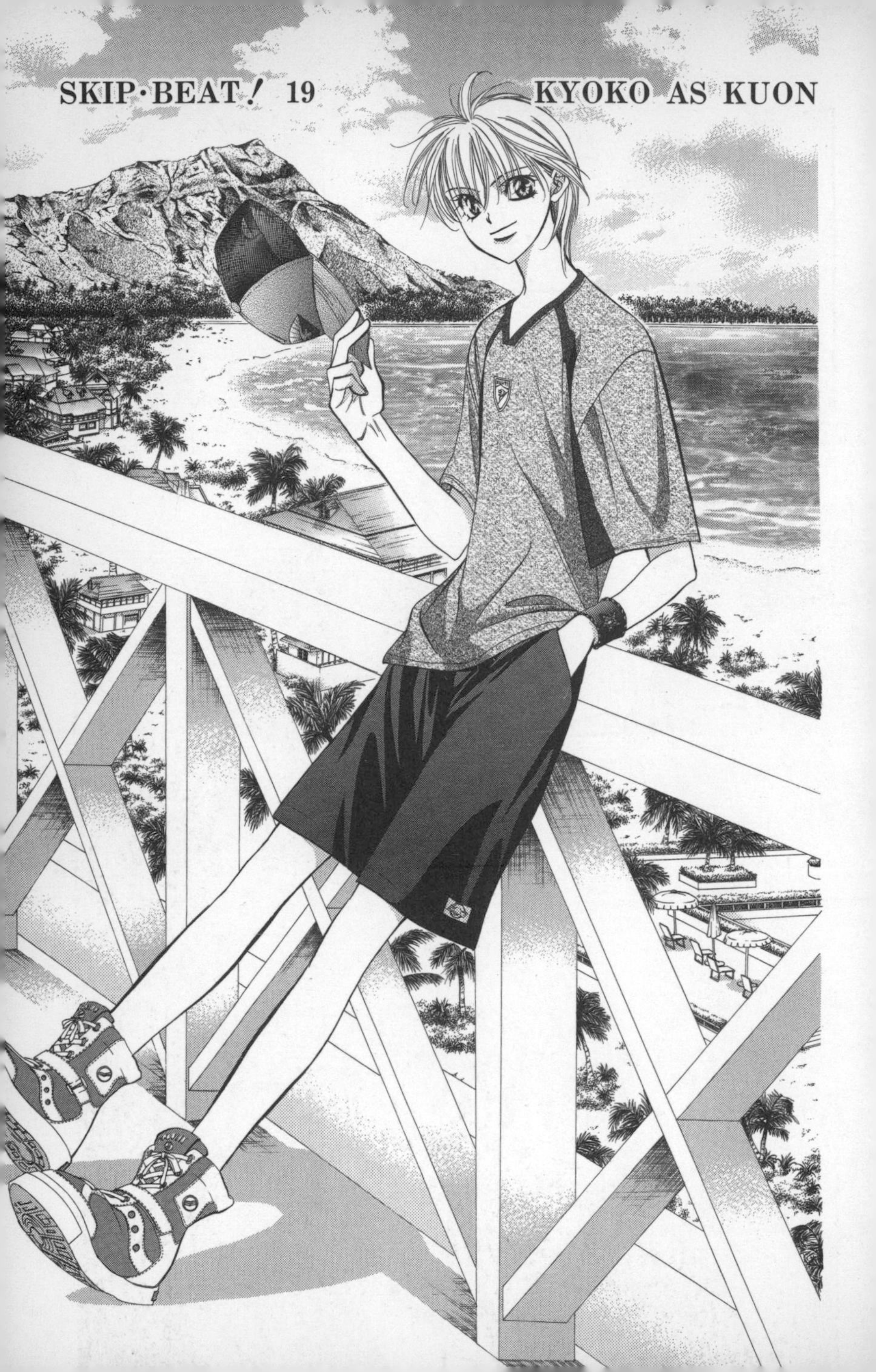
SKIP·BEAT! 19
KYOKO AS KUON

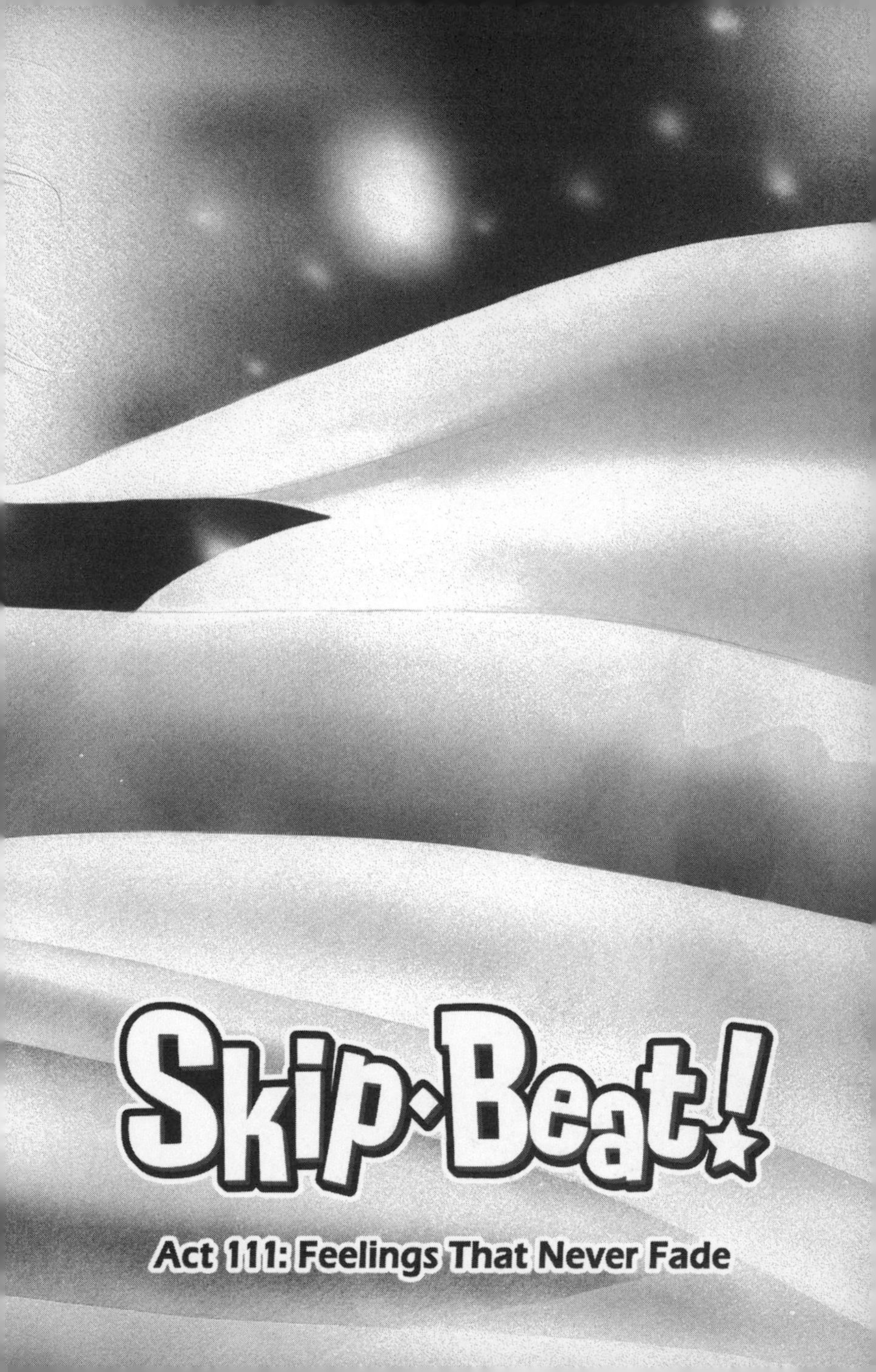
Skip·Beat!
Act 111: Feelings That Never Fade

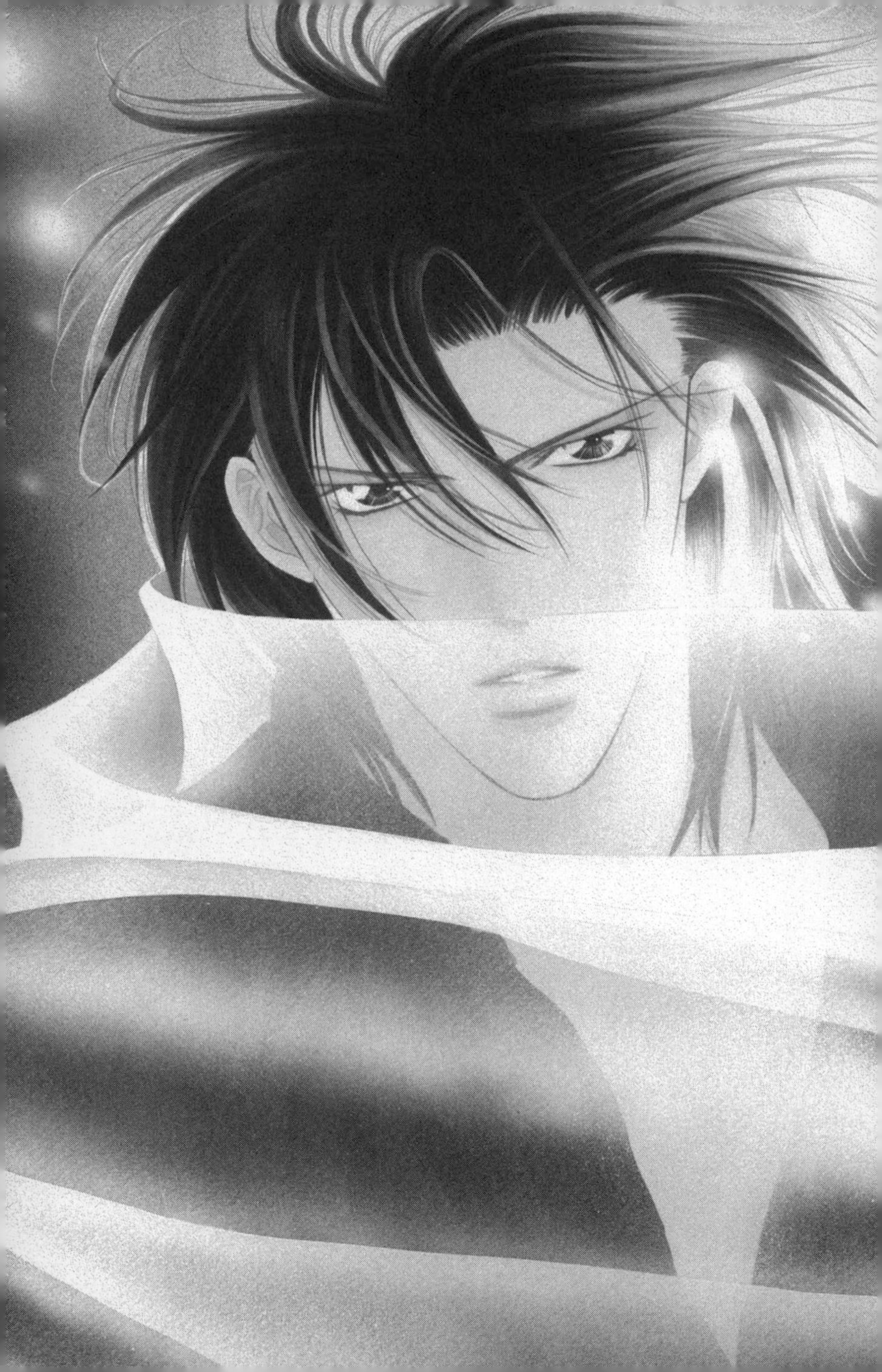

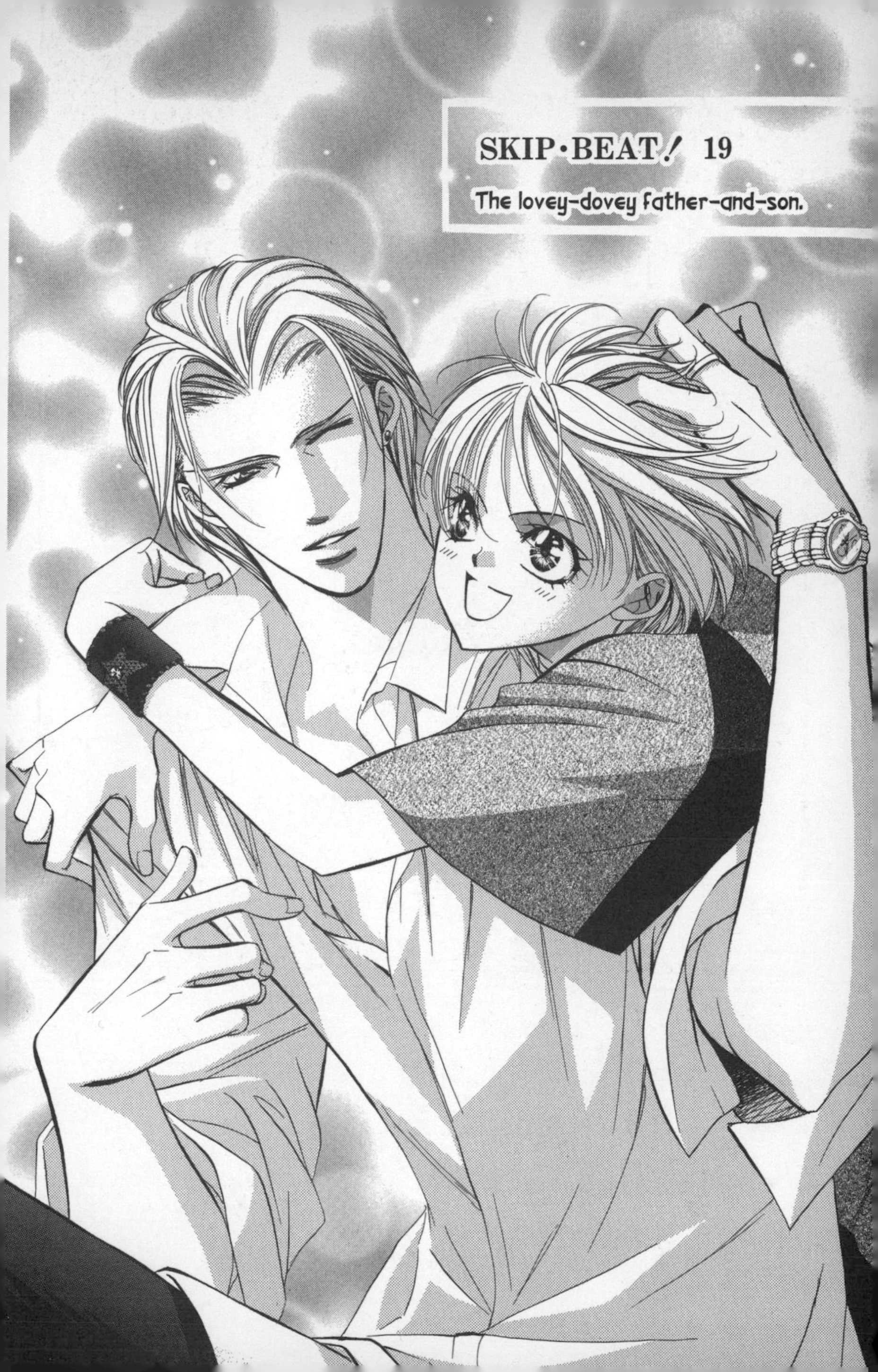
SKIP·BEAT! 19
The lovey-dovey father-and-son.

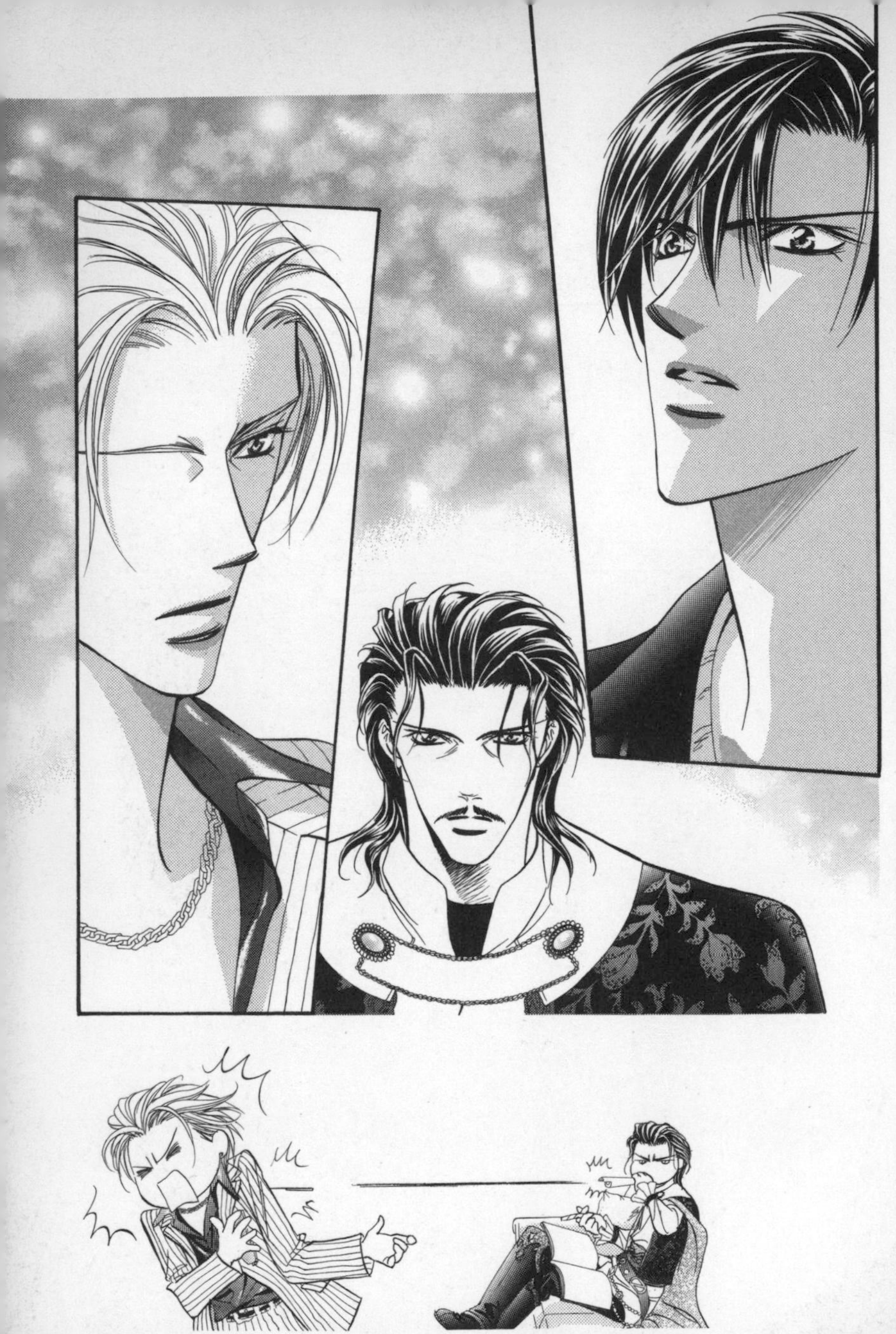

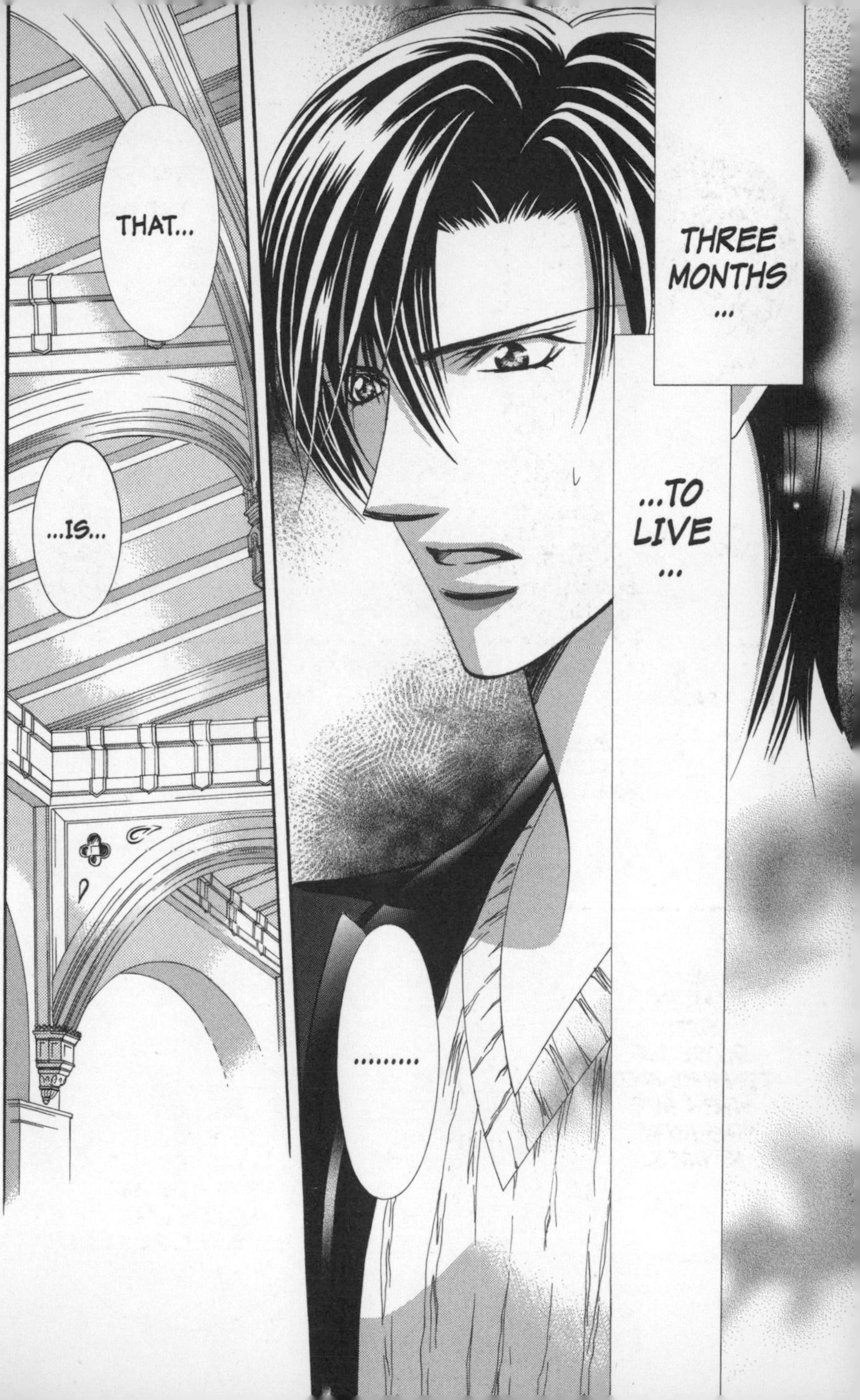
THREE MONTHS ...
...TO LIVE ...
.........
THAT...
...IS...

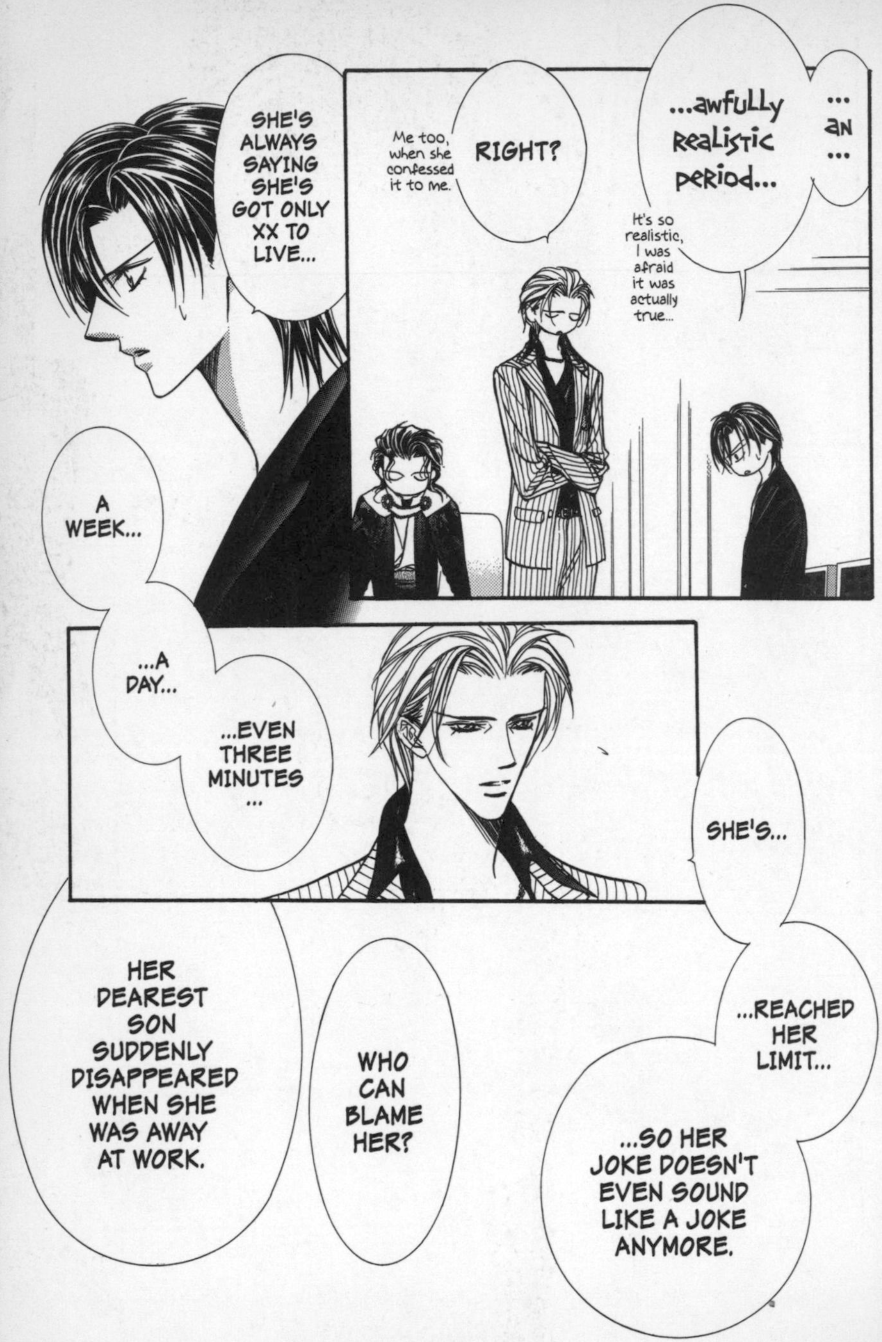

... an ...
...awfully realistic period...
It's so realistic, I was afraid it was actually true...
RIGHT?
Me too, when she confessed it to me.
SHE'S ALWAYS SAYING SHE'S GOT ONLY XX TO LIVE...
A WEEK...
...A DAY...
...EVEN THREE MINUTES ...
SHE'S...
...REACHED HER LIMIT...
...SO HER JOKE DOESN'T EVEN SOUND LIKE A JOKE ANYMORE.
WHO CAN BLAME HER?
HER DEAREST SON SUDDENLY DISAPPEARED WHEN SHE WAS AWAY AT WORK.

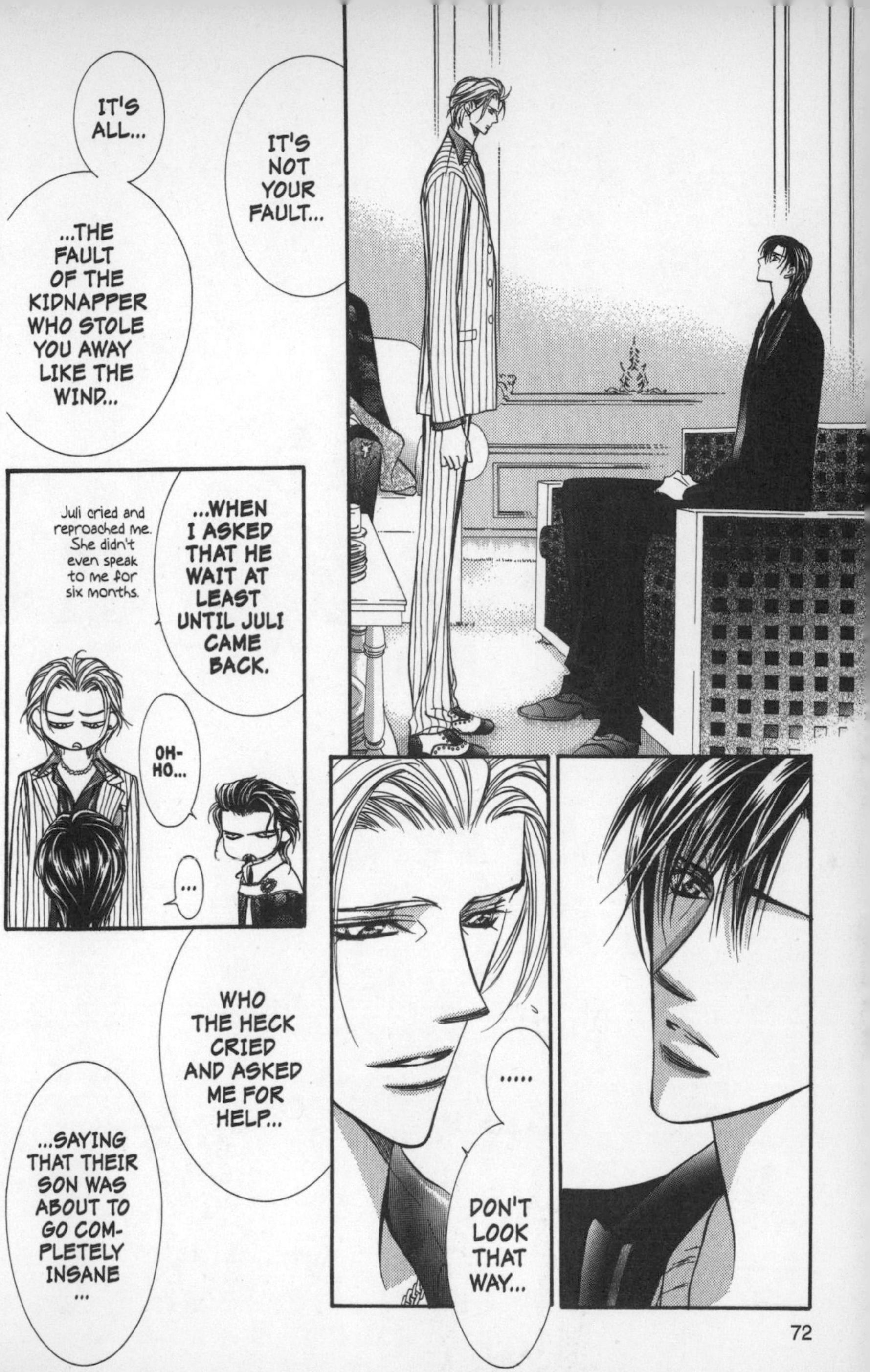
IT'S NOT YOUR FAULT...
IT'S ALL...
...THE FAULT OF THE KIDNAPPER WHO STOLE YOU AWAY LIKE THE WIND...
...WHEN I ASKED THAT HE WAIT AT LEAST UNTIL JULI CAME BACK.
Juli cried and reproached me. She didn't even speak to me for six months.
OH-HO...
...
WHO THE HECK CRIED AND ASKED ME FOR HELP...
...SAYING THAT THEIR SON WAS ABOUT TO GO COM-PLETELY INSANE ...
.....
DON'T LOOK THAT WAY...

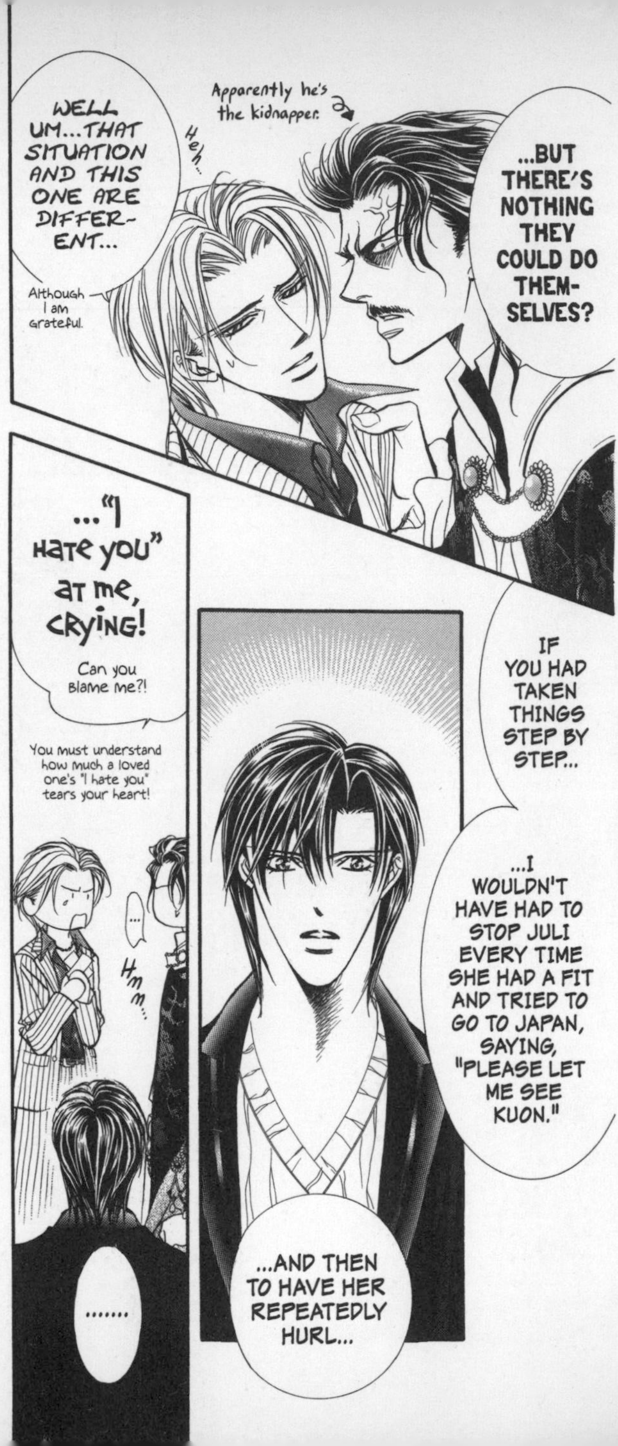
...BUT THERE'S NOTHING THEY COULD DO THEMSELVES?
Apparently he's the kidnapper.
Heh...
WELL UM...THAT SITUATION AND THIS ONE ARE DIFFERENT...
Although I am grateful.
IF YOU HAD TAKEN THINGS STEP BY STEP...
...I WOULDN'T HAVE HAD TO STOP JULI EVERY TIME SHE HAD A FIT AND TRIED TO GO TO JAPAN, SAYING, "PLEASE LET ME SEE KUON."
...AND THEN TO HAVE HER REPEATEDLY HURL...
..."I hate you" at me, crying!
Can you blame me?!
You must understand how much a loved one's "I hate you" tears your heart!
...
Hmm...
.......

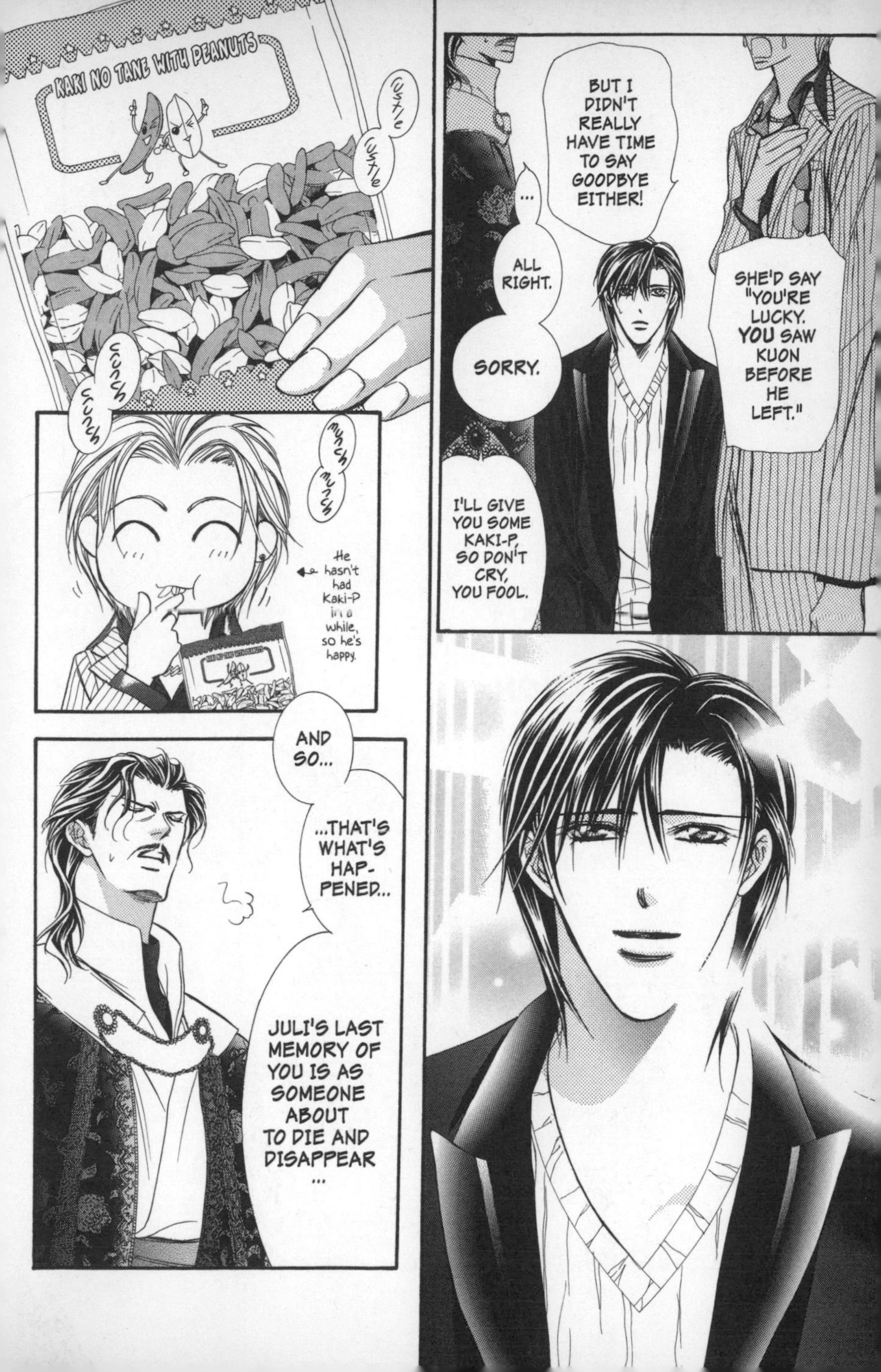

BUT I DIDN'T REALLY HAVE TIME TO SAY GOODBYE EITHER!
SHE'D SAY "YOU'RE LUCKY. YOU SAW KUON BEFORE HE LEFT."
...
ALL RIGHT.
SORRY.
I'LL GIVE YOU SOME KAKI-P, SO DON'T CRY, YOU FOOL.
KAKI NO TANE WITH PEANUTS
rustle rustle
crunch crunch
munch munch
He hasn't had Kaki-P in a while, so he's happy.
AND SO...
...THAT'S WHAT'S HAP-PENED...
JULI'S LAST MEMORY OF YOU IS AS SOMEONE ABOUT TO DIE AND DISAPPEAR ...

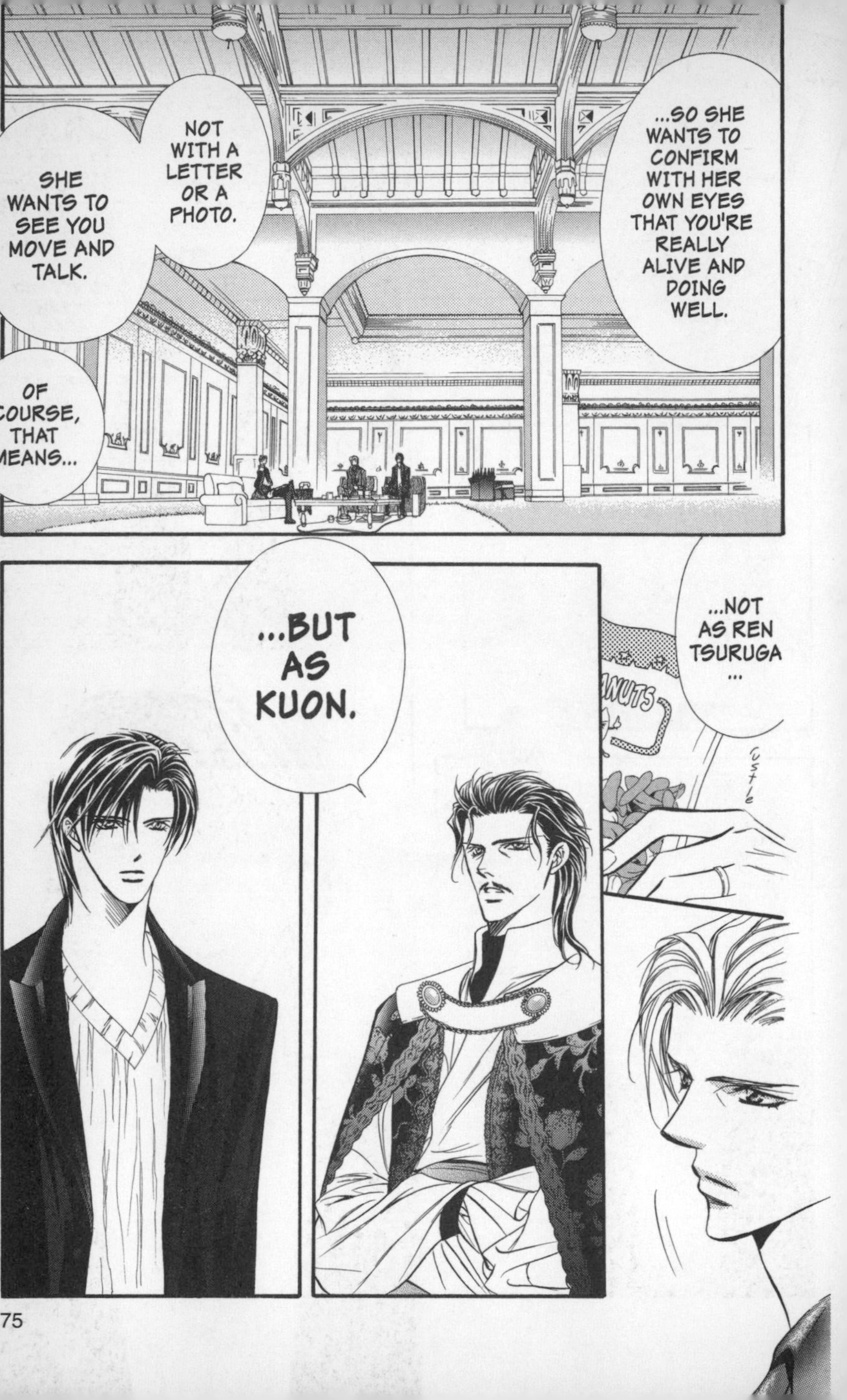
...SO SHE WANTS TO CONFIRM WITH HER OWN EYES THAT YOU'RE REALLY ALIVE AND DOING WELL.
NOT WITH A LETTER OR A PHOTO.
SHE WANTS TO SEE YOU MOVE AND TALK.
OF COURSE, THAT MEANS...
...NOT AS REN TSURUGA ...
rustle
...BUT AS KUON.

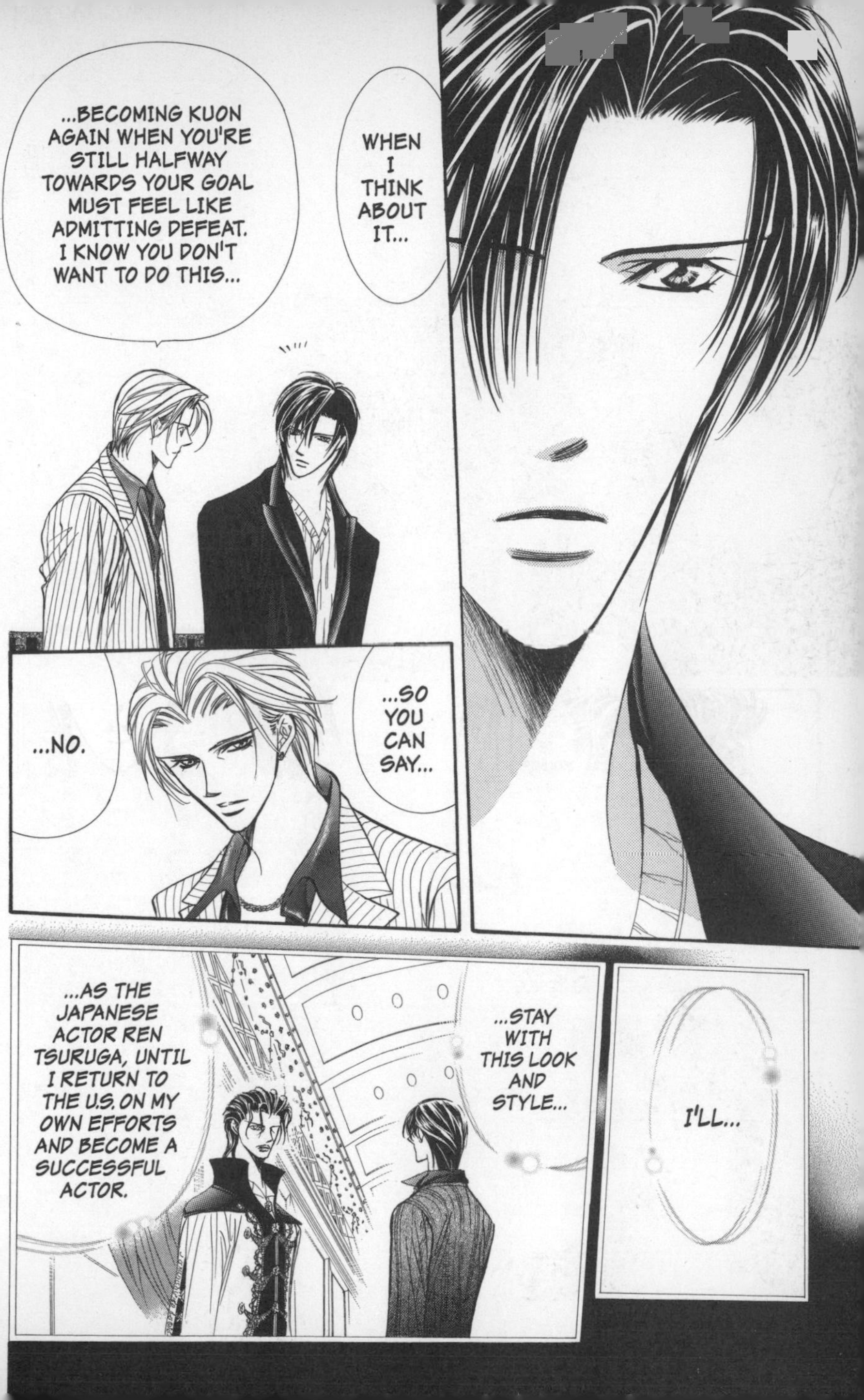
WHEN I THINK ABOUT IT...
...BECOMING KUON AGAIN WHEN YOU'RE STILL HALFWAY TOWARDS YOUR GOAL MUST FEEL LIKE ADMITTING DEFEAT. I KNOW YOU DON'T WANT TO DO THIS...
...SO YOU CAN SAY...
...NO.
I'LL...
...STAY WITH THIS LOOK AND STYLE...
...AS THE JAPANESE ACTOR REN TSURUGA, UNTIL I RETURN TO THE U.S. ON MY OWN EFFORTS AND BECOME A SUCCESSFUL ACTOR.

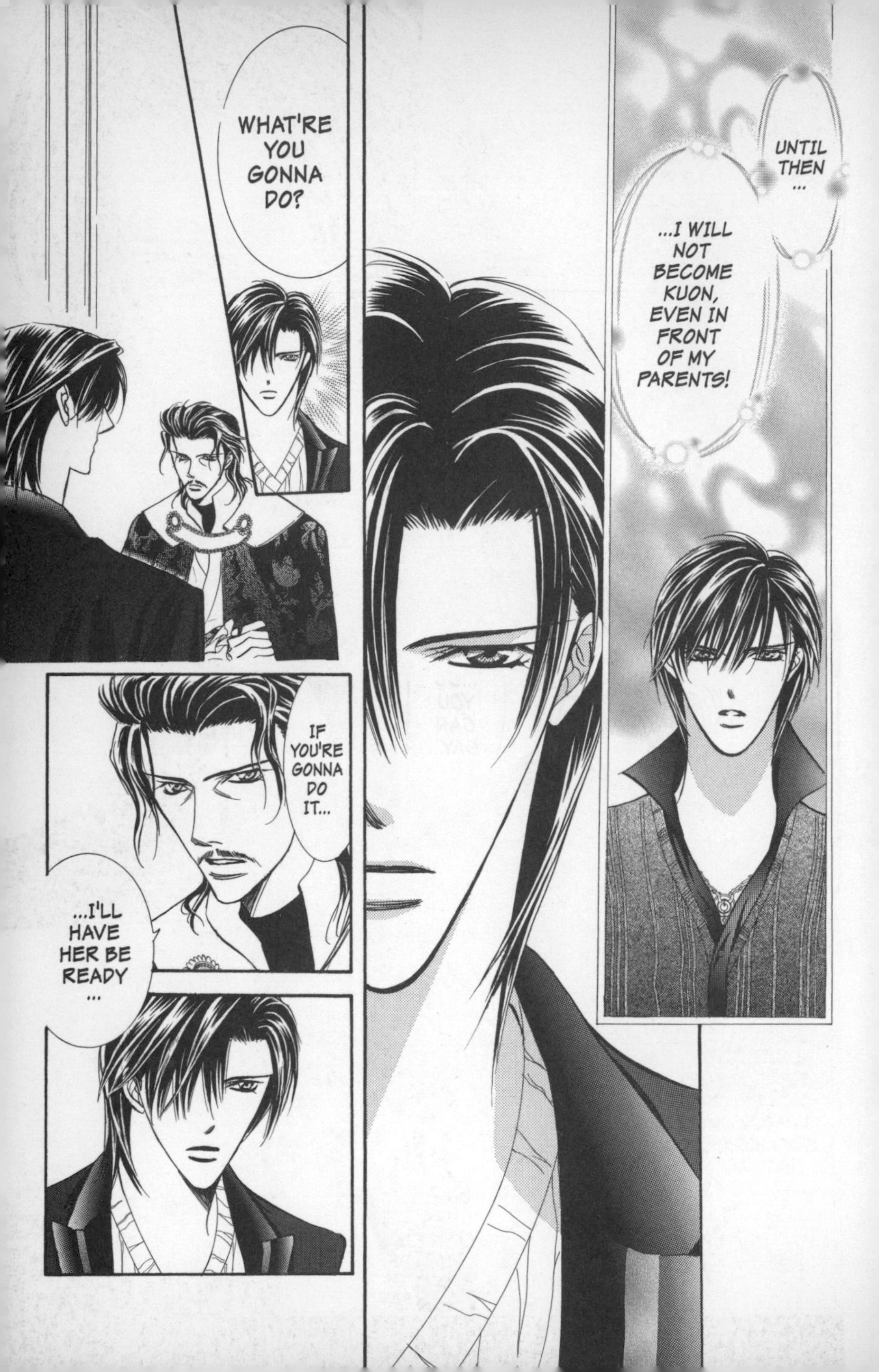
UNTIL THEN ...
...I WILL NOT BECOME KUON, EVEN IN FRONT OF MY PARENTS!
WHAT'RE YOU GONNA DO?
IF YOU'RE GONNA DO IT...
...I'LL HAVE HER BE READY ...

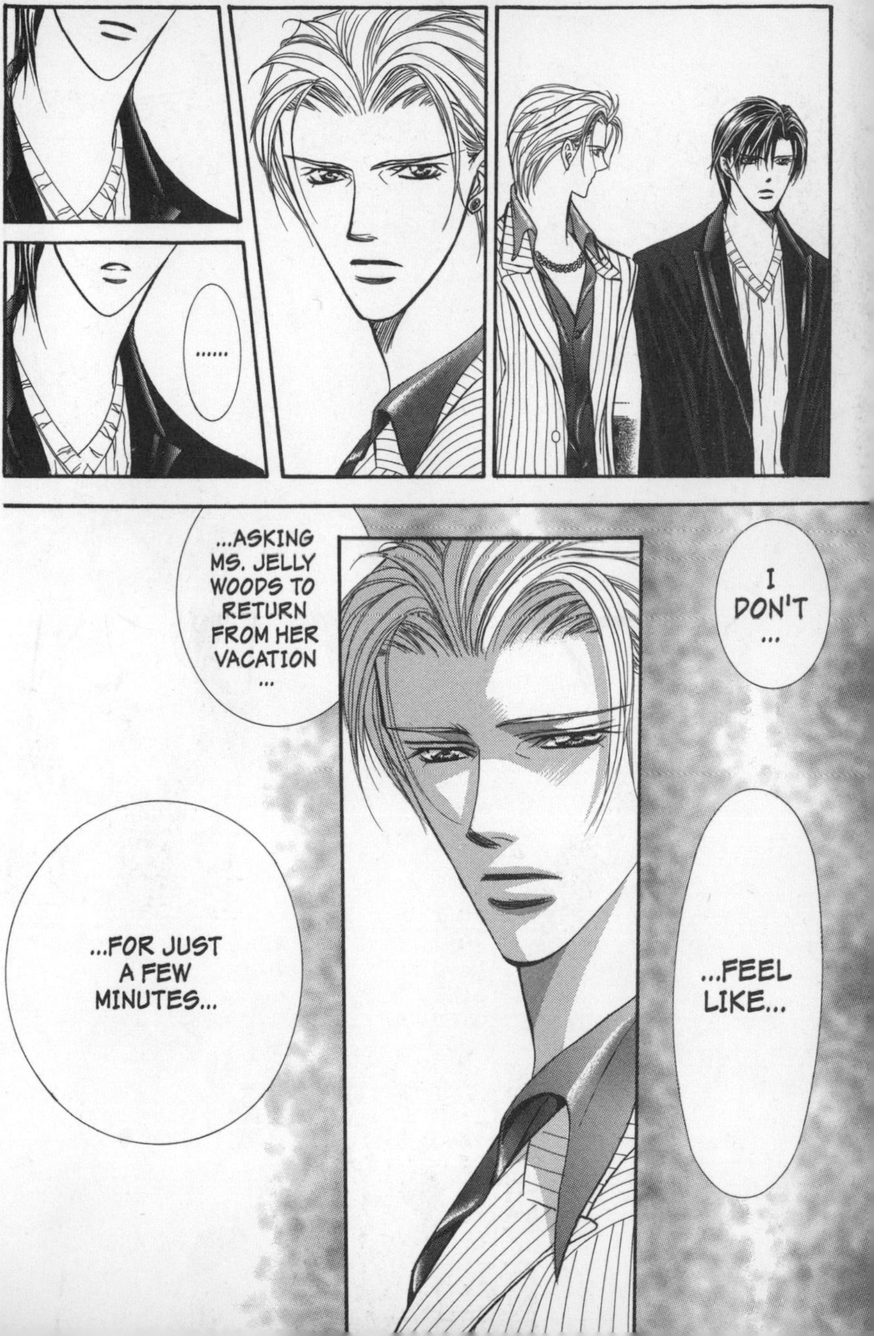
......
I DON'T ...
...FEEL LIKE...
...ASKING MS. JELLY WOODS TO RETURN FROM HER VACATION ...
...FOR JUST A FEW MINUTES...

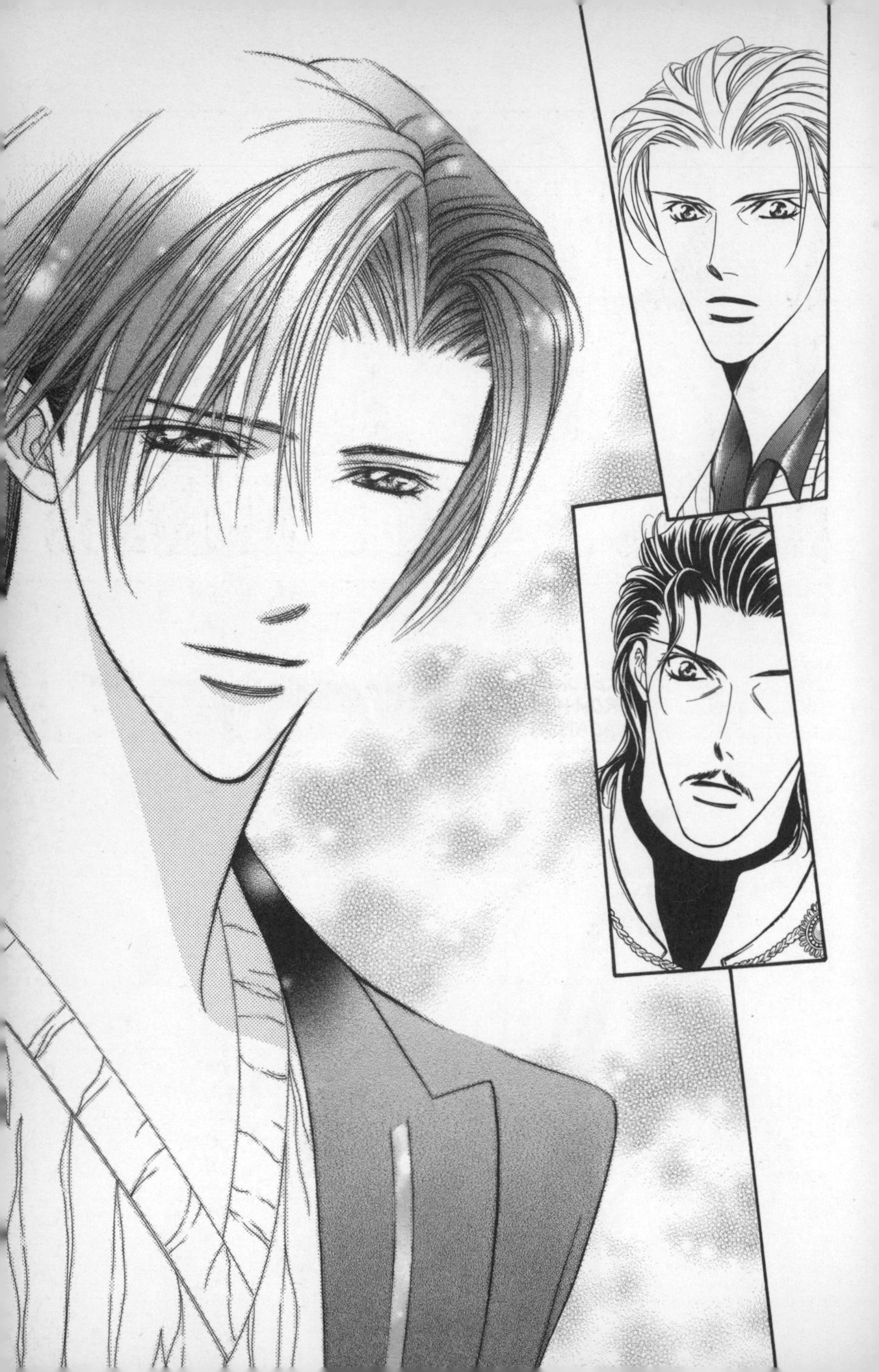

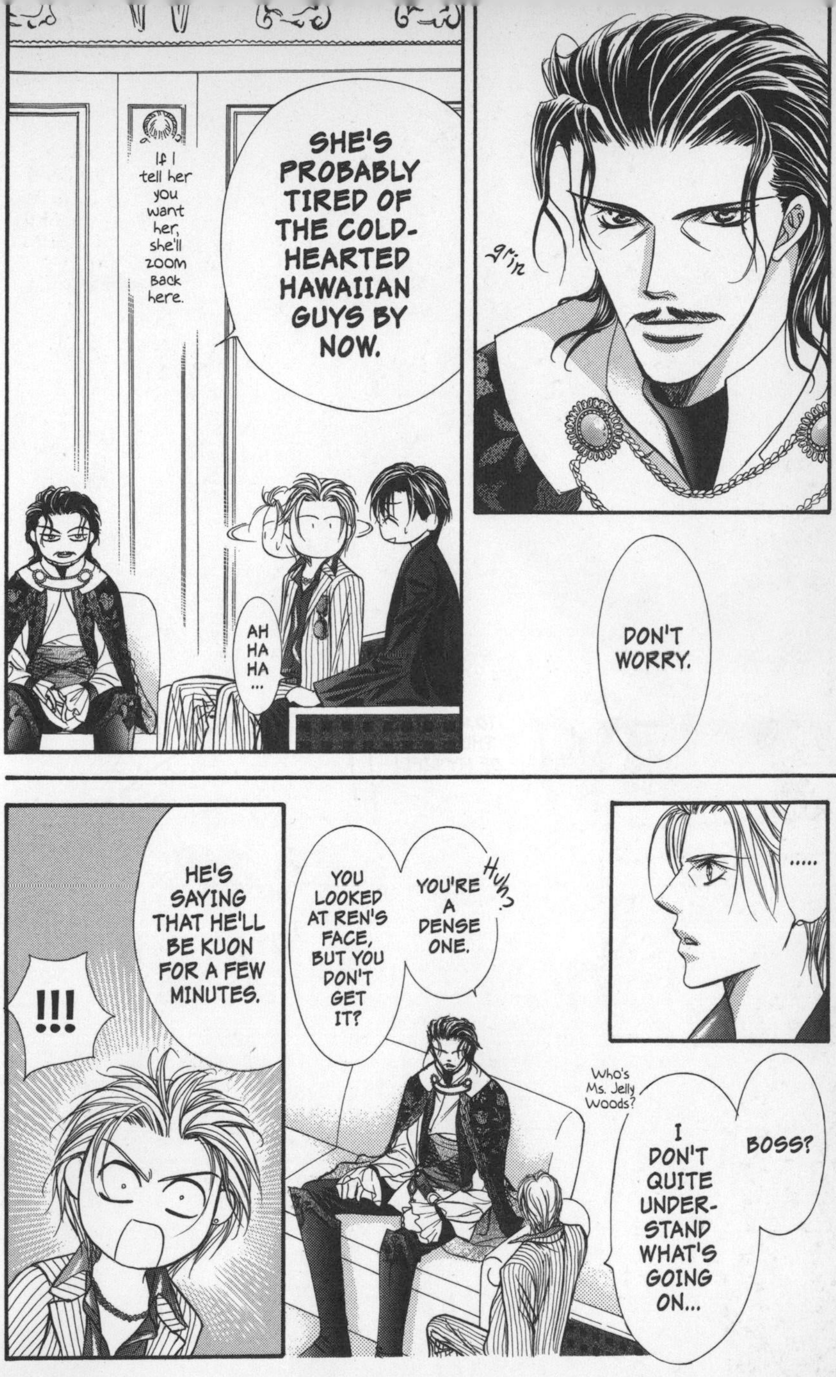
grin
DON'T WORRY.
SHE'S PROBABLY TIRED OF THE COLD-HEARTED HAWAIIAN GUYS BY NOW.
If I tell her you want her, she'll zoom back here.
AH HA HA...
.....
BOSS?
I DON'T QUITE UNDER-STAND WHAT'S GOING ON...
Who's Ms. Jelly Woods?
YOU'RE A DENSE ONE.
Huh?
YOU LOOKED AT REN'S FACE, BUT YOU DON'T GET IT?
HE'S SAYING THAT HE'LL BE KUON FOR A FEW MINUTES.
!!!

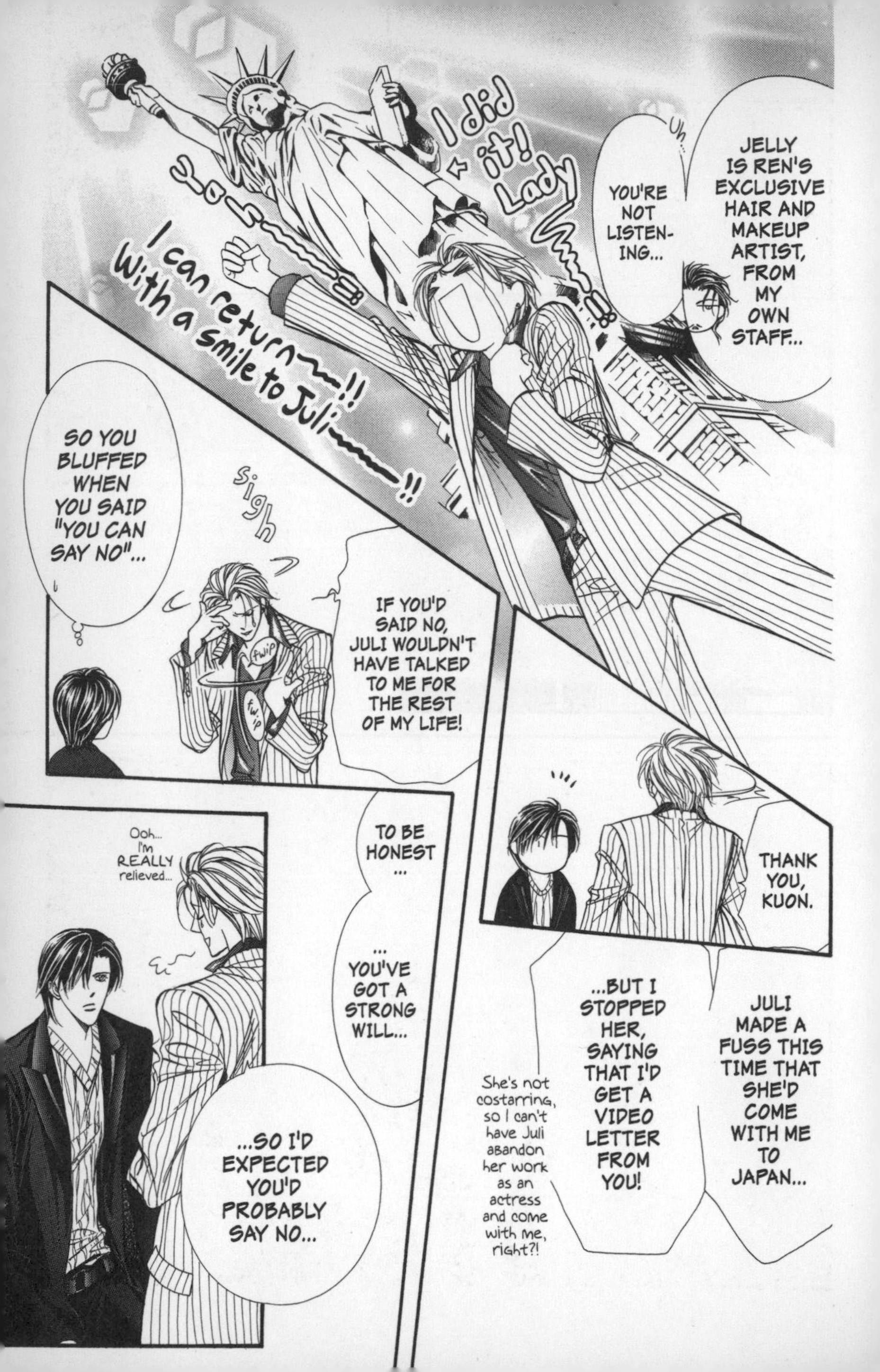

JELLY IS REN'S EXCLUSIVE HAIR AND MAKEUP ARTIST, FROM MY OWN STAFF...
Uh...
YOU'RE NOT LISTENING...
I did it!
Lady
I can return~~!!
With a smile to Juli~~!!
THANK YOU, KUON.
JULI MADE A FUSS THIS TIME THAT SHE'D COME WITH ME TO JAPAN...
...BUT I STOPPED HER, SAYING THAT I'D GET A VIDEO LETTER FROM YOU!
She's not costarring, so I can't have Juli abandon her work as an actress and come with me, right?!
sigh
IF YOU'D SAID NO, JULI WOULDN'T HAVE TALKED TO ME FOR THE REST OF MY LIFE!
fwip
fwip
SO YOU BLUFFED WHEN YOU SAID "YOU CAN SAY NO"...
TO BE HONEST ...
... YOU'VE GOT A STRONG WILL...
...SO I'D EXPECTED YOU'D PROBABLY SAY NO...
Ooh... I'm REALLY relieved...

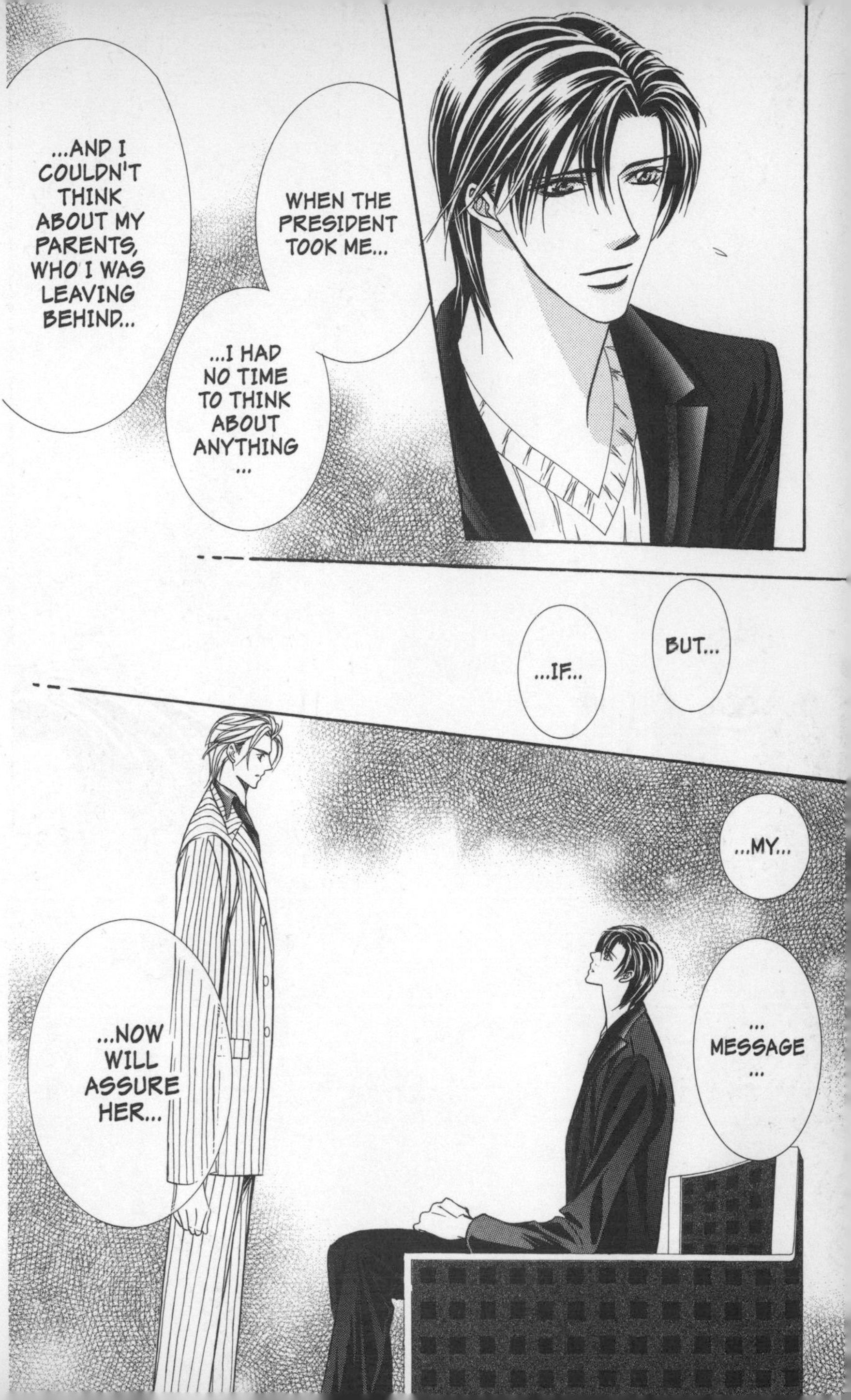
WHEN THE PRESIDENT TOOK ME...
...I HAD NO TIME TO THINK ABOUT ANYTHING ...
...AND I COULDN'T THINK ABOUT MY PARENTS, WHO I WAS LEAVING BEHIND...
BUT...
...IF...
...MY...
... MESSAGE ...
...NOW WILL ASSURE HER...

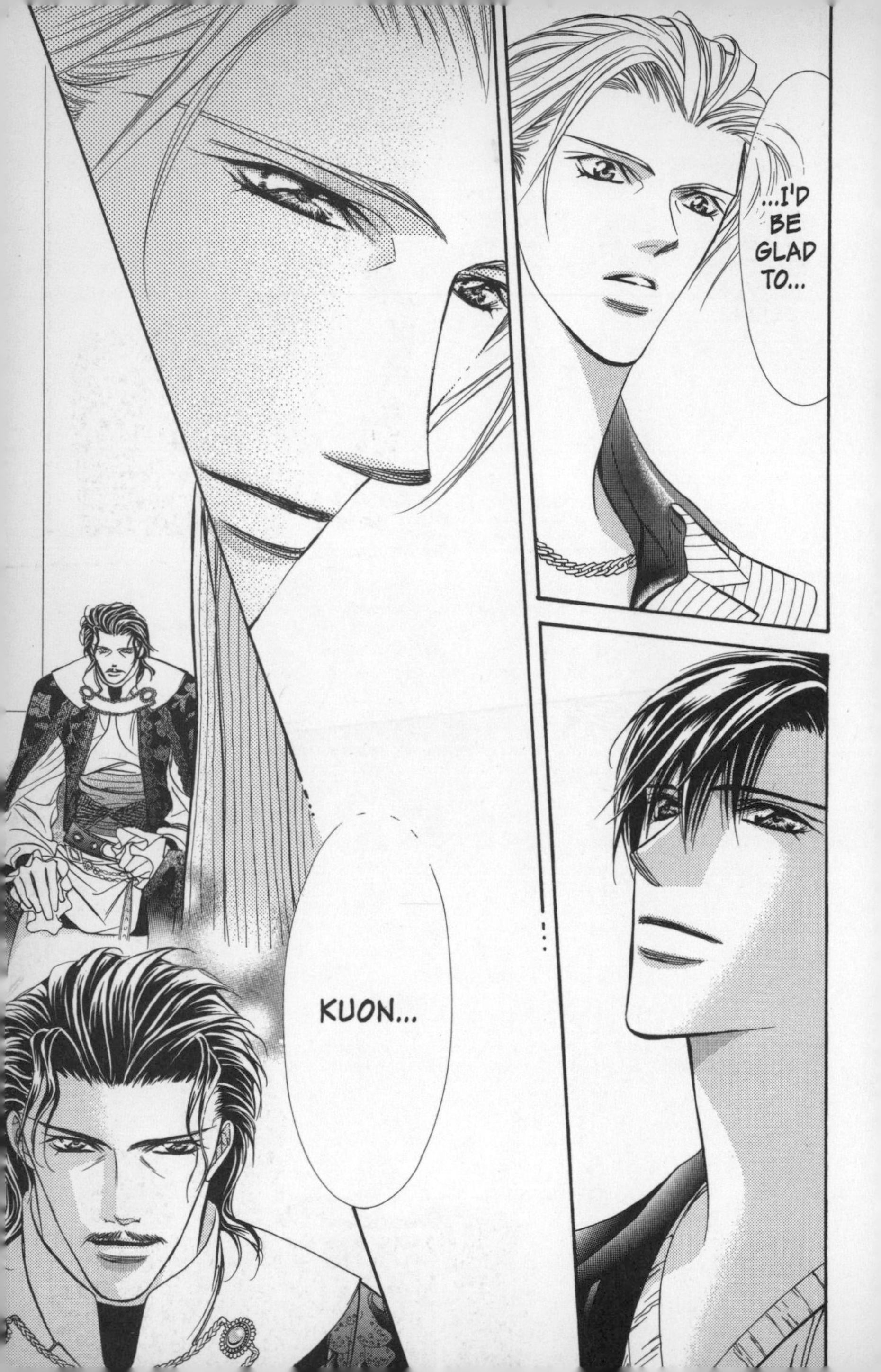
...I'D BE GLAD TO...
KUON...

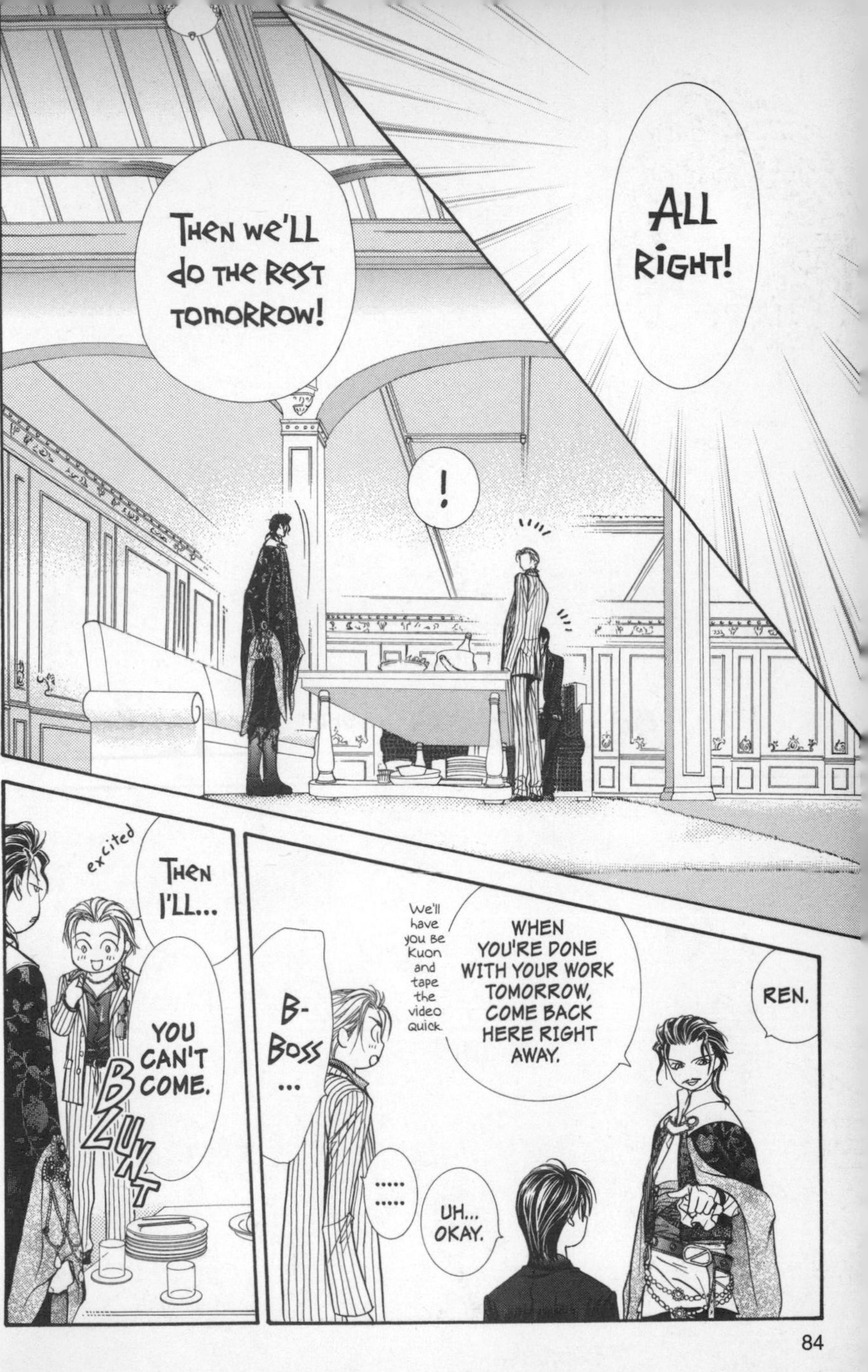
ALL RIGHT!
THEN WE'LL DO THE REST TOMORROW!
!
REN.
WHEN YOU'RE DONE WITH YOUR WORK TOMORROW, COME BACK HERE RIGHT AWAY.
We'll have you be Kuon and tape the video quick.
B-BOSS...
UH... OKAY.
...... ......
excited
THEN I'LL...
YOU CAN'T COME.
BLUNT

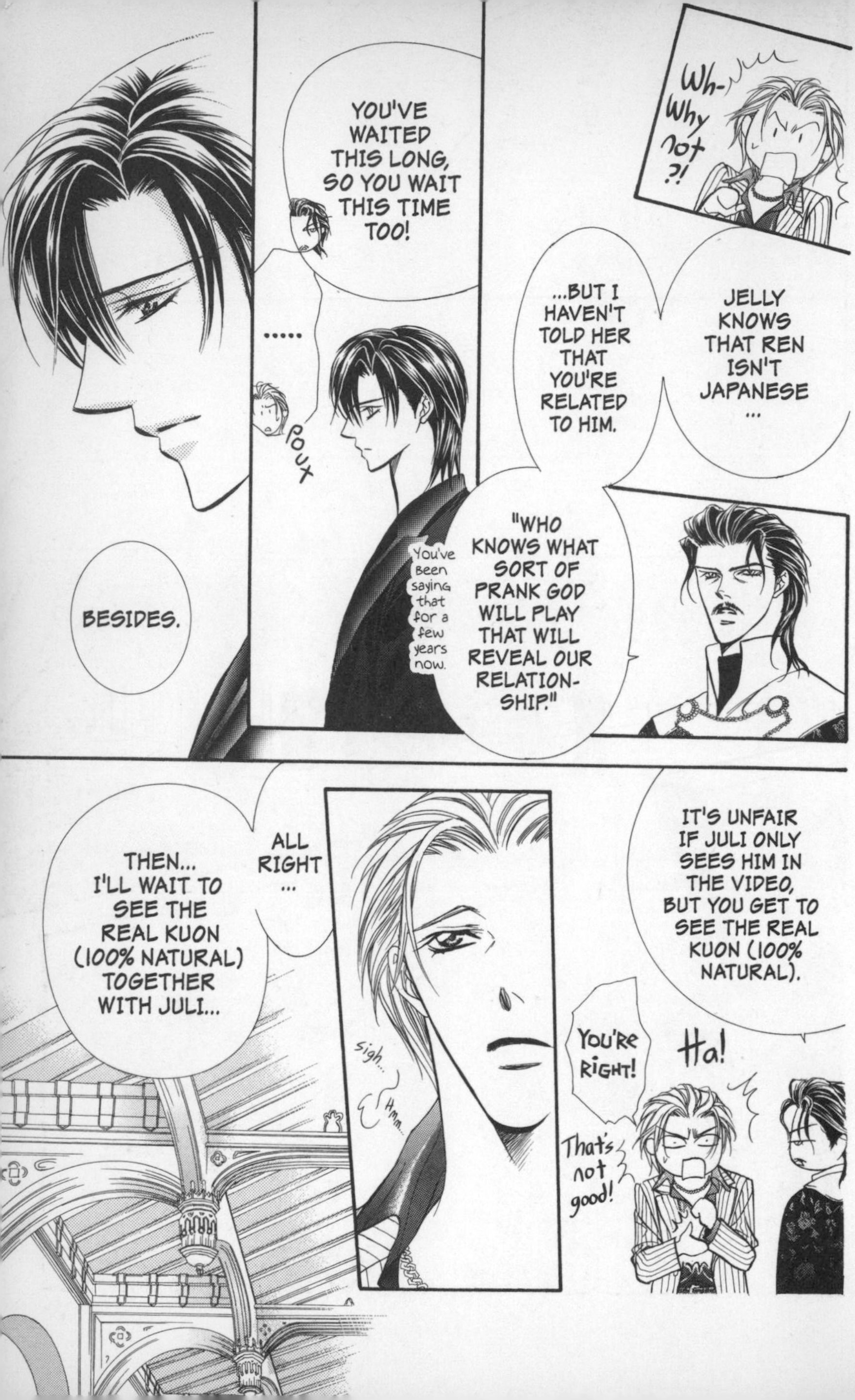
Wh-Why not ?!
JELLY KNOWS THAT REN ISN'T JAPANESE ...
...BUT I HAVEN'T TOLD HER THAT YOU'RE RELATED TO HIM.
"WHO KNOWS WHAT SORT OF PRANK GOD WILL PLAY THAT WILL REVEAL OUR RELATION-SHIP."
YOU'VE WAITED THIS LONG, SO YOU WAIT THIS TIME TOO!
.....
Pout
You've Been saying that for a few years now.
BESIDES.
IT'S UNFAIR IF JULI ONLY SEES HIM IN THE VIDEO, BUT YOU GET TO SEE THE REAL KUON (100% NATURAL).
Ha!
You're Right!
That's not good!
ALL RIGHT ...
sigh...
Hmm...
THEN... I'LL WAIT TO SEE THE REAL KUON (100% NATURAL) TOGETHER WITH JULI...

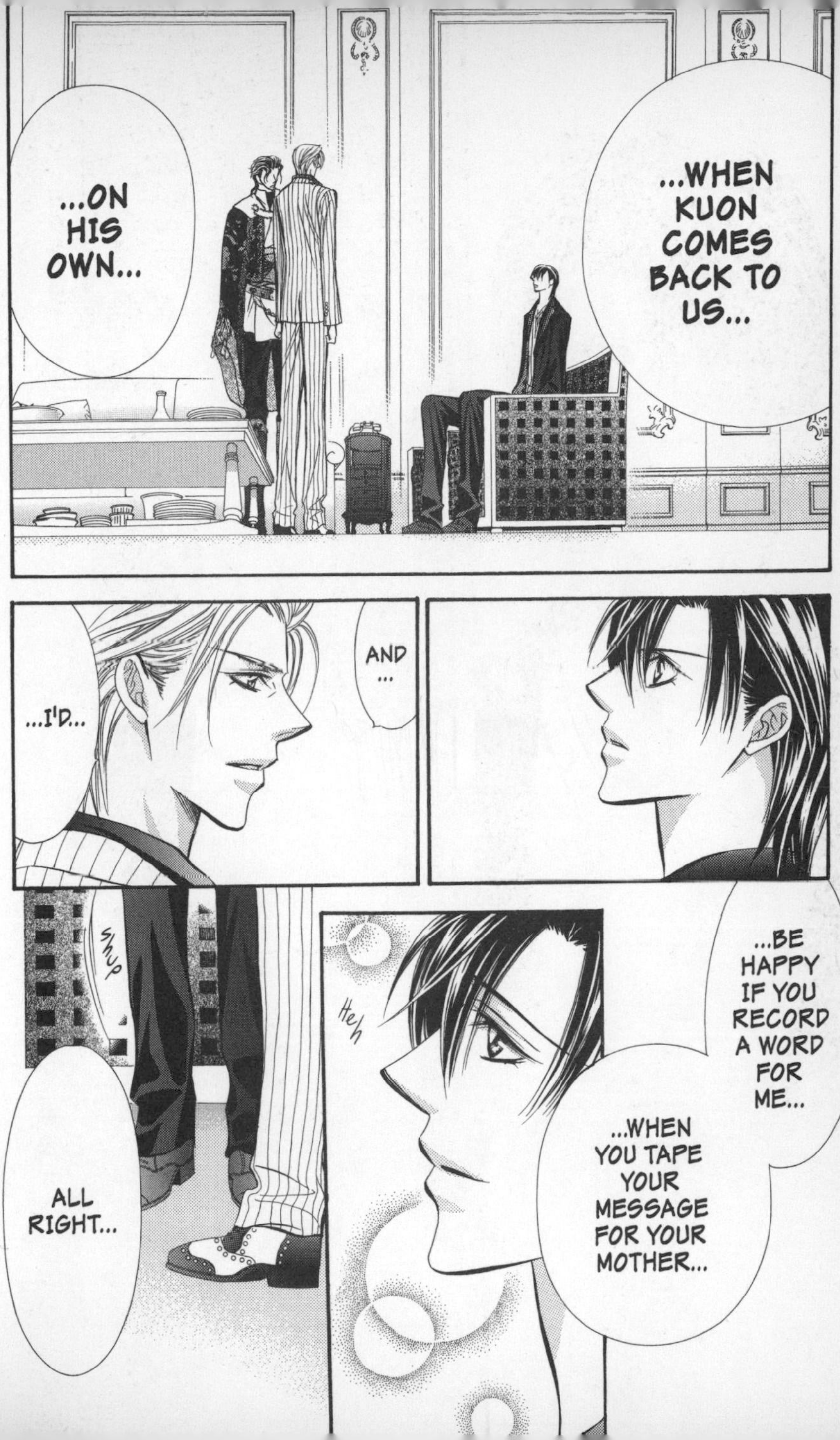
...WHEN KUON COMES BACK TO US...
...ON HIS OWN...
AND ...
...I'D...
...BE HAPPY IF YOU RECORD A WORD FOR ME...
...WHEN YOU TAPE YOUR MESSAGE FOR YOUR MOTHER...
Heh
Shup
ALL RIGHT...

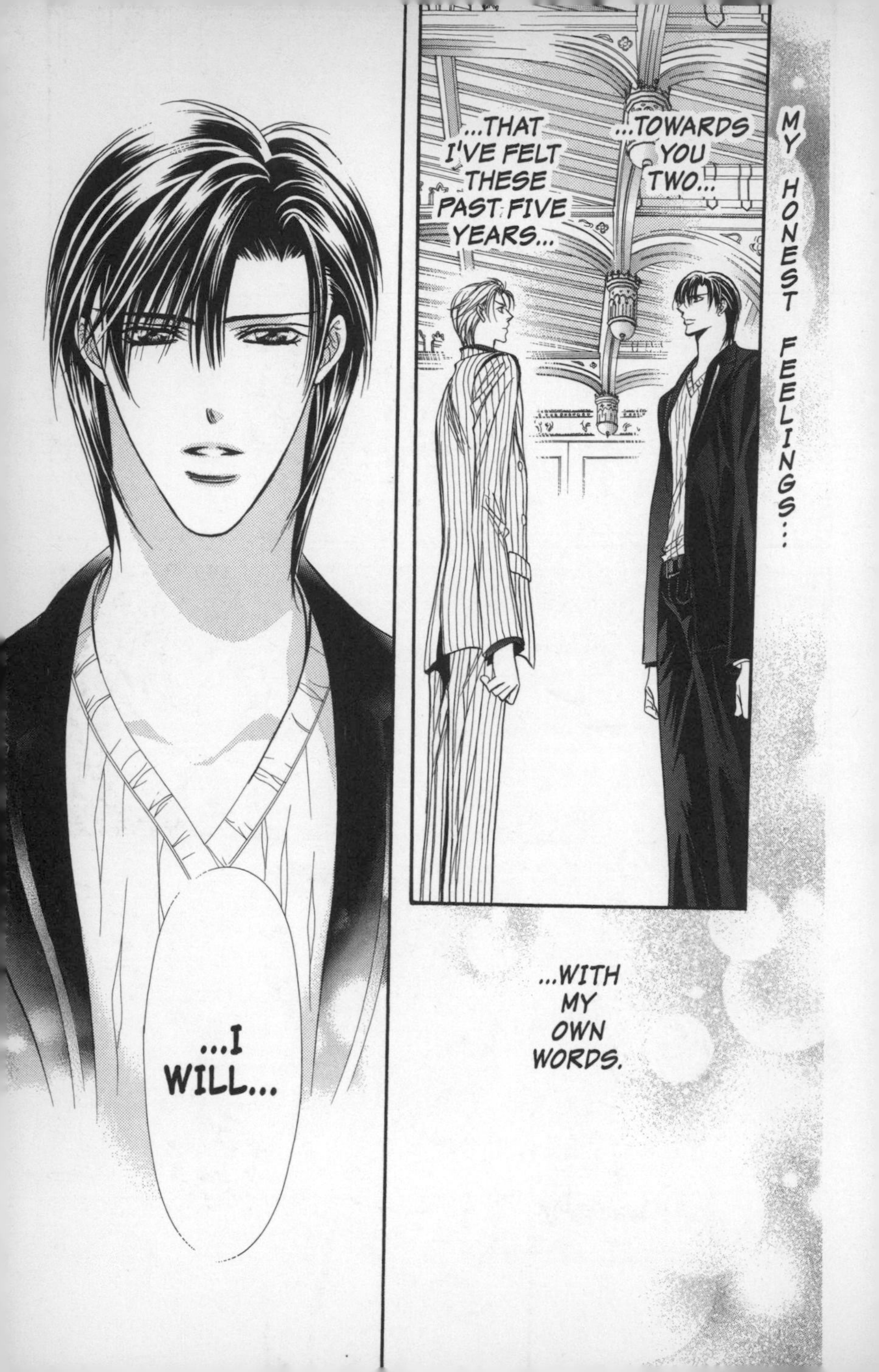
MY HONEST FEELINGS...
...TOWARDS YOU TWO...
...THAT I'VE FELT THESE PAST FIVE YEARS...
...WITH MY OWN WORDS.
...I WILL...

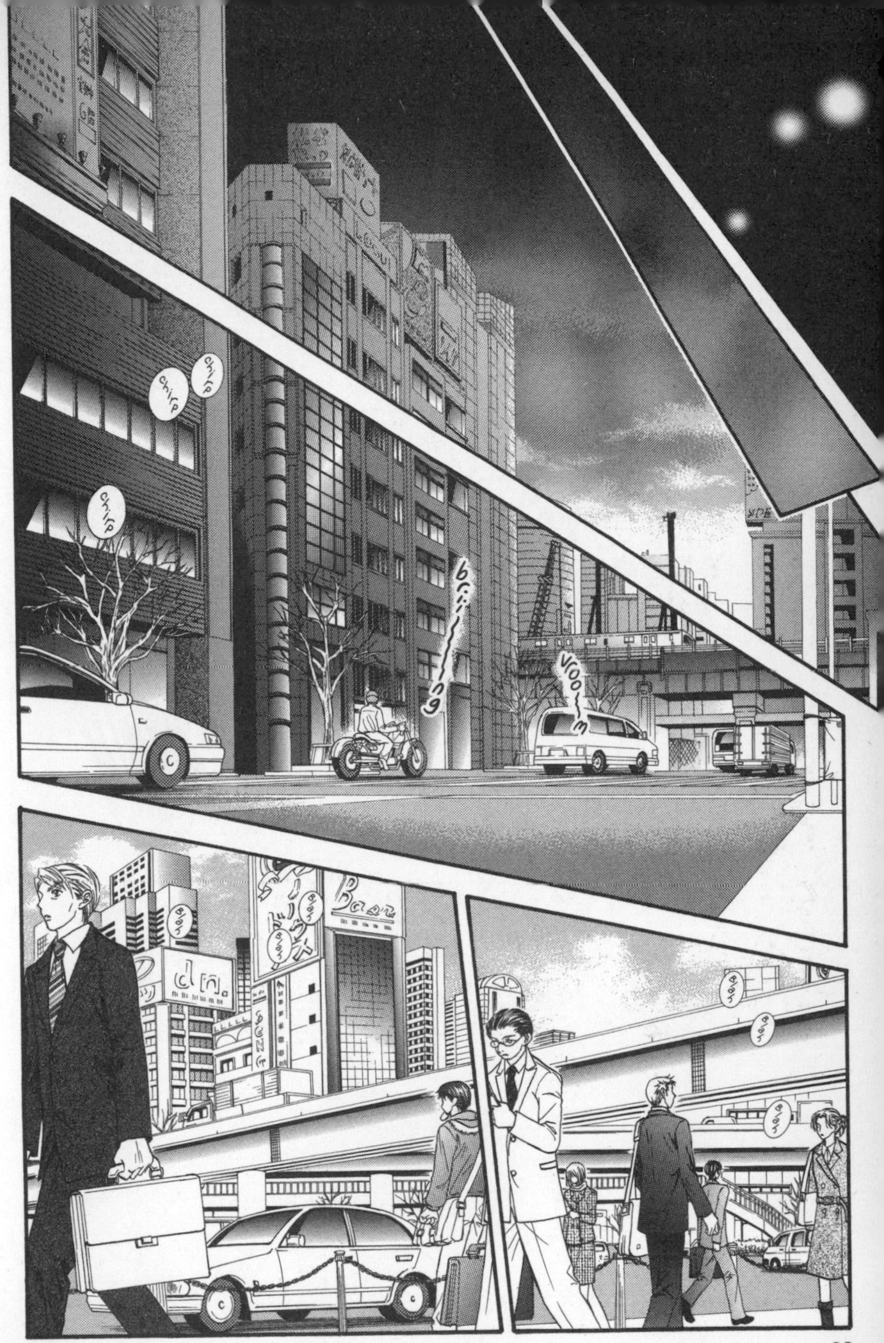
chirp
chirp
chirp
vroo~m
brii——ng

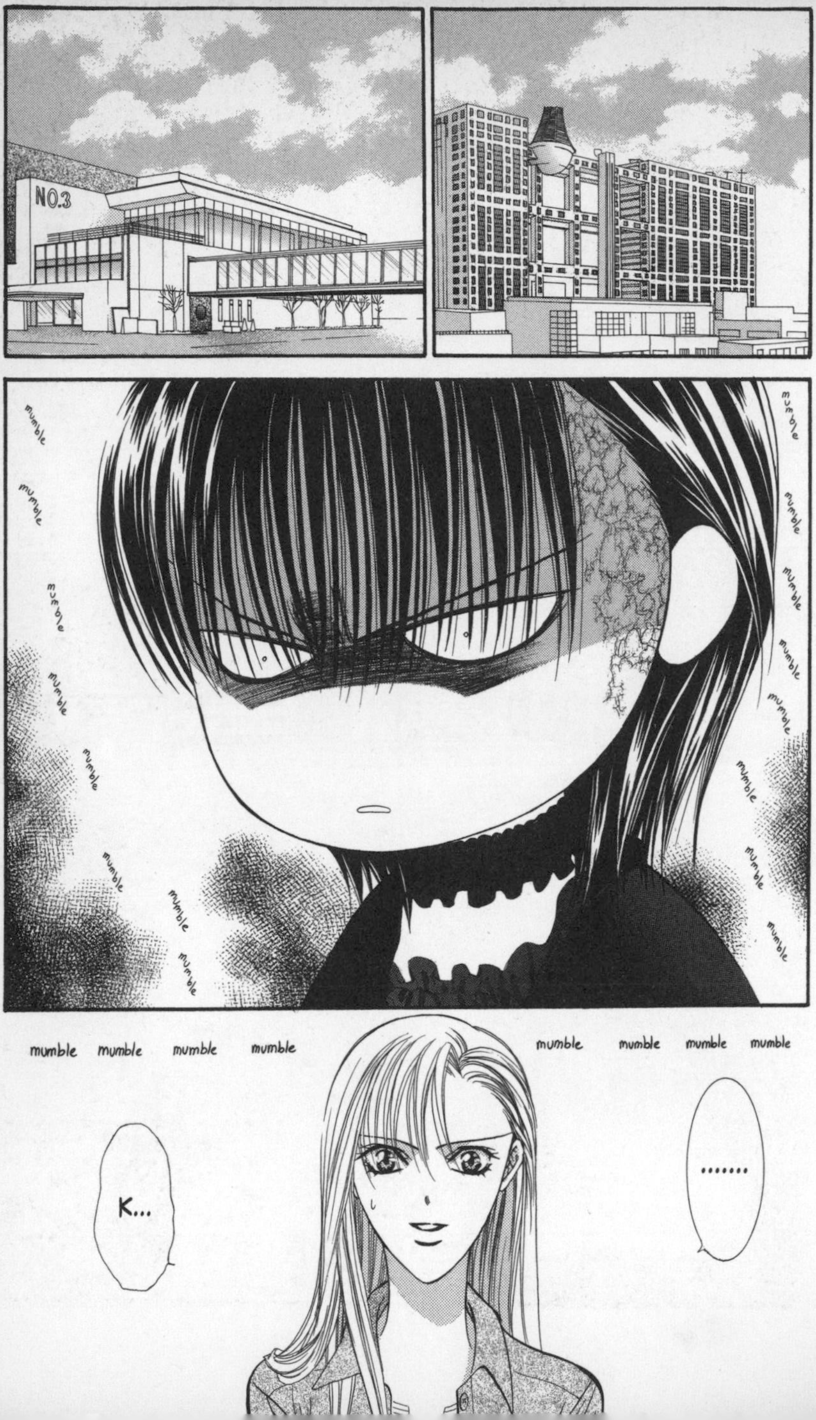
mumble
mumble
mumble
mumble
mumble
mumble
mumble
mumble
mumble
mumble
mumble
mumble
mumble
mumble
mumble
mumble
mumble
mumble
mumble mumble mumble mumble
mumble mumble mumble mumble
........
K...

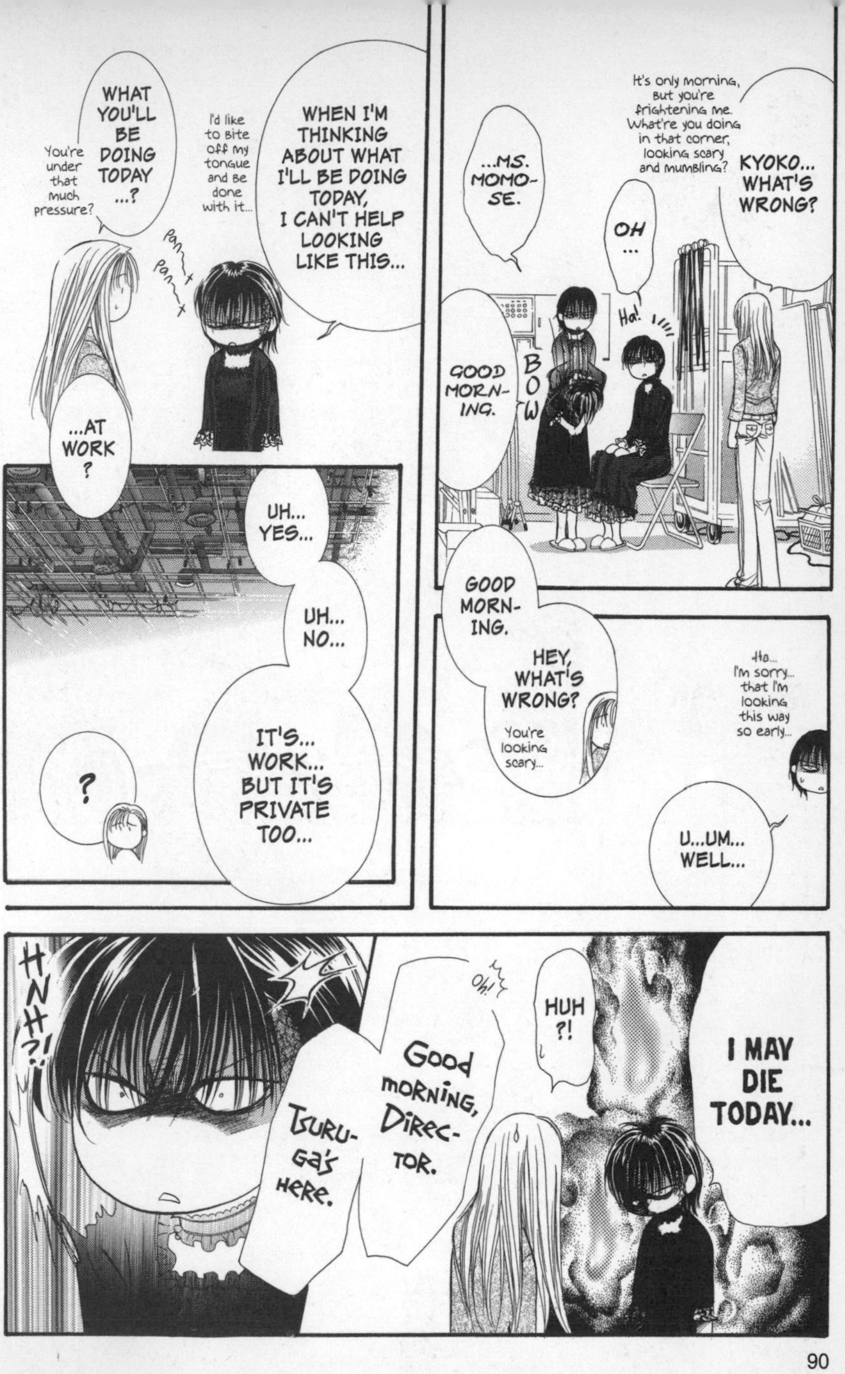
It's only morning, but you're frightening me. What're you doing in that corner, looking scary and mumbling?
KYOKO... WHAT'S WRONG?
OH...
Ha!
...MS. MOMOSE.
BOW
GOOD MORNING.
GOOD MORNING.
HEY, WHAT'S WRONG?
You're looking scary...
Ho... I'm sorry... that I'm looking this way so early...
U...UM... WELL...
WHEN I'M THINKING ABOUT WHAT I'LL BE DOING TODAY, I CAN'T HELP LOOKING LIKE THIS...
I'd like to bite off my tongue and be done with it...
Pan-t Pan-t
WHAT YOU'LL BE DOING TODAY...?
You're under that much pressure?
...AT WORK?
UH... YES...
UH... NO...
IT'S... WORK... BUT IT'S PRIVATE TOO...
?
I MAY DIE TODAY...
HUH?!
Oh!
Good morning, Director.
Tsuruga's here.
HNH?!

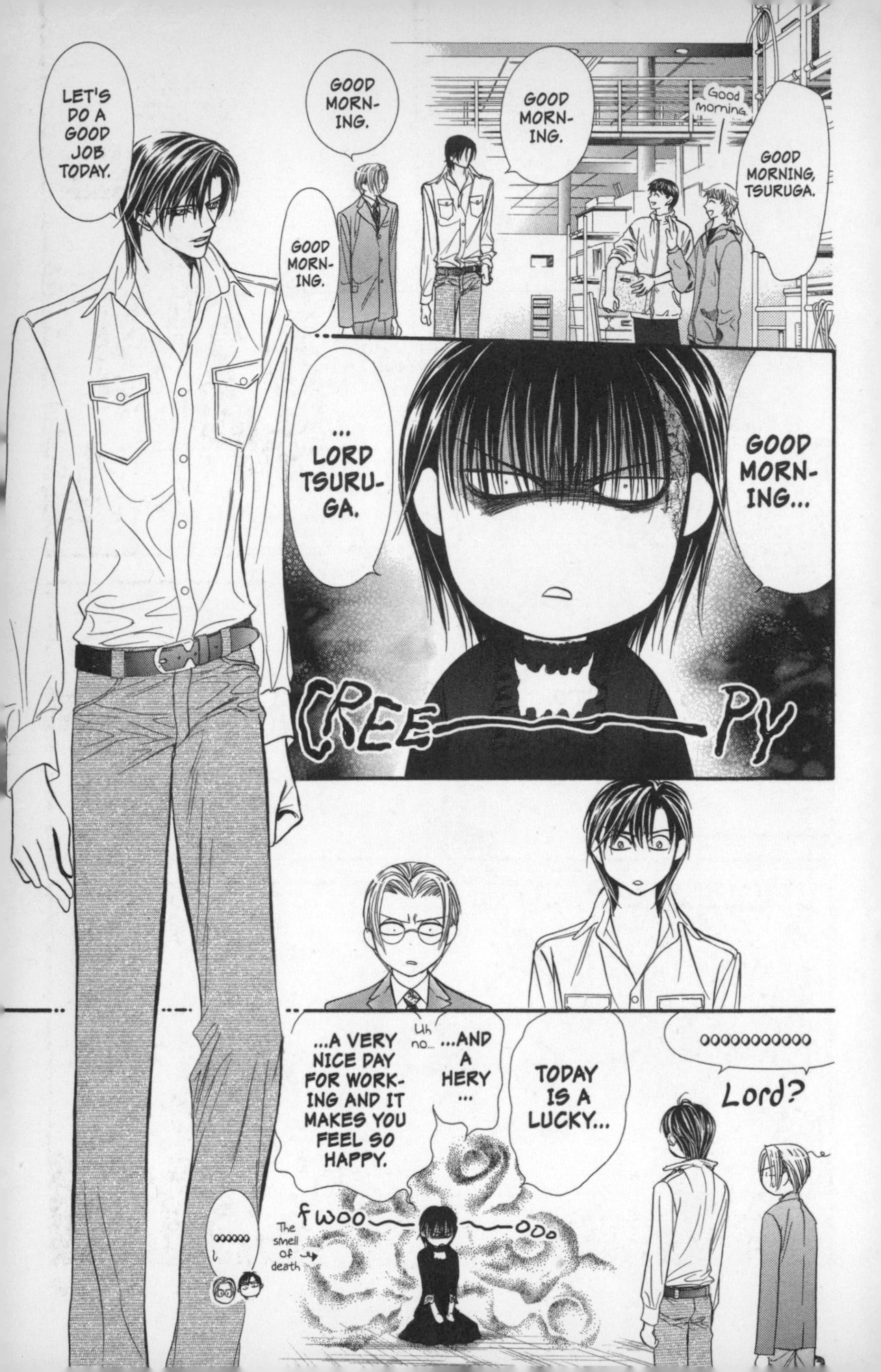
GOOD MORNING, TSURUGA.
Good morning.
GOOD MORN-ING.
GOOD MORN-ING.
GOOD MORN-ING.
GOOD MORN-ING...
... LORD TSURU-GA.
CREE——PY
OOOOOOOOOOO
Lord?
TODAY IS A LUCKY...
...AND A HERY ...
Uh no...
...A VERY NICE DAY FOR WORK-ING AND IT MAKES YOU FEEL SO HAPPY.
FWOO——OOO
The smell of death
OOOOOO
LET'S DO A GOOD JOB TODAY.

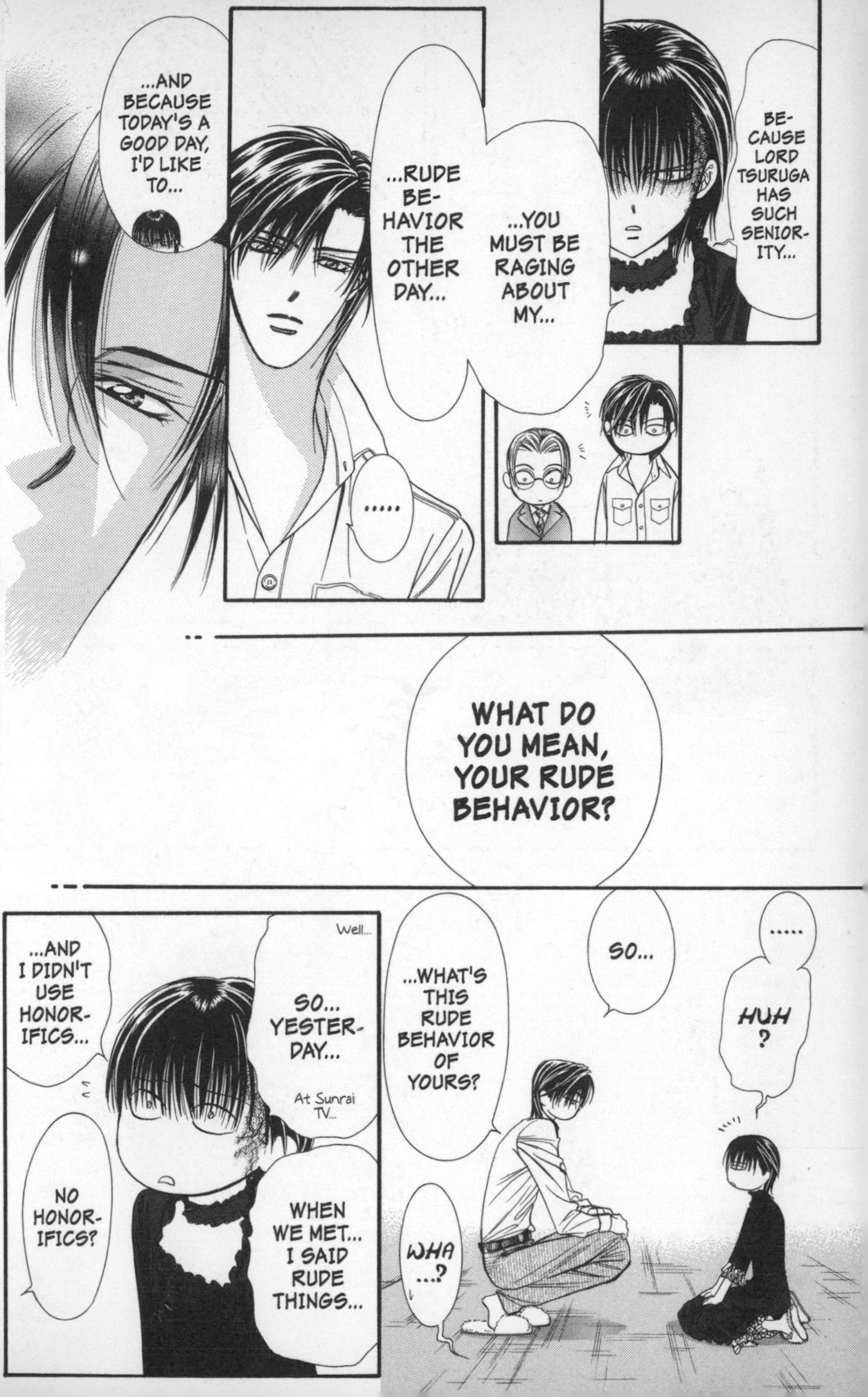
BECAUSE LORD TSURUGA HAS SUCH SENIORITY...
...YOU MUST BE RAGING ABOUT MY...
...RUDE BEHAVIOR THE OTHER DAY...
.....
...AND BECAUSE TODAY'S A GOOD DAY, I'D LIKE TO...
WHAT DO YOU MEAN, YOUR RUDE BEHAVIOR?
.....
HUH?
SO...
...WHAT'S THIS RUDE BEHAVIOR OF YOURS?
WHA...?
Well...
SO... YESTERDAY...
At Sunrai TV...
WHEN WE MET... I SAID RUDE THINGS...
...AND I DIDN'T USE HONORIFICS...
NO HONORIFICS?

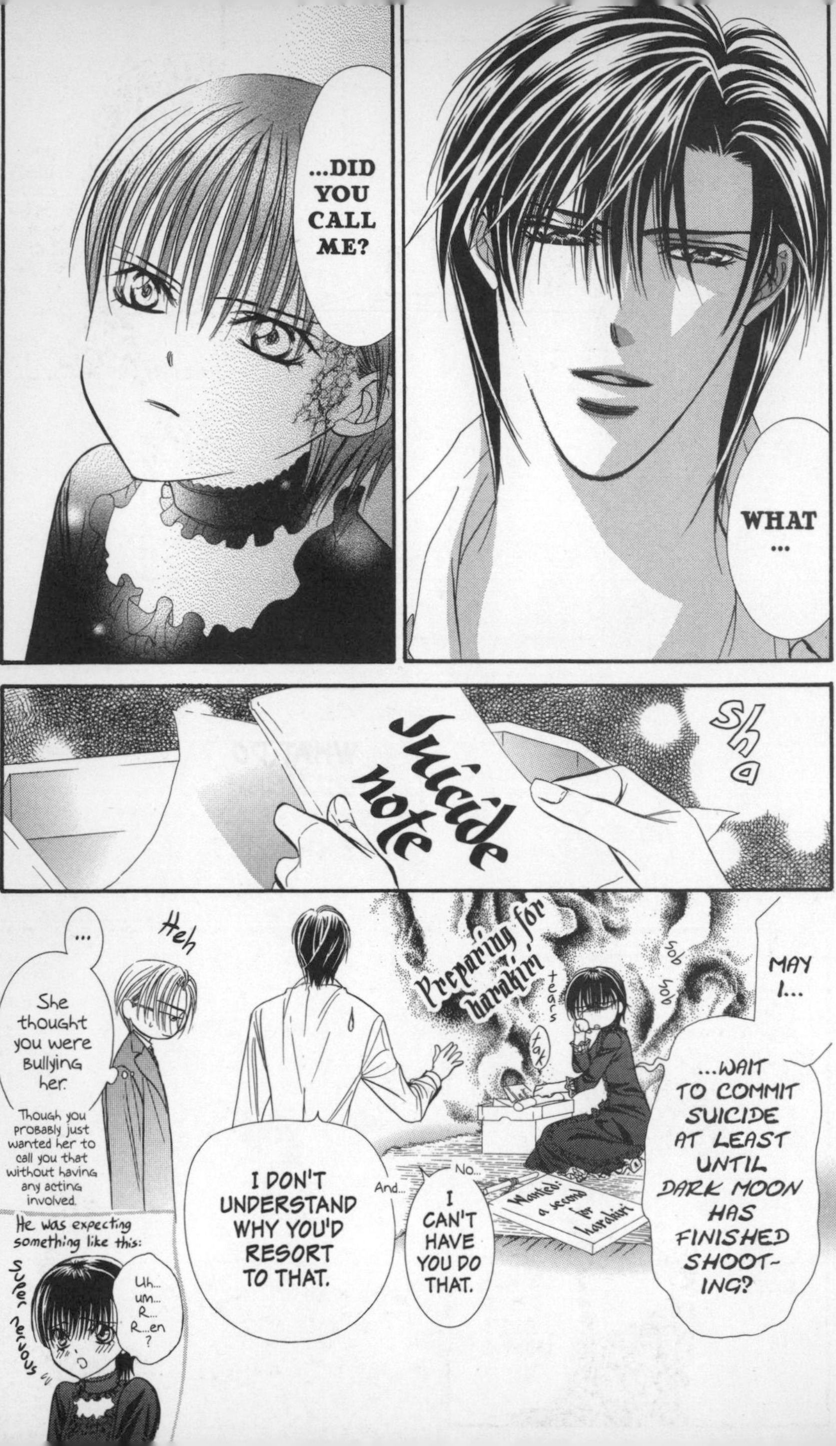

WHAT ...
...DID YOU CALL ME?
Suicide note
Sha
MAY I...
...WAIT TO COMMIT SUICIDE AT LEAST UNTIL DARK MOON HAS FINISHED SHOOT-ING?
Preparing for harakiri
sob sob
tears
tak
Wanted: a second for harakiri
No...
I CAN'T HAVE YOU DO THAT.
And...
I DON'T UNDERSTAND WHY YOU'D RESORT TO THAT.
Heh
...
She thought you were bullying her.
Though you probably just wanted her to call you that without having any acting involved.
He was expecting something like this:
Uh... um... R... R...en ?
Super nervous

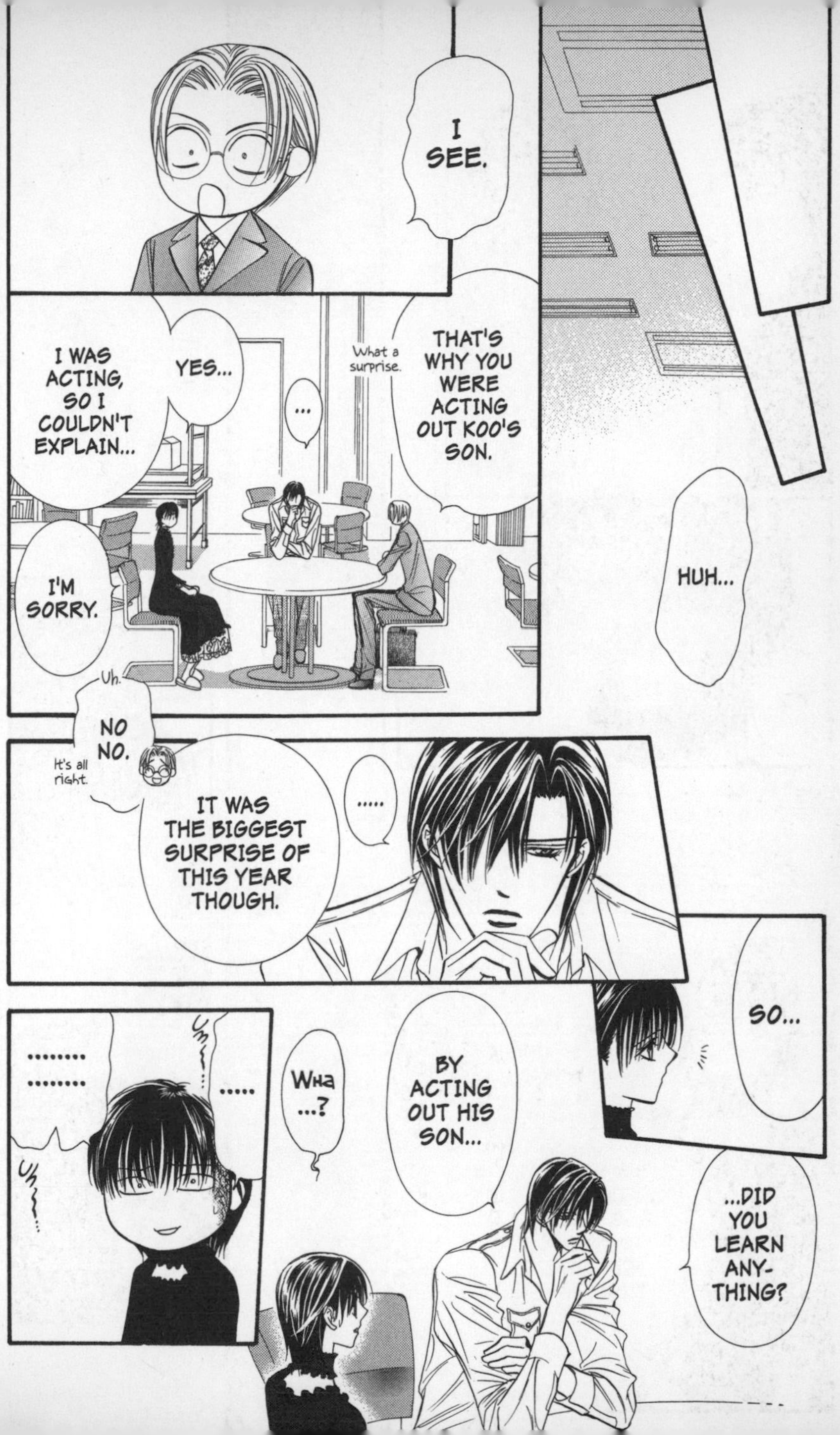
HUH...
I SEE.
THAT'S WHY YOU WERE ACTING OUT KOO'S SON.
What a surprise.
...
YES...
I WAS ACTING, SO I COULDN'T EXPLAIN...
I'M SORRY.
Uh.
NO NO.
It's all right.
IT WAS THE BIGGEST SURPRISE OF THIS YEAR THOUGH.
.....
SO...
...DID YOU LEARN ANYTHING?
BY ACTING OUT HIS SON...
Wha...?
.....
Um~...
........
........
Uh~...

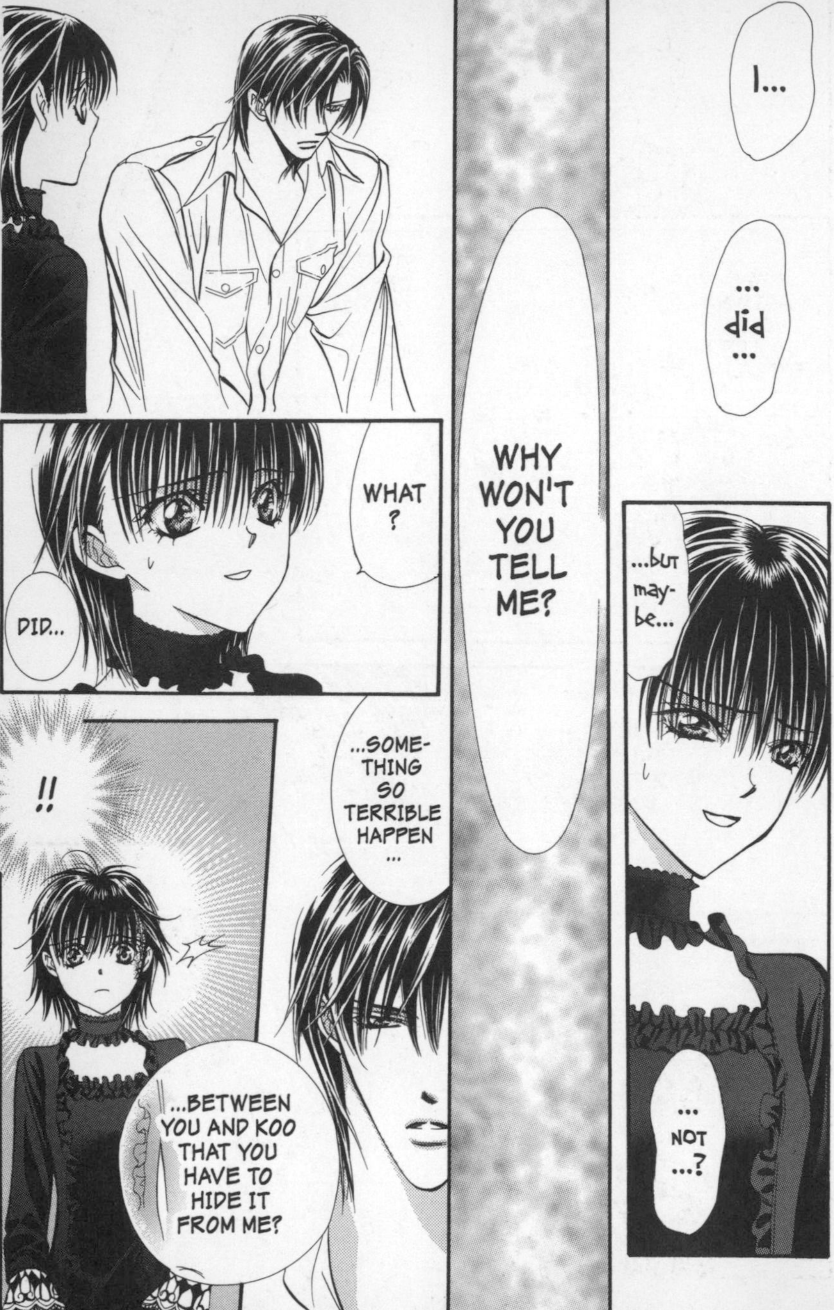
I...
...did...
...but may-be...
...NOT...?
WHY WON'T YOU TELL ME?
WHAT?
DID...
...SOME-THING SO TERRIBLE HAPPEN...
!!
...BETWEEN YOU AND KOO THAT YOU HAVE TO HIDE IT FROM ME?

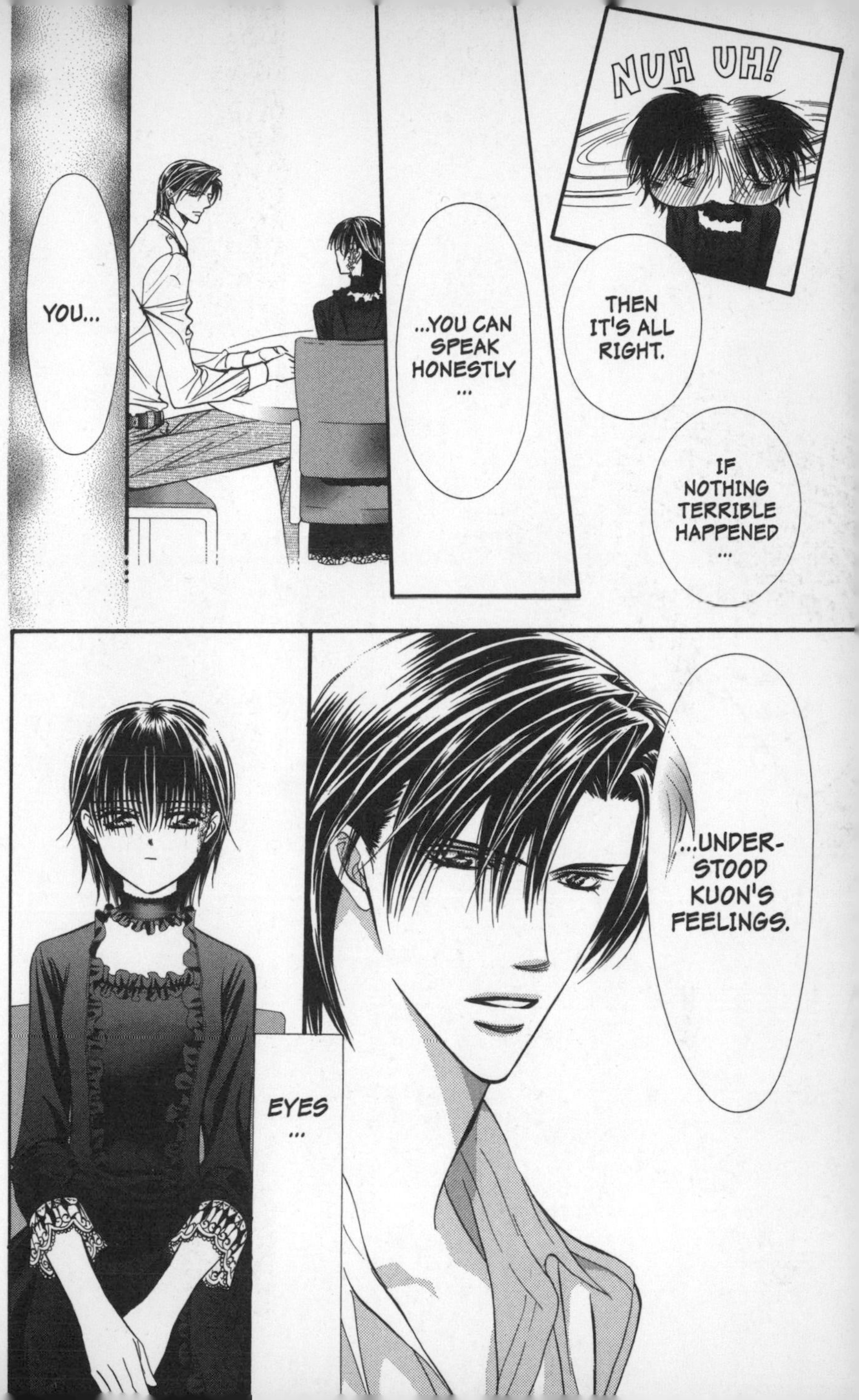
NUH UH!
THEN IT'S ALL RIGHT.
IF NOTHING TERRIBLE HAPPENED...
...YOU CAN SPEAK HONESTLY...
YOU...
...UNDER-STOOD KUON'S FEELINGS.
EYES...

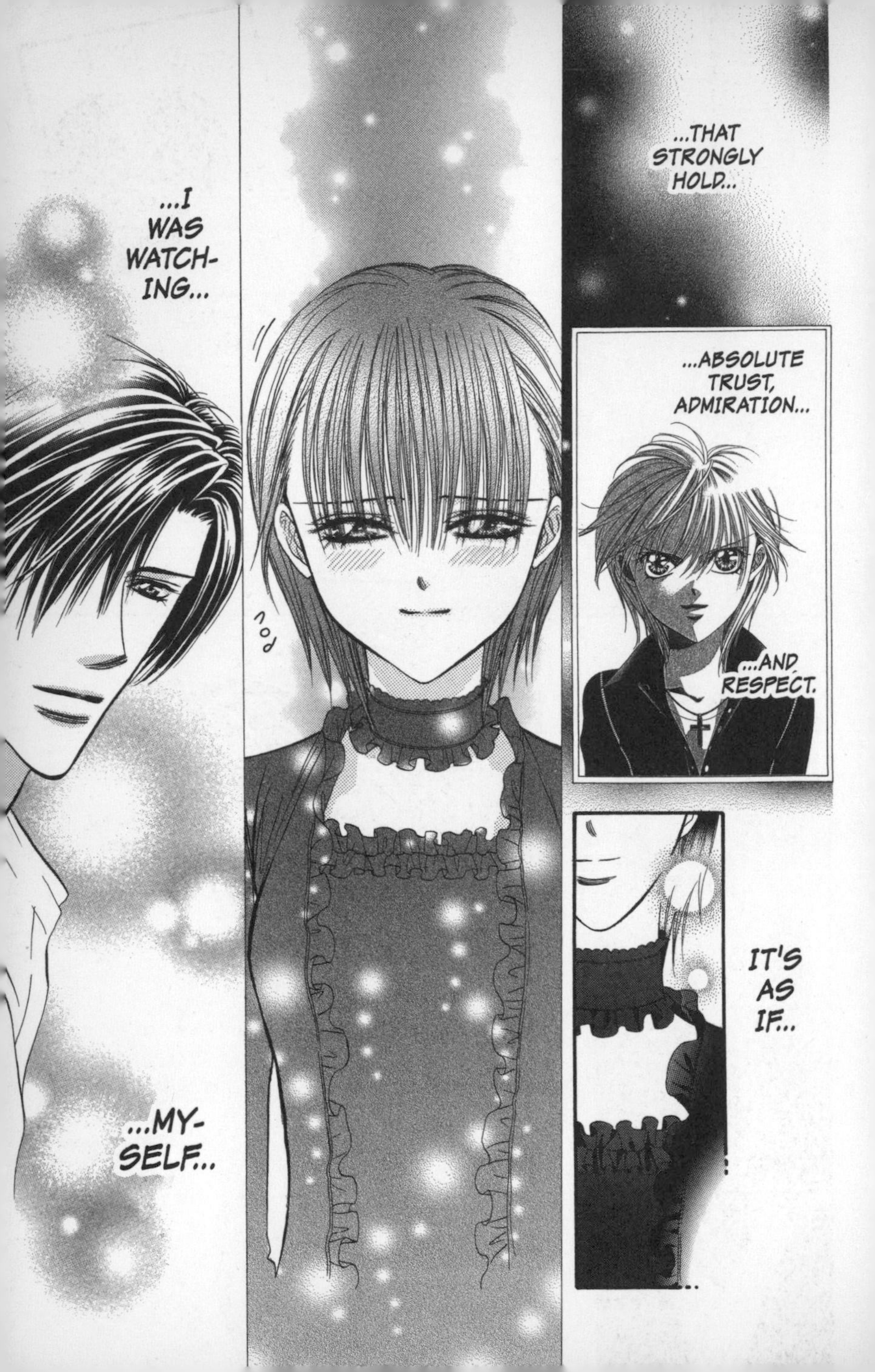
...THAT STRONGLY HOLD...
...ABSOLUTE TRUST, ADMIRATION...
...AND RESPECT.
IT'S AS IF...
pon
...I WAS WATCHING...
...MYSELF...

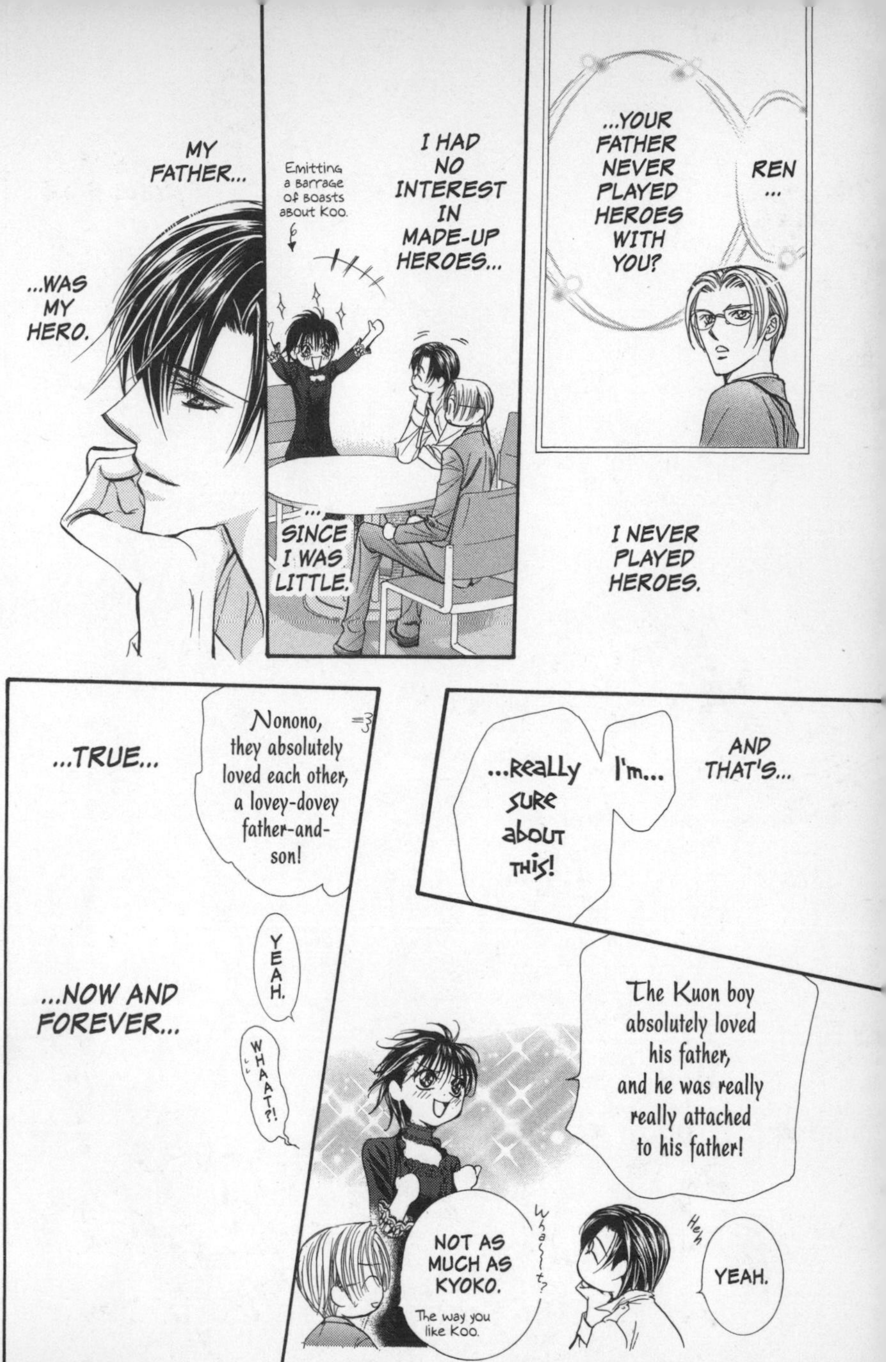
REN...
...YOUR FATHER NEVER PLAYED HEROES WITH YOU?
I NEVER PLAYED HEROES.
I HAD NO INTEREST IN MADE-UP HEROES...
Emitting a Barrage of Boasts about Koo.
...SINCE I WAS LITTLE.
MY FATHER...
...WAS MY HERO.
AND THAT'S...
I'm...
...really sure about this!
Nonono, they absolutely loved each other, a lovey-dovey father-and-son!
...TRUE...
YEAH.
...NOW AND FOREVER...
WHAAT?!
The Kuon boy absolutely loved his father, and he was really really attached to his father!
Heh
YEAH.
Wha~t?
NOT AS MUCH AS KYOKO.
The way you like Koo.

**End of Act 111**

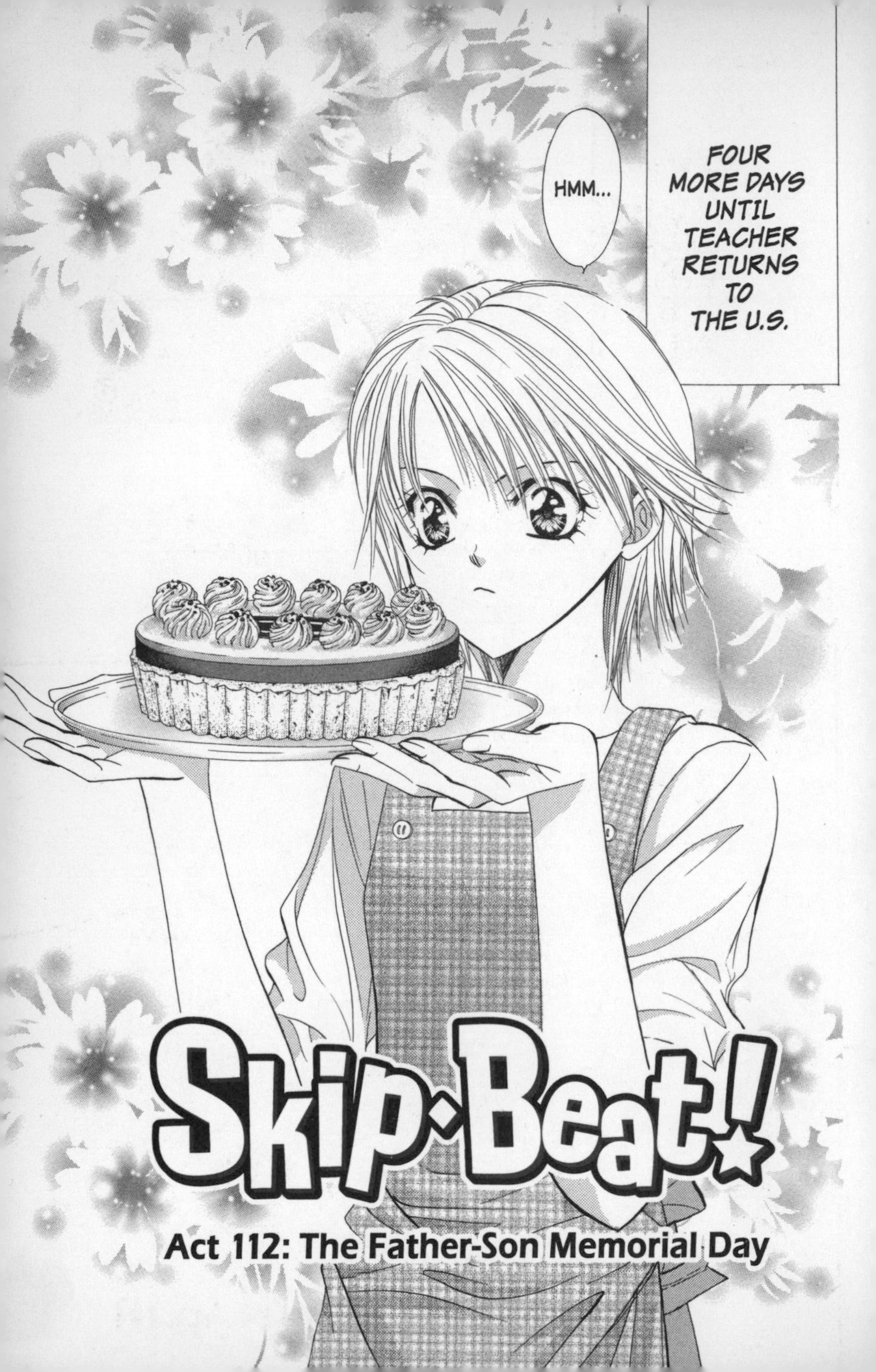
FOUR MORE DAYS UNTIL TEACHER RETURNS TO THE U.S.
HMM...
Skip·Beat!
Act 112: The Father-Son Memorial Day

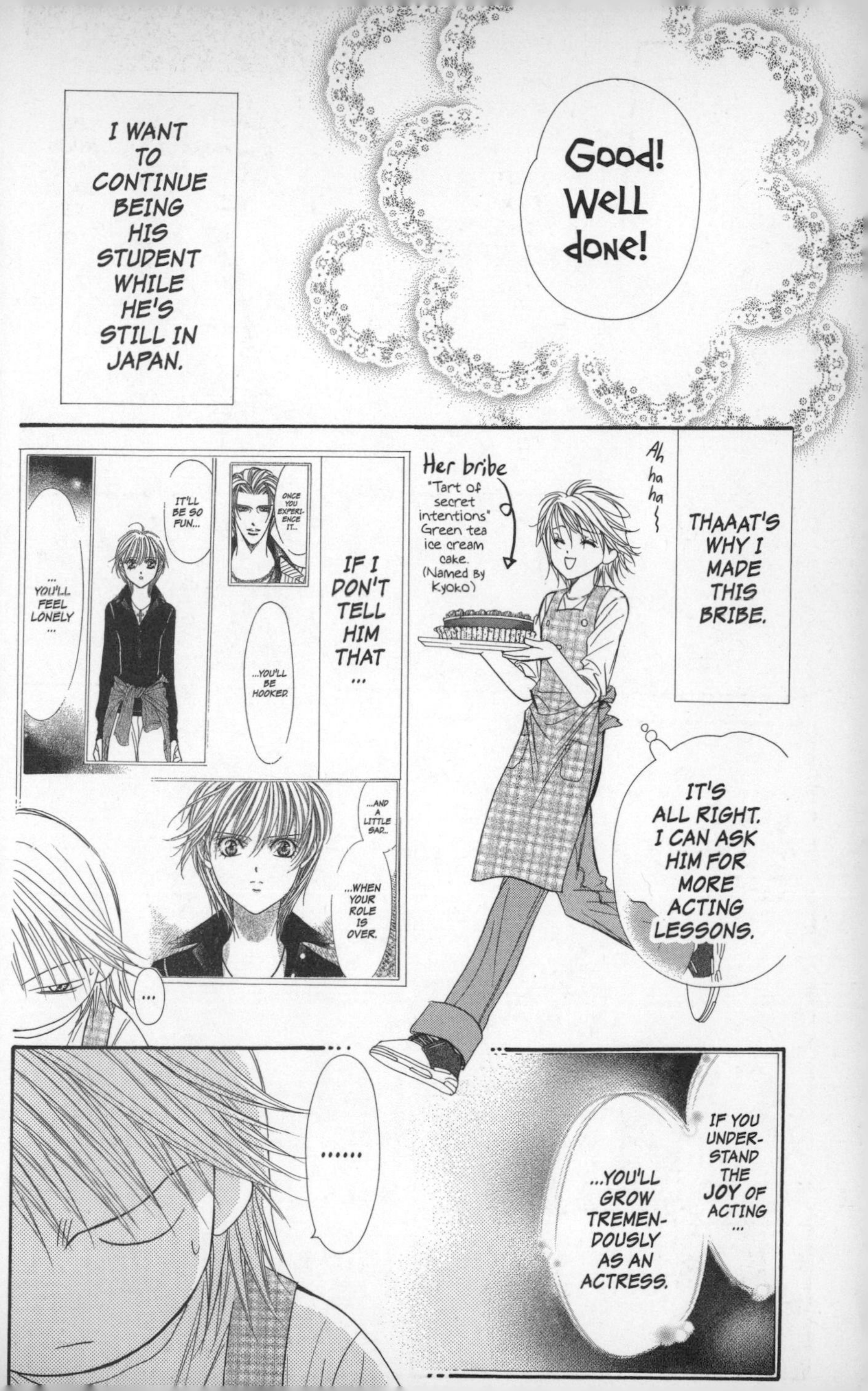
Good! Well done!
I WANT TO CONTINUE BEING HIS STUDENT WHILE HE'S STILL IN JAPAN.
THAAAT'S WHY I MADE THIS BRIBE.
Ah ha ha ~
Her bribe
"Tart of secret intentions" Green tea ice cream cake. (Named By Kyoko)
IT'S ALL RIGHT. I CAN ASK HIM FOR MORE ACTING LESSONS.
IF I DON'T TELL HIM THAT ...
ONCE YOU EXPERIENCE IT...
...YOU'LL BE HOOKED.
IT'LL BE SO FUN...
...YOU'LL FEEL LONELY ...
...AND A LITTLE SAD...
...WHEN YOUR ROLE IS OVER.
...
IF YOU UNDERSTAND THE JOY OF ACTING ...
...YOU'LL GROW TREMENDOUSLY AS AN ACTRESS.
......

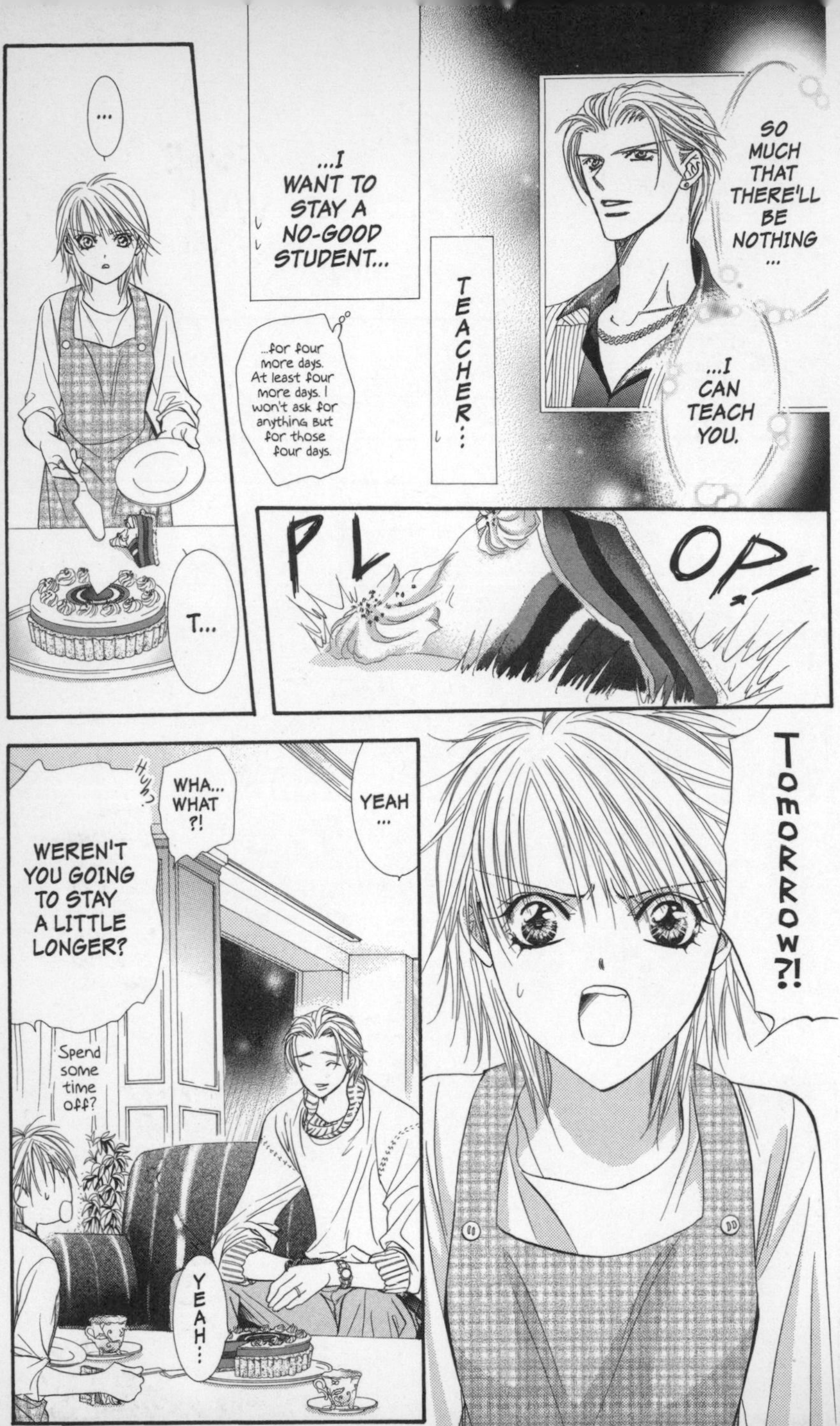
SO MUCH THAT THERE'LL BE NOTHING ...
...I CAN TEACH YOU.
TEACHER...
...I WANT TO STAY A NO-GOOD STUDENT...
...for four more days. At least four more days. I won't ask for anything but for those four days.
PLOP!
...
T...
TOMORROW?!
YEAH ...
WHA... WHAT?!
Huh?
WEREN'T YOU GOING TO STAY A LITTLE LONGER?
Spend some time off?
YEAH...

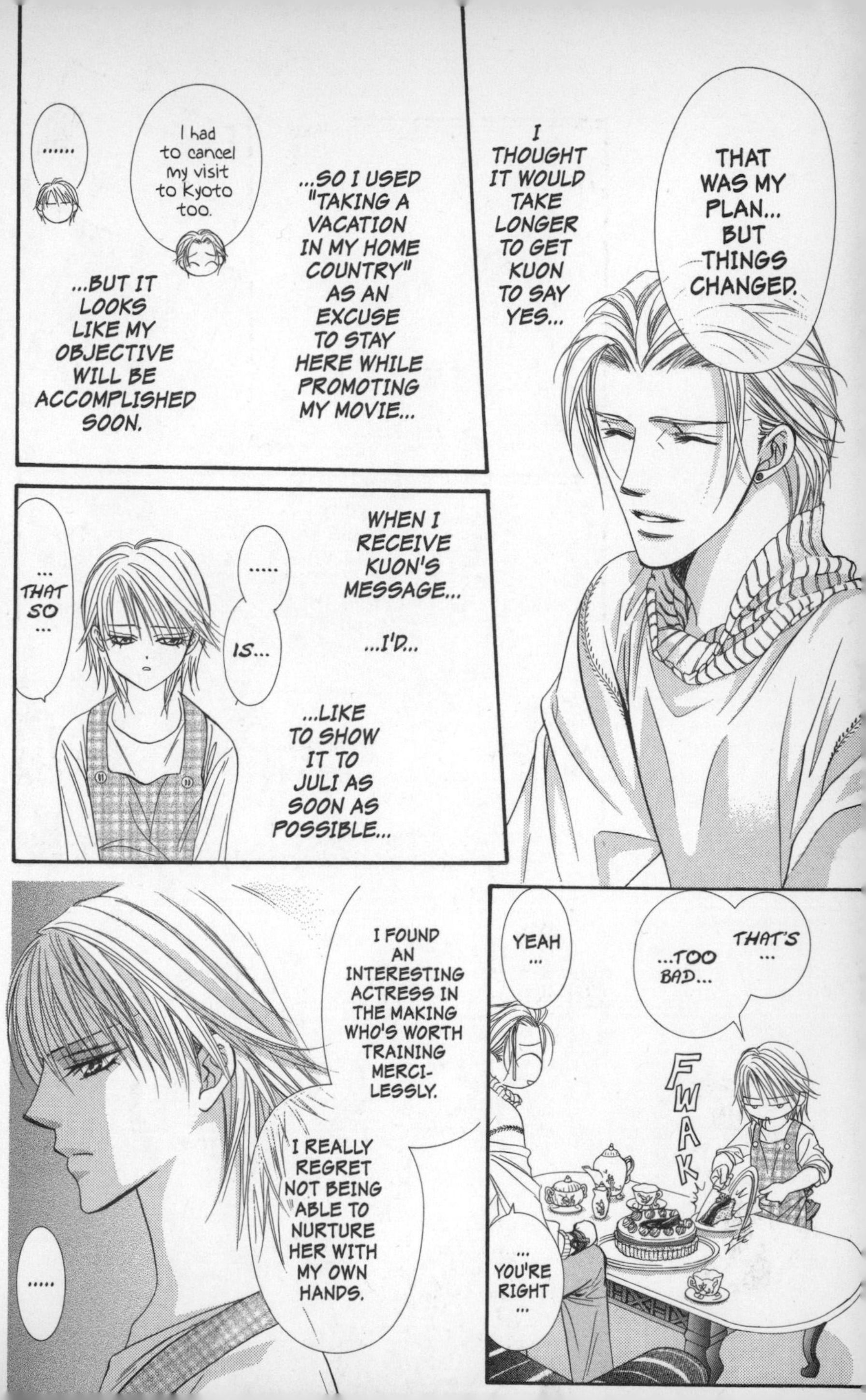
THAT WAS MY PLAN... BUT THINGS CHANGED.
I THOUGHT IT WOULD TAKE LONGER TO GET KUON TO SAY YES...
...SO I USED "TAKING A VACATION IN MY HOME COUNTRY" AS AN EXCUSE TO STAY HERE WHILE PROMOTING MY MOVIE...
I had to cancel my visit to Kyoto too.
......
...BUT IT LOOKS LIKE MY OBJECTIVE WILL BE ACCOMPLISHED SOON.
WHEN I RECEIVE KUON'S MESSAGE...
...I'D...
...LIKE TO SHOW IT TO JULI AS SOON AS POSSIBLE...
.....
IS...
... THAT SO ...
THAT'S ... ...TOO BAD...
YEAH ...
FWAK
... YOU'RE RIGHT ...
I FOUND AN INTERESTING ACTRESS IN THE MAKING WHO'S WORTH TRAINING MERCI-LESSLY.
I REALLY REGRET NOT BEING ABLE TO NURTURE HER WITH MY OWN HANDS.
.....

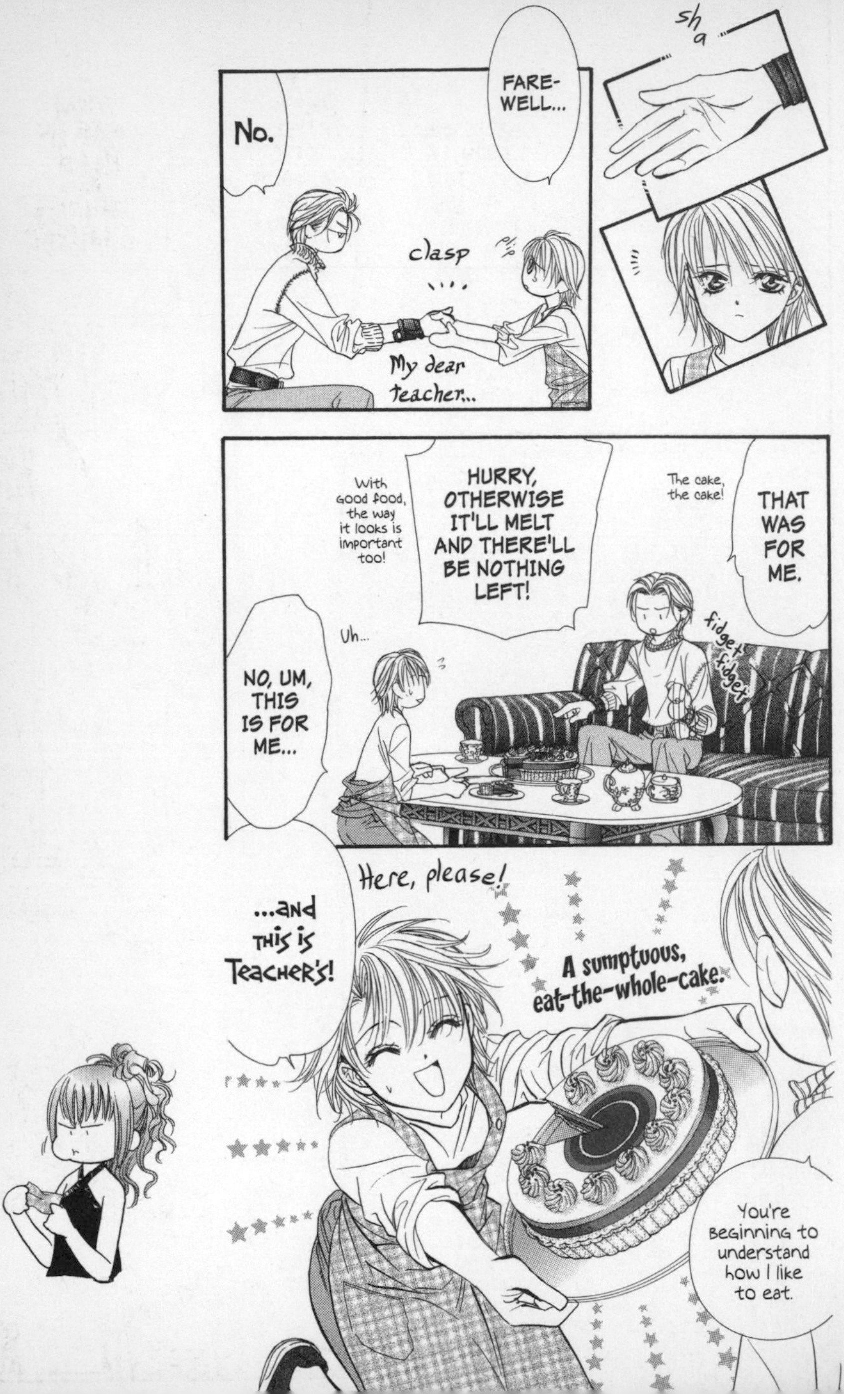
sha
FARE-WELL...
No.
clasp
My dear teacher...
THAT WAS FOR ME.
The cake, the cake!
HURRY, OTHERWISE IT'LL MELT AND THERE'LL BE NOTHING LEFT!
With good food, the way it looks is important too!
Uh...
NO, UM, THIS IS FOR ME...
Here, please!
...and THIS is Teacher's!
A sumptuous, eat-the-whole-cake.
You're beginning to understand how I like to eat.

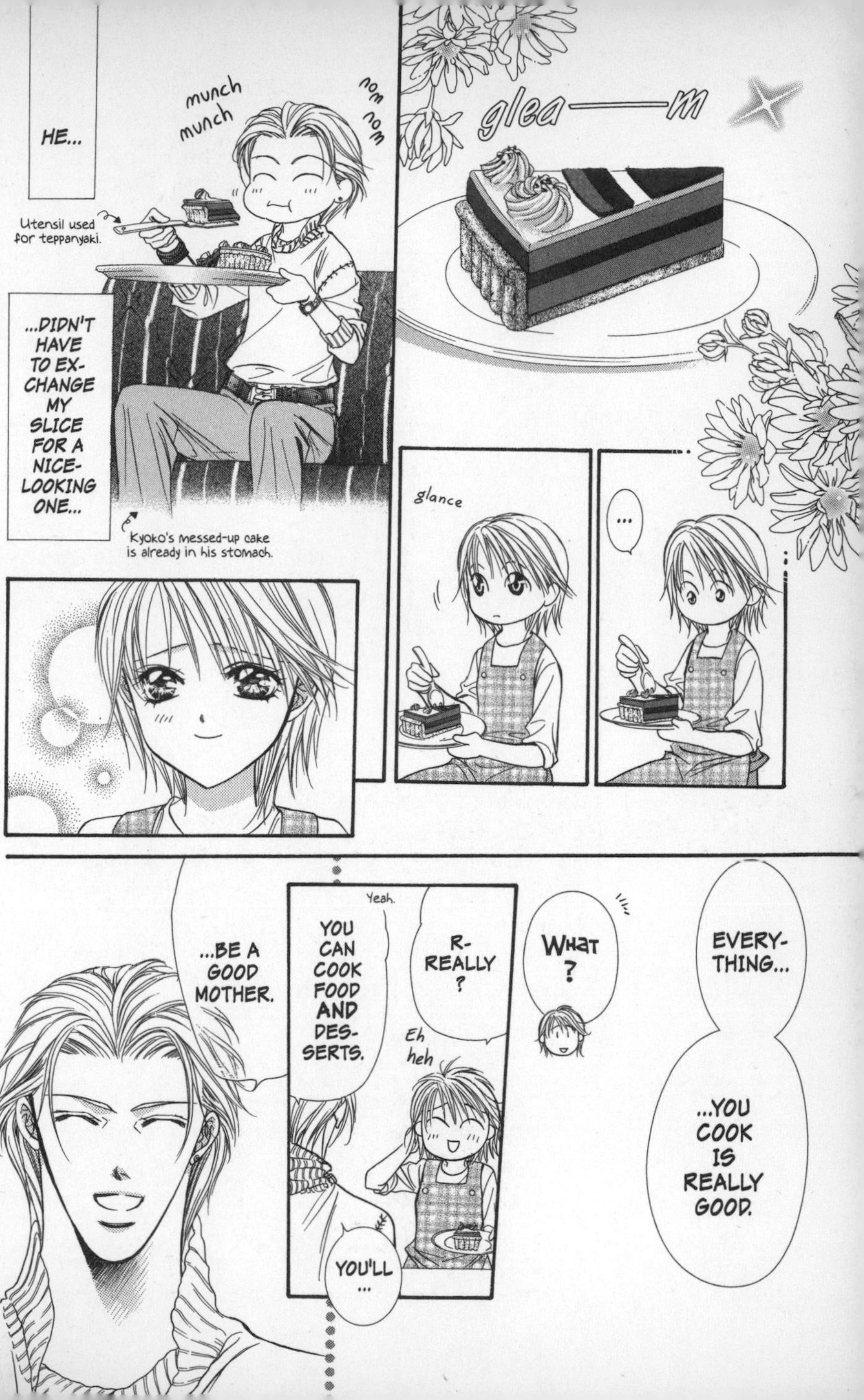
glea——m
nom nom
munch munch
HE...
Utensil used for teppanyaki.
...DIDN'T HAVE TO EX-CHANGE MY SLICE FOR A NICE-LOOKING ONE...
Kyoko's messed-up cake is already in his stomach.
...
glance
EVERY-THING...
...YOU COOK IS REALLY GOOD.
WHAT ?
R-REALLY ?
Eh heh
Yeah.
YOU CAN COOK FOOD AND DES-SERTS.
YOU'LL ...
...BE A GOOD MOTHER.

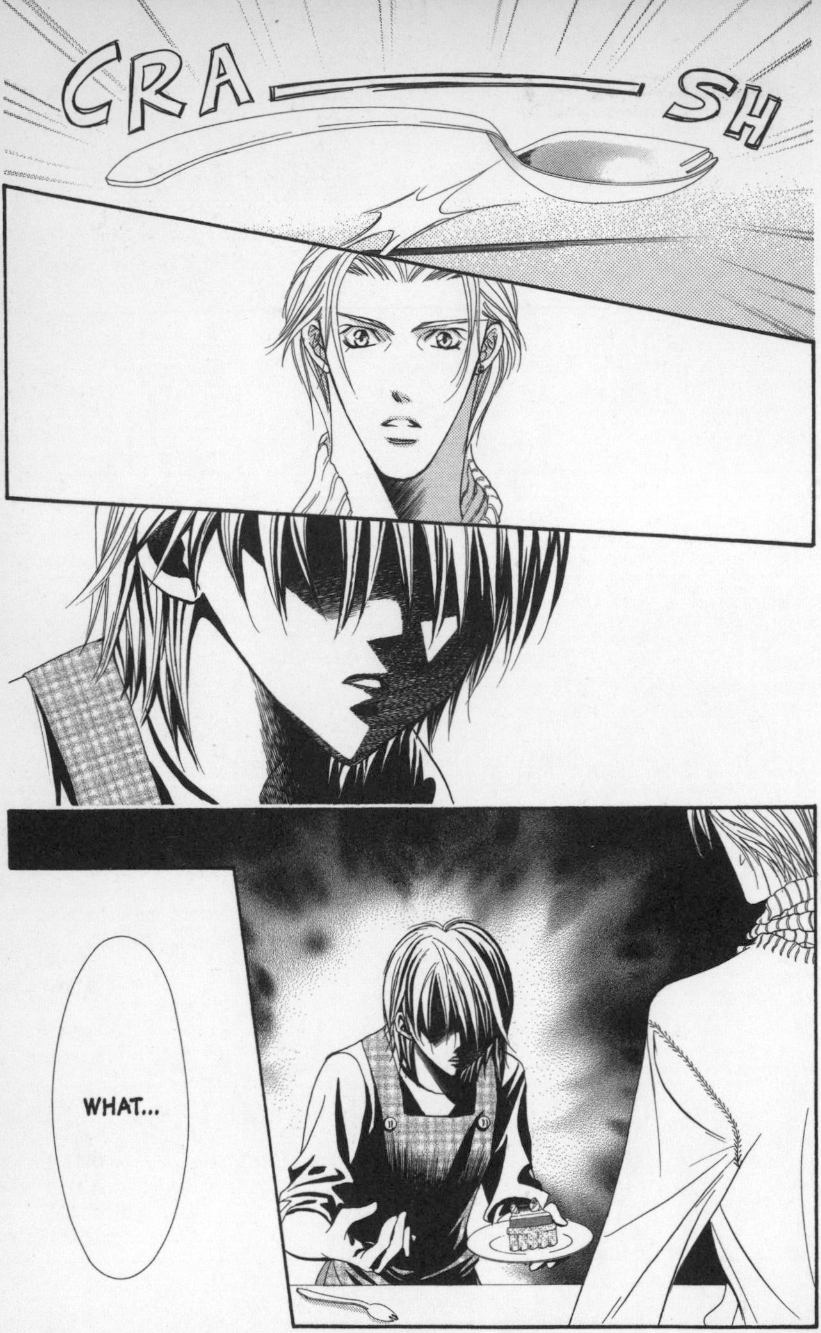
CRA——SH
WHAT...

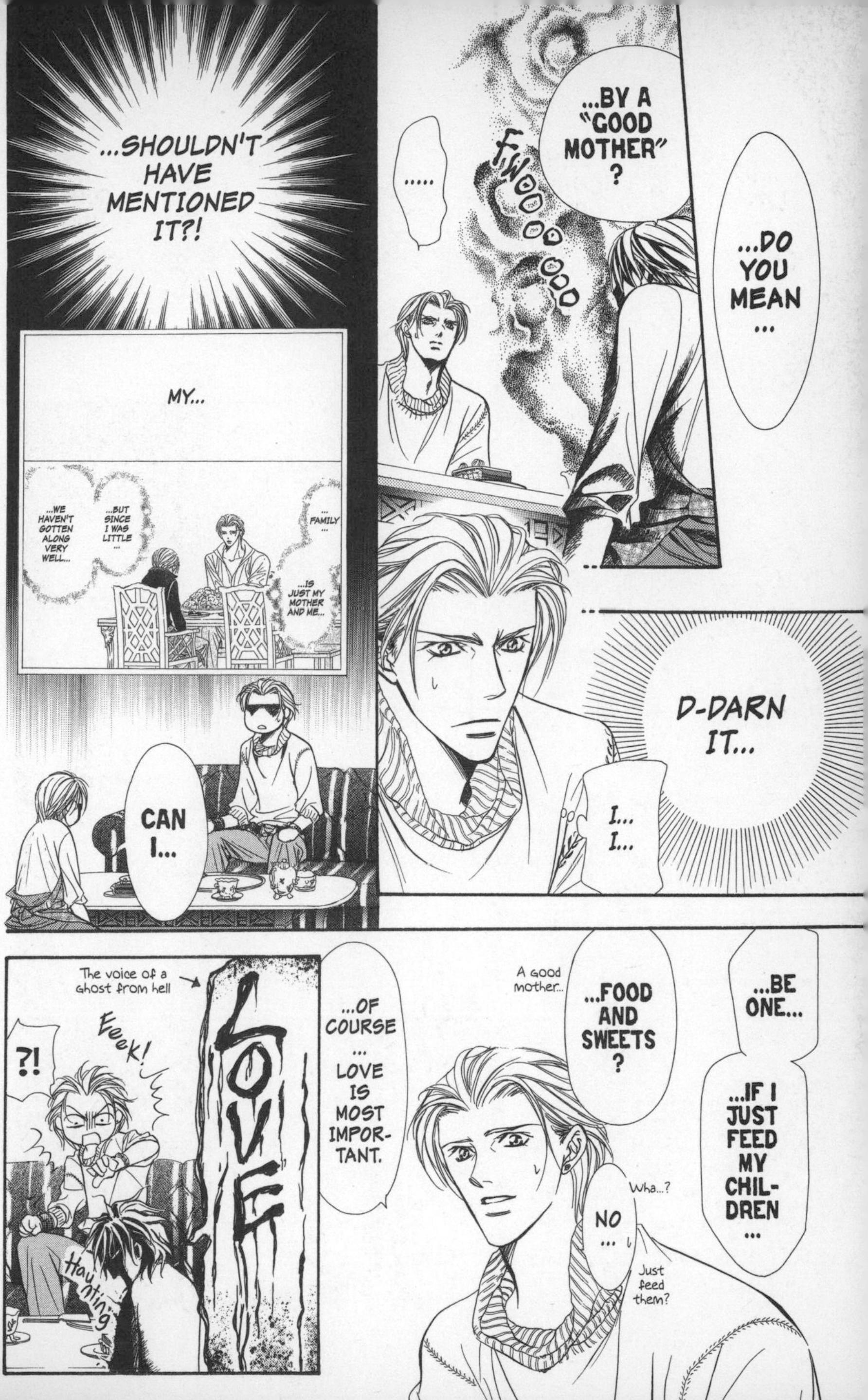
...DO YOU MEAN...
...BY A "GOOD MOTHER"?
FWOOOOOOO
.....
...
...
D-DARN IT...
I... I...
...SHOULDN'T HAVE MENTIONED IT?!
MY...
...FAMILY...
...IS JUST MY MOTHER AND ME...
...BUT SINCE I WAS LITTLE...
...WE HAVEN'T GOTTEN ALONG VERY WELL...
CAN I...
...BE ONE...
...IF I JUST FEED MY CHILDREN...
A good mother...
...FOOD AND SWEETS?
Wha...?
NO...
Just feed them?
...OF COURSE... LOVE IS MOST IMPOR-TANT.
The voice of a ghost from hell
LOVE
Eeek!
?!
Haunting

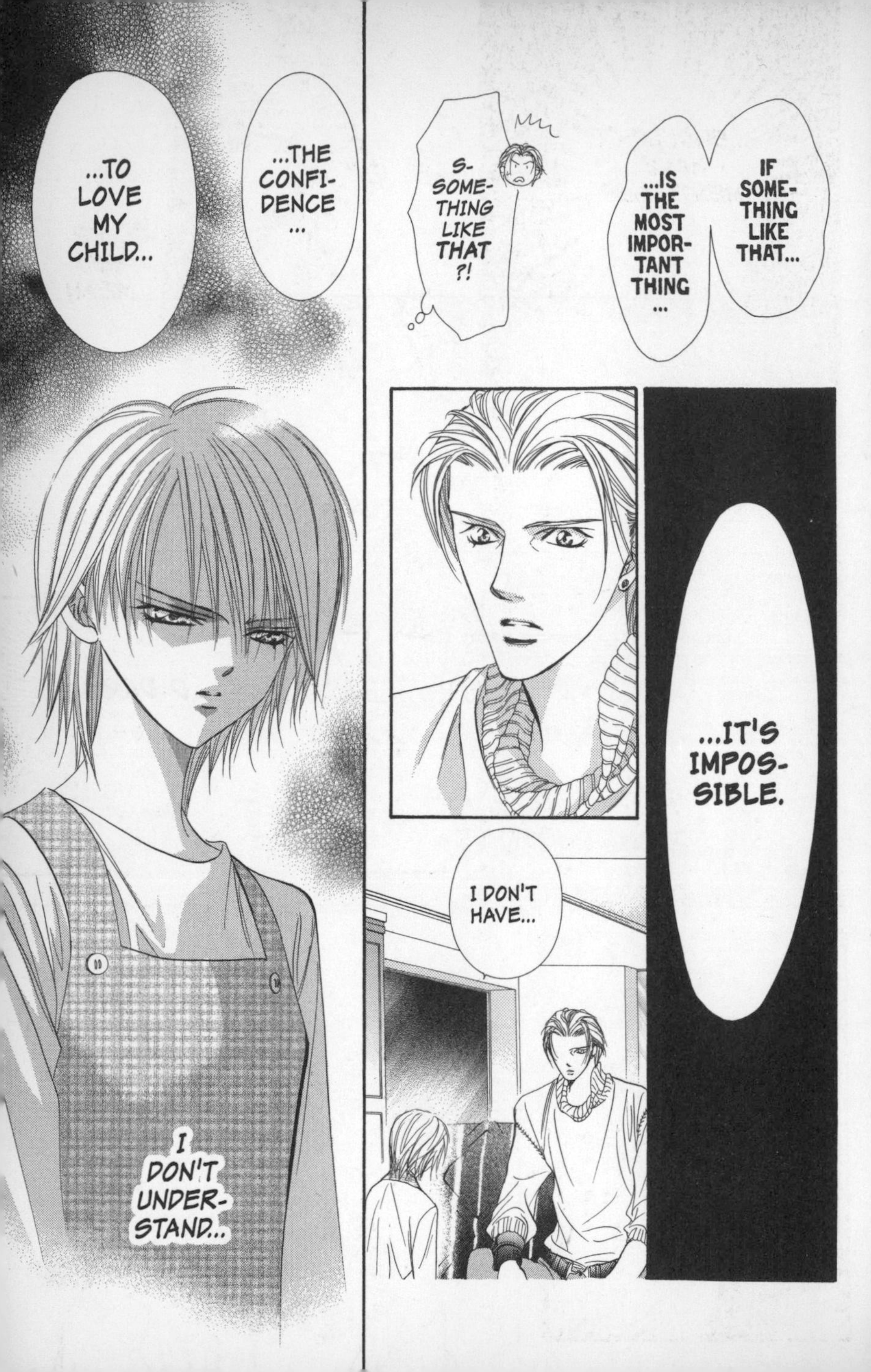
IF SOMETHING LIKE THAT...
...IS THE MOST IMPORTANT THING...
S-SOMETHING LIKE THAT?!
...IT'S IMPOSSIBLE.
I DON'T HAVE...
...THE CONFIDENCE...
...TO LOVE MY CHILD...
I DON'T UNDERSTAND...

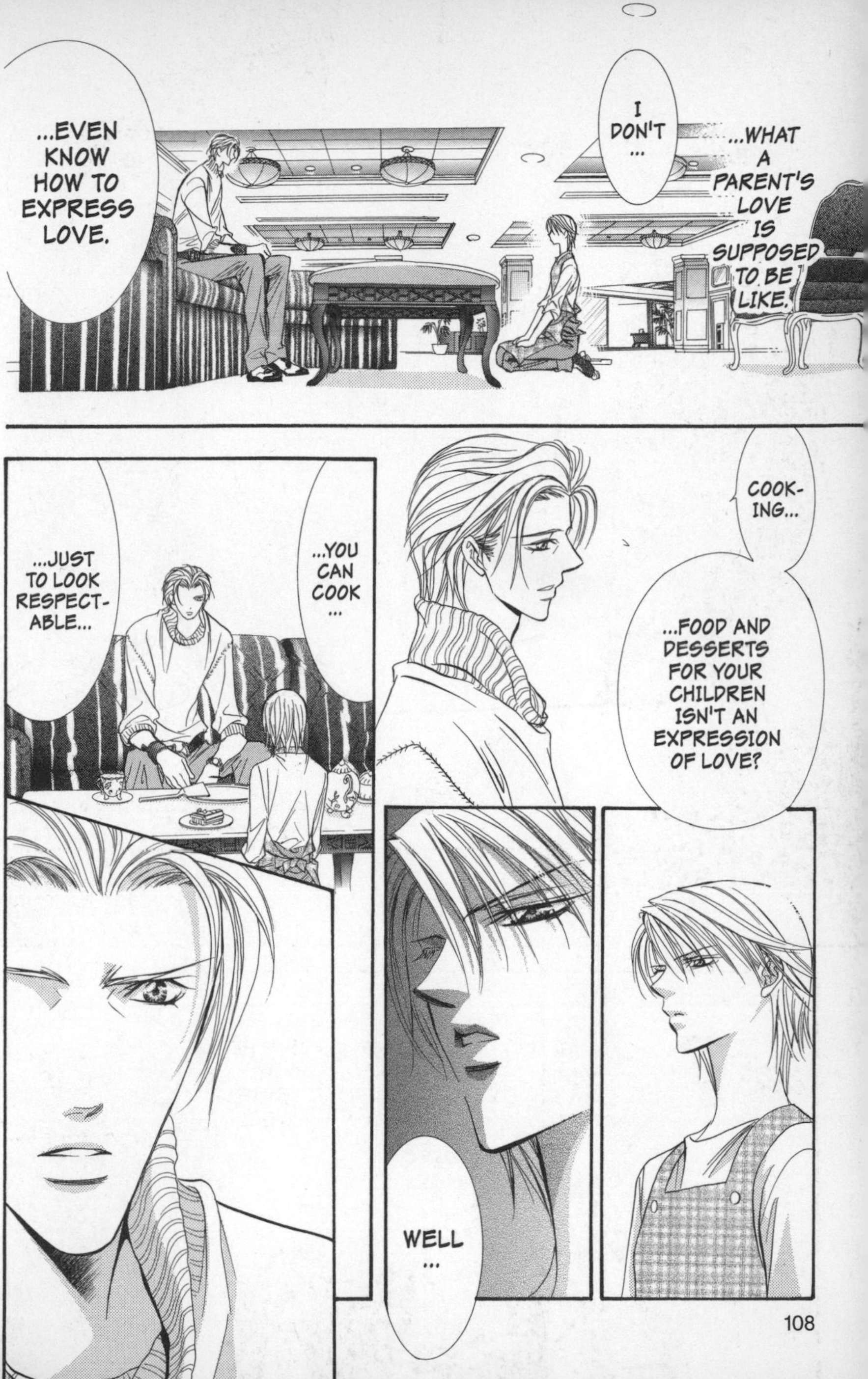
I DON'T ...
...WHAT A PARENT'S LOVE IS SUPPOSED TO BE LIKE.
...EVEN KNOW HOW TO EXPRESS LOVE.
COOK-ING...
...FOOD AND DESSERTS FOR YOUR CHILDREN ISN'T AN EXPRESSION OF LOVE?
...YOU CAN COOK ...
...JUST TO LOOK RESPECT-ABLE...
WELL ...

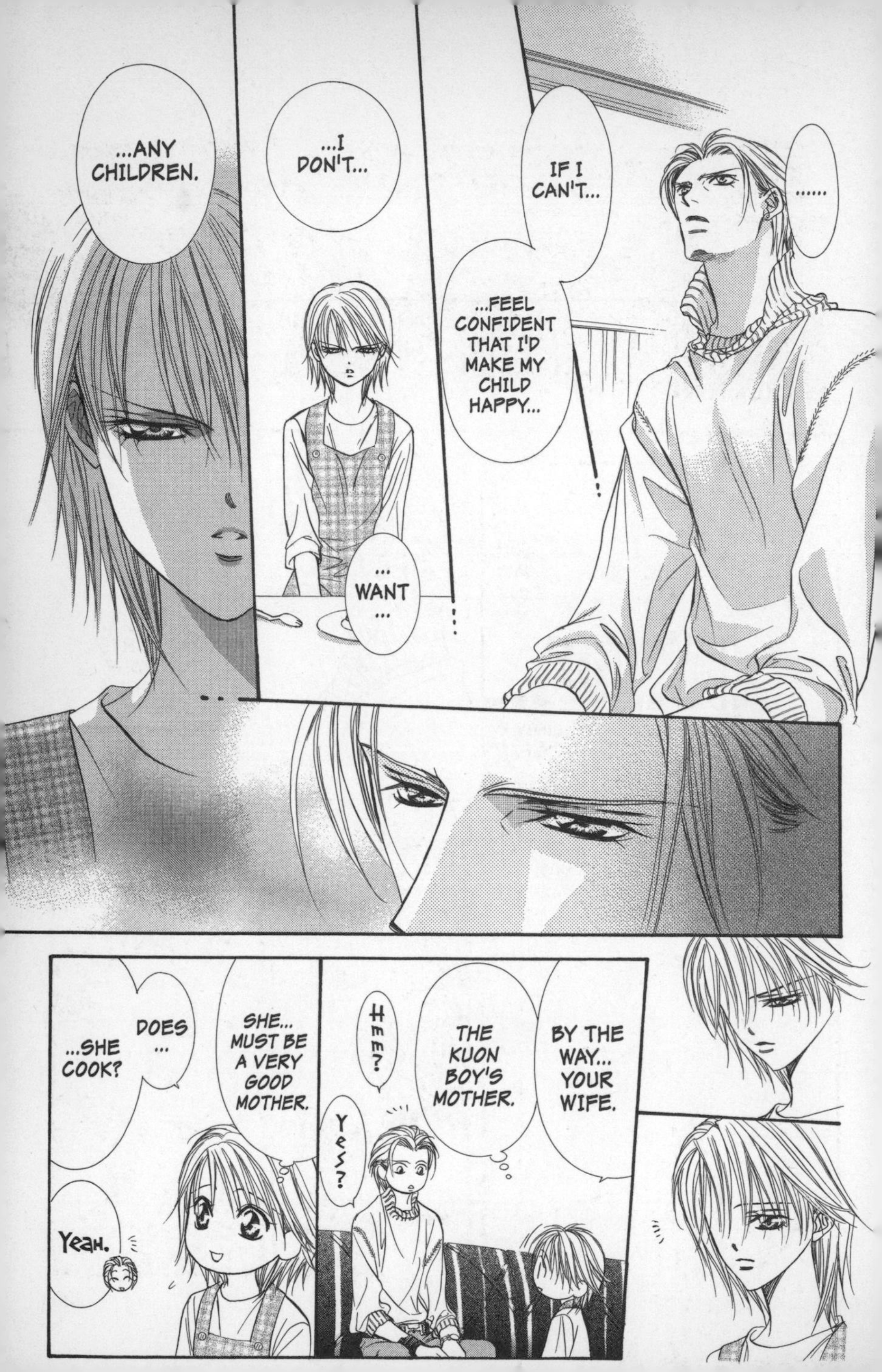
......
IF I CAN'T...
...FEEL CONFIDENT THAT I'D MAKE MY CHILD HAPPY...
...I DON'T...
...WANT...
...ANY CHILDREN.
BY THE WAY... YOUR WIFE.
THE KUON BOY'S MOTHER.
Hmm?
Yes?
SHE... MUST BE A VERY GOOD MOTHER.
DOES...
...SHE COOK?
Yeah.

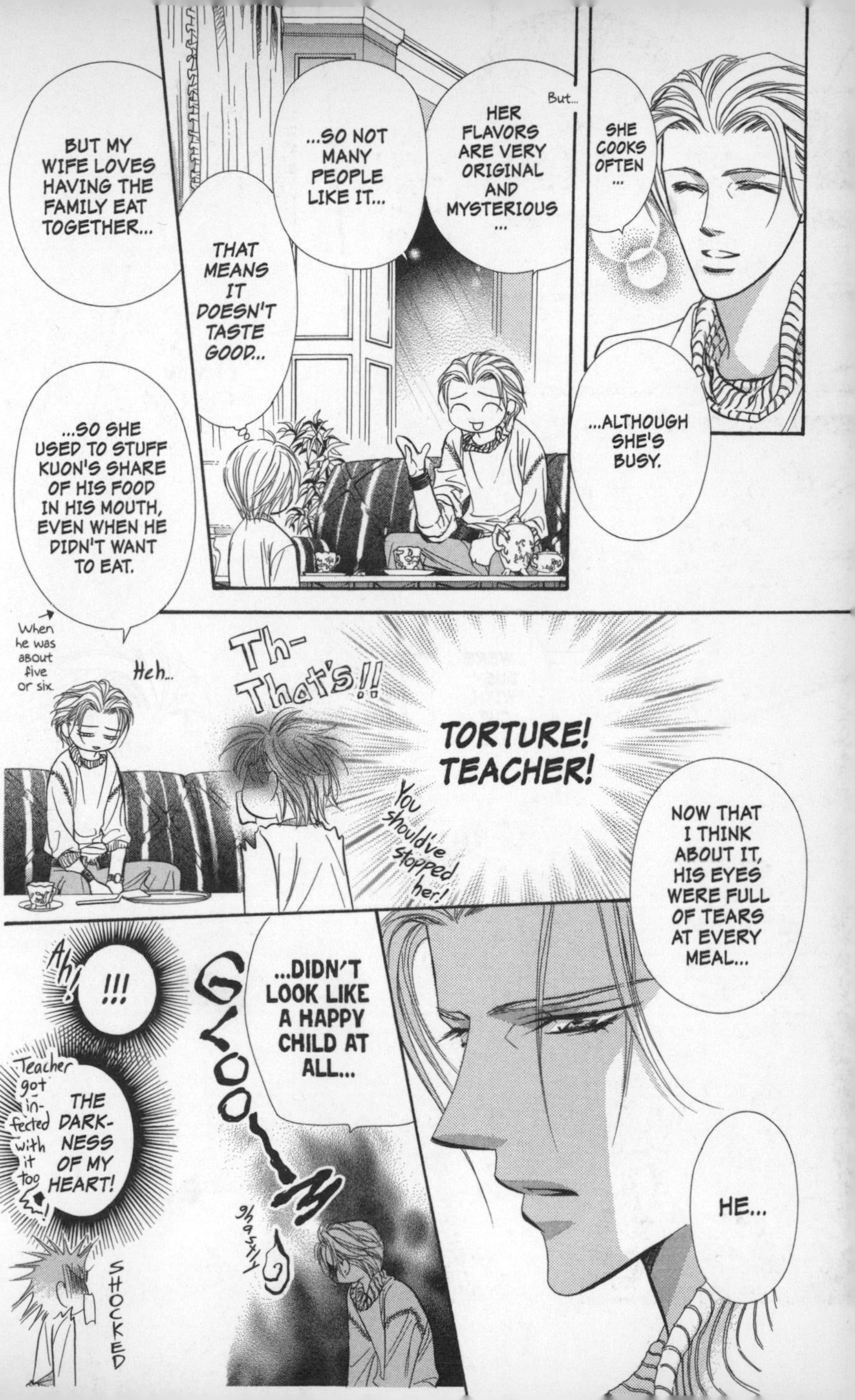

SHE COOKS OFTEN ...
...ALTHOUGH SHE'S BUSY.
But...
HER FLAVORS ARE VERY ORIGINAL AND MYSTERIOUS ...
...SO NOT MANY PEOPLE LIKE IT...
THAT MEANS IT DOESN'T TASTE GOOD...
BUT MY WIFE LOVES HAVING THE FAMILY EAT TOGETHER...
...SO SHE USED TO STUFF KUON'S SHARE OF HIS FOOD IN HIS MOUTH, EVEN WHEN HE DIDN'T WANT TO EAT.
When he was about five or six.
Heh...
Th- That's!!
TORTURE! TEACHER!
You should've stopped her!
NOW THAT I THINK ABOUT IT, HIS EYES WERE FULL OF TEARS AT EVERY MEAL...
HE...
...DIDN'T LOOK LIKE A HAPPY CHILD AT ALL...
GLOO~M
ghastly
Ah!
!!!
THE DARKNESS OF MY HEART!
Teacher got infected with it too
SHOCKED

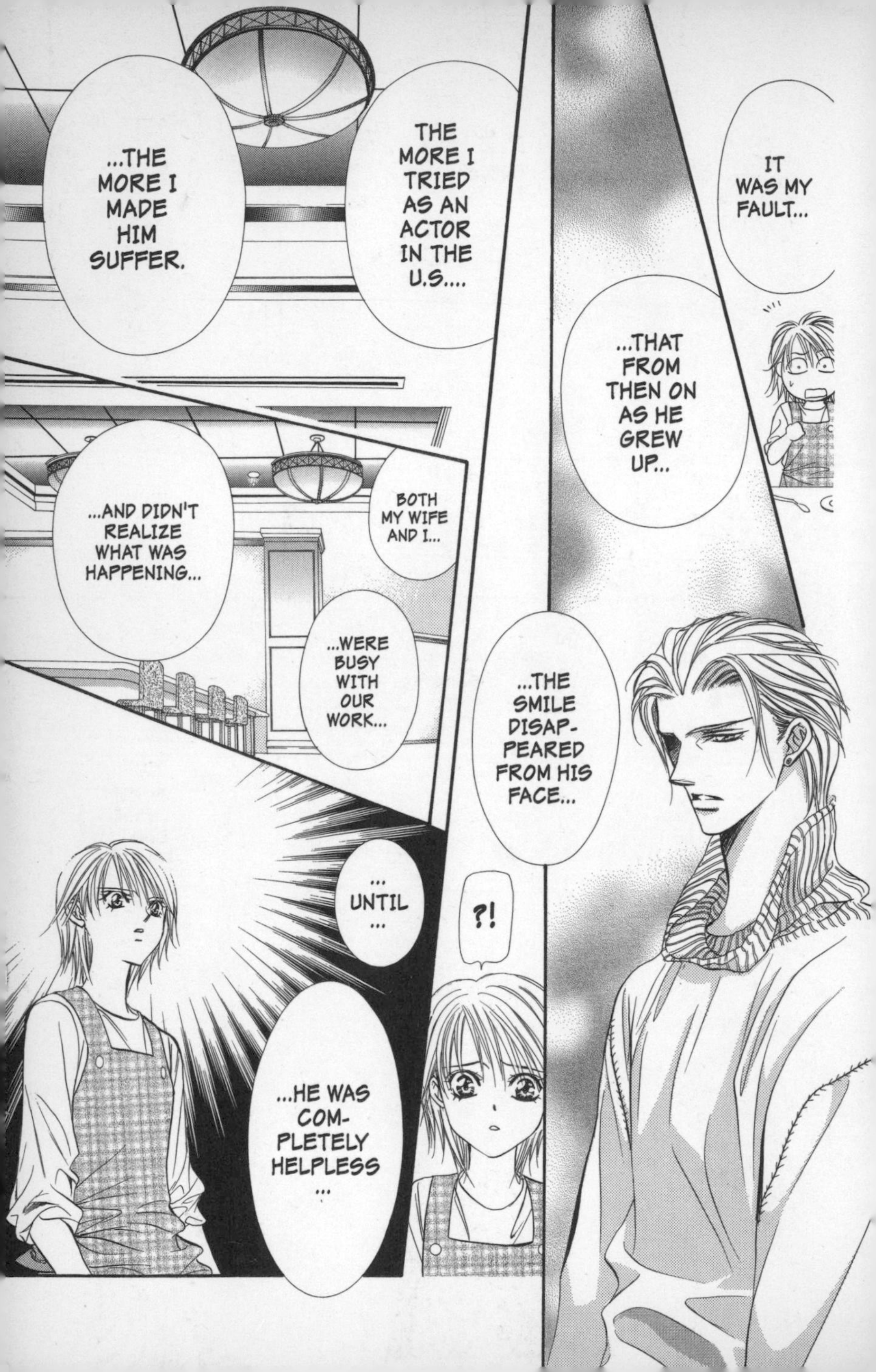
IT WAS MY FAULT...
...THAT FROM THEN ON AS HE GREW UP...
...THE SMILE DISAP-PEARED FROM HIS FACE...
THE MORE I TRIED AS AN ACTOR IN THE U.S....
...THE MORE I MADE HIM SUFFER.
BOTH MY WIFE AND I...
...WERE BUSY WITH OUR WORK...
...AND DIDN'T REALIZE WHAT WAS HAPPENING...
?!
... UNTIL ...
...HE WAS COM-PLETELY HELPLESS ...

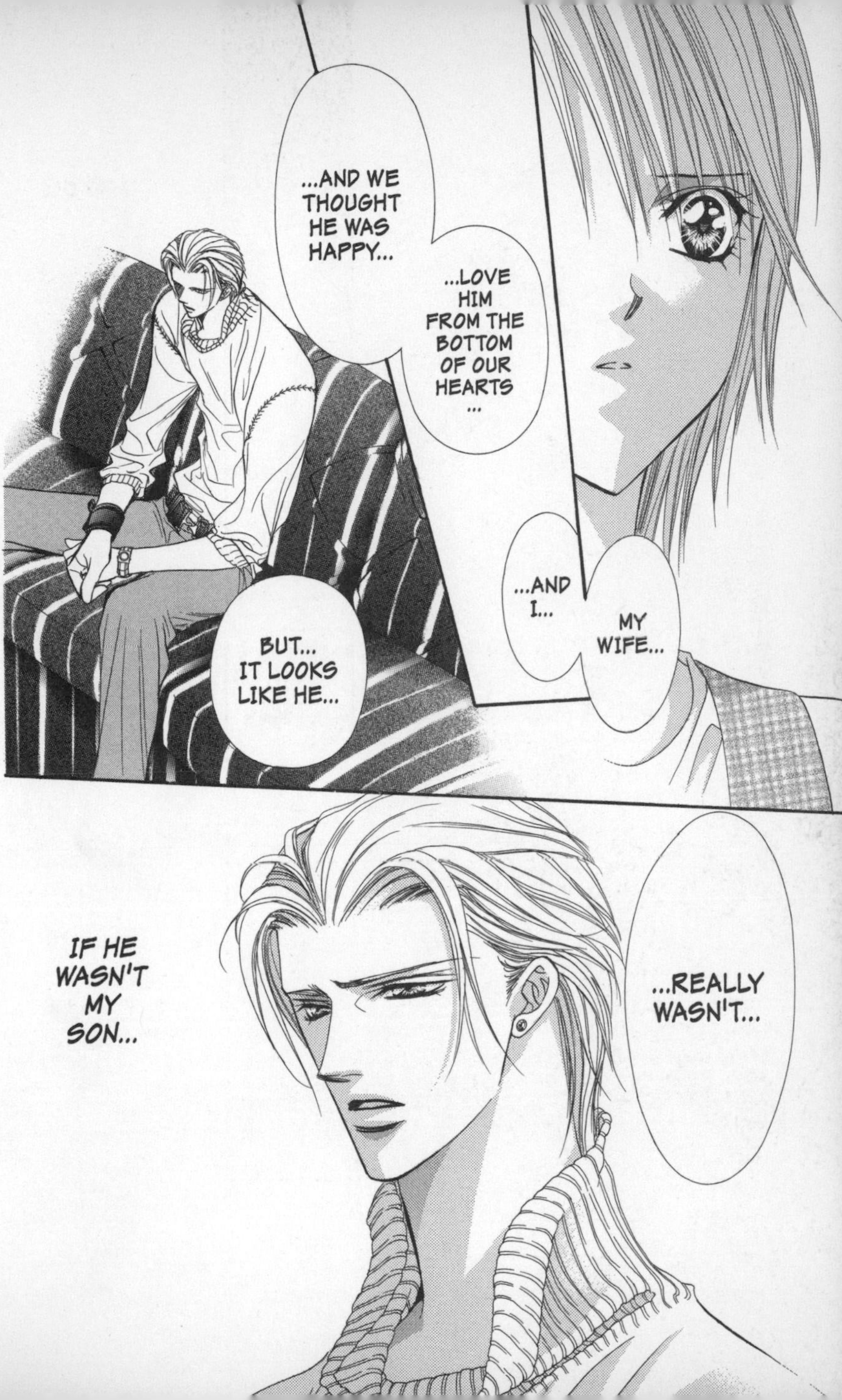
MY WIFE...
...AND I...
...LOVE HIM FROM THE BOTTOM OF OUR HEARTS...
...AND WE THOUGHT HE WAS HAPPY...
BUT... IT LOOKS LIKE HE...
...REALLY WASN'T...
IF HE WASN'T MY SON...

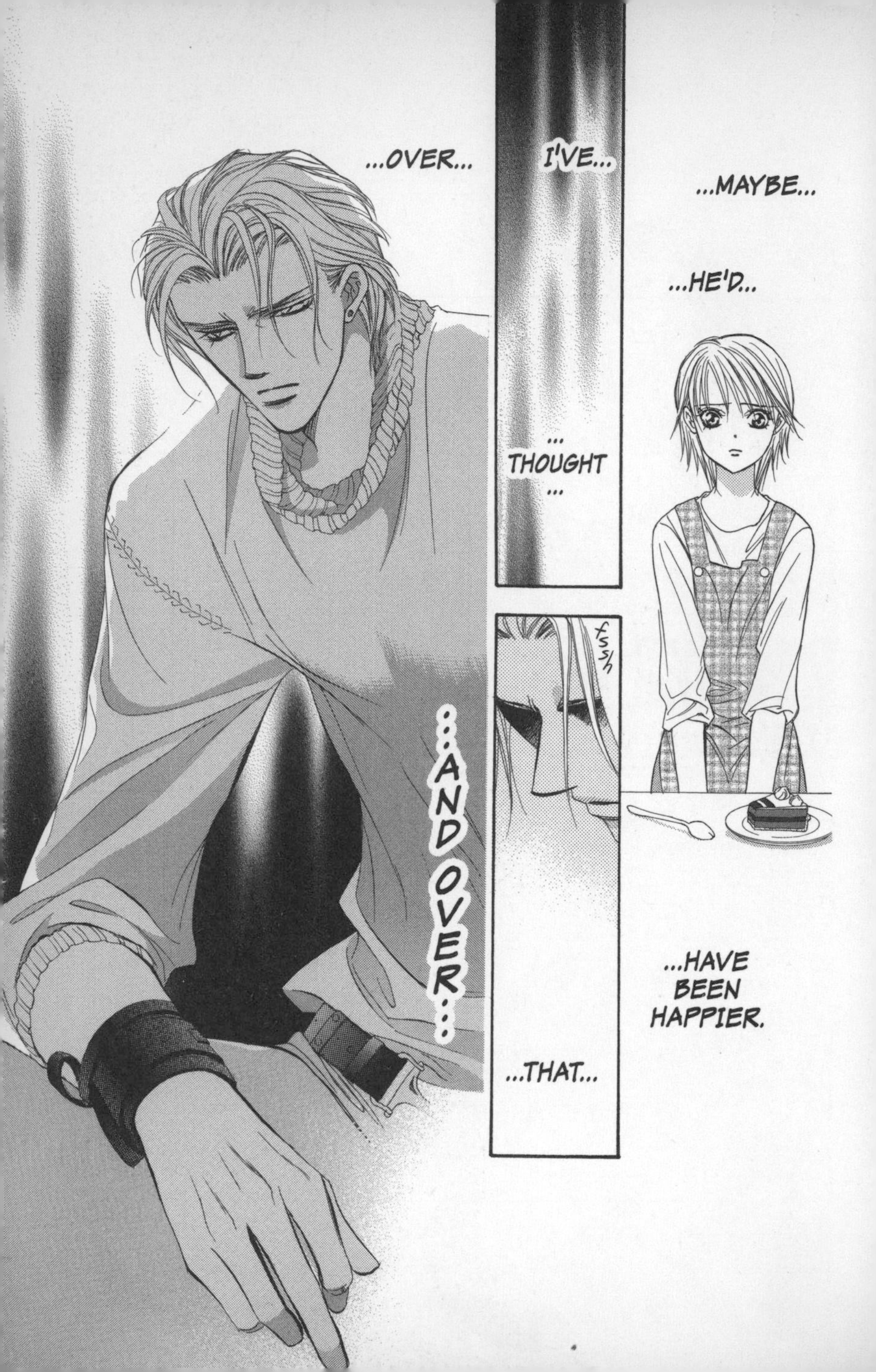
...MAYBE...
...HE'D...
...HAVE BEEN HAPPIER.
I'VE...
...THOUGHT...
fssh
...THAT...
...OVER...
...AND OVER...

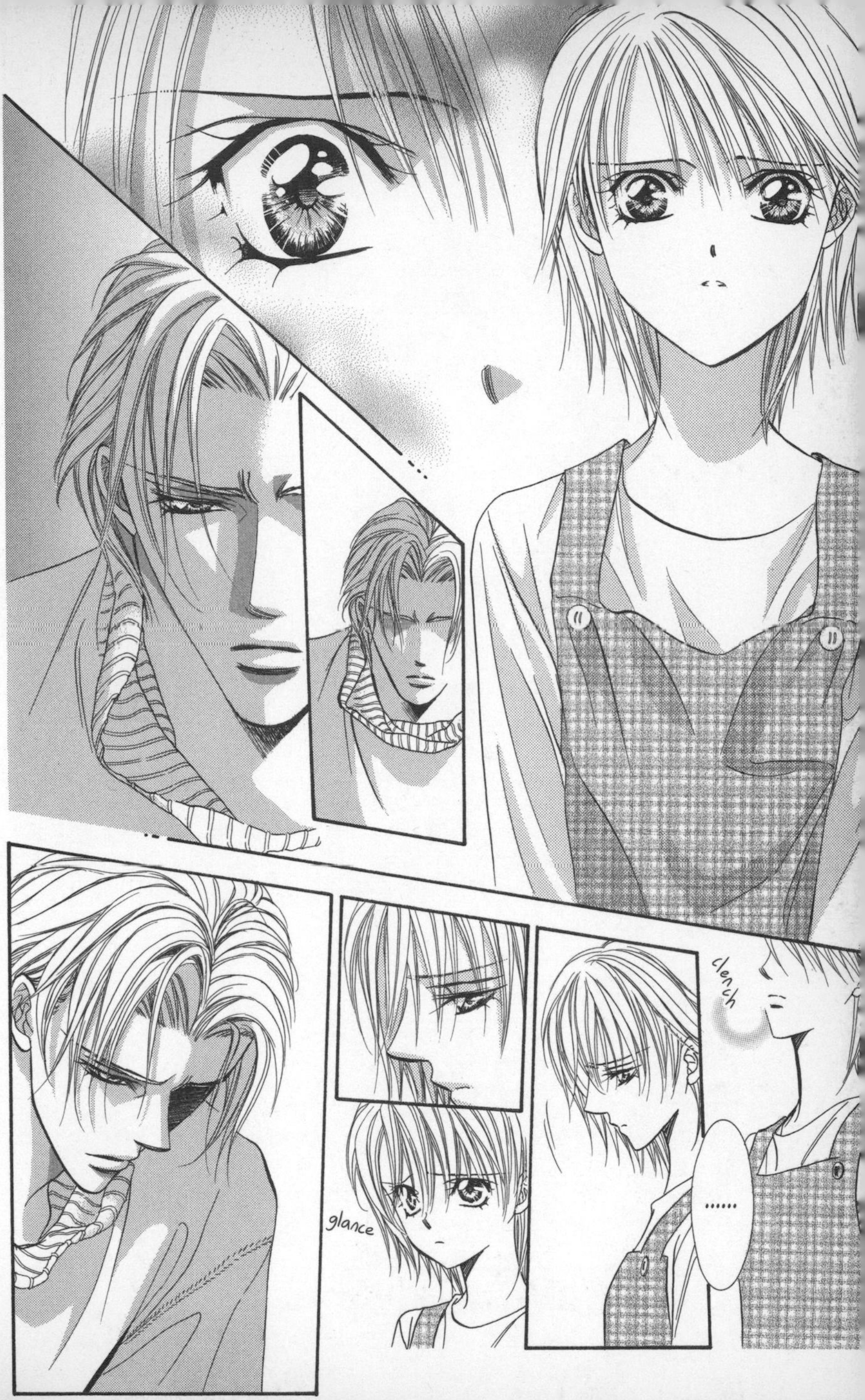
...
clench
......
glance

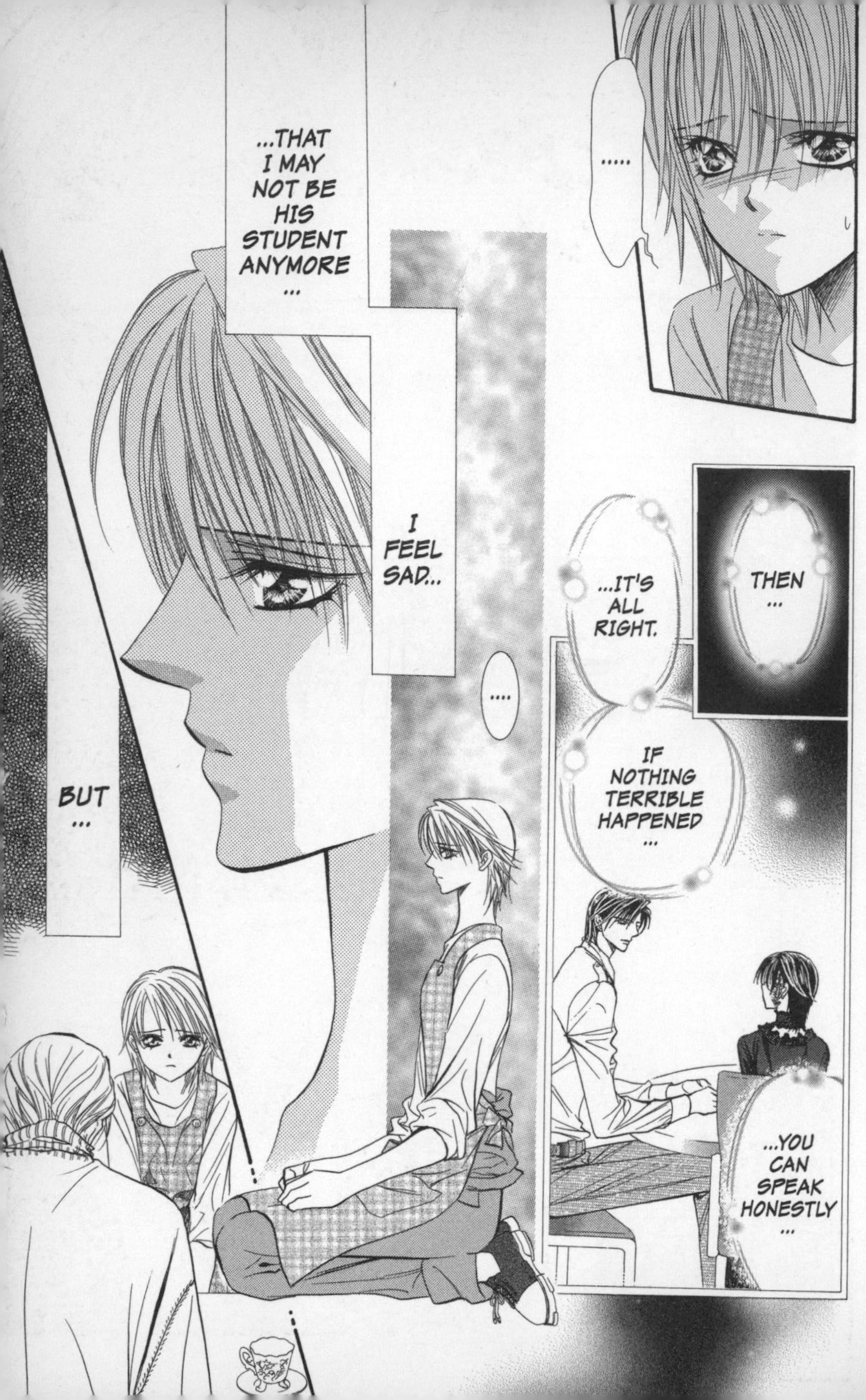
.....
THEN ...
...IT'S ALL RIGHT.
IF NOTHING TERRIBLE HAPPENED ...
...YOU CAN SPEAK HONESTLY ...
...THAT I MAY NOT BE HIS STUDENT ANYMORE ...
I FEEL SAD...
....
BUT ...

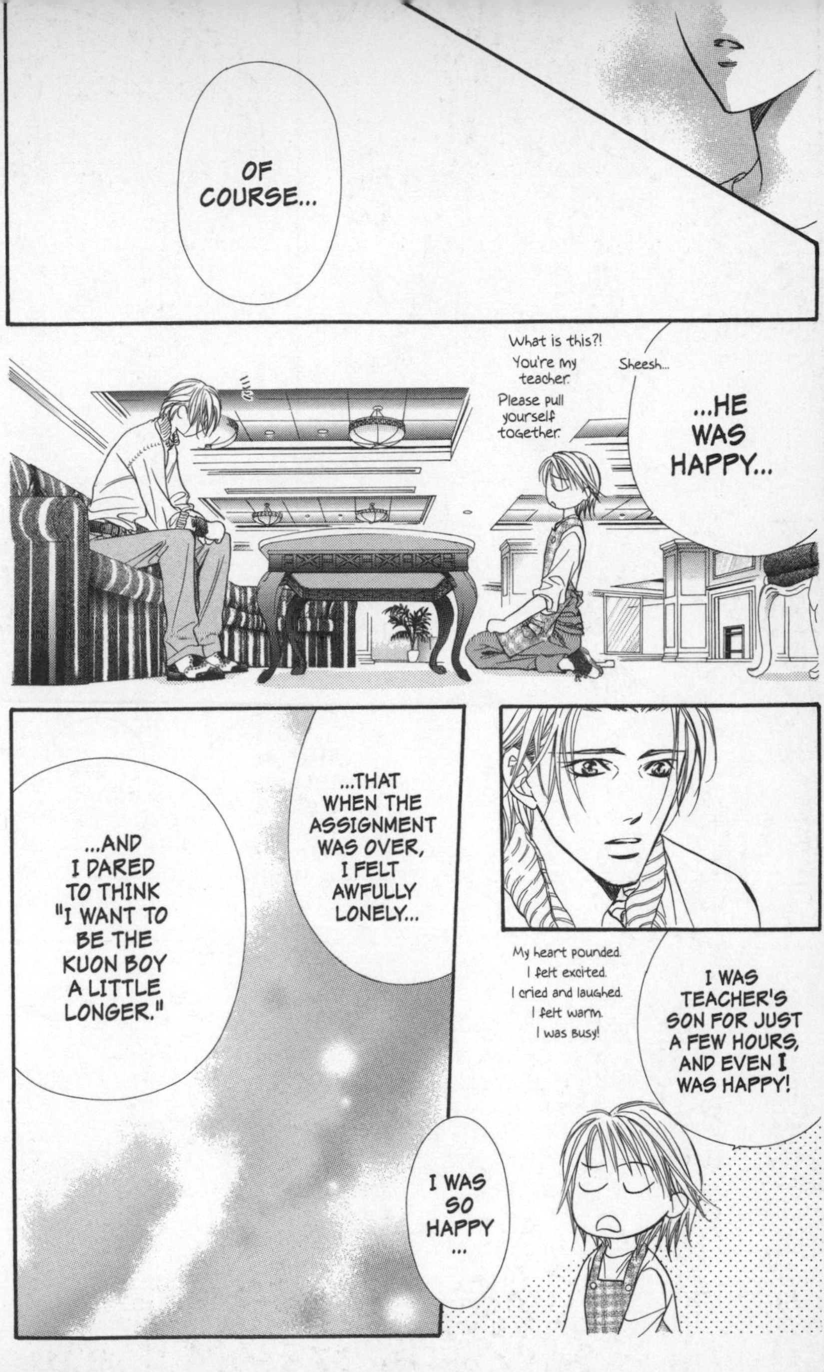
OF COURSE...
...HE WAS HAPPY...
Sheesh...
What is this?! You're my teacher. Please pull yourself together.
I WAS TEACHER'S SON FOR JUST A FEW HOURS, AND EVEN I WAS HAPPY!
My heart pounded. I felt excited. I cried and laughed. I felt warm. I was busy!
I WAS SO HAPPY ...
...THAT WHEN THE ASSIGNMENT WAS OVER, I FELT AWFULLY LONELY...
...AND I DARED TO THINK "I WANT TO BE THE KUON BOY A LITTLE LONGER."

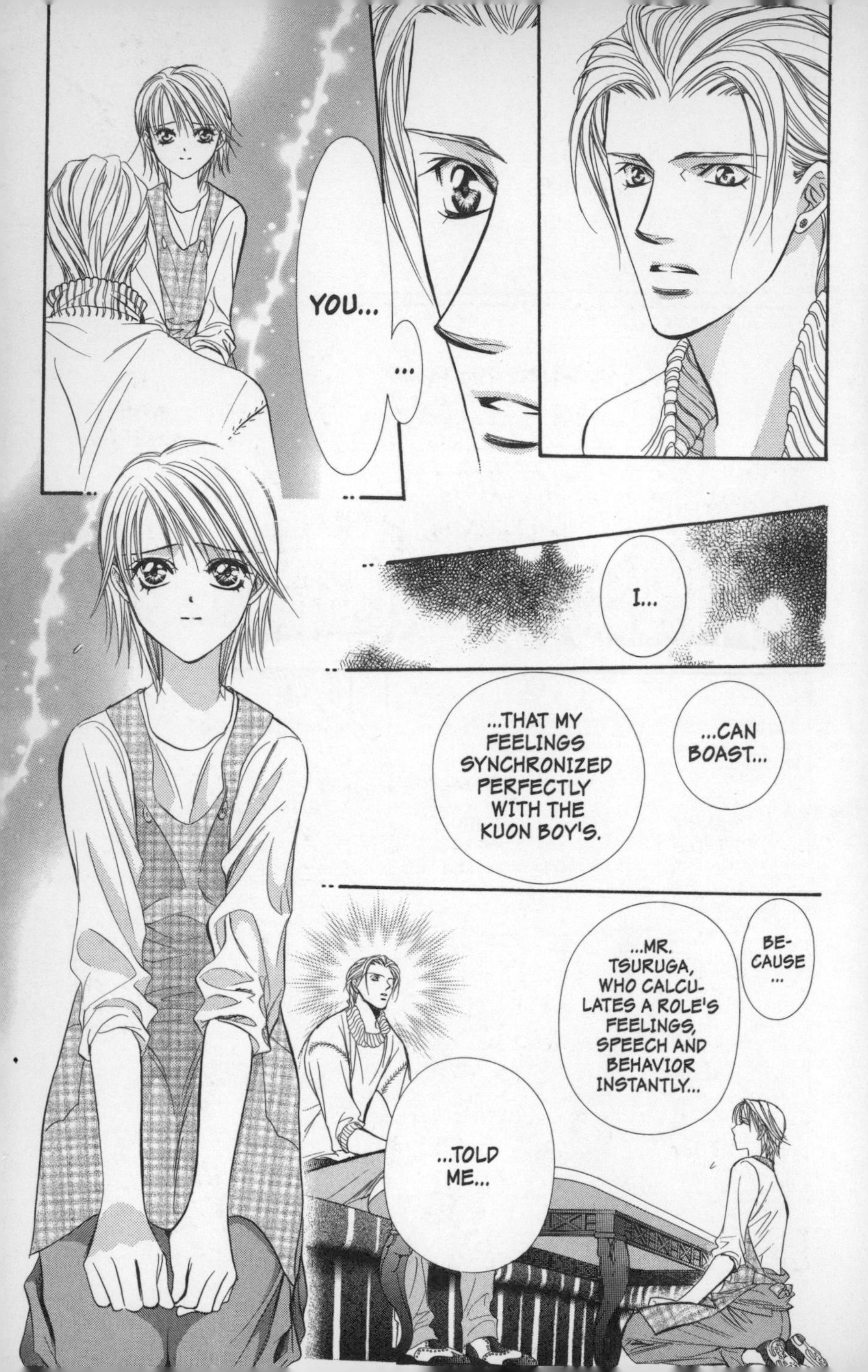
YOU...
...
I...
...CAN BOAST...
...THAT MY FEELINGS SYNCHRONIZED PERFECTLY WITH THE KUON BOY'S.
BE-CAUSE...
...MR. TSURUGA, WHO CALCU-LATES A ROLE'S FEELINGS, SPEECH AND BEHAVIOR INSTANTLY...
...TOLD ME...

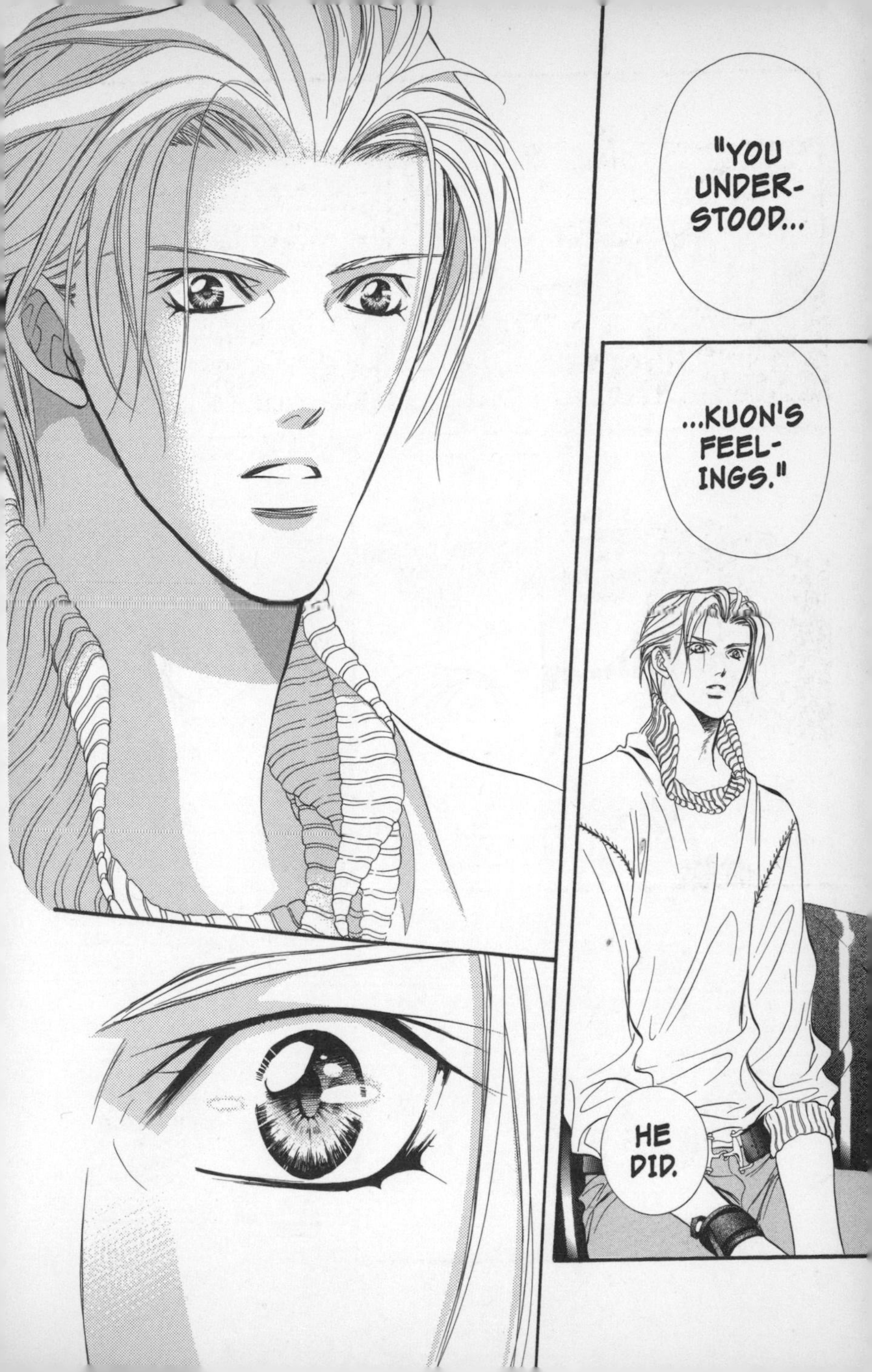
"YOU UNDER-STOOD...
...KUON'S FEEL-INGS."
HE DID.

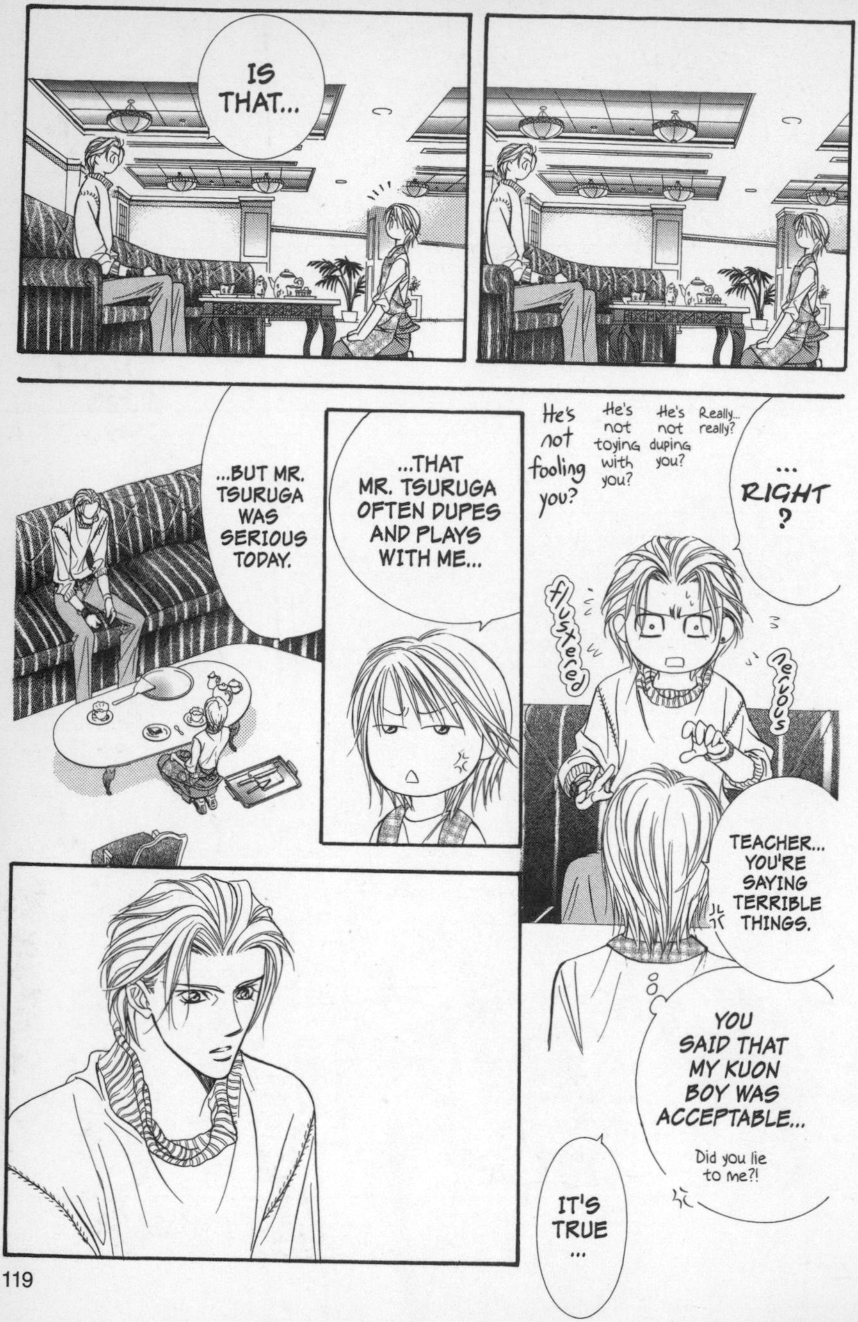

IS THAT...
...RIGHT?
Really... really?
He's not duping you?
He's not toying with you?
He's not fooling you?
flustered
nervous
TEACHER... YOU'RE SAYING TERRIBLE THINGS.
...THAT MR. TSURUGA OFTEN DUPES AND PLAYS WITH ME...
...BUT MR. TSURUGA WAS SERIOUS TODAY.
YOU SAID THAT MY KUON BOY WAS ACCEPTABLE...
Did you lie to me?!
IT'S TRUE...

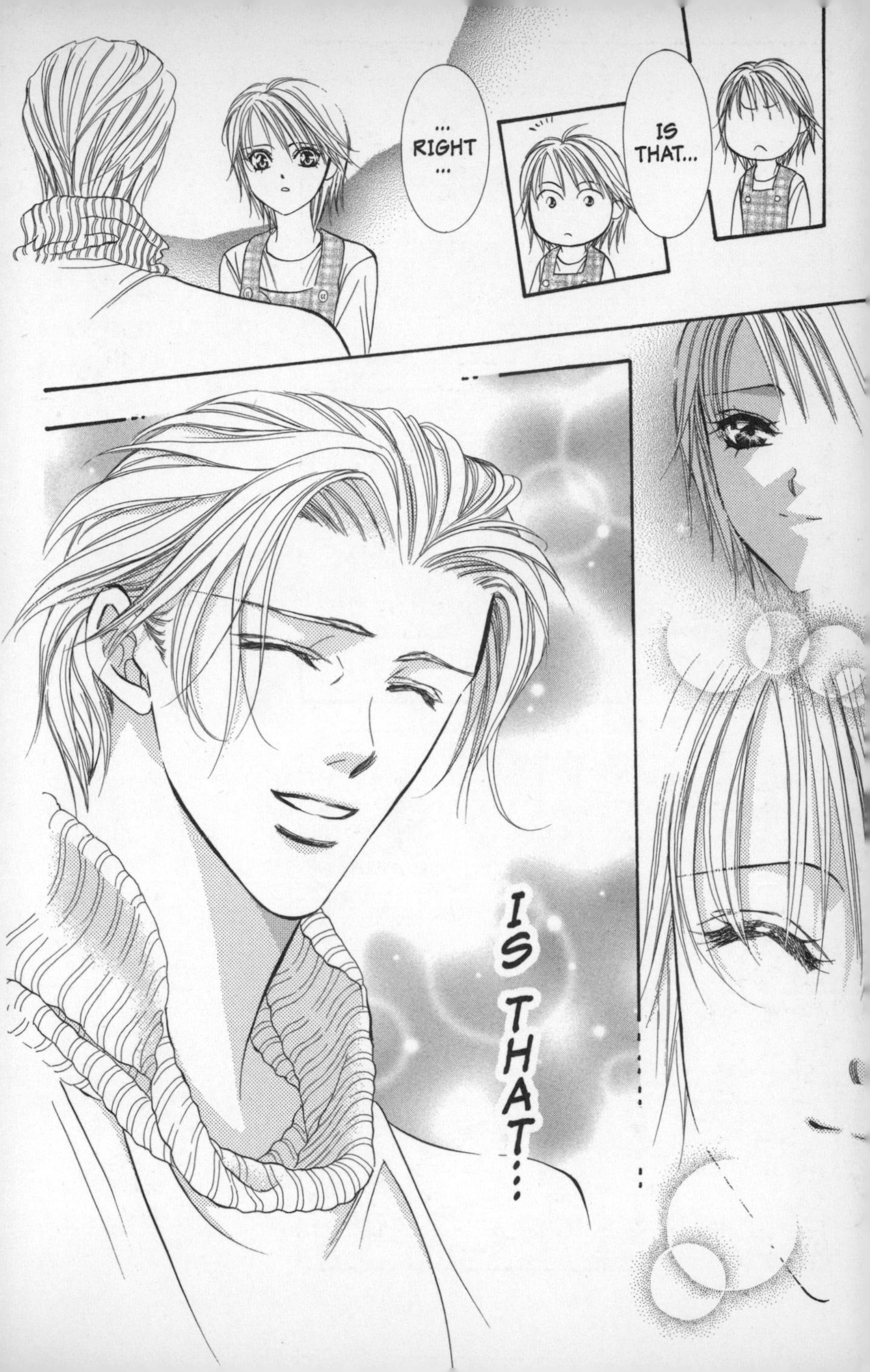
IS THAT...
... RIGHT ...
IS THAT...

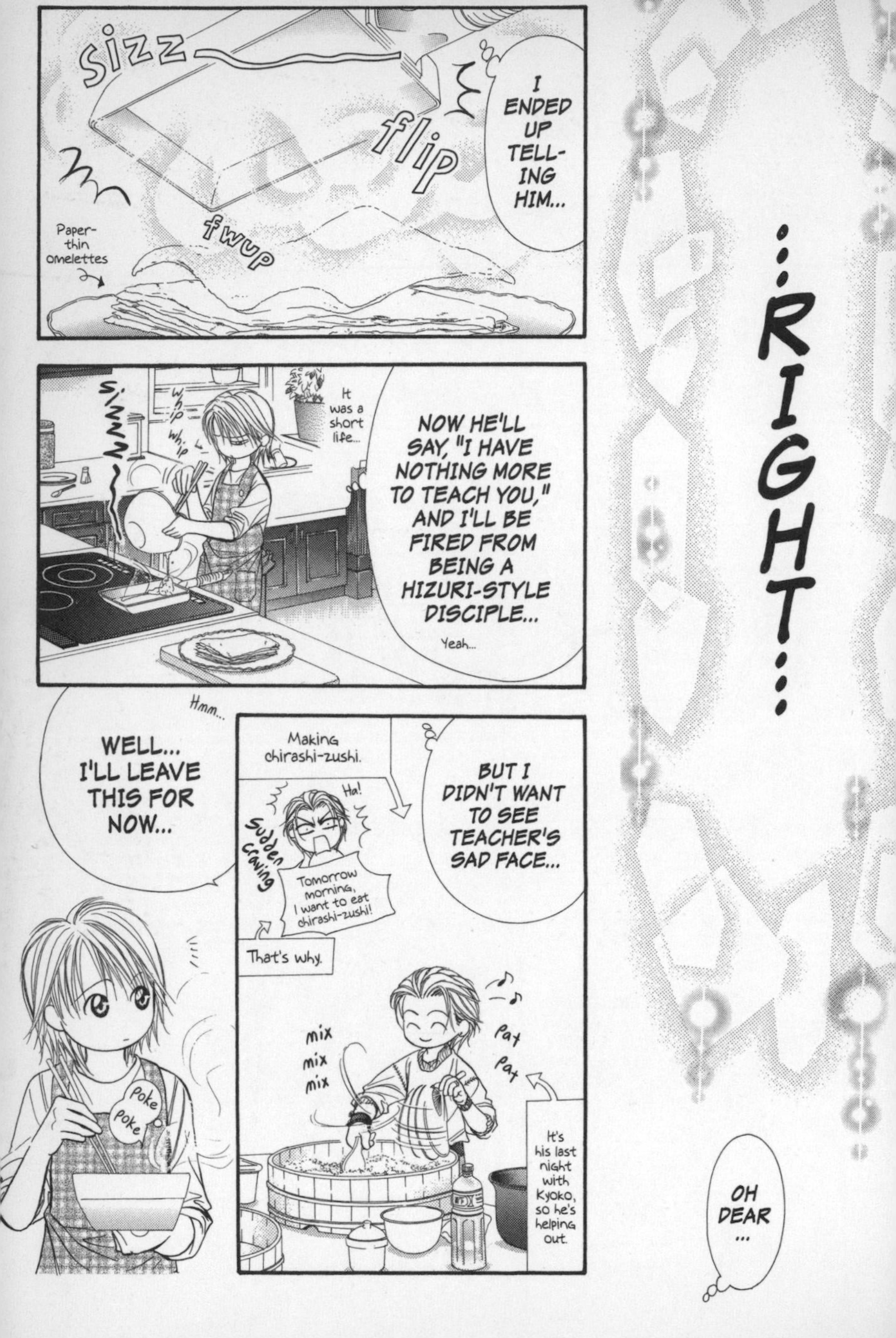
...RIGHT...
OH DEAR ...
I ENDED UP TELLING HIM...
flip
sizz
fwup
Paper-thin omelettes
NOW HE'LL SAY, "I HAVE NOTHING MORE TO TEACH YOU," AND I'LL BE FIRED FROM BEING A HIZURI-STYLE DISCIPLE...
Yeah...
It was a short life...
whip whip
sizzz
BUT I DIDN'T WANT TO SEE TEACHER'S SAD FACE...
Making chirashi-zushi.
Ha!
Sudden craving
Tomorrow morning, I want to eat chirashi-zushi!
That's why.
Pat Pat
mix mix mix
It's his last night with Kyoko, so he's helping out.
Hmm...
WELL... I'LL LEAVE THIS FOR NOW...
Poke Poke

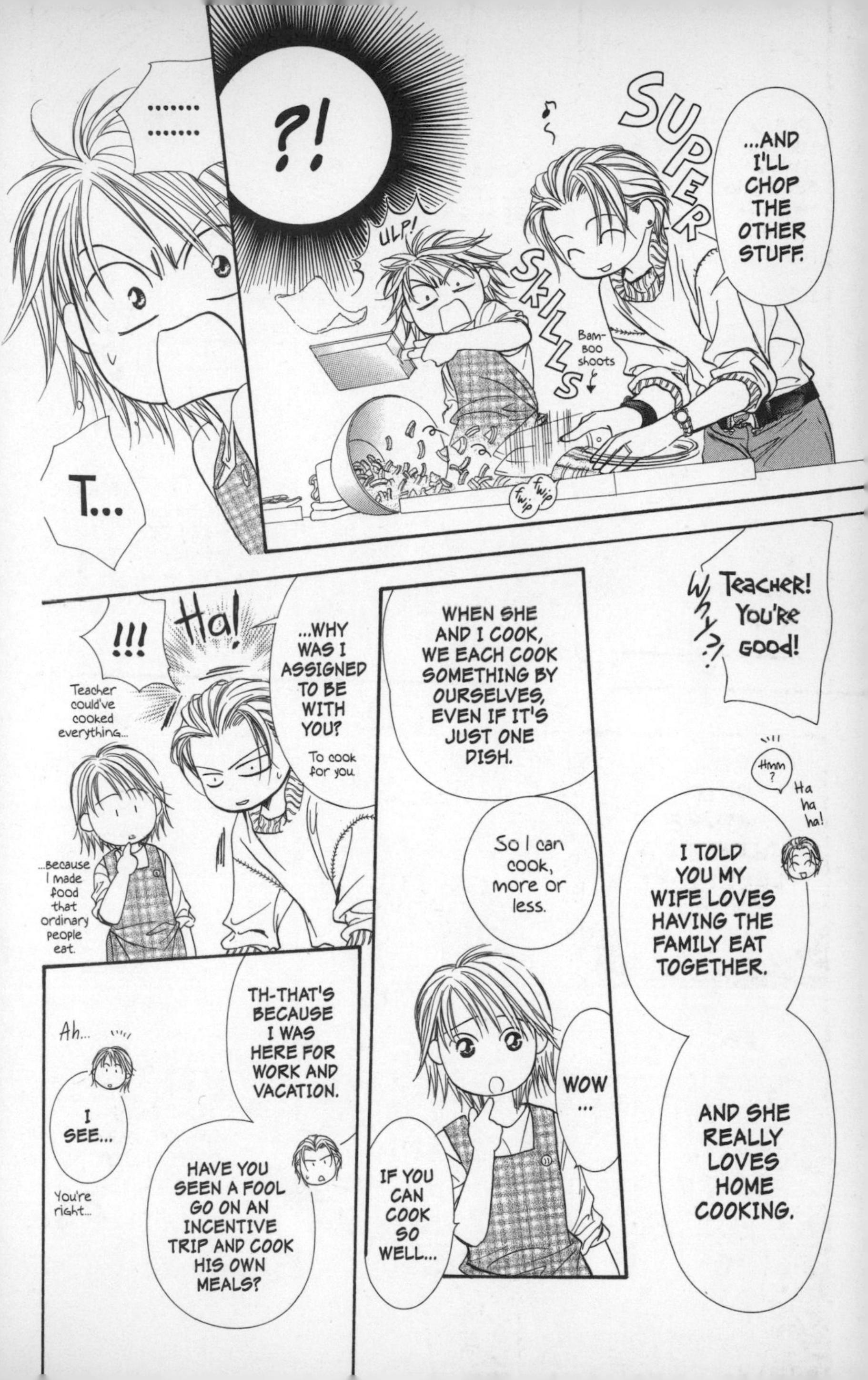

...AND I'LL CHOP THE OTHER STUFF.
SUPER SKILLS
Bam-boo shoots
fwip fwip
ULP!
?!
......
......
T...
Why?!
Teacher! You're good!
Hmm?
Ha ha ha!
I TOLD YOU MY WIFE LOVES HAVING THE FAMILY EAT TOGETHER.
AND SHE REALLY LOVES HOME COOKING.
WHEN SHE AND I COOK, WE EACH COOK SOMETHING BY OURSELVES, EVEN IF IT'S JUST ONE DISH.
So I can cook, more or less.
WOW...
IF YOU CAN COOK SO WELL...
...WHY WAS I ASSIGNED TO BE WITH YOU?
To cook for you
Ha!
!!!
Teacher could've cooked everything...
...Because I made food that ordinary people eat.
TH-THAT'S BECAUSE I WAS HERE FOR WORK AND VACATION.
HAVE YOU SEEN A FOOL GO ON AN INCENTIVE TRIP AND COOK HIS OWN MEALS?
Ah...
I SEE...
You're right...

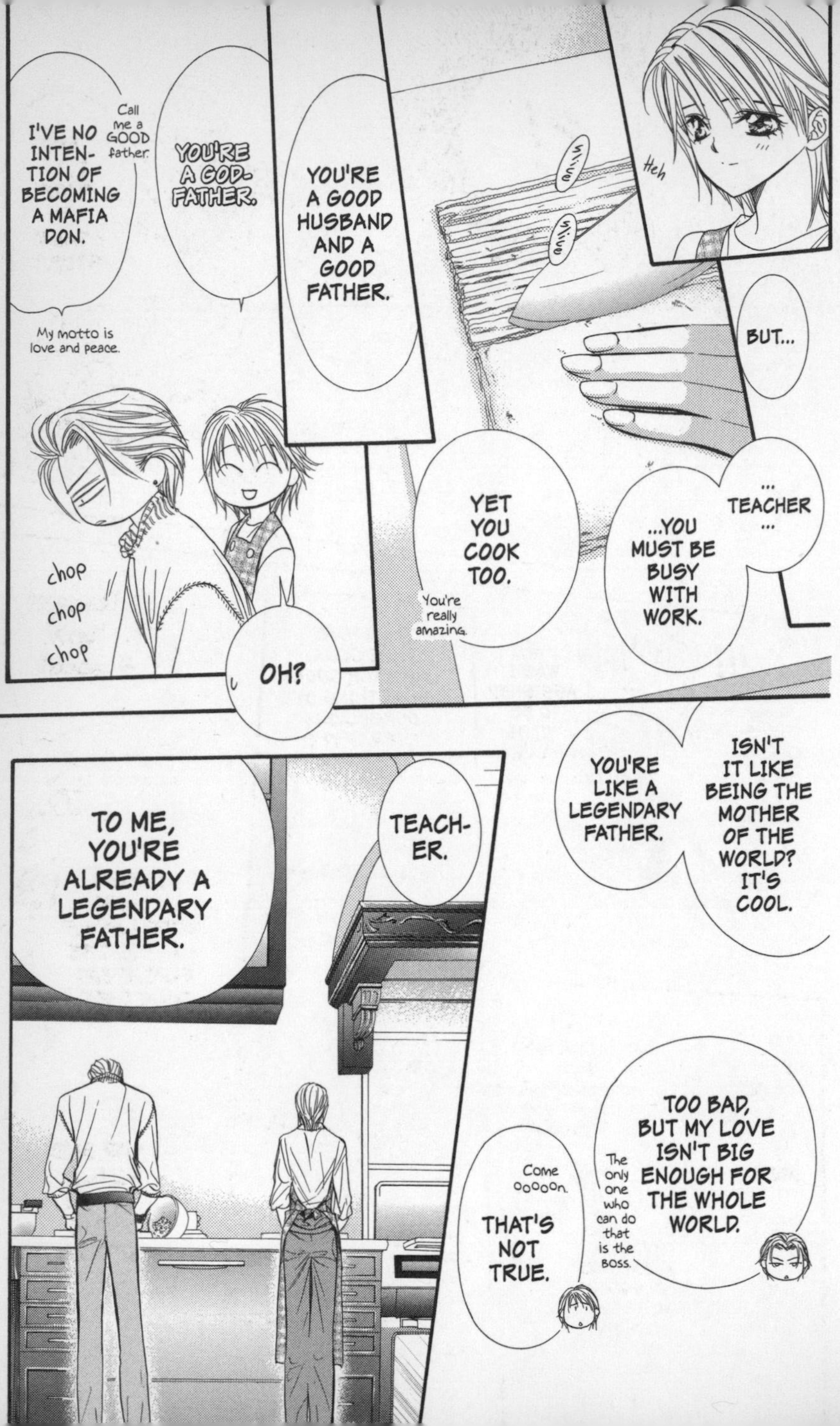

slice
slice
Heh
BUT...
... TEACHER ...
...YOU MUST BE BUSY WITH WORK.
YET YOU COOK TOO.
You're really amazing.
OH?
YOU'RE A GOOD HUSBAND AND A GOOD FATHER.
YOU'RE A GOD-FATHER.
Call me a GOOD father.
I'VE NO INTEN-TION OF BECOMING A MAFIA DON.
My motto is love and peace.
chop
chop
chop
YOU'RE LIKE A LEGENDARY FATHER.
ISN'T IT LIKE BEING THE MOTHER OF THE WORLD? IT'S COOL.
TEACH-ER.
TO ME, YOU'RE ALREADY A LEGENDARY FATHER.
TOO BAD, BUT MY LOVE ISN'T BIG ENOUGH FOR THE WHOLE WORLD.
The only one who can do that is the BOSS.
THAT'S NOT TRUE.
Come oooooon.

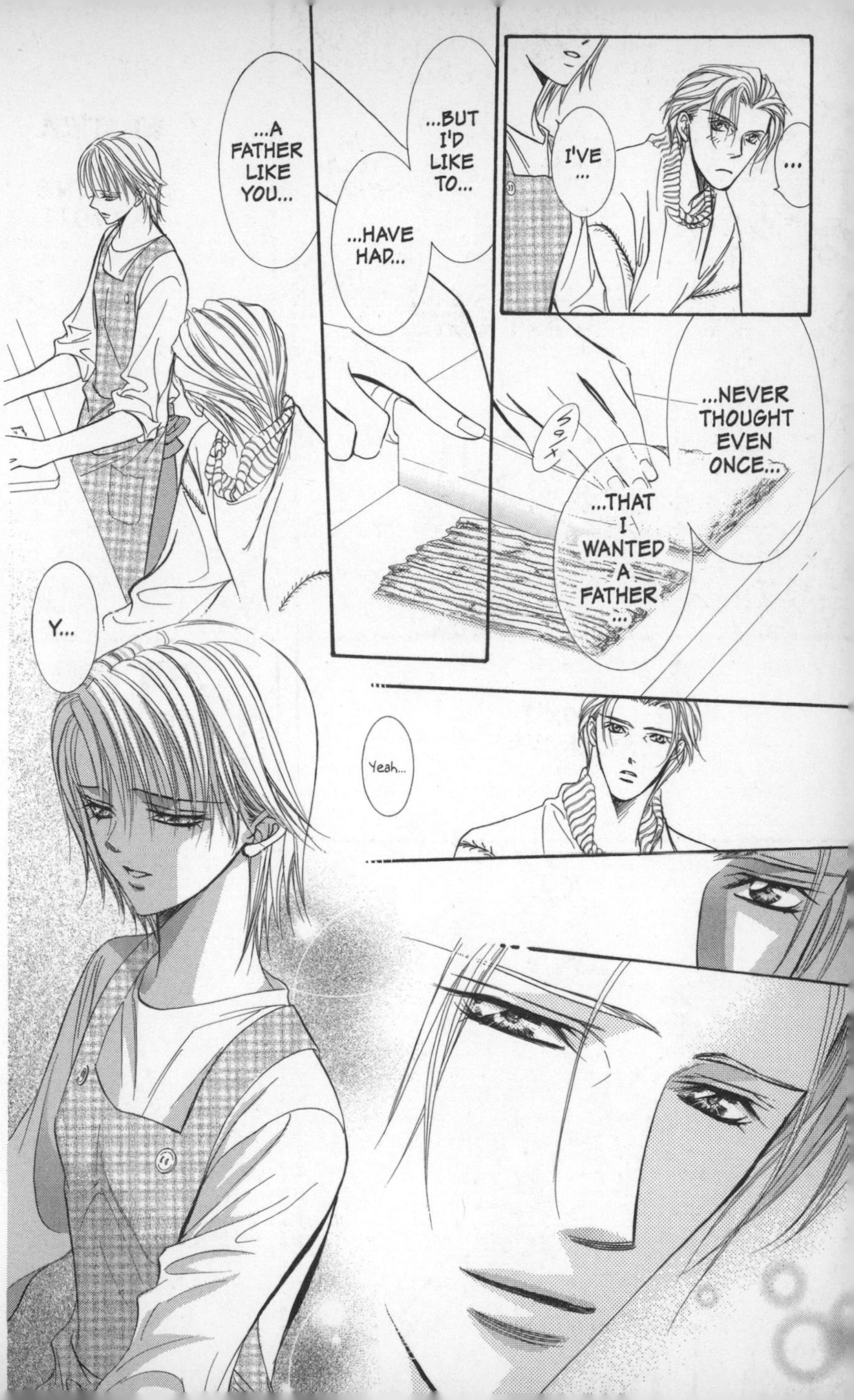
...
I'VE ...
...NEVER THOUGHT EVEN ONCE...
...THAT I WANTED A FATHER ...
...BUT I'D LIKE TO...
...HAVE HAD...
...A FATHER LIKE YOU...
Y...
Yeah...

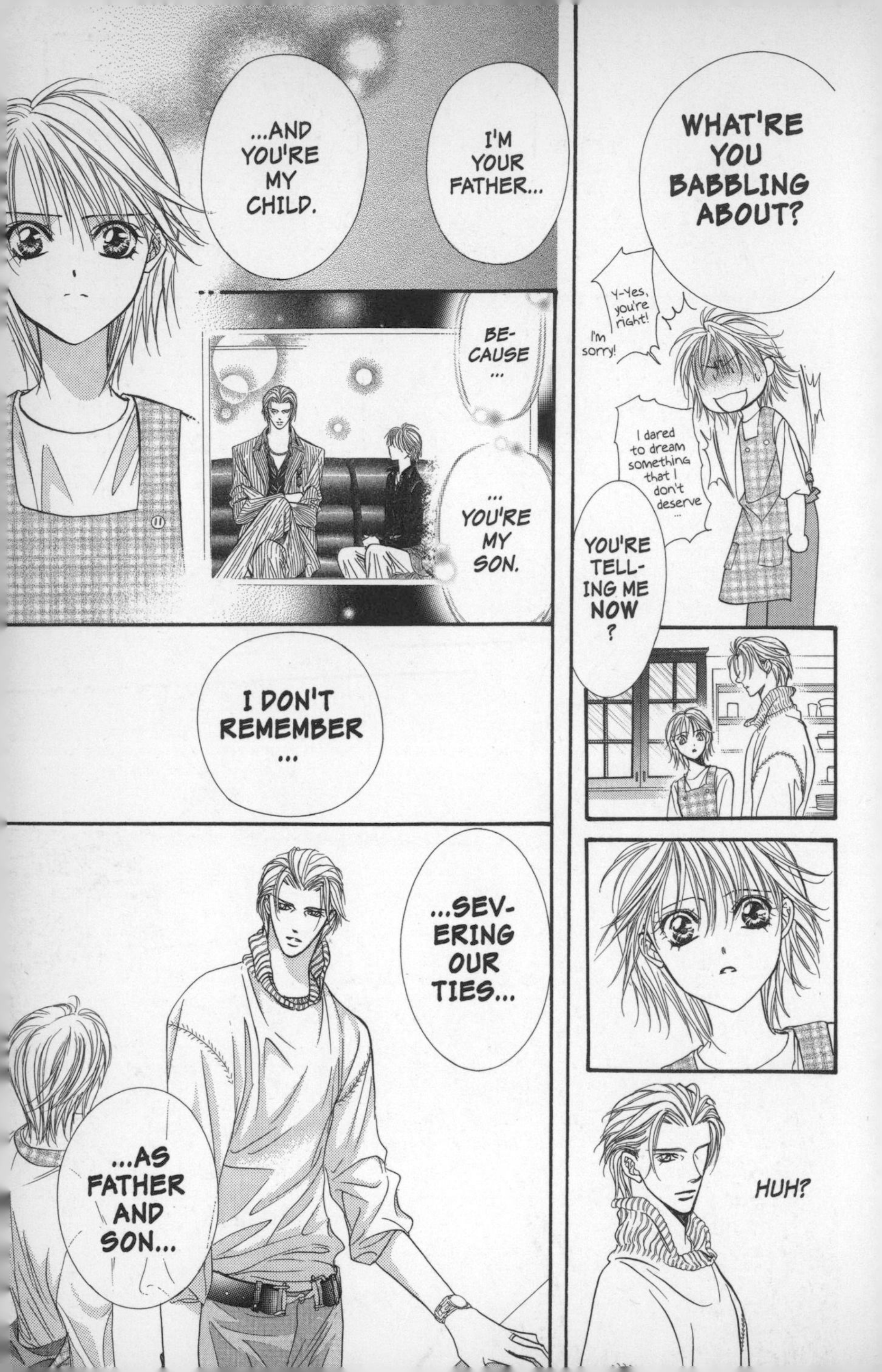
WHAT'RE YOU BABBLING ABOUT?
Y-Yes, you're right! I'm sorry!
I dared to dream something that I don't deserve...
YOU'RE TELL-ING ME NOW?
HUH?
I'M YOUR FATHER...
...AND YOU'RE MY CHILD.
BE-CAUSE...
...YOU'RE MY SON.
I DON'T REMEMBER...
...SEV-ERING OUR TIES...
...AS FATHER AND SON...

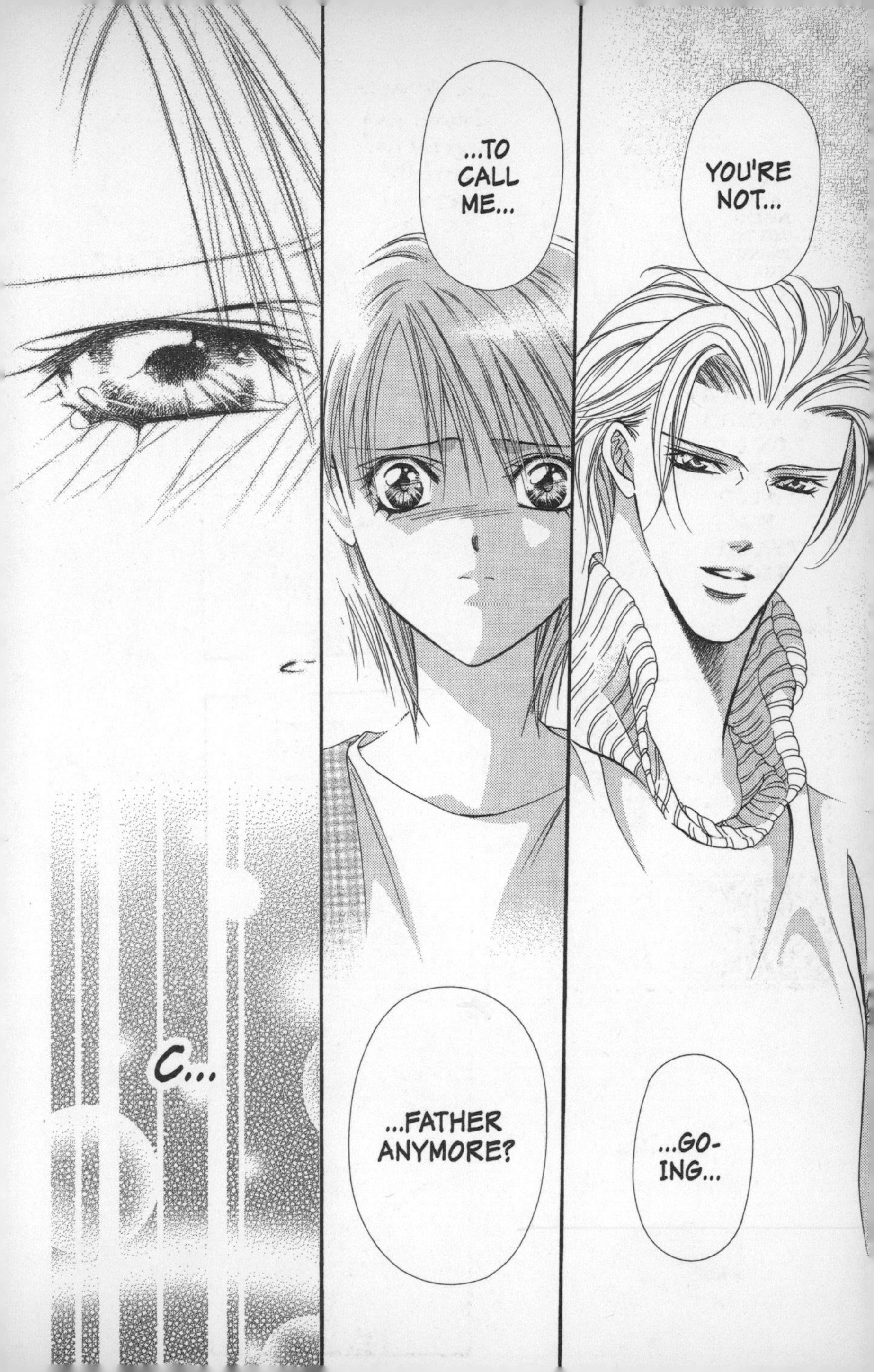
YOU'RE NOT...
...GO-
ING...
...TO CALL ME...
...FATHER ANYMORE?
C...

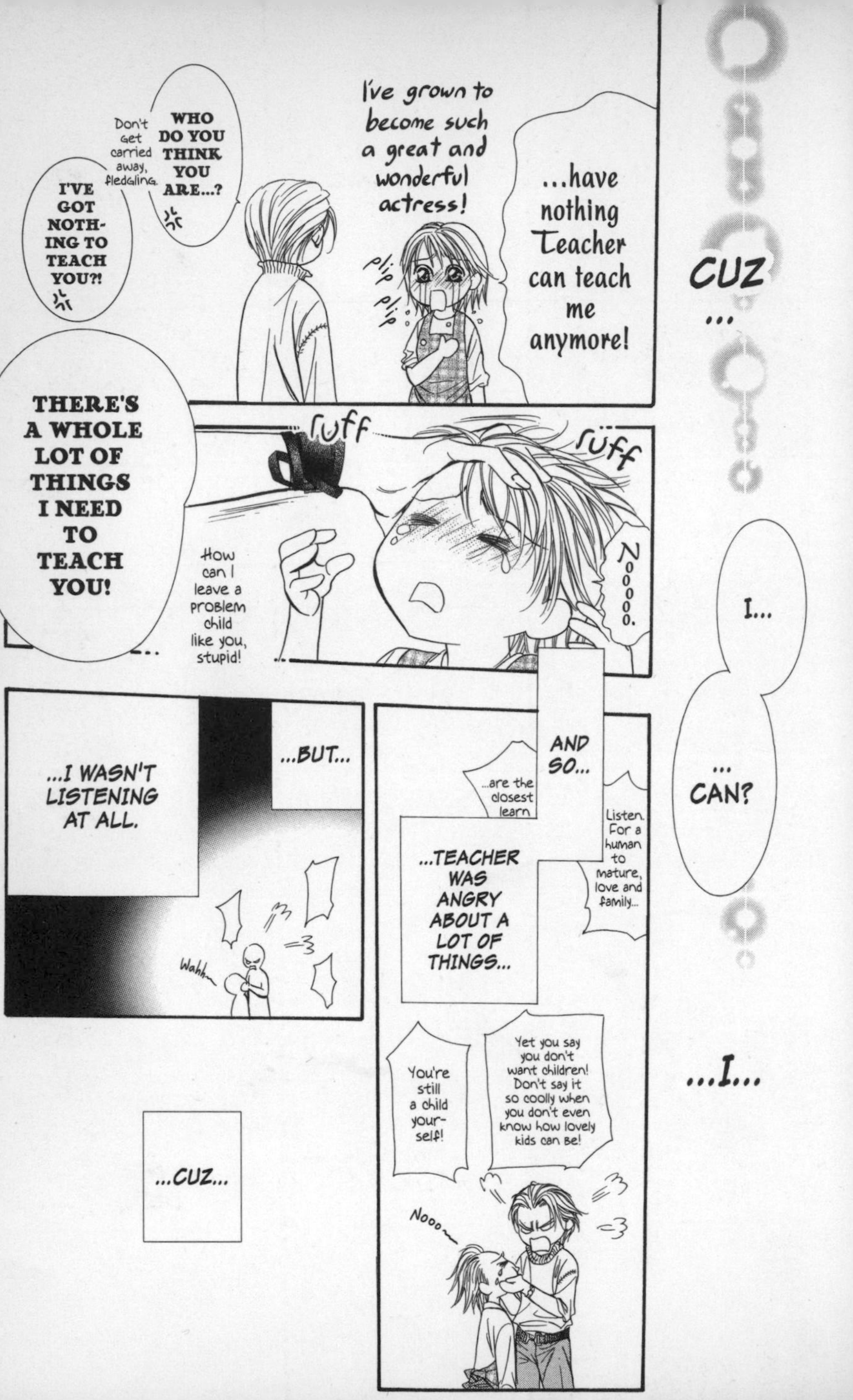
CUZ...
I...
...CAN?
...I...
...have nothing Teacher can teach me anymore!
I've grown to become such a great and wonderful actress!
plip plip
WHO DO YOU THINK YOU ARE...?
Don't get carried away, fledgling.
I'VE GOT NOTHING TO TEACH YOU?!
ruff
ruff
Nooooo.
How can I leave a problem child like you, stupid!
THERE'S A WHOLE LOT OF THINGS I NEED TO TEACH YOU!
AND SO...
...are the closest learn
Listen. For a human to mature, love and family...
...TEACHER WAS ANGRY ABOUT A LOT OF THINGS...
Yet you say you don't want children! Don't say it so coolly when you don't even know how lovely kids can be!
You're still a child your-self!
Nooo~
...BUT...
...I WASN'T LISTENING AT ALL.
Wahh~
...CUZ...

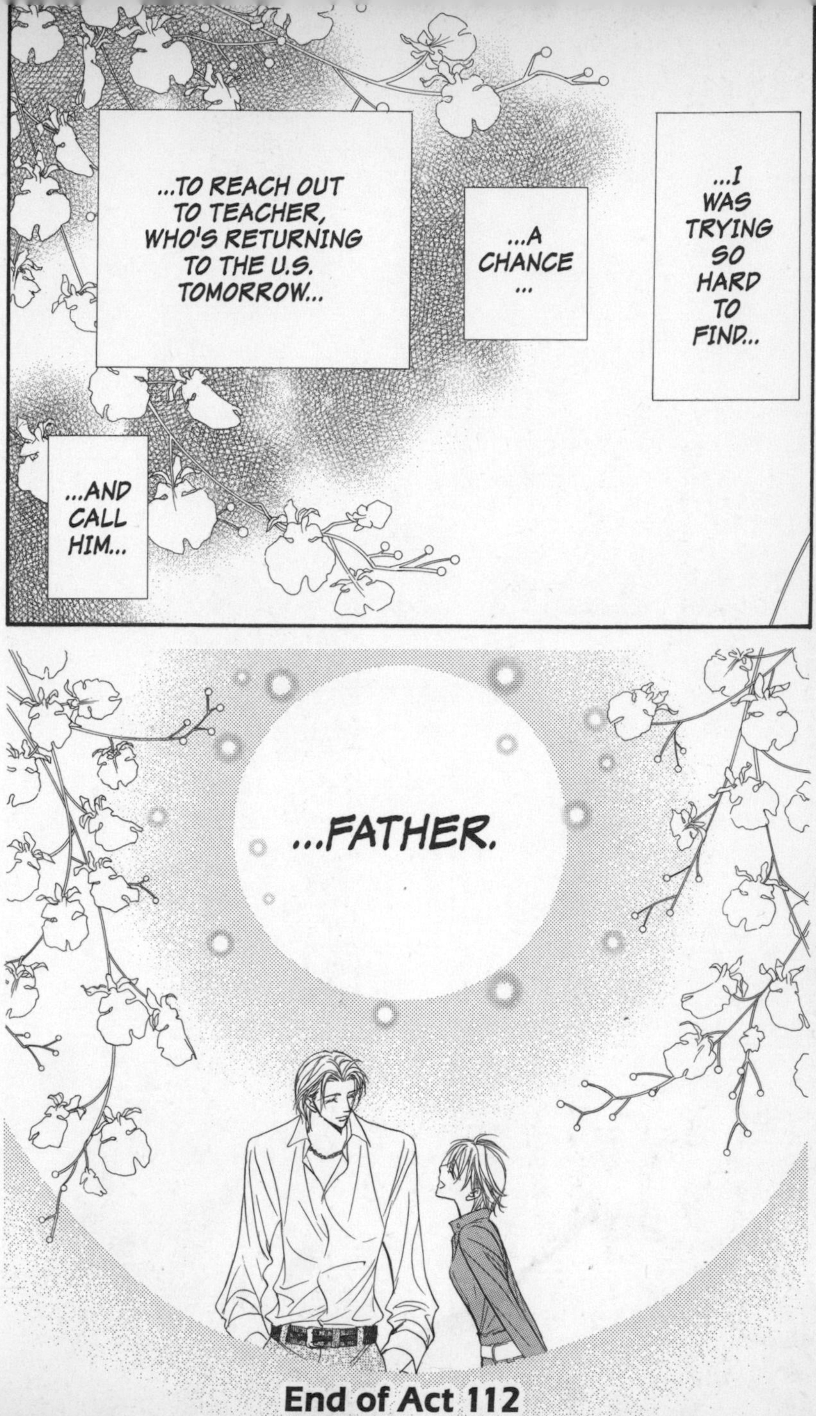
...I WAS TRYING SO HARD TO FIND...
...A CHANCE...
...TO REACH OUT TO TEACHER, WHO'S RETURNING TO THE U.S. TOMORROW...
...AND CALL HIM...
...FATHER.

End of Act 112

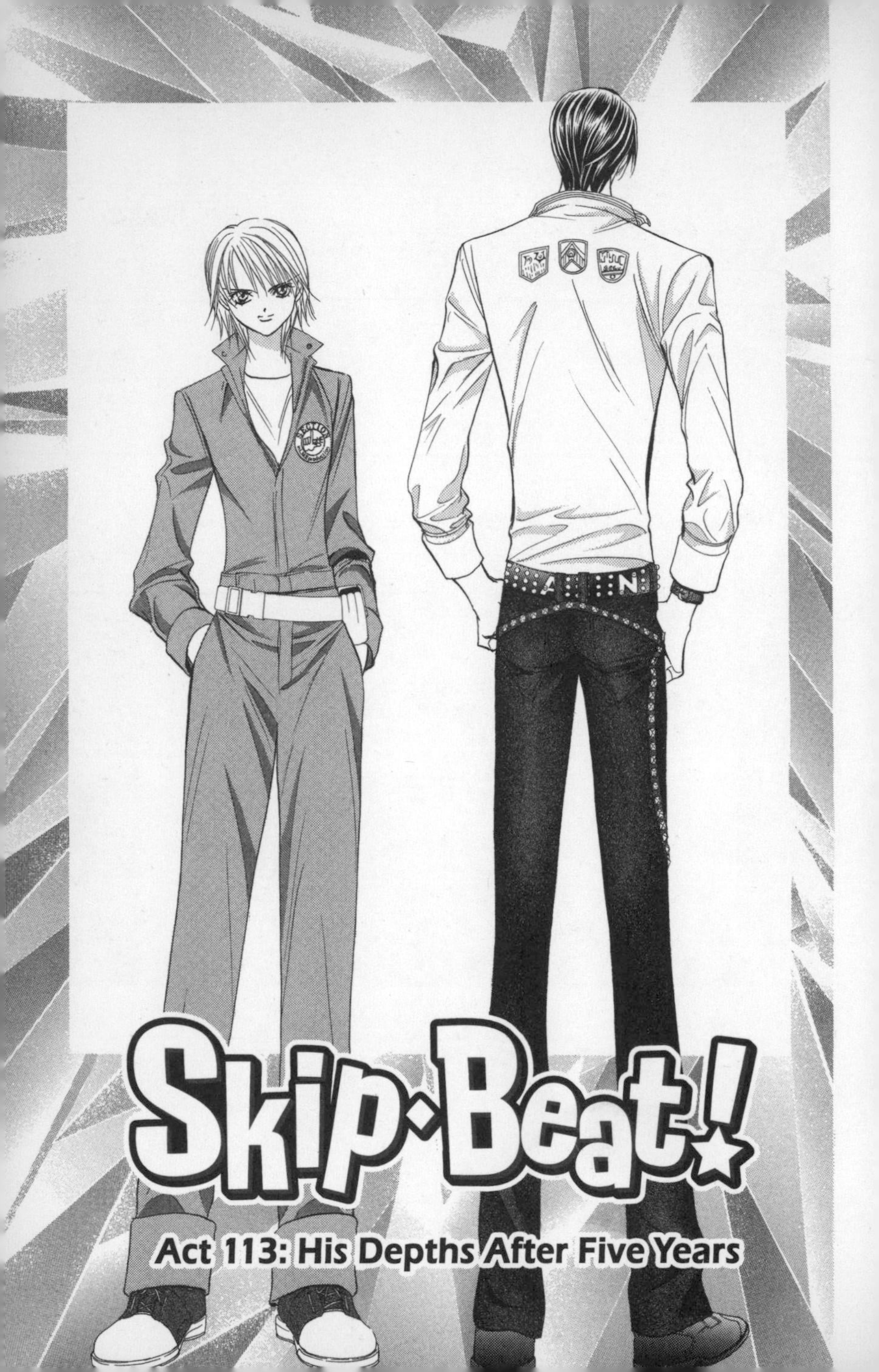
Skip·Beat!
Act 113: His Depths After Five Years

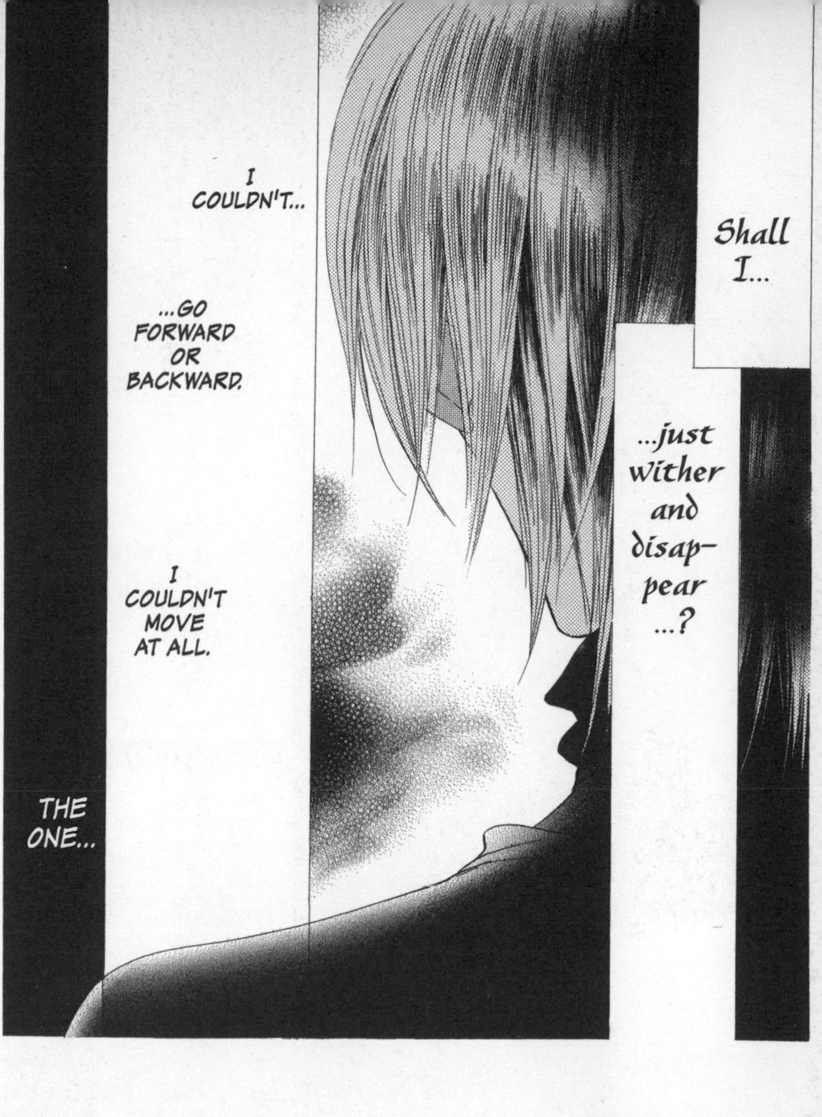
Shall I...
...just wither and disap-pear ...?
I COULDN'T...
...GO FORWARD OR BACKWARD.
I COULDN'T MOVE AT ALL.
THE ONE...

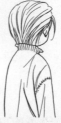

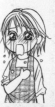

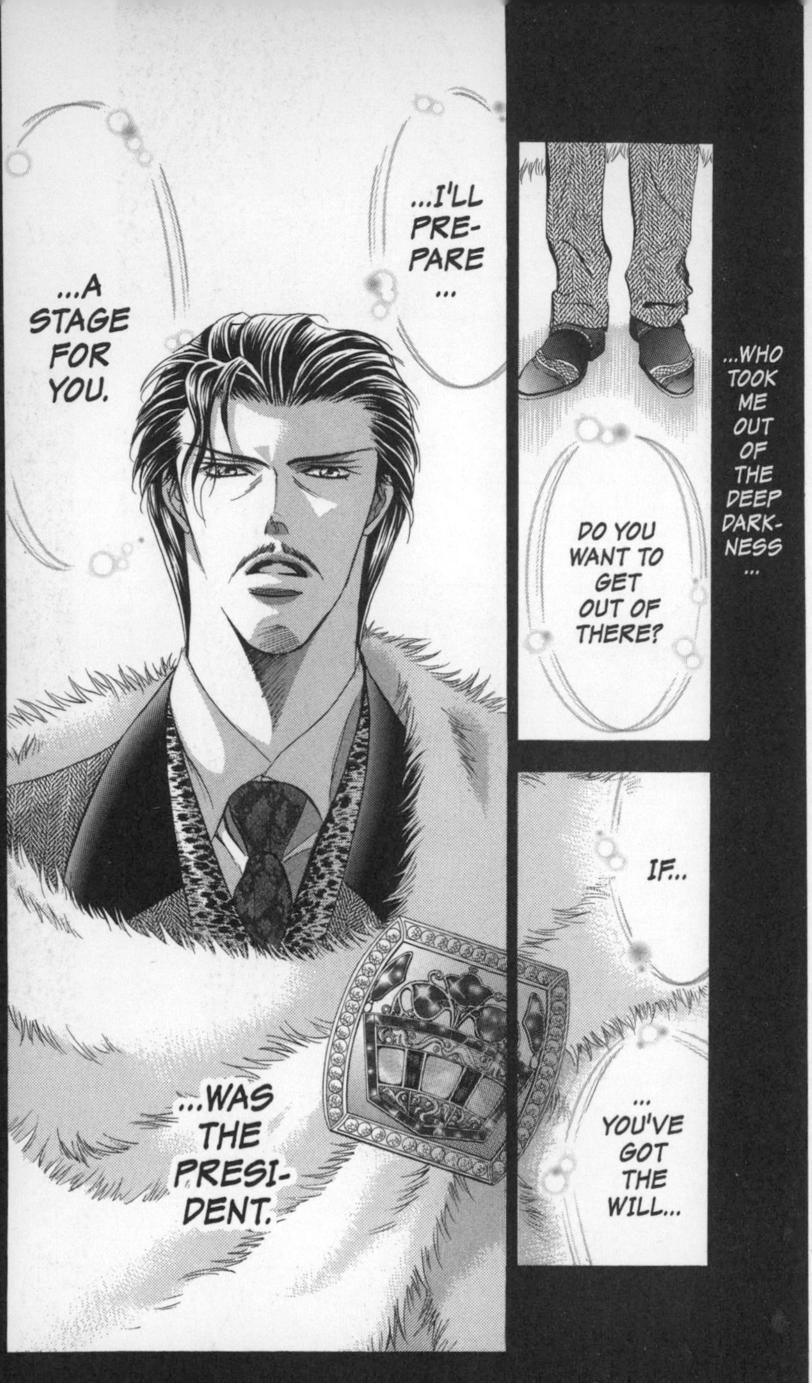
DO YOU WANT TO GET OUT OF THERE?
IF...
...YOU'VE GOT THE WILL...
...I'LL PREPARE...
...A STAGE FOR YOU.
...WHO TOOK ME OUT OF THE DEEP DARKNESS...
...WAS THE PRESIDENT.

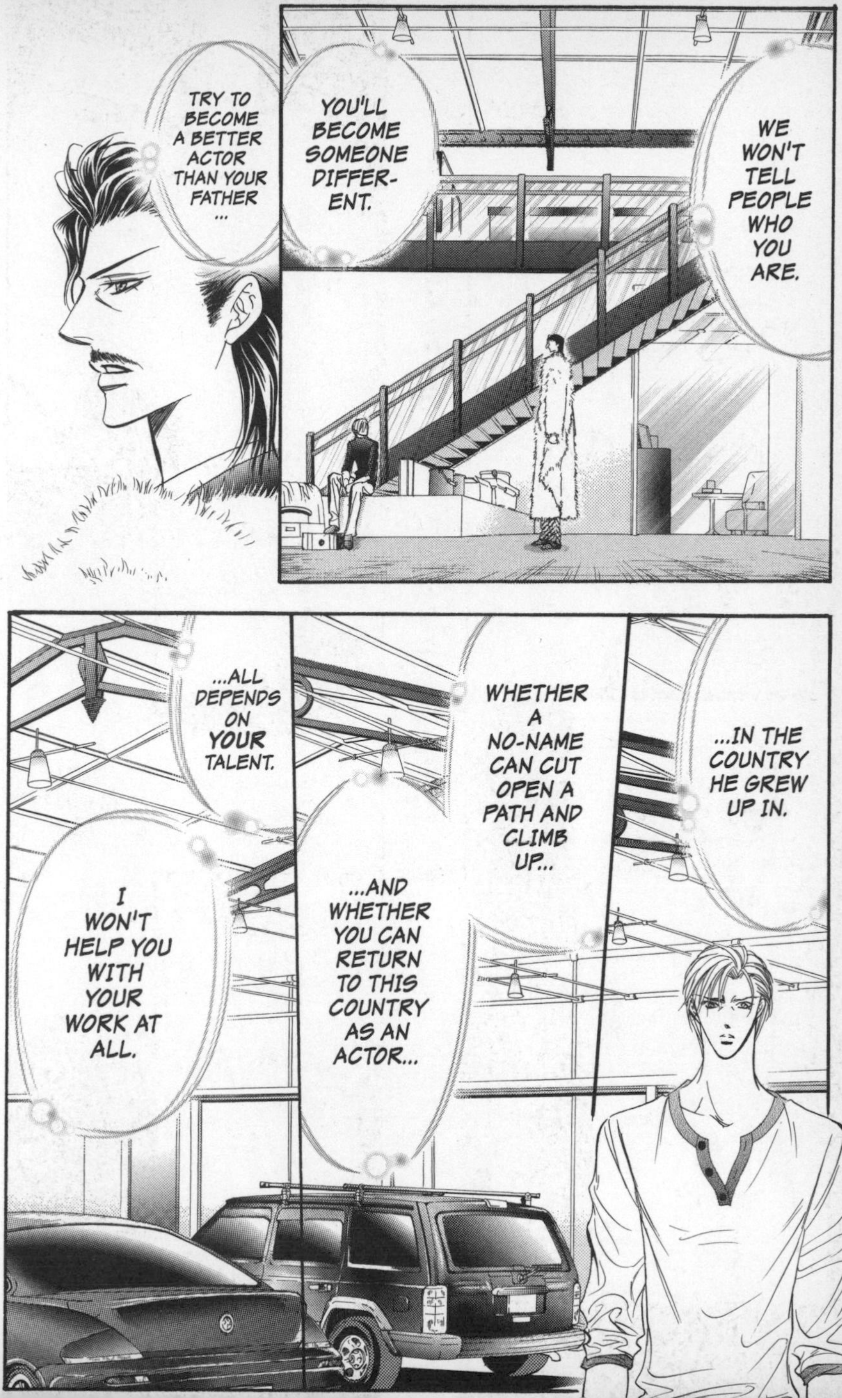
WE WON'T TELL PEOPLE WHO YOU ARE.
YOU'LL BECOME SOMEONE DIFFER-ENT.
TRY TO BECOME A BETTER ACTOR THAN YOUR FATHER ...
...IN THE COUNTRY HE GREW UP IN.
WHETHER A NO-NAME CAN CUT OPEN A PATH AND CLIMB UP...
...ALL DEPENDS ON YOUR TALENT.
...AND WHETHER YOU CAN RETURN TO THIS COUNTRY AS AN ACTOR...
I WON'T HELP YOU WITH YOUR WORK AT ALL.

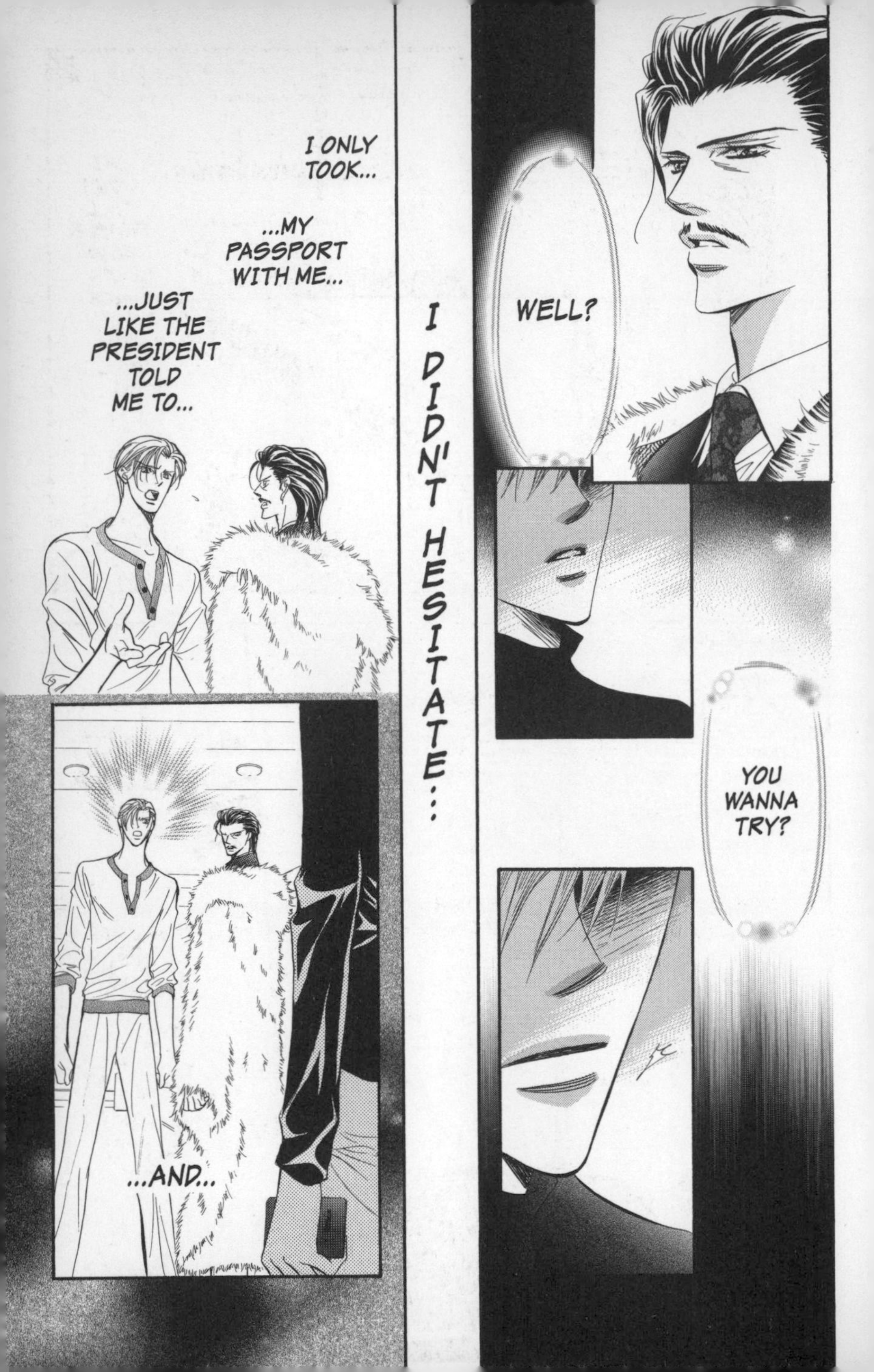
WELL?
YOU WANNA TRY?
I DIDN'T HESITATE...
I ONLY TOOK...
...MY PASSPORT WITH ME...
...JUST LIKE THE PRESIDENT TOLD ME TO...
...AND...

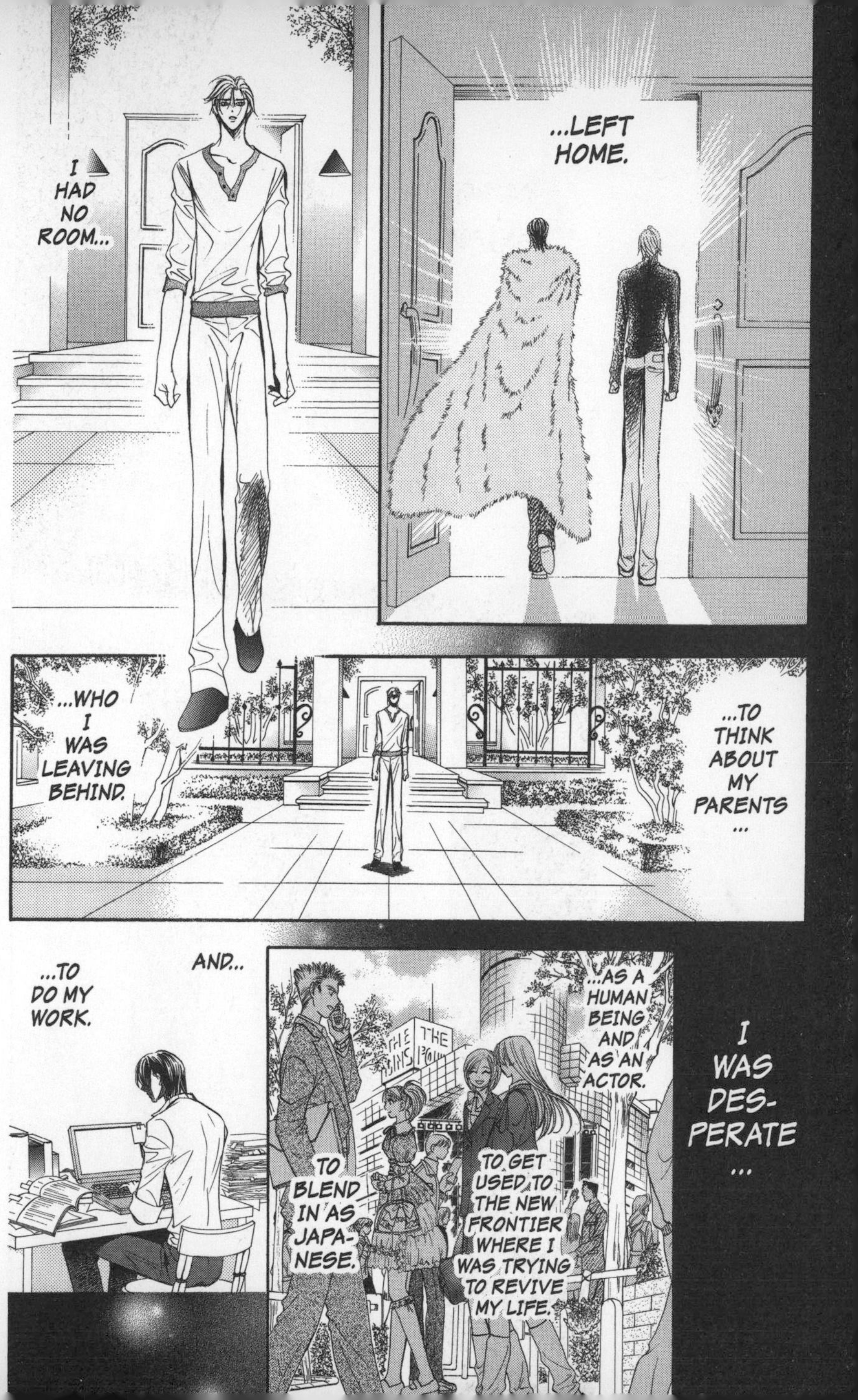
...LEFT HOME.
I HAD NO ROOM...
...TO THINK ABOUT MY PARENTS...
...WHO I WAS LEAVING BEHIND.
I WAS DES-PERATE...
...AS A HUMAN BEING AND AS AN ACTOR.
TO GET USED TO THE NEW FRONTIER WHERE I WAS TRYING TO REVIVE MY LIFE.
TO BLEND IN AS JAPA-NESE.
AND...
...TO DO MY WORK.

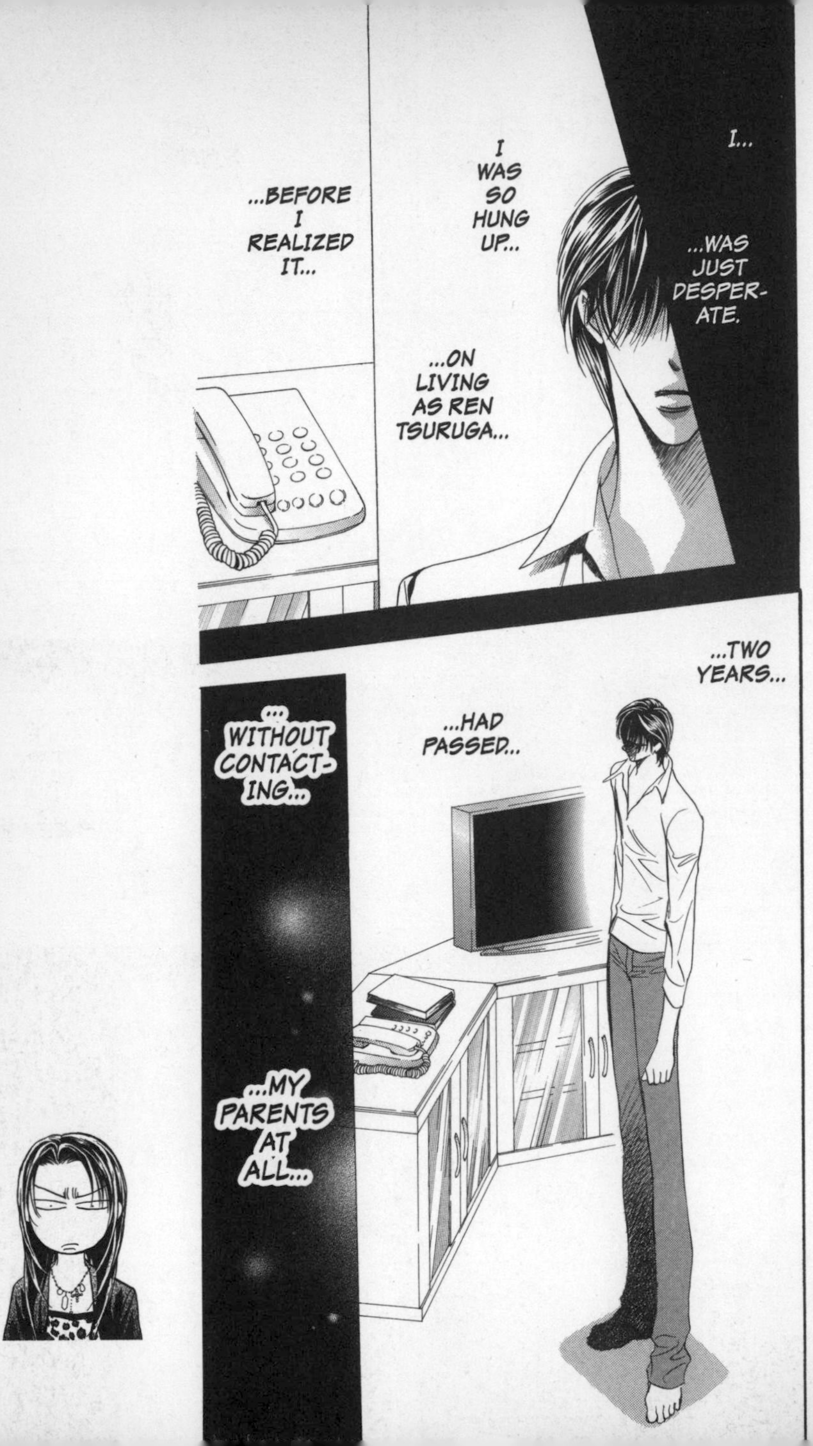
I...
...WAS JUST DESPERATE.
I WAS SO HUNG UP...
...ON LIVING AS REN TSURUGA...
...BEFORE I REALIZED IT...
...TWO YEARS...
...HAD PASSED...
...WITHOUT CONTACTING...
...MY PARENTS AT ALL...

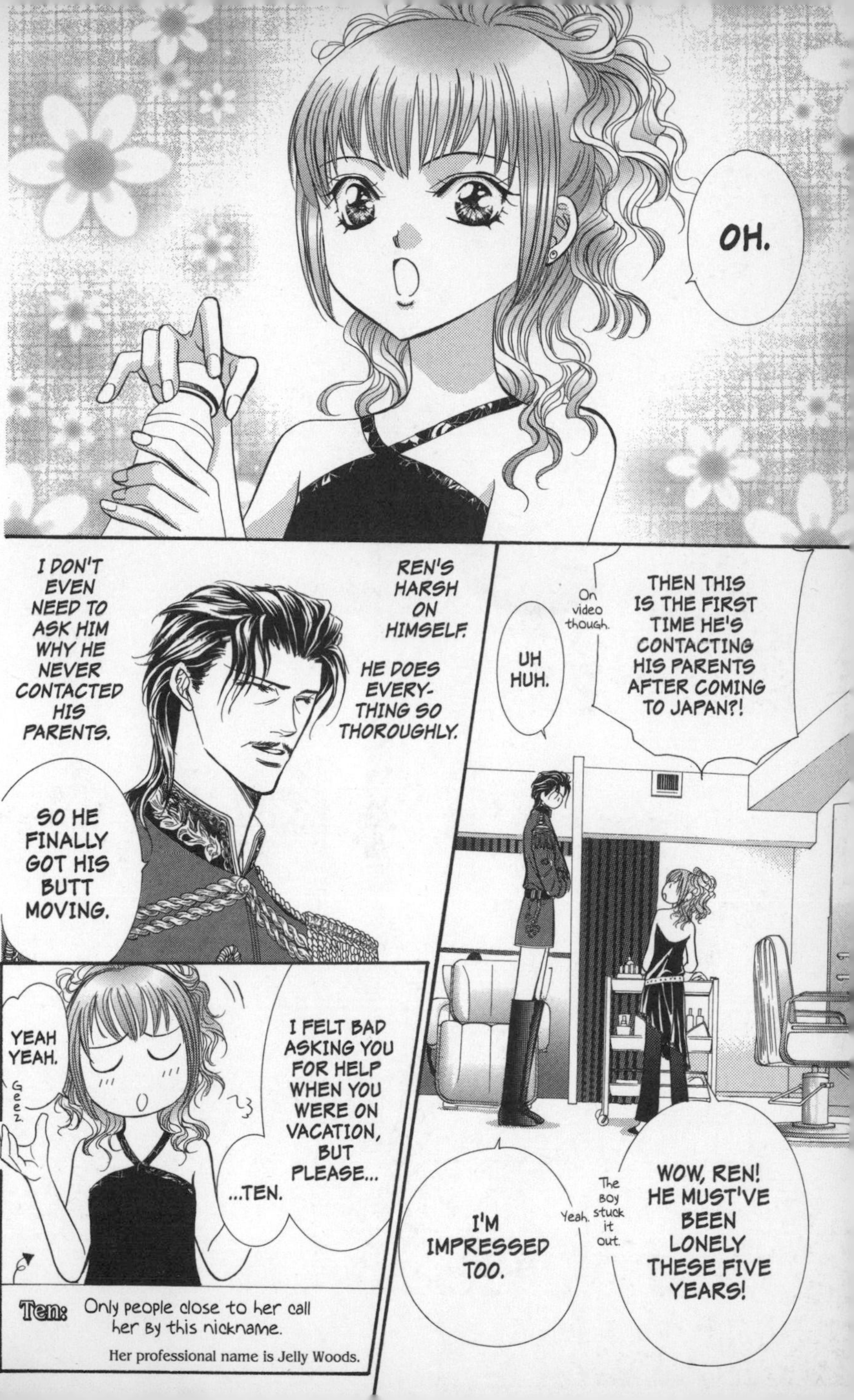
OH.
THEN THIS IS THE FIRST TIME HE'S CONTACTING HIS PARENTS AFTER COMING TO JAPAN?!
On video though.
UH HUH.
WOW, REN! HE MUST'VE BEEN LONELY THESE FIVE YEARS!
The Boy stuck it out.
Yeah.
I'M IMPRESSED TOO.
REN'S HARSH ON HIMSELF.
HE DOES EVERY-THING SO THOROUGHLY.
I DON'T EVEN NEED TO ASK HIM WHY HE NEVER CONTACTED HIS PARENTS.
SO HE FINALLY GOT HIS BUTT MOVING.
I FELT BAD ASKING YOU FOR HELP WHEN YOU WERE ON VACATION, BUT PLEASE...
...TEN.
YEAH YEAH.
Geez.
Ten: Only people close to her call her By this nickname.
Her professional name is Jelly Woods.

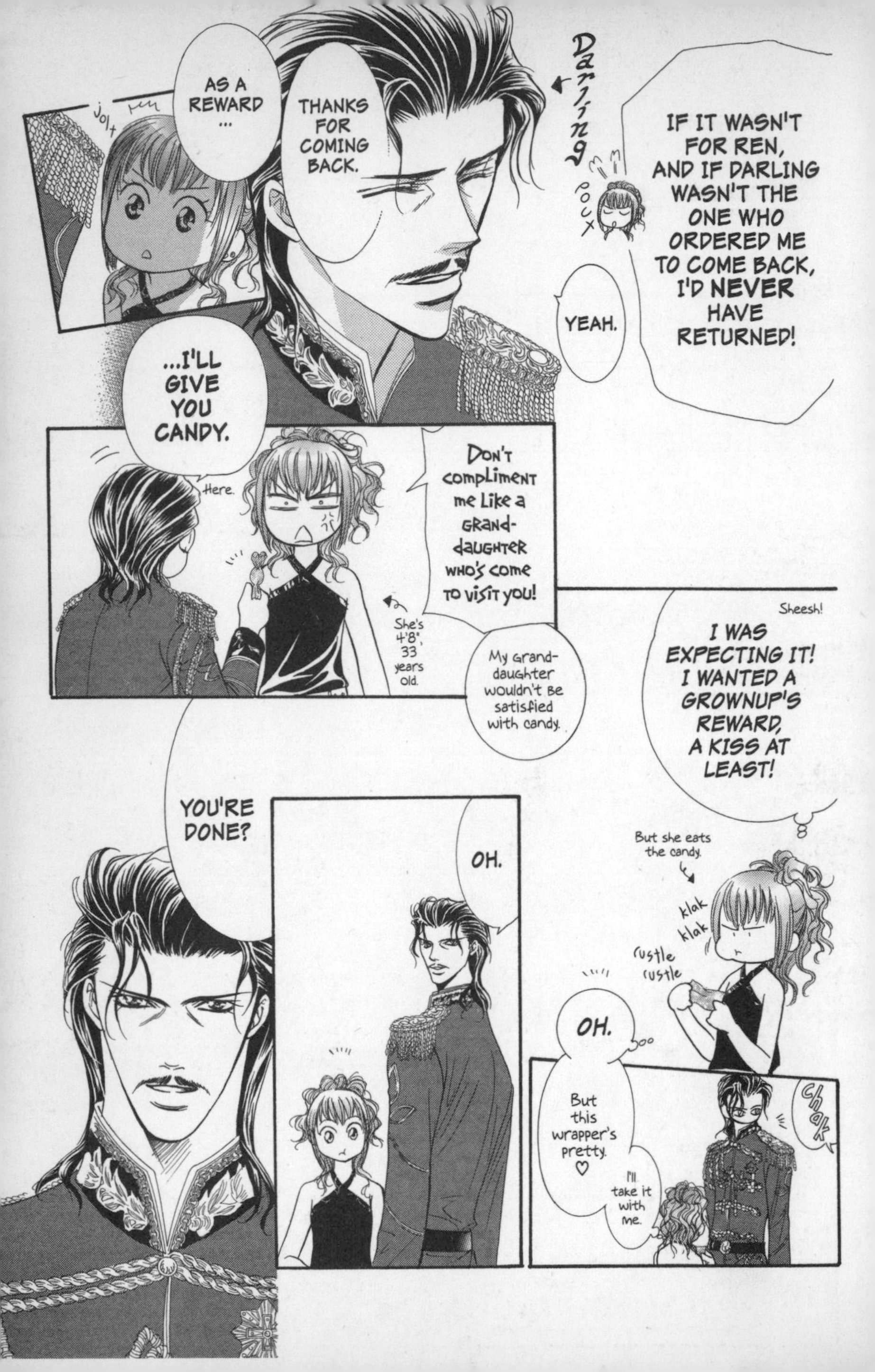
Darling
pout
IF IT WASN'T FOR REN, AND IF DARLING WASN'T THE ONE WHO ORDERED ME TO COME BACK, I'D NEVER HAVE RETURNED!
YEAH.
THANKS FOR COMING BACK.
AS A REWARD...
jolt
...I'LL GIVE YOU CANDY.
Here.
Don't compliment me like a grand-daughter who's come to visit you!
She's 4'8", 33 years old.
My grand-daughter wouldn't be satisfied with candy.
Sheesh!
I WAS EXPECTING IT! I WANTED A GROWNUP'S REWARD, A KISS AT LEAST!
But she eats the candy.
klak klak
rustle rustle
OH.
But this wrapper's pretty. ♡
I'll take it with me.
Chak
OH.
YOU'RE DONE?

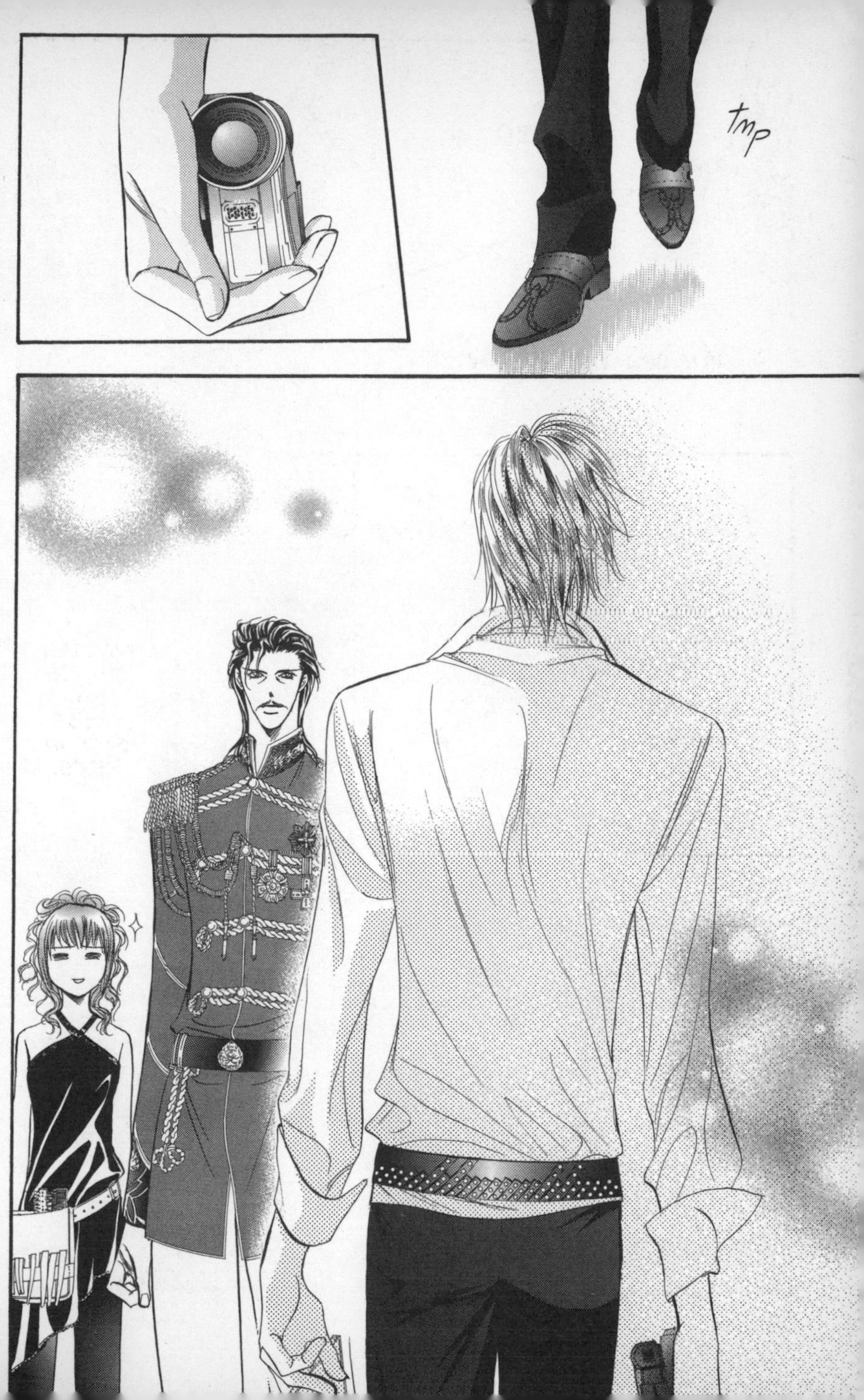
tmp

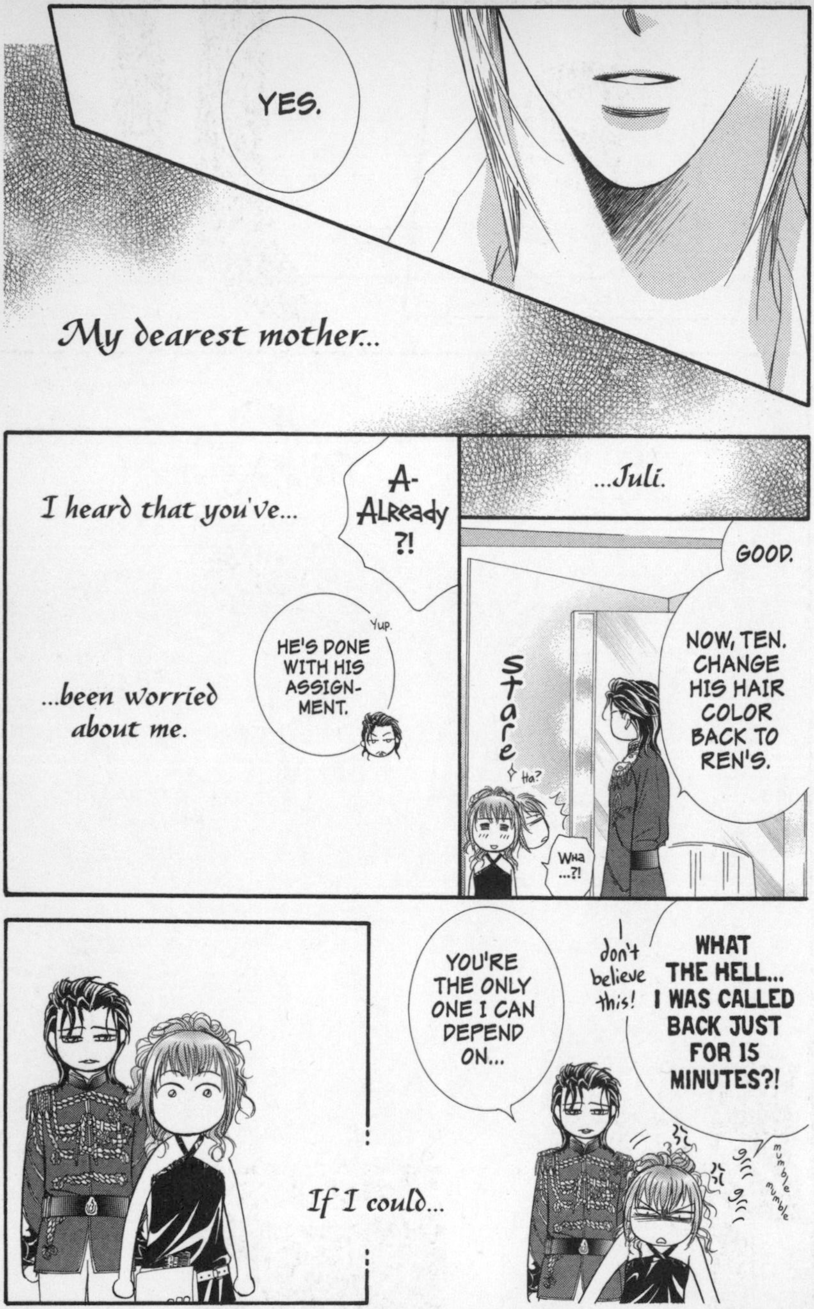
YES.
My dearest mother...
...Juli.
GOOD.
NOW, TEN. CHANGE HIS HAIR COLOR BACK TO REN'S.
Stare
Ha?
Wha...?!
I heard that you've...
A-Already?!
Yup.
HE'S DONE WITH HIS ASSIGNMENT.
...been worried about me.
WHAT THE HELL... I WAS CALLED BACK JUST FOR 15 MINUTES?!
I don't believe this!
YOU'RE THE ONLY ONE I CAN DEPEND ON...
grrr grrr
mumble mumble
If I could...

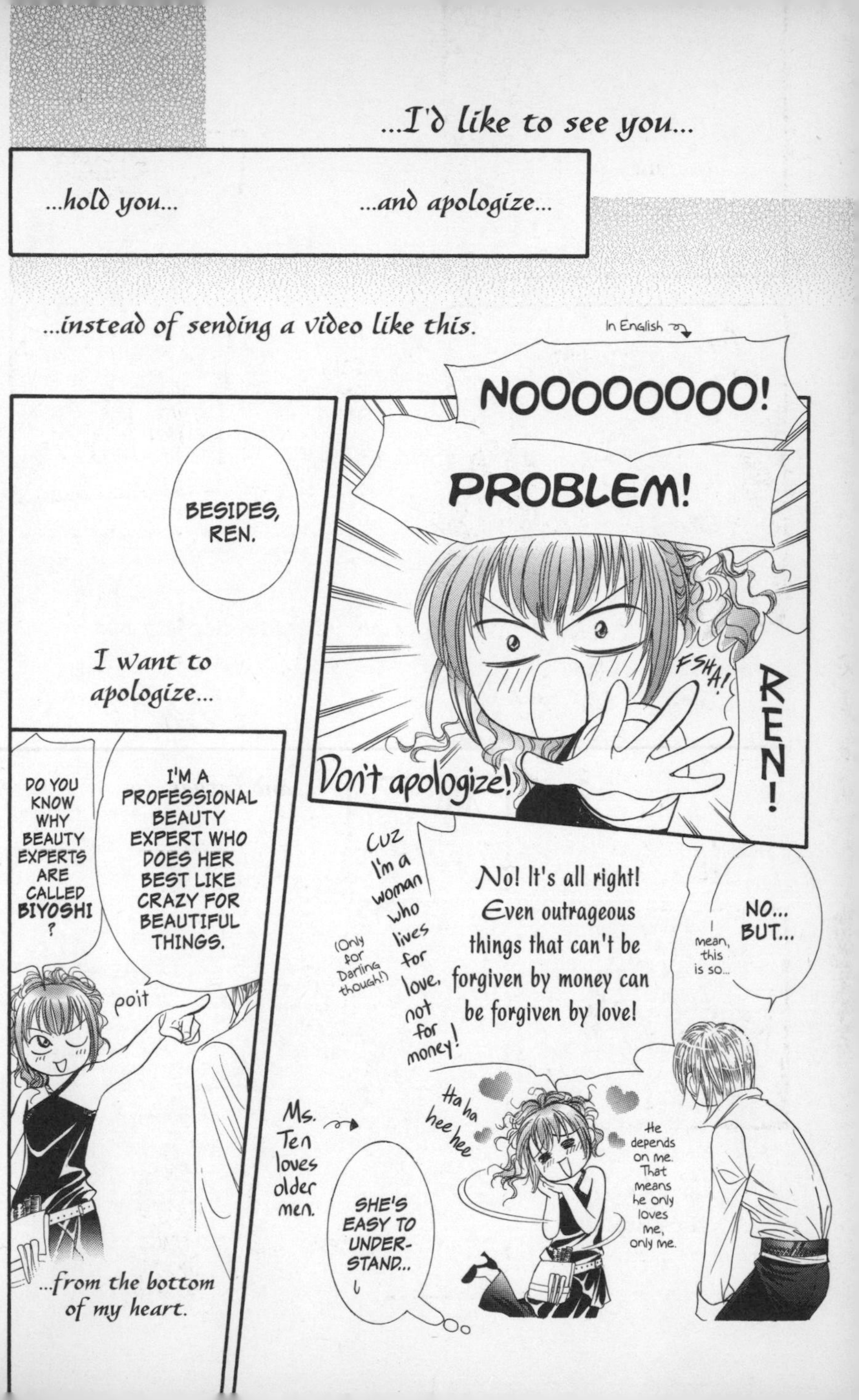

...I'd like to see you...
...hold you...
...and apologize...
...instead of sending a video like this.
BESIDES, REN.
I want to apologize...
I'M A PROFESSIONAL BEAUTY EXPERT WHO DOES HER BEST LIKE CRAZY FOR BEAUTIFUL THINGS.
DO YOU KNOW WHY BEAUTY EXPERTS ARE CALLED BIYOSHI?
poit
...from the bottom of my heart.
In English
NOOOOOOOO!
PROBLEM!
REN!
FSHA!
Don't apologize!
NO... BUT...
I mean, this is so...
No! It's all right! Even outrageous things that can't be forgiven by money can be forgiven by love!
Cuz I'm a woman who lives for love, not for money!
(Only for Darling though!)
He depends on me. That means he only loves me, only me.
Ha ha hee hee
Ms. Ten loves older men.
SHE'S EASY TO UNDERSTAND...

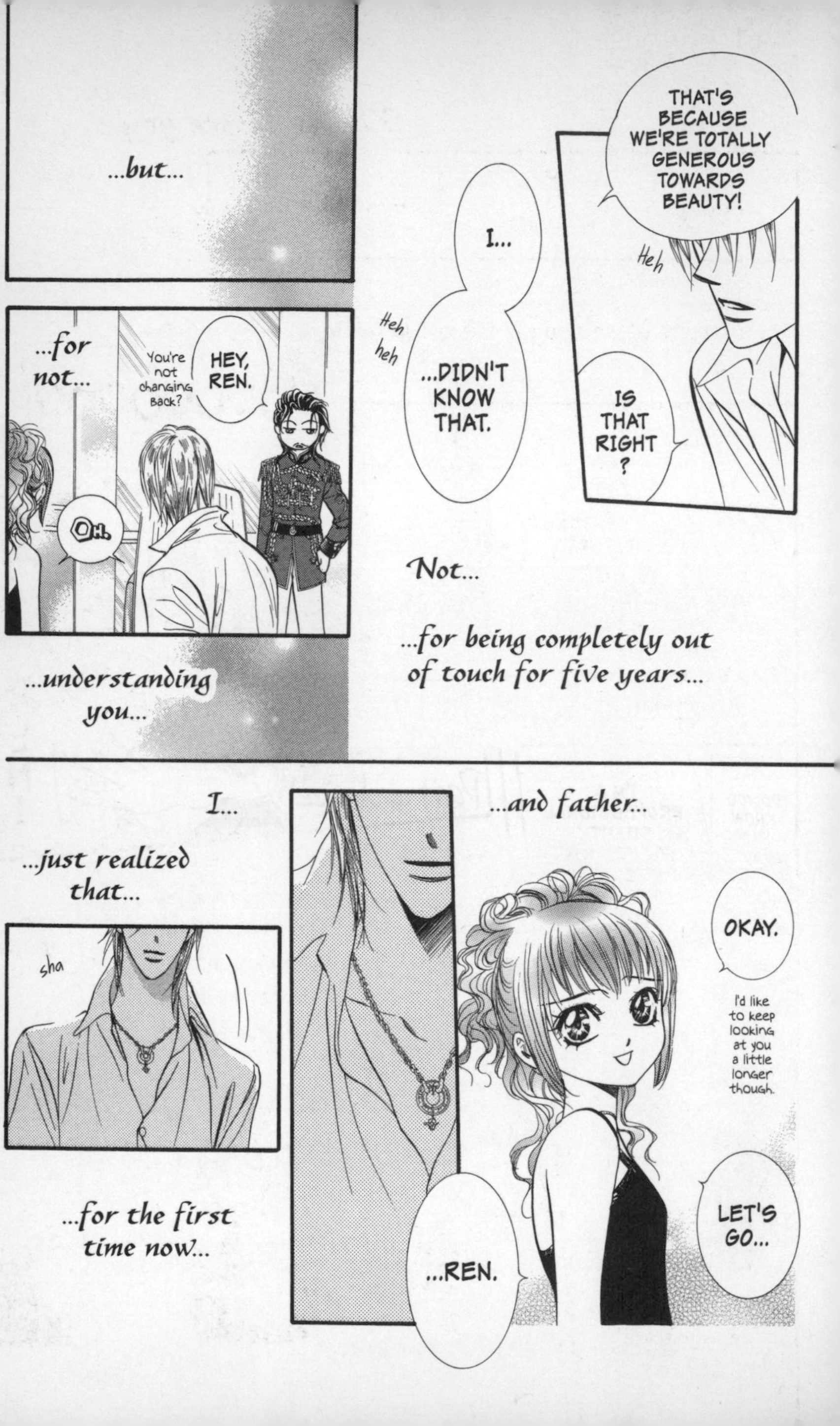
THAT'S BECAUSE WE'RE TOTALLY GENEROUS TOWARDS BEAUTY!
Heh
IS THAT RIGHT?
I...
...DIDN'T KNOW THAT.
Heh heh
Not...
...for being completely out of touch for five years...
...but...
...for not...
HEY, REN.
You're not changing back?
OH.
...understanding you...
...and father...
OKAY.
I'd like to keep looking at you a little longer though.
LET'S GO...
...REN.
I...
...just realized that...
sha
...for the first time now...

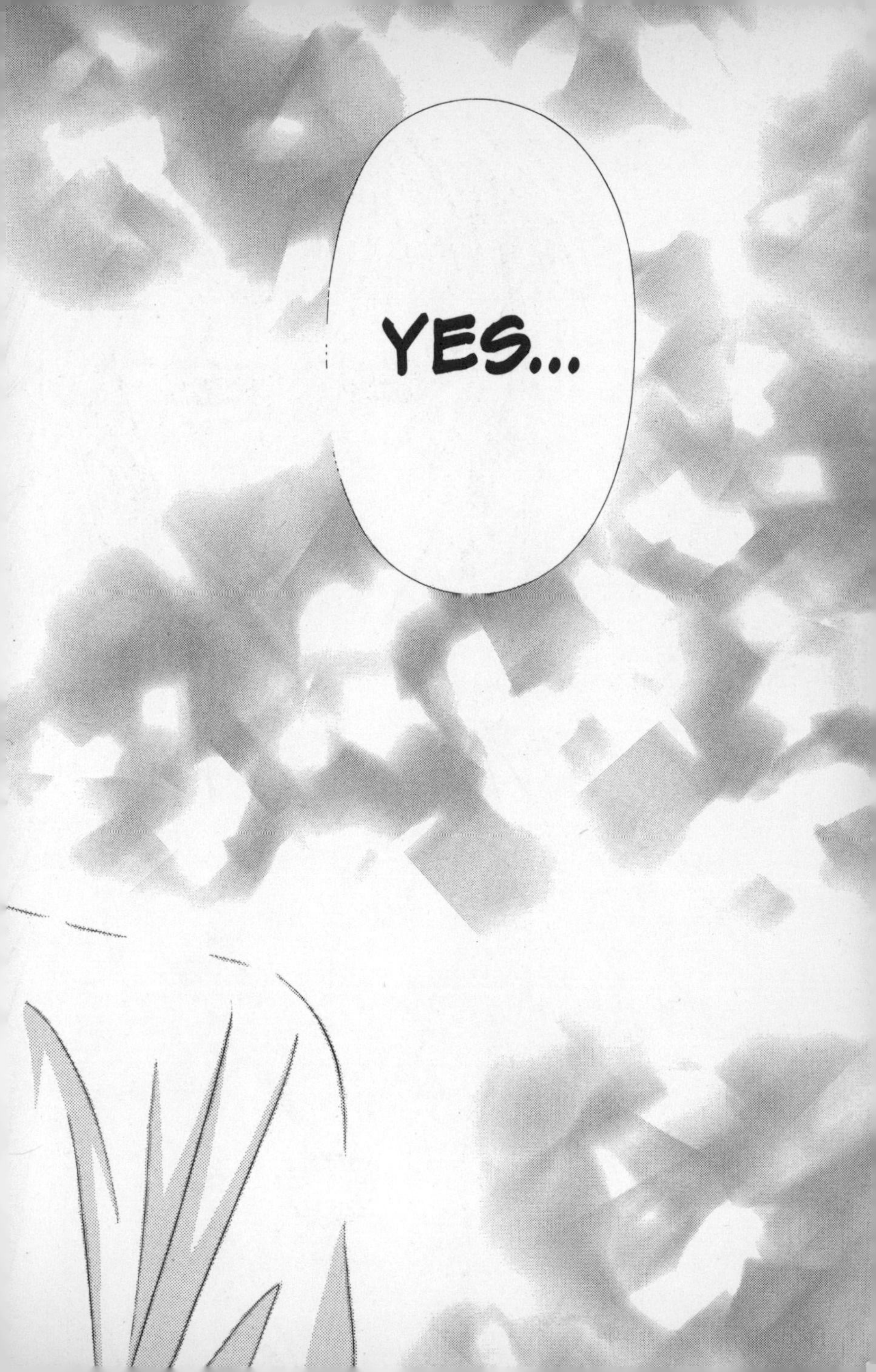
YES...

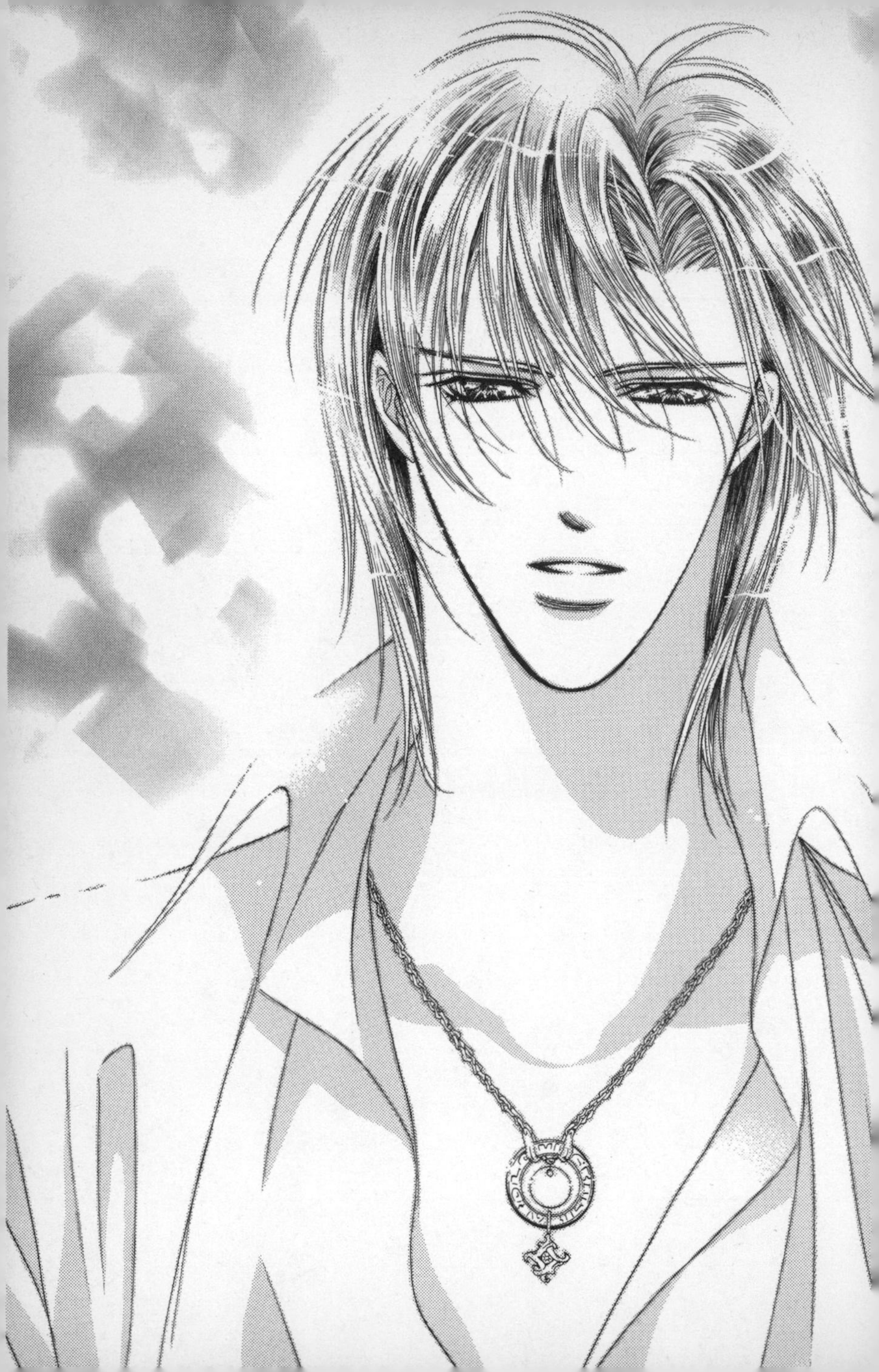

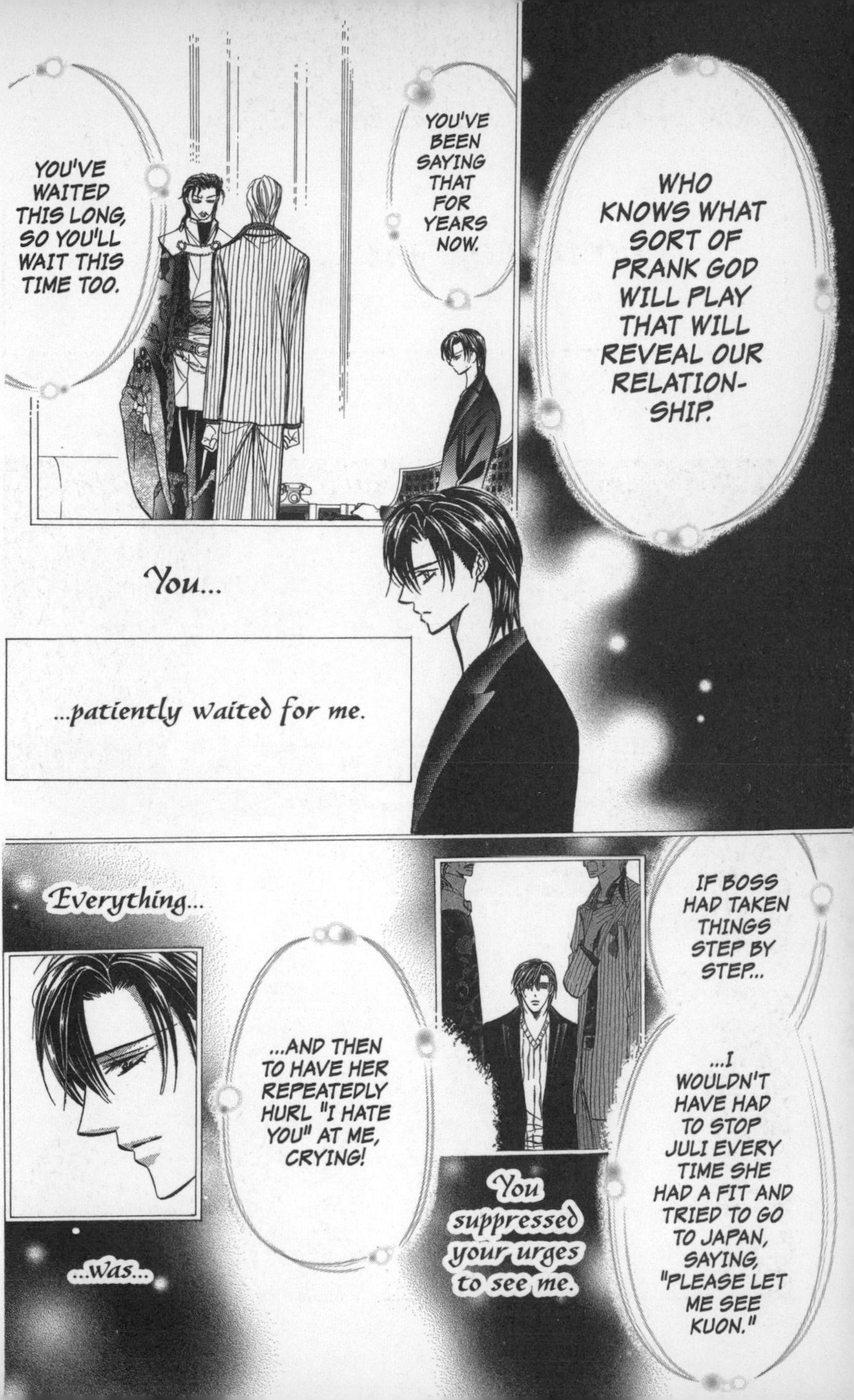
WHO KNOWS WHAT SORT OF PRANK GOD WILL PLAY THAT WILL REVEAL OUR RELATION-SHIP.
YOU'VE BEEN SAYING THAT FOR YEARS NOW.
YOU'VE WAITED THIS LONG, SO YOU'LL WAIT THIS TIME TOO.
You...
...patiently waited for me.
IF BOSS HAD TAKEN THINGS STEP BY STEP...
...I WOULDN'T HAVE HAD TO STOP JULI EVERY TIME SHE HAD A FIT AND TRIED TO GO TO JAPAN, SAYING, "PLEASE LET ME SEE KUON."
You suppressed your urges to see me.
...AND THEN TO HAVE HER REPEATEDLY HURL "I HATE YOU" AT ME, CRYING!
Everything...
...was...

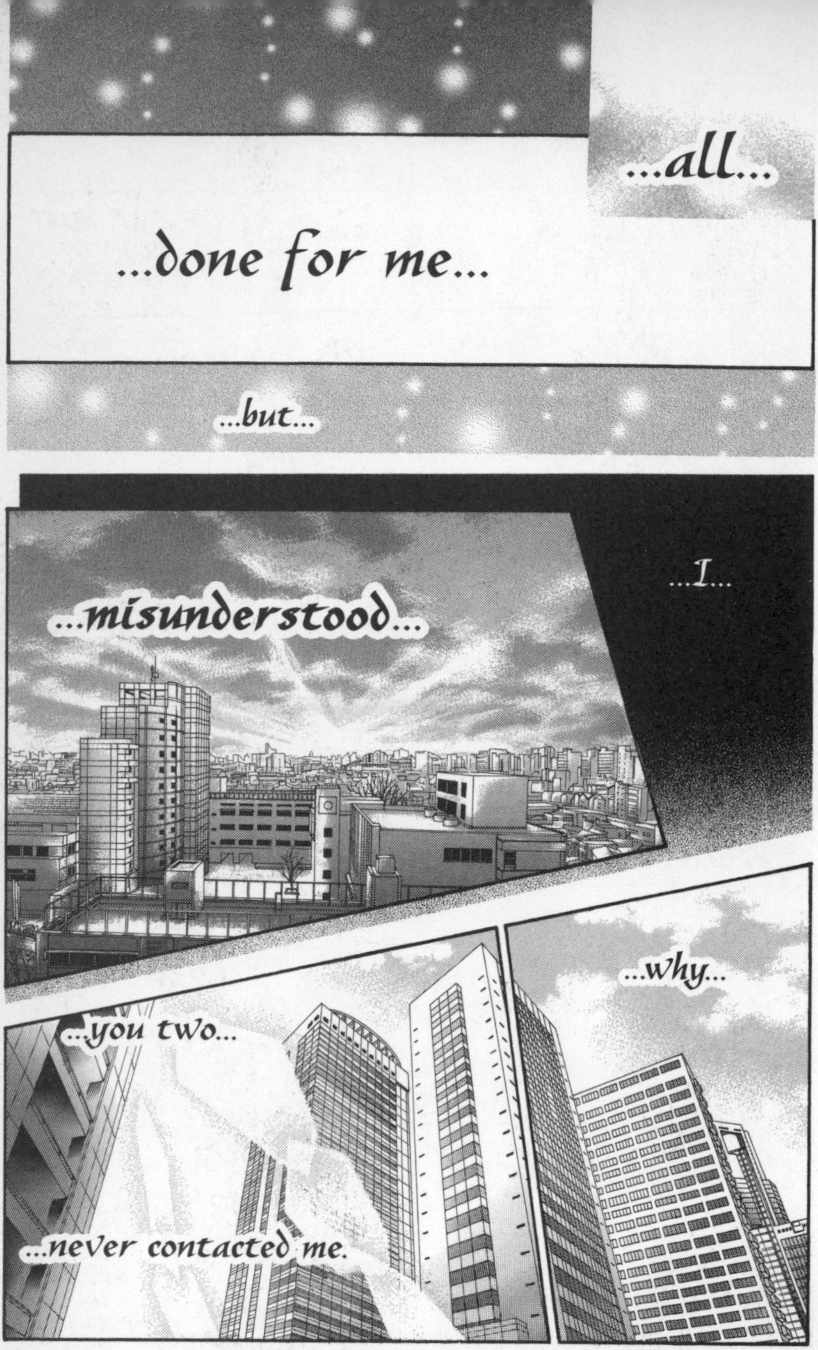
...all...
...done for me...
...but...
...I...
...misunderstood...
...why...
...you two...
...never contacted me.

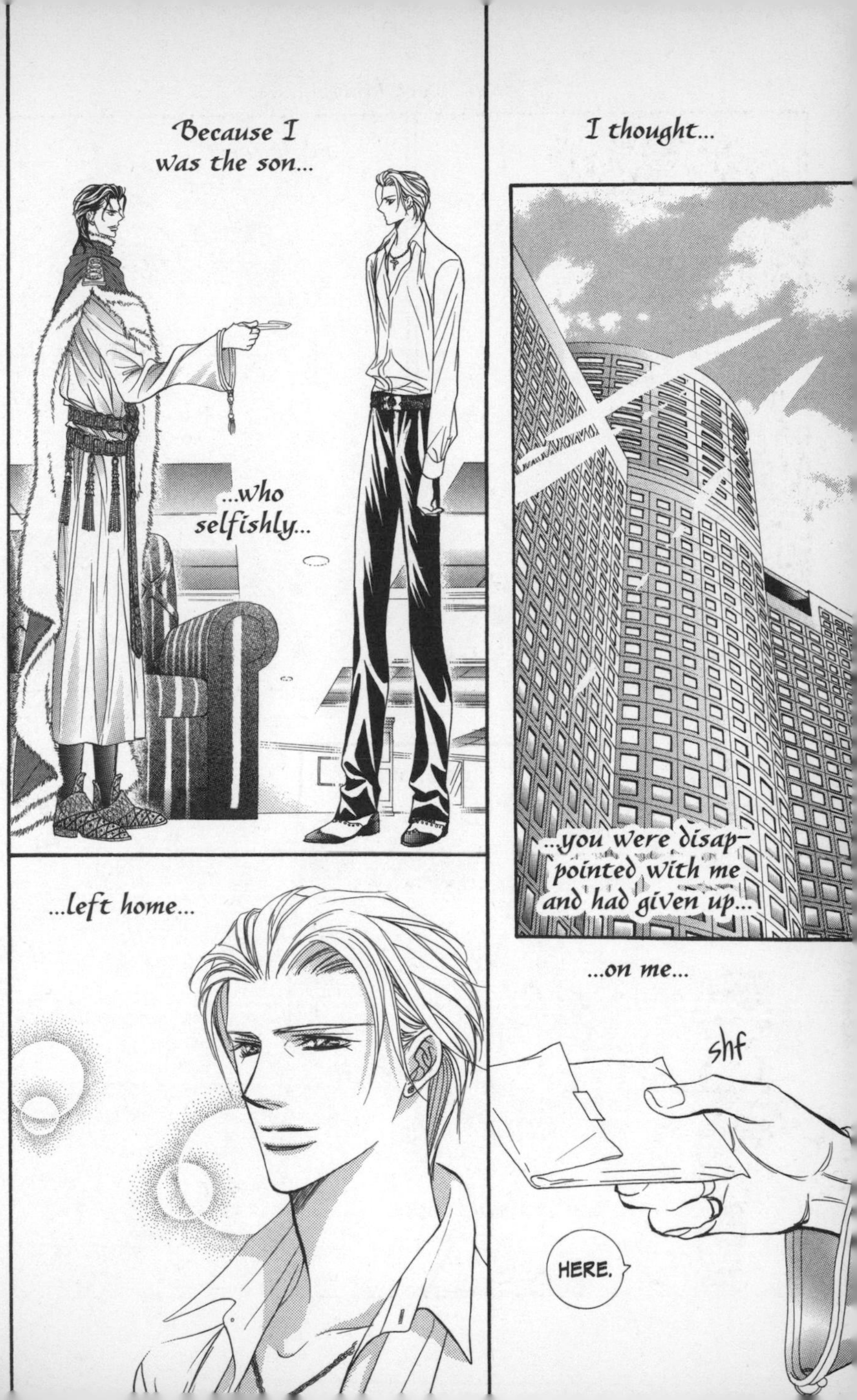
Because I was the son...
...who selfishly...
...left home...
I thought...
...you were disap-pointed with me and had given up...
...on me...
shf
HERE.

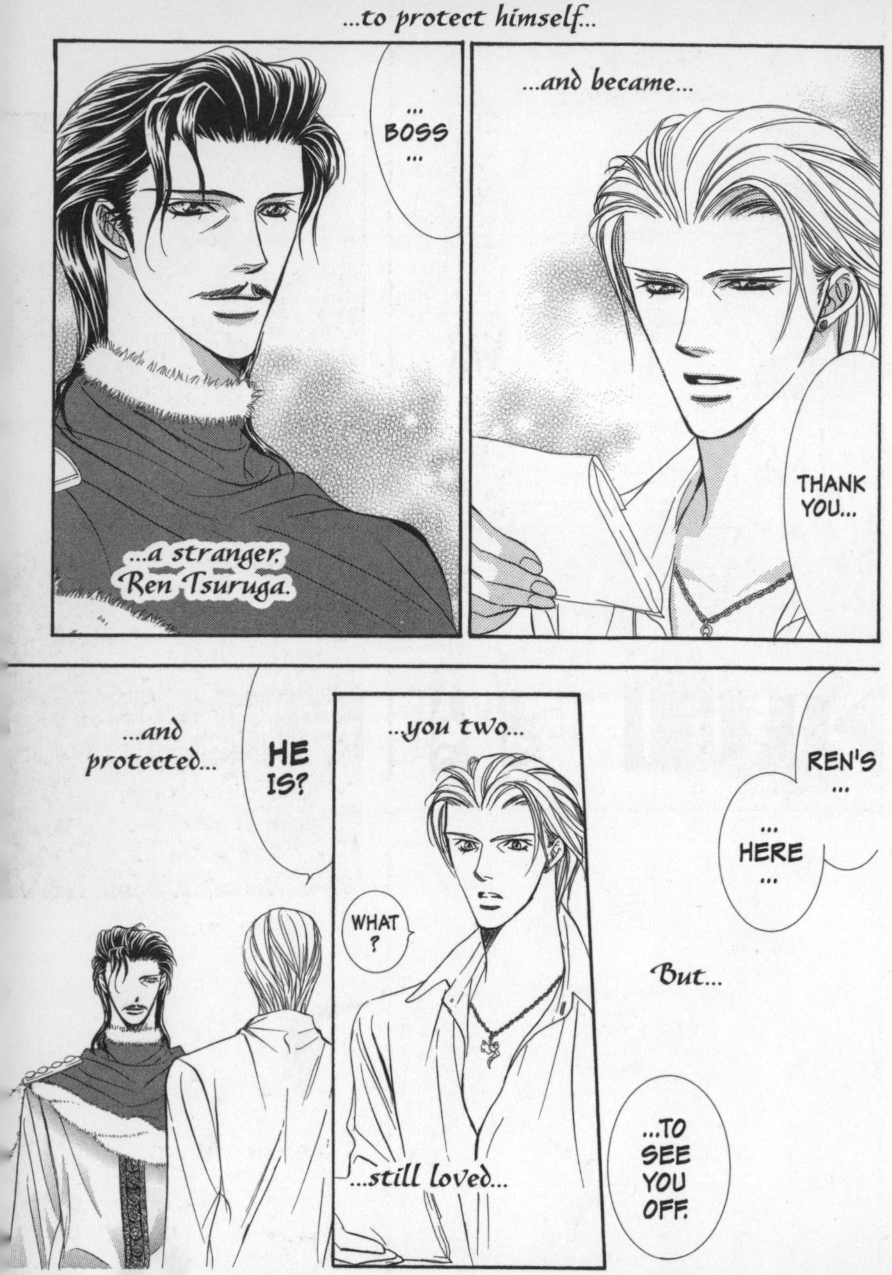
...to protect himself...
...and became...
THANK YOU...
... BOSS ...
...a stranger, Ren Tsuruga.
REN'S ...
... HERE ...
But...
...TO SEE YOU OFF.
...you two...
WHAT ?
...still loved...
...and protected...
HE IS?

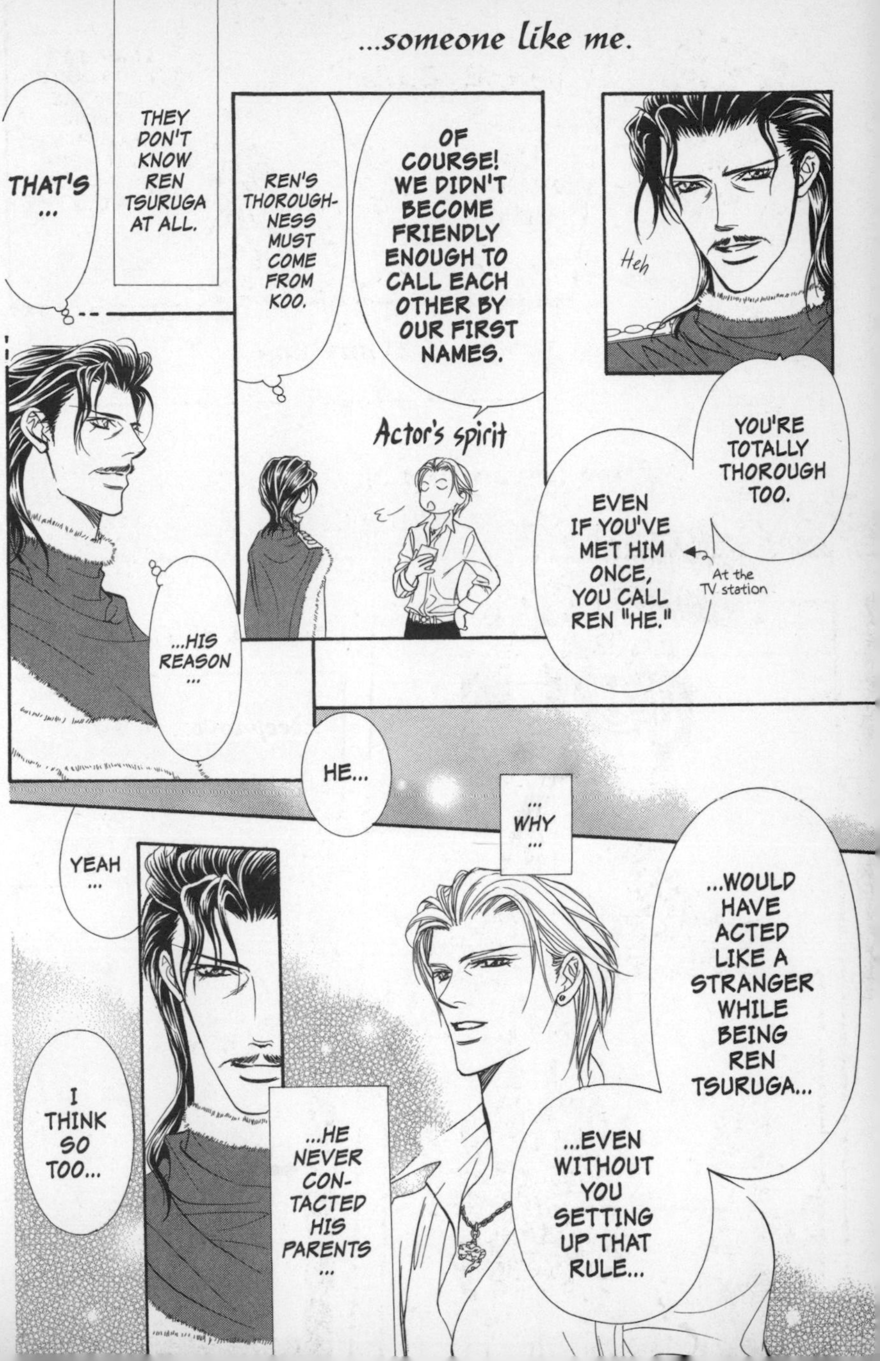
...someone like me.
Heh
YOU'RE TOTALLY THOROUGH TOO.
EVEN IF YOU'VE MET HIM ONCE, YOU CALL REN "HE."
At the TV station
OF COURSE! WE DIDN'T BECOME FRIENDLY ENOUGH TO CALL EACH OTHER BY OUR FIRST NAMES.
Actor's spirit
REN'S THOROUGH-NESS MUST COME FROM KOO.
THEY DON'T KNOW REN TSURUGA AT ALL.
THAT'S...
...HIS REASON...
HE...
...WHY...
...WOULD HAVE ACTED LIKE A STRANGER WHILE BEING REN TSURUGA...
...EVEN WITHOUT YOU SETTING UP THAT RULE...
...HE NEVER CON-TACTED HIS PARENTS...
YEAH...
I THINK SO TOO...

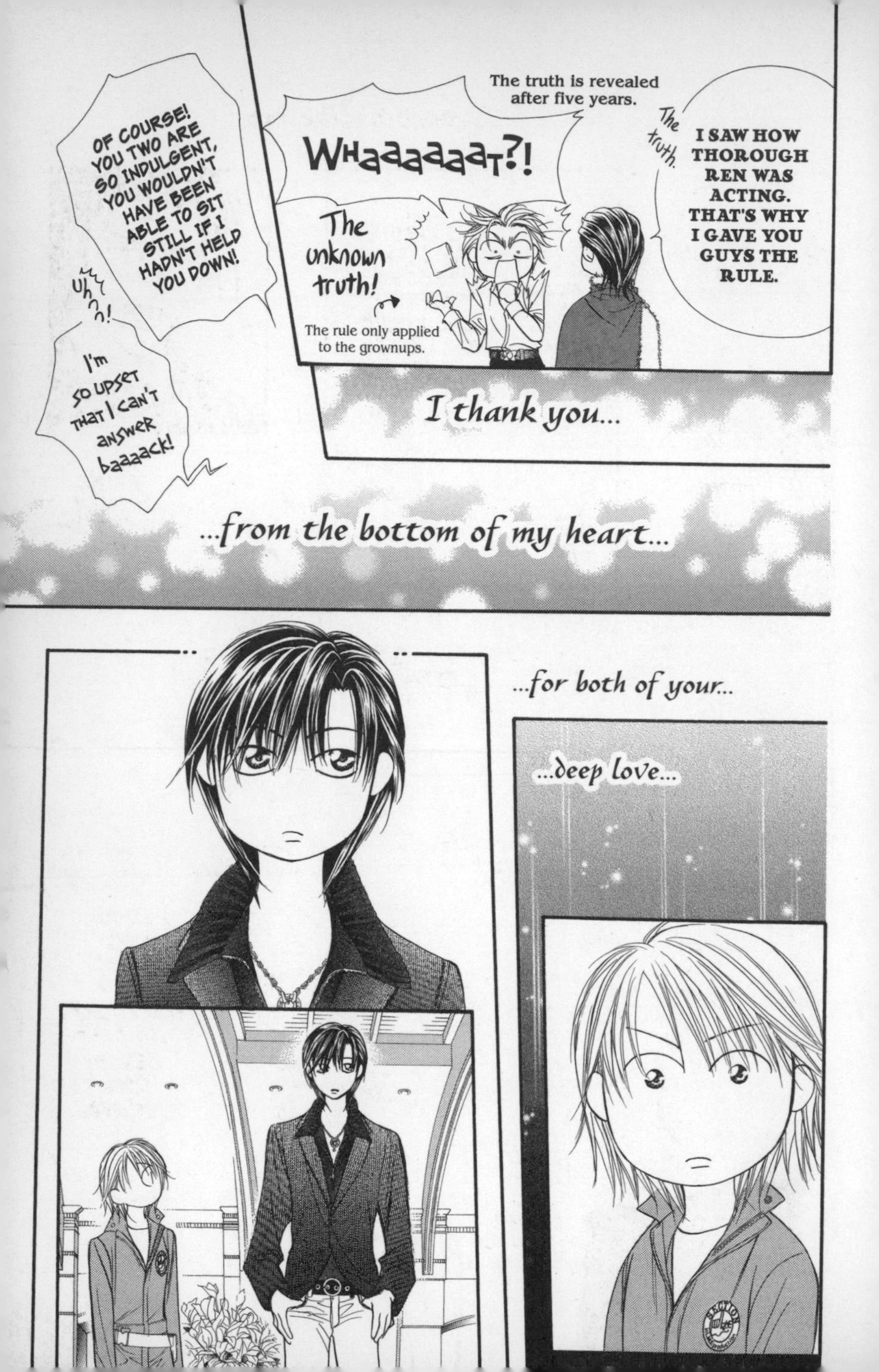
I SAW HOW THOROUGH REN WAS ACTING. THAT'S WHY I GAVE YOU GUYS THE RULE.
The truth.
The truth is revealed after five years.
WHaaaaaaaT?!
The unknown truth!
The rule only applied to the grownups.
OF COURSE! YOU TWO ARE SO INDULGENT, YOU WOULDN'T HAVE BEEN ABLE TO SIT STILL IF I HADN'T HELD YOU DOWN!
Uh?!
I'm so upset that I can't answer baaaack!
I thank you...
...from the bottom of my heart...
...for both of your...
...deep love...

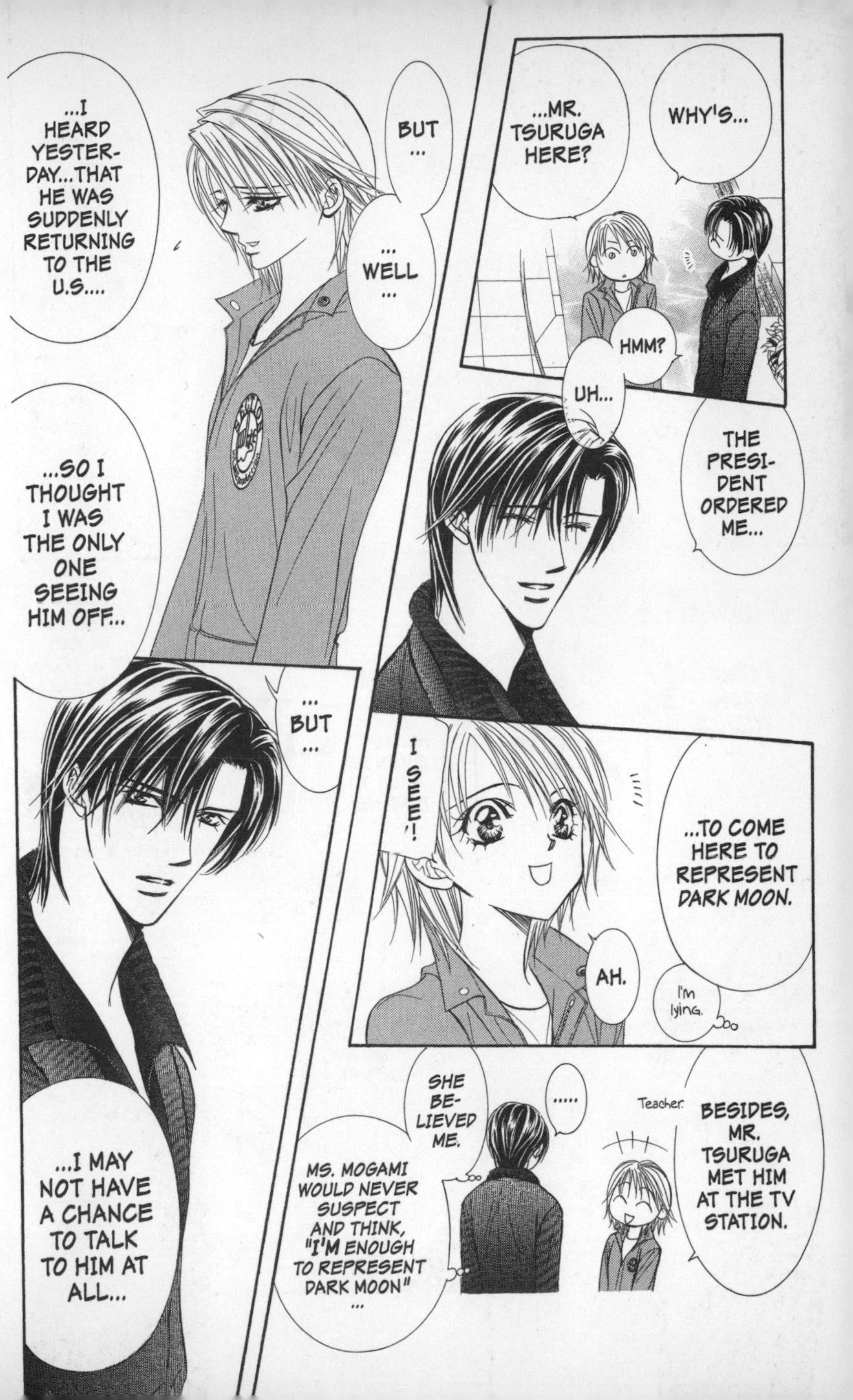
WHY'S...
...MR. TSURUGA HERE?
HMM?
UH...
THE PRESIDENT ORDERED ME...
...TO COME HERE TO REPRESENT DARK MOON.
I SEE!
AH.
I'm lying.
BESIDES, MR. TSURUGA MET HIM AT THE TV STATION.
Teacher.
......
SHE BELIEVED ME.
MS. MOGAMI WOULD NEVER SUSPECT AND THINK, "I'M ENOUGH TO REPRESENT DARK MOON"...
BUT...
...WELL...
...I HEARD YESTERDAY...THAT HE WAS SUDDENLY RETURNING TO THE U.S....
...SO I THOUGHT I WAS THE ONLY ONE SEEING HIM OFF...
...BUT...
...I MAY NOT HAVE A CHANCE TO TALK TO HIM AT ALL...

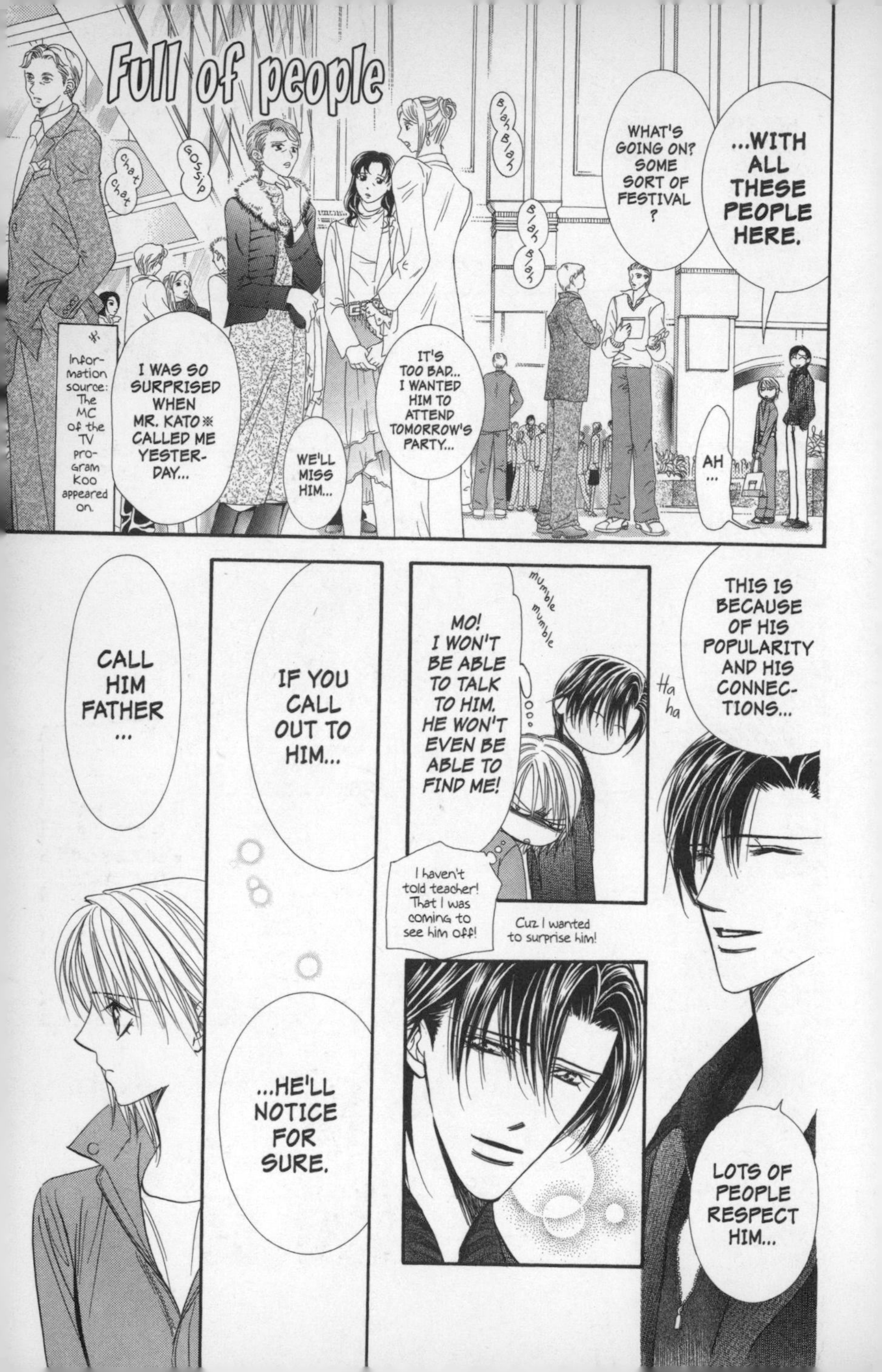
...WITH ALL THESE PEOPLE HERE.
WHAT'S GOING ON? SOME SORT OF FESTIVAL ?
AH ...
Blah Blah
Blah Blah
Full of people
IT'S TOO BAD... I WANTED HIM TO ATTEND TOMORROW'S PARTY...
WE'LL MISS HIM...
GOSSIP
Chat chat
I WAS SO SURPRISED WHEN MR. KATO※ CALLED ME YESTERDAY...
※ Information source: The MC of the TV program Koo appeared on.
THIS IS BECAUSE OF HIS POPULARITY AND HIS CONNECTIONS...
Ha ha
LOTS OF PEOPLE RESPECT HIM...
MO! I WON'T BE ABLE TO TALK TO HIM. HE WON'T EVEN BE ABLE TO FIND ME!
mumble mumble
I haven't told teacher! That I was coming to see him off!
Cuz I wanted to surprise him!
IF YOU CALL OUT TO HIM...
...HE'LL NOTICE FOR SURE.
CALL HIM FATHER ...

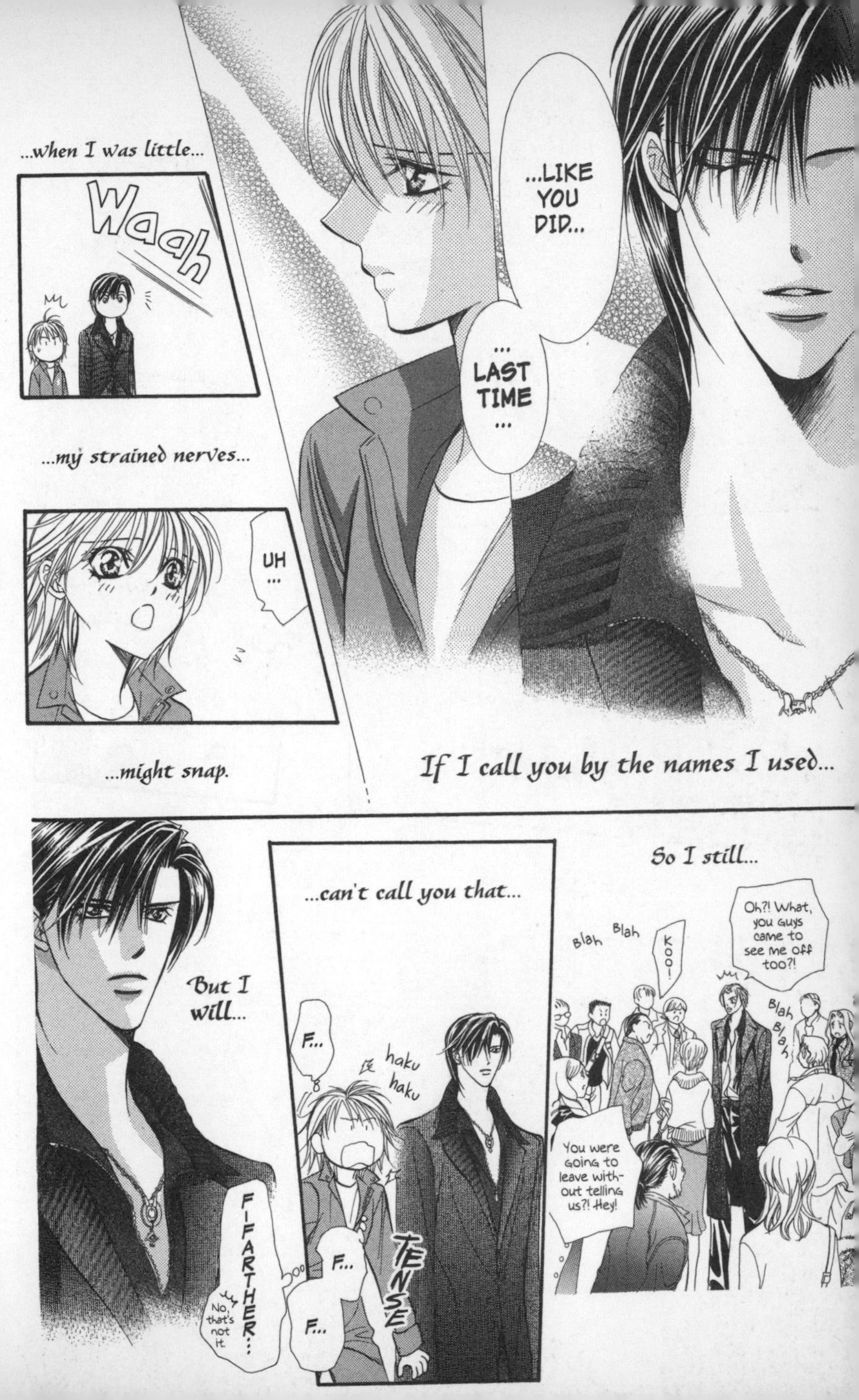
...LIKE YOU DID...
...LAST TIME...
If I call you by the names I used...
...when I was little...
Waah
...my strained nerves...
UH...
...might snap.
So I still...
Oh?! What, you guys came to see me off too?!
Blah Blah
KOO!
Blah Blah
Blah Blah
You were going to leave without telling us?! Hey!
...can't call you that...
F...
haku haku
TENSE
F...
F...
FIFARTHER...
No, that's not it.
But I will...

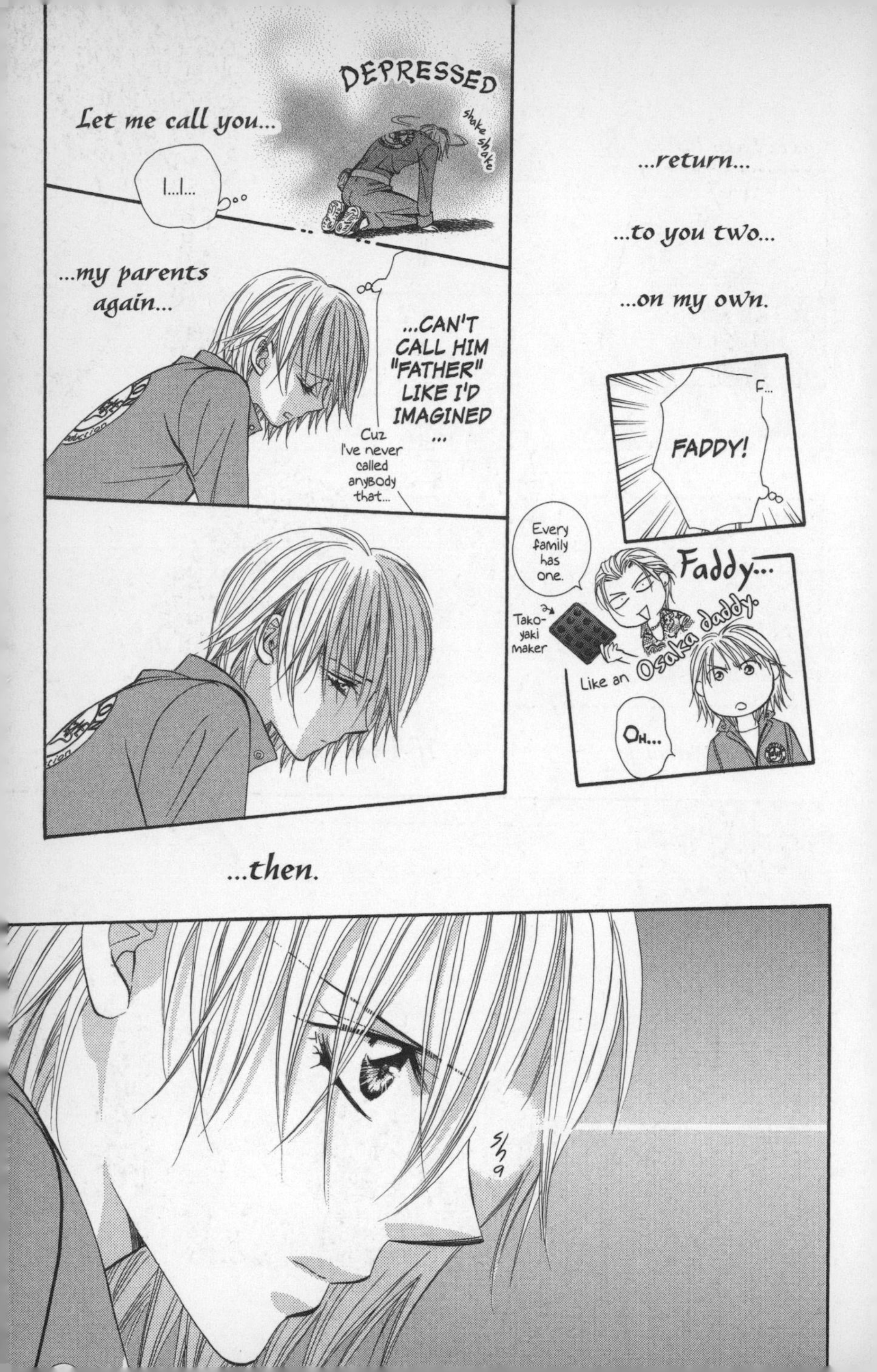
...return...
...to you two...
...on my own.
F...
FADDY!
Faddy...
Like an Osaka daddy.
Every family has one.
Tako-yaki maker
Oh...
Let me call you...
DEPRESSED
shake shake
I...I...
...my parents again...
...CAN'T CALL HIM "FATHER" LIKE I'D IMAGINED...
Cuz I've never called anybody that...
...then.
sha

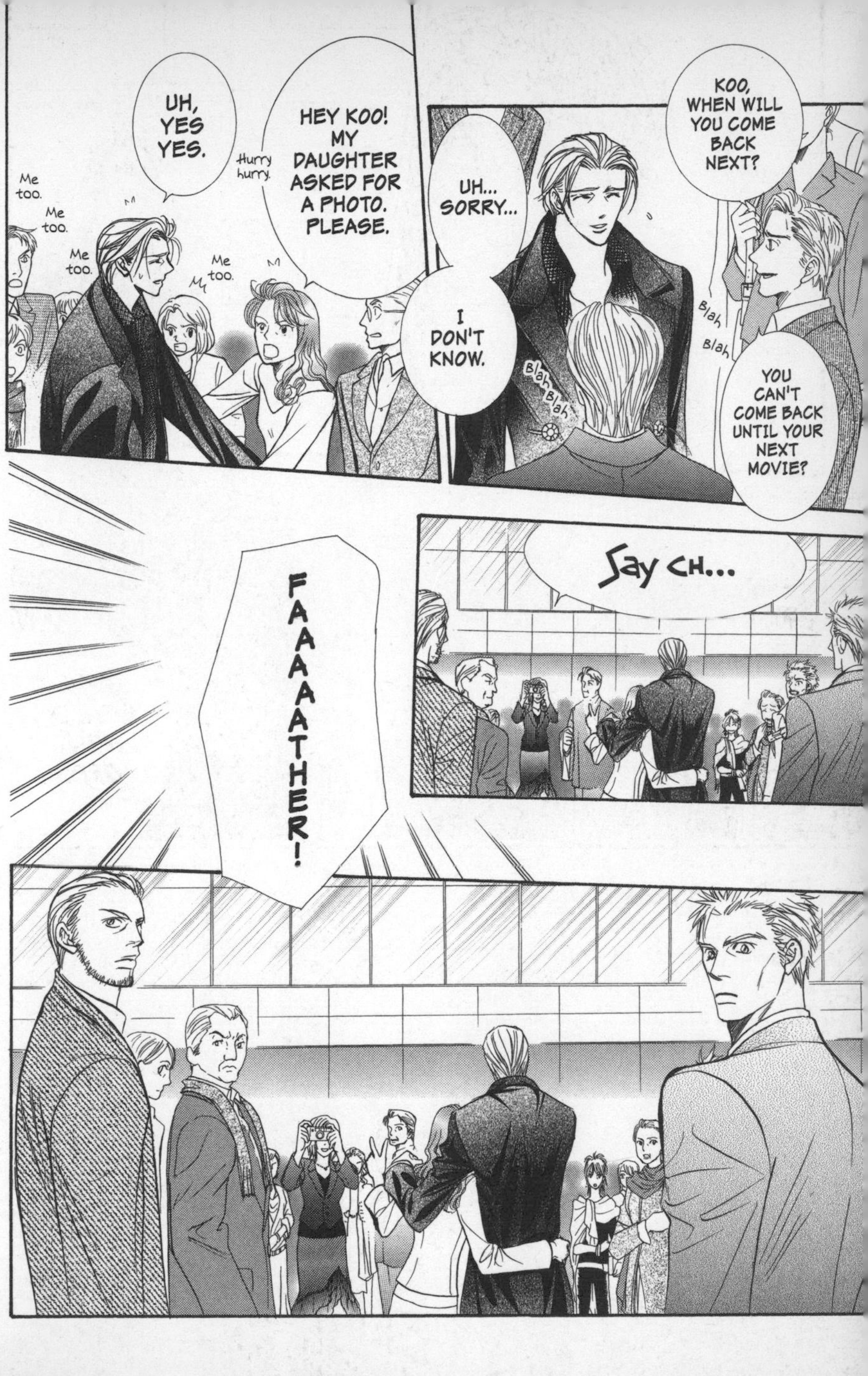
KOO, WHEN WILL YOU COME BACK NEXT?
UH... SORRY...
I DON'T KNOW.
Blah Blah
YOU CAN'T COME BACK UNTIL YOUR NEXT MOVIE?
Blah Blah
HEY KOO! MY DAUGHTER ASKED FOR A PHOTO. PLEASE.
UH, YES YES.
Hurry hurry.
Me too.
Me too.
Me too.
Me too.
Say ch...
FAAAAATHER!

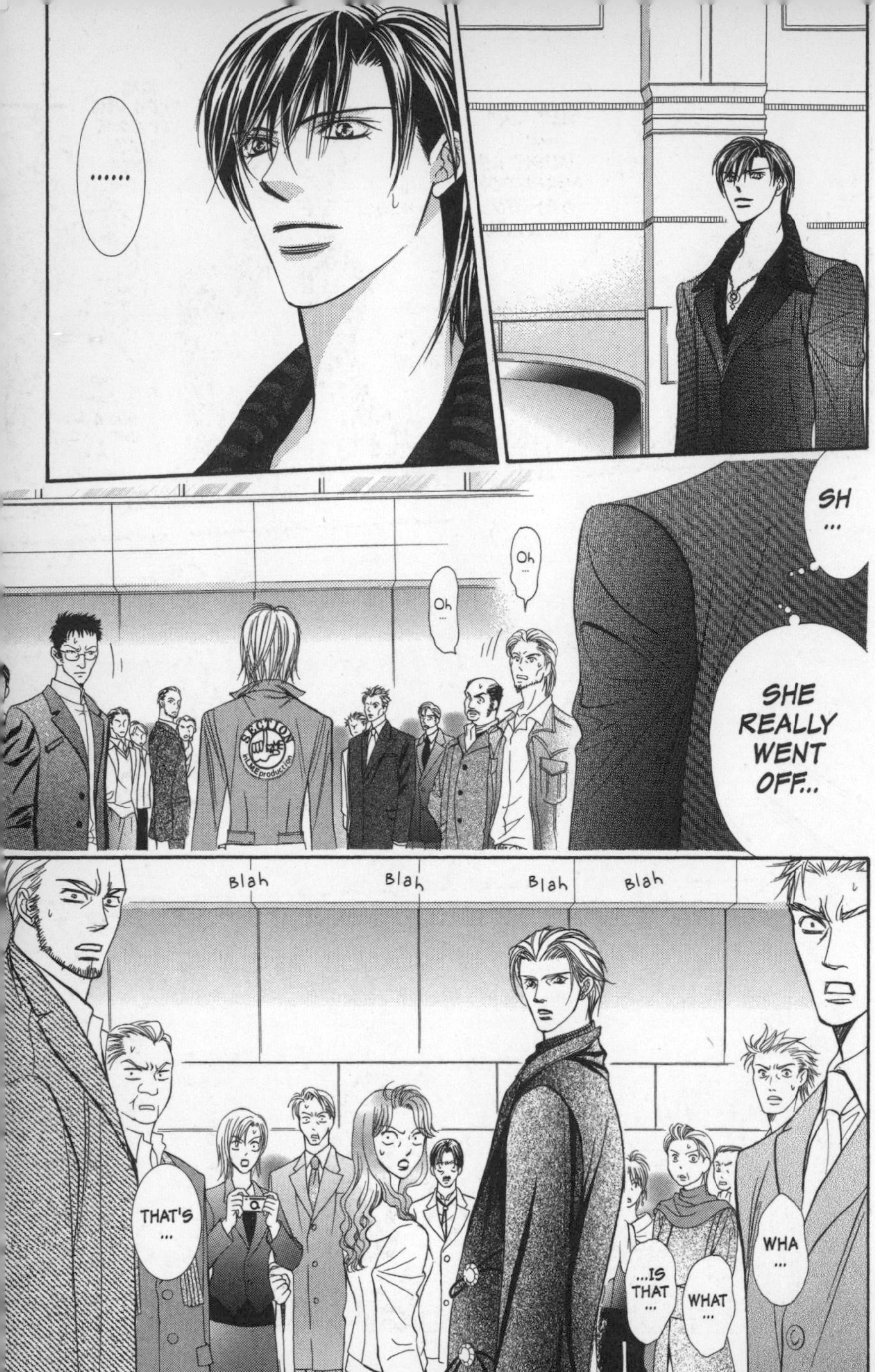
......
SH...
SHE REALLY WENT OFF...
Oh...
Oh...
Blah
Blah
Blah
Blah
WHA...
WHAT...
...IS THAT...
THAT'S...

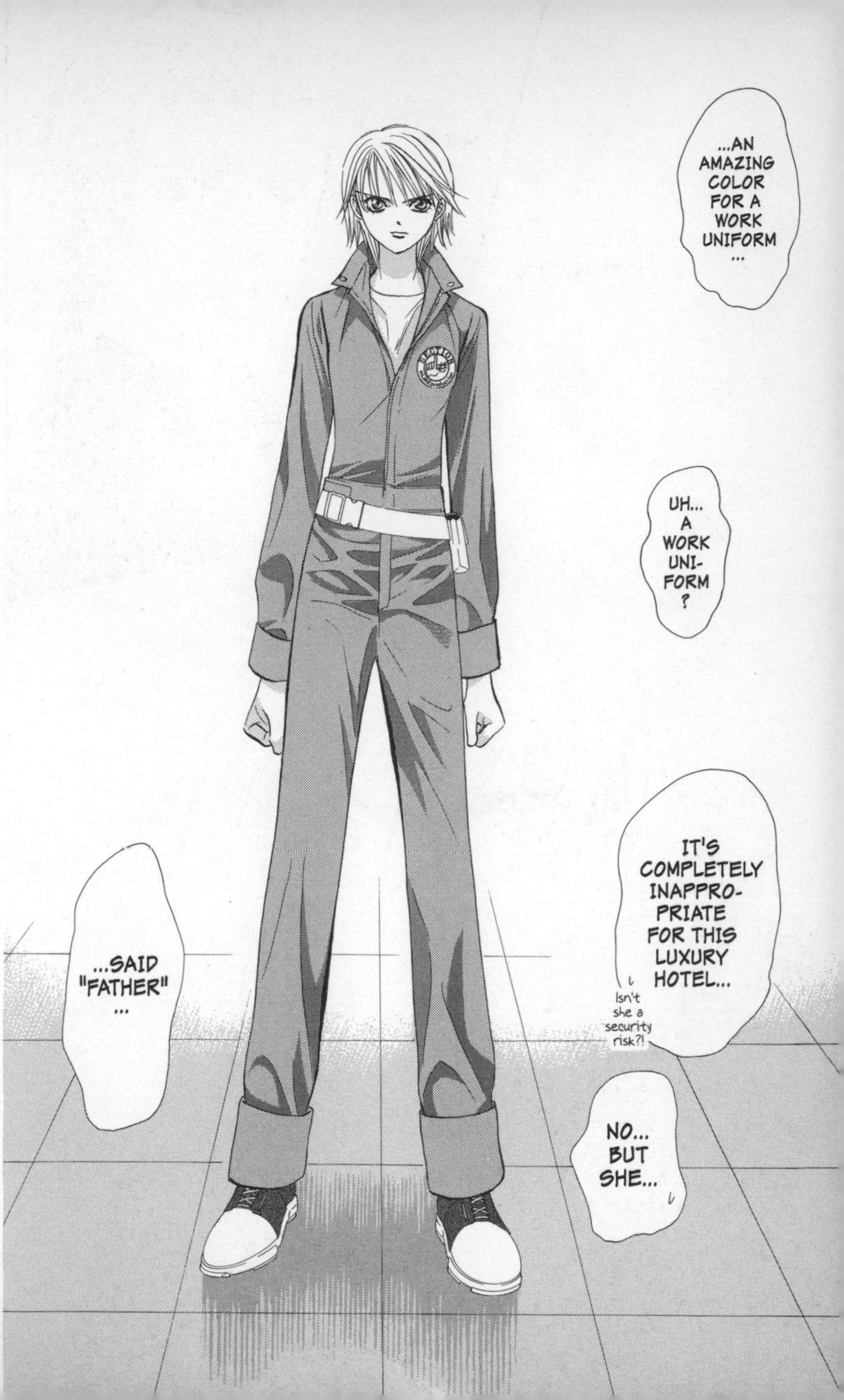
...AN AMAZING COLOR FOR A WORK UNIFORM ...
UH... A WORK UNI-FORM ?
IT'S COMPLETELY INAPPRO-PRIATE FOR THIS LUXURY HOTEL...
Isn't she a security risk?!
NO... BUT SHE...
...SAID "FATHER" ...

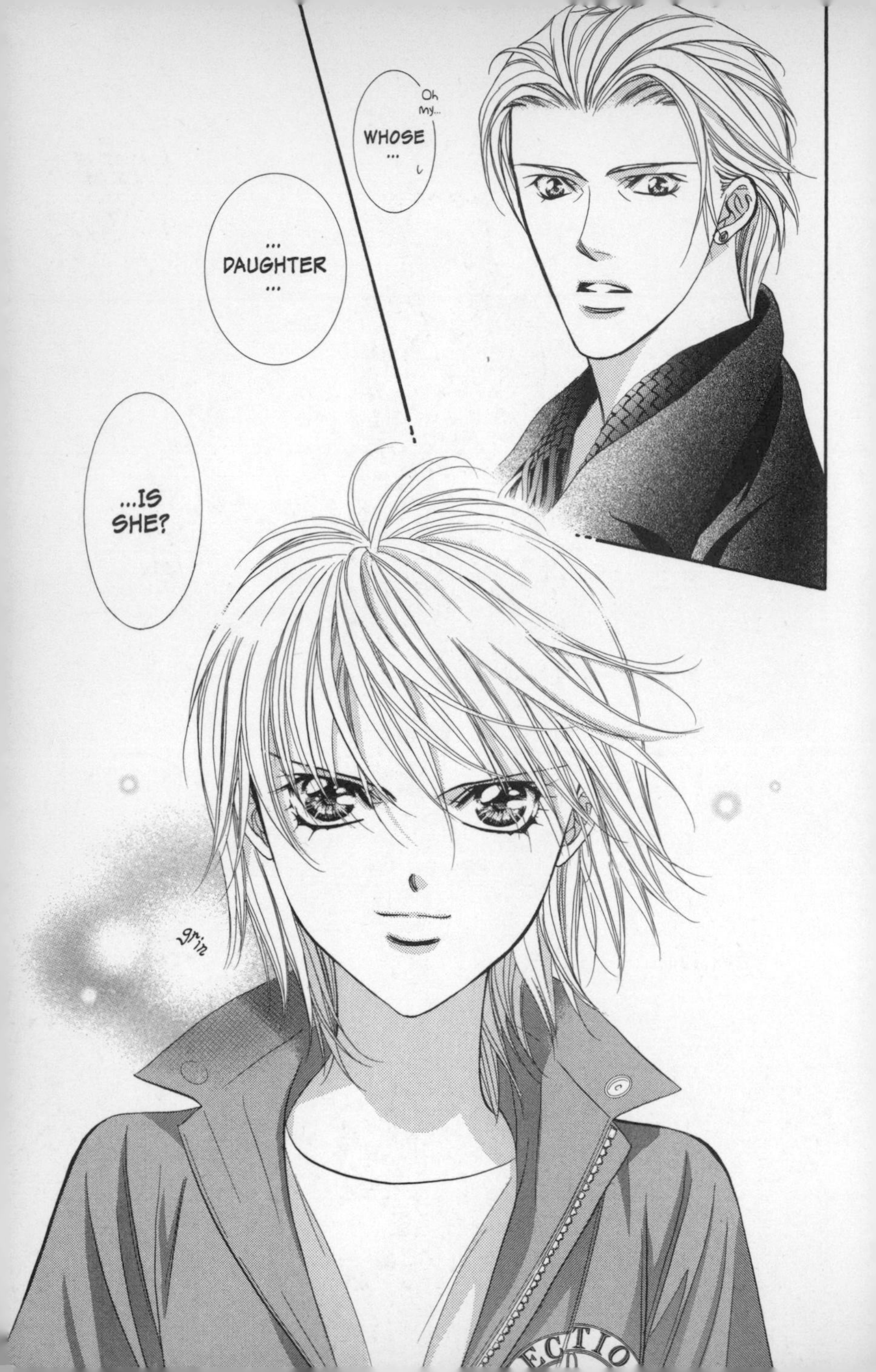
Oh my...
WHOSE...
...DAUGHTER...
...IS SHE?
grin

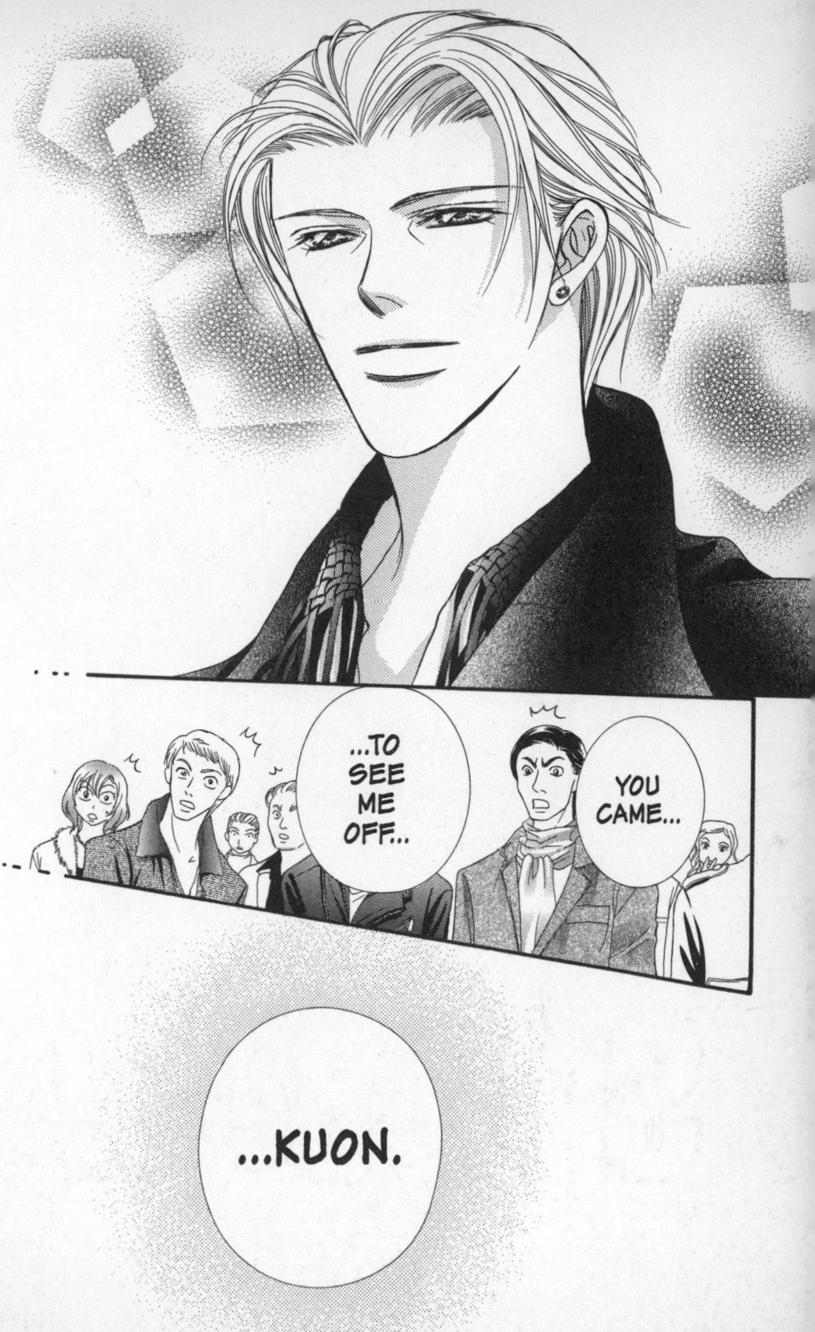
YOU CAME...
...TO SEE ME OFF...
...KUON.

End of Act 113

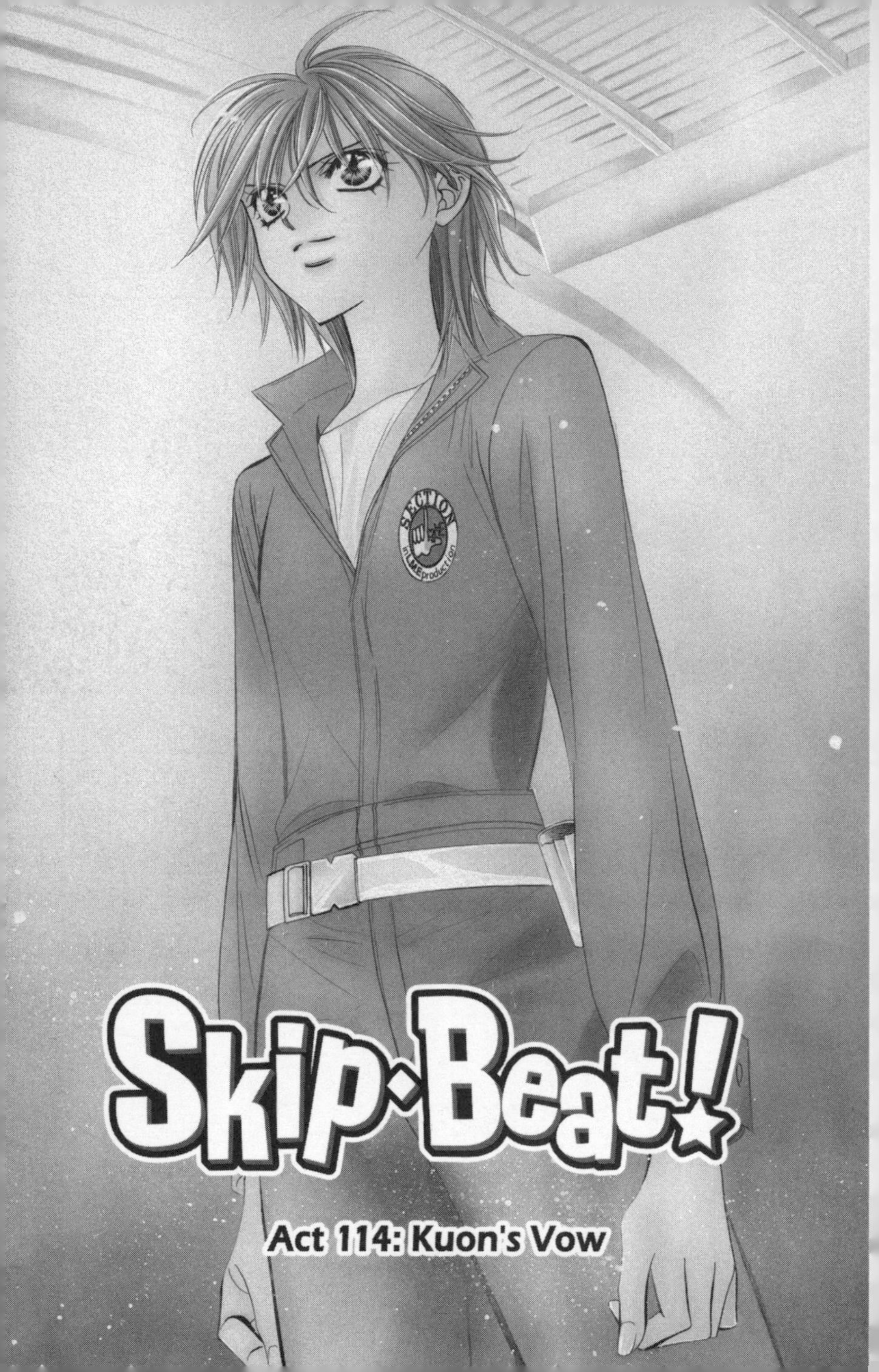
Skip·Beat!
Act 114: Kuon's Vow

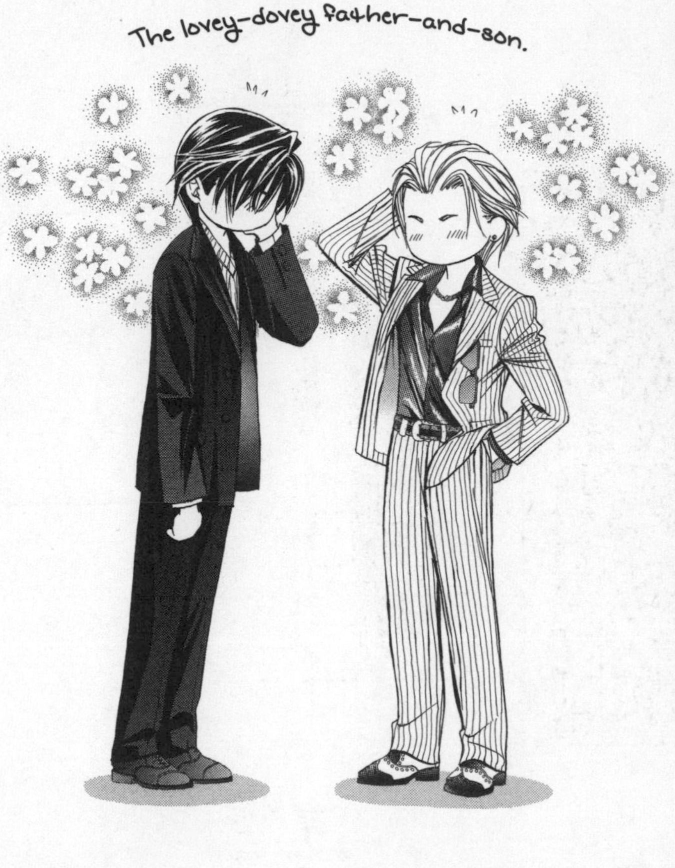
The lovey-dovey father-and-son.

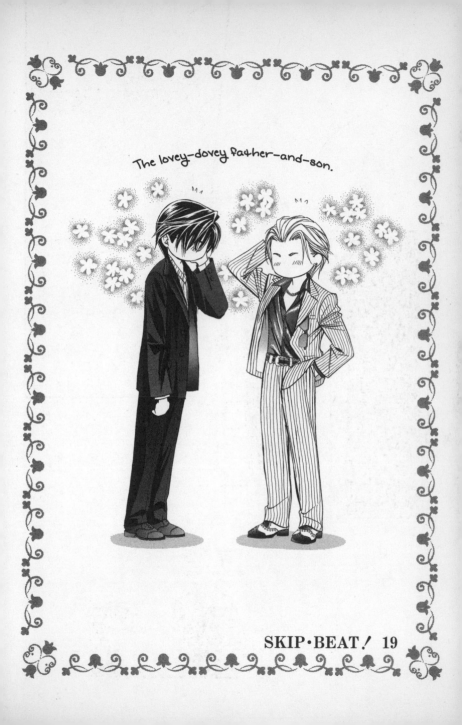

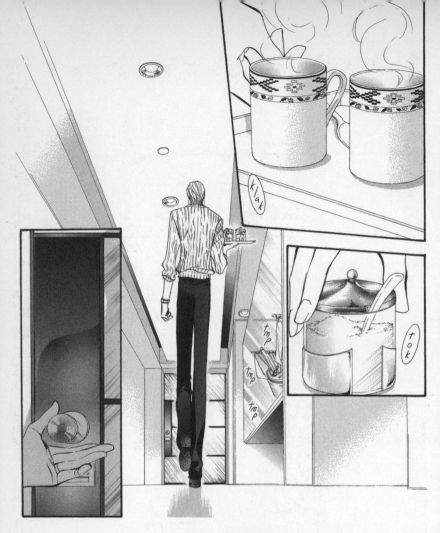

klak

tmp
tmp
tmp

tok

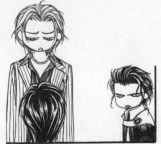

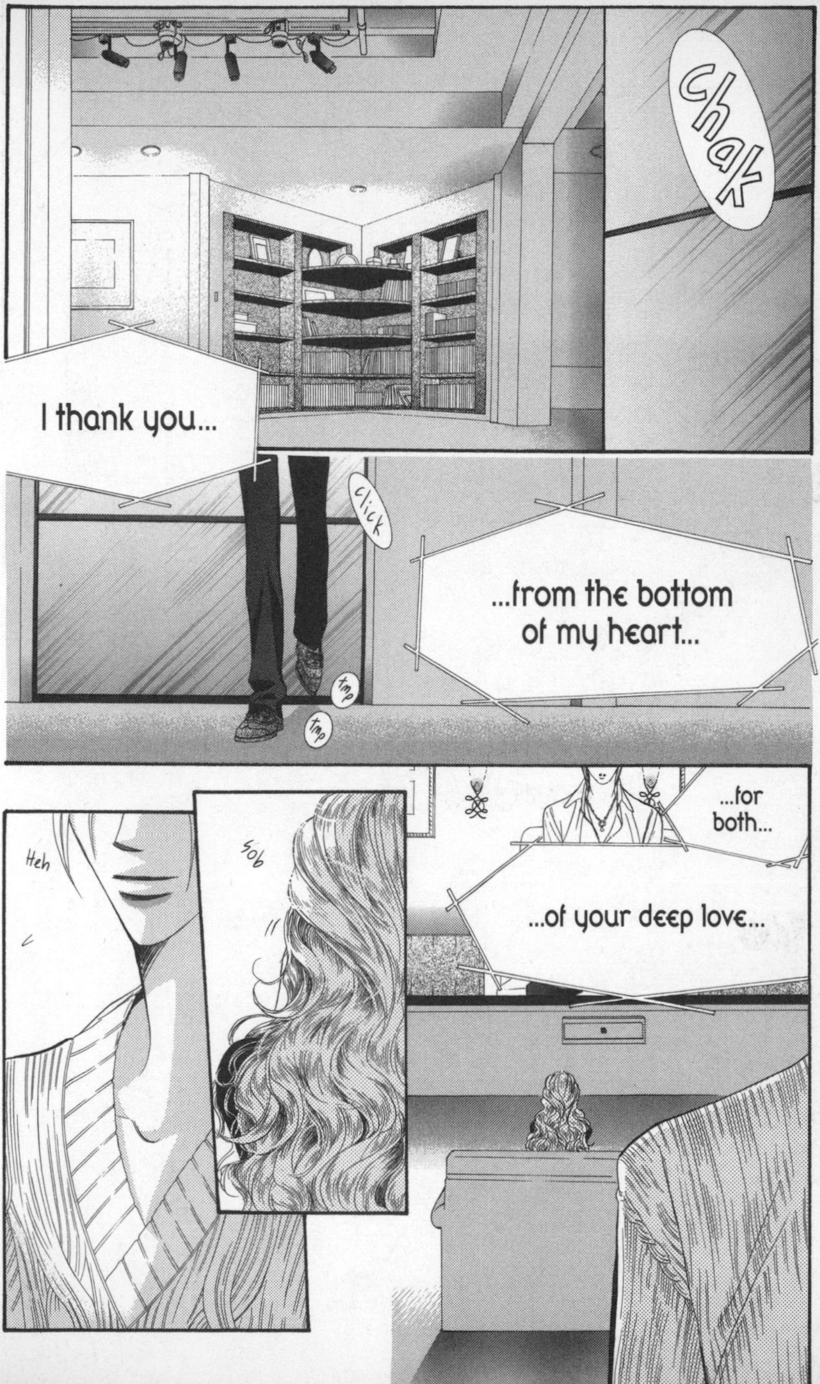
Chak
I thank you...
...from the bottom of my heart...
click
tmp
tmp
...for both...
...of your deep love...
sob
Heh

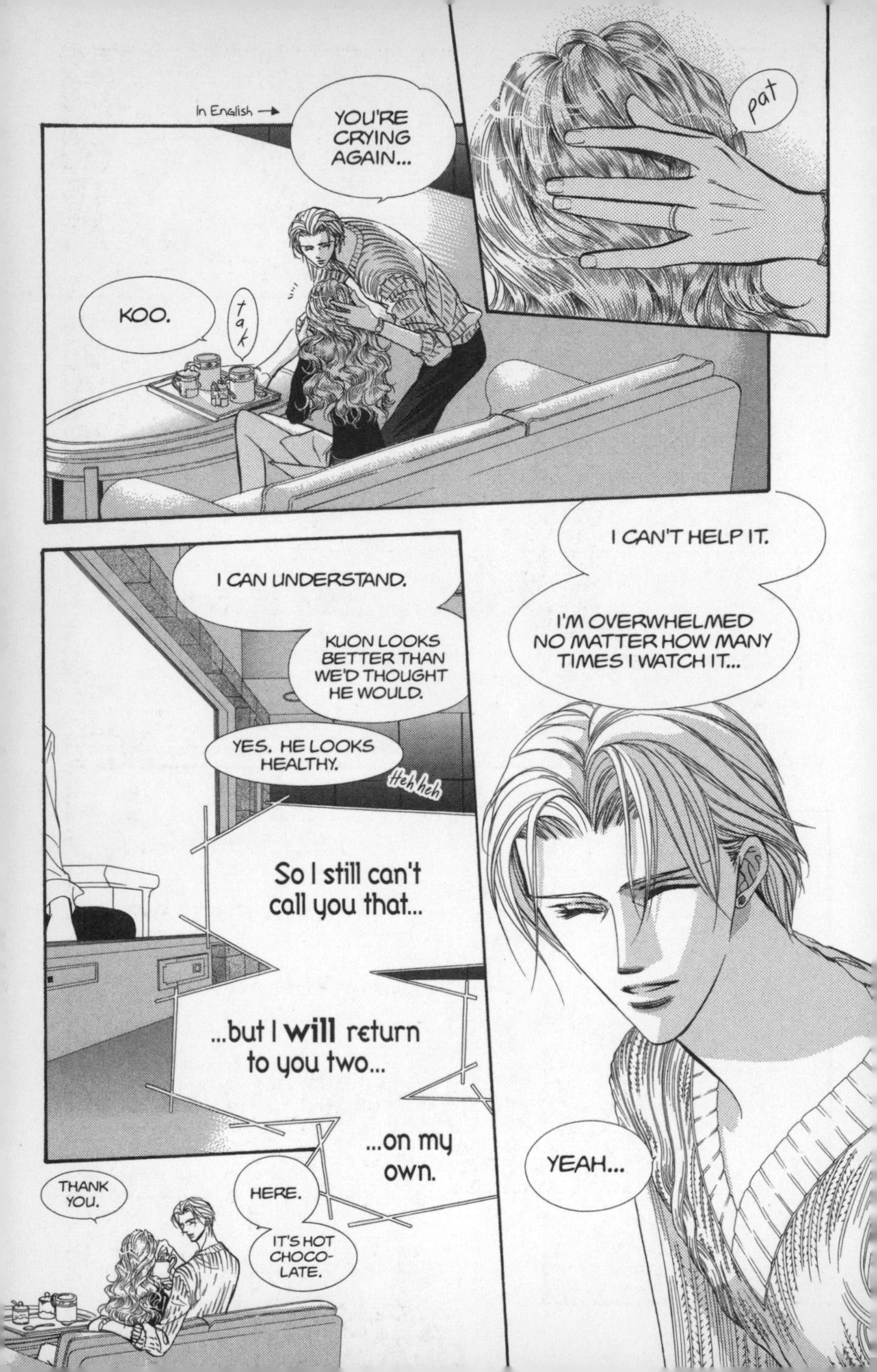
pat
In English →
YOU'RE CRYING AGAIN...
tak
KOO.
I CAN'T HELP IT.
I'M OVERWHELMED NO MATTER HOW MANY TIMES I WATCH IT...
YEAH...
I CAN UNDERSTAND.
KUON LOOKS BETTER THAN WE'D THOUGHT HE WOULD.
YES. HE LOOKS HEALTHY.
Heh heh
So I still can't call you that...
...but I **will** return to you two...
...on my own.
HERE.
IT'S HOT CHOCOLATE.
THANK YOU.

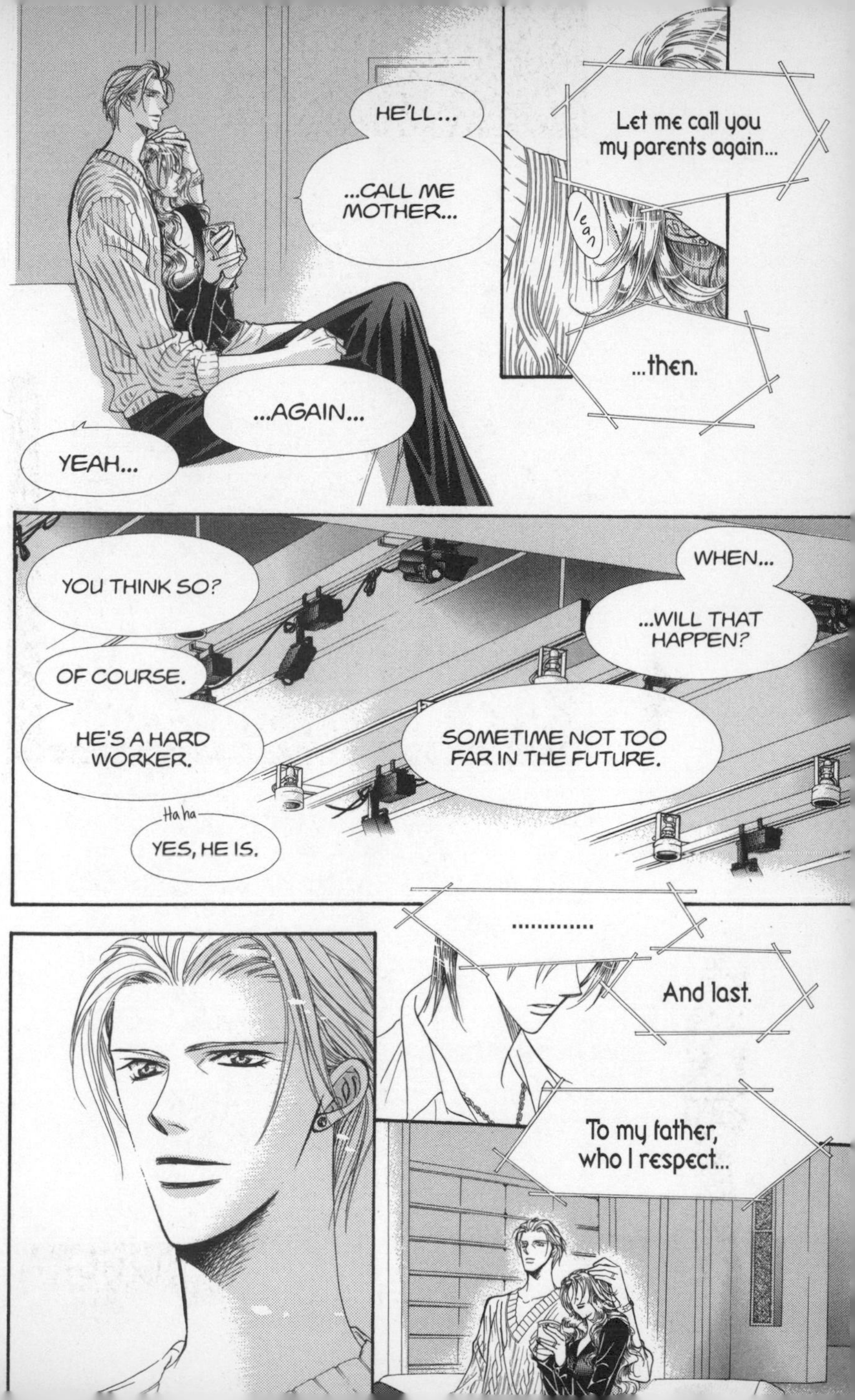
Let me call you my parents again...
...then.
HE'LL...
...CALL ME MOTHER...
...AGAIN...
YEAH...
WHEN...
...WILL THAT HAPPEN?
SOMETIME NOT TOO FAR IN THE FUTURE.
YOU THINK SO?
OF COURSE.
HE'S A HARD WORKER.
Ha ha
YES, HE IS.
............
And last.
To my father, who I respect...

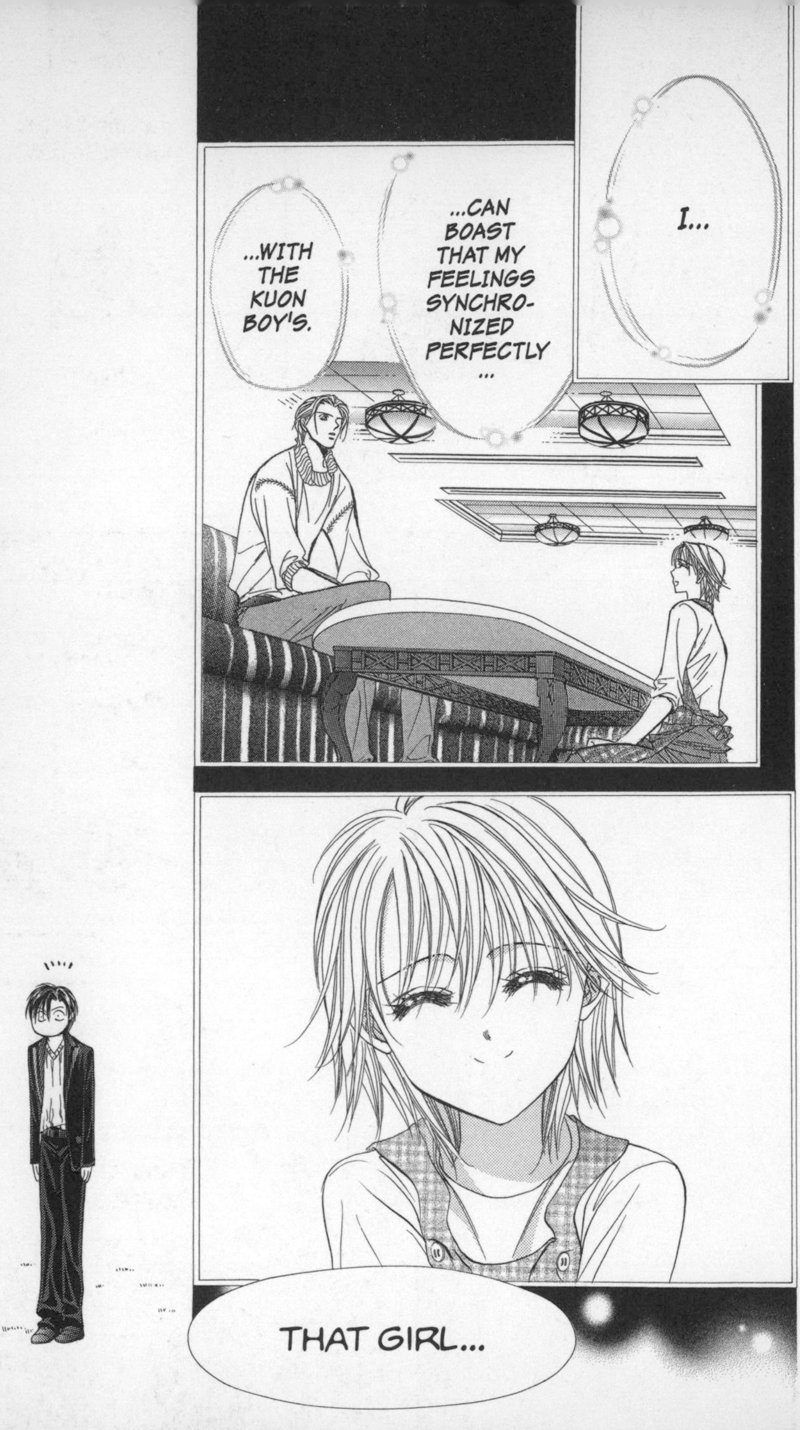
I...
...CAN BOAST THAT MY FEELINGS SYNCHRONIZED PERFECTLY...
...WITH THE KUON BOY'S.
THAT GIRL...

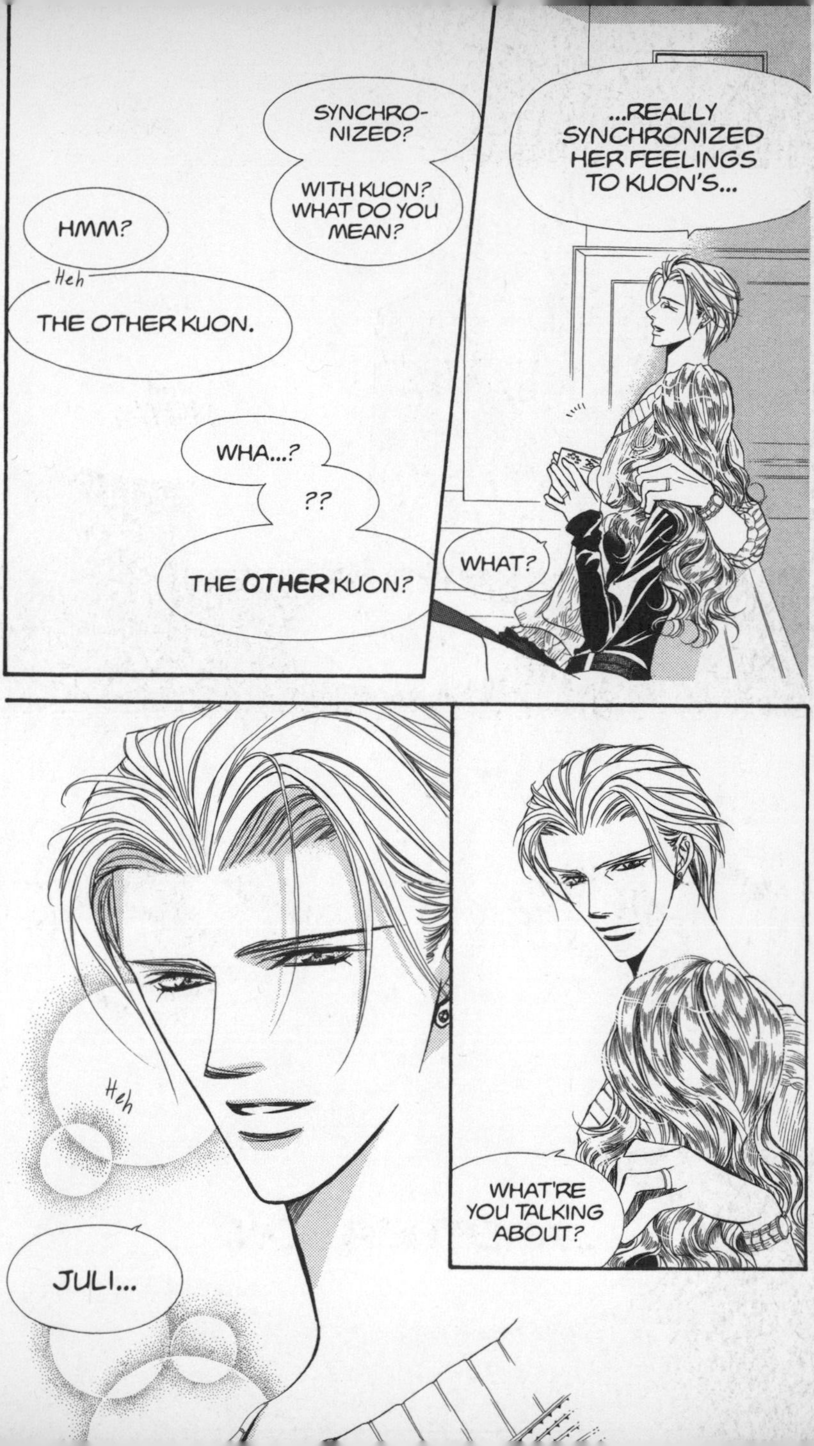
...REALLY SYNCHRONIZED HER FEELINGS TO KUON'S...
WHAT?
SYNCHRO-NIZED?
WITH KUON? WHAT DO YOU MEAN?
HMM?
Heh
THE OTHER KUON.
WHA...?
??
THE **OTHER** KUON?
WHAT'RE YOU TALKING ABOUT?
Heh
JULI...

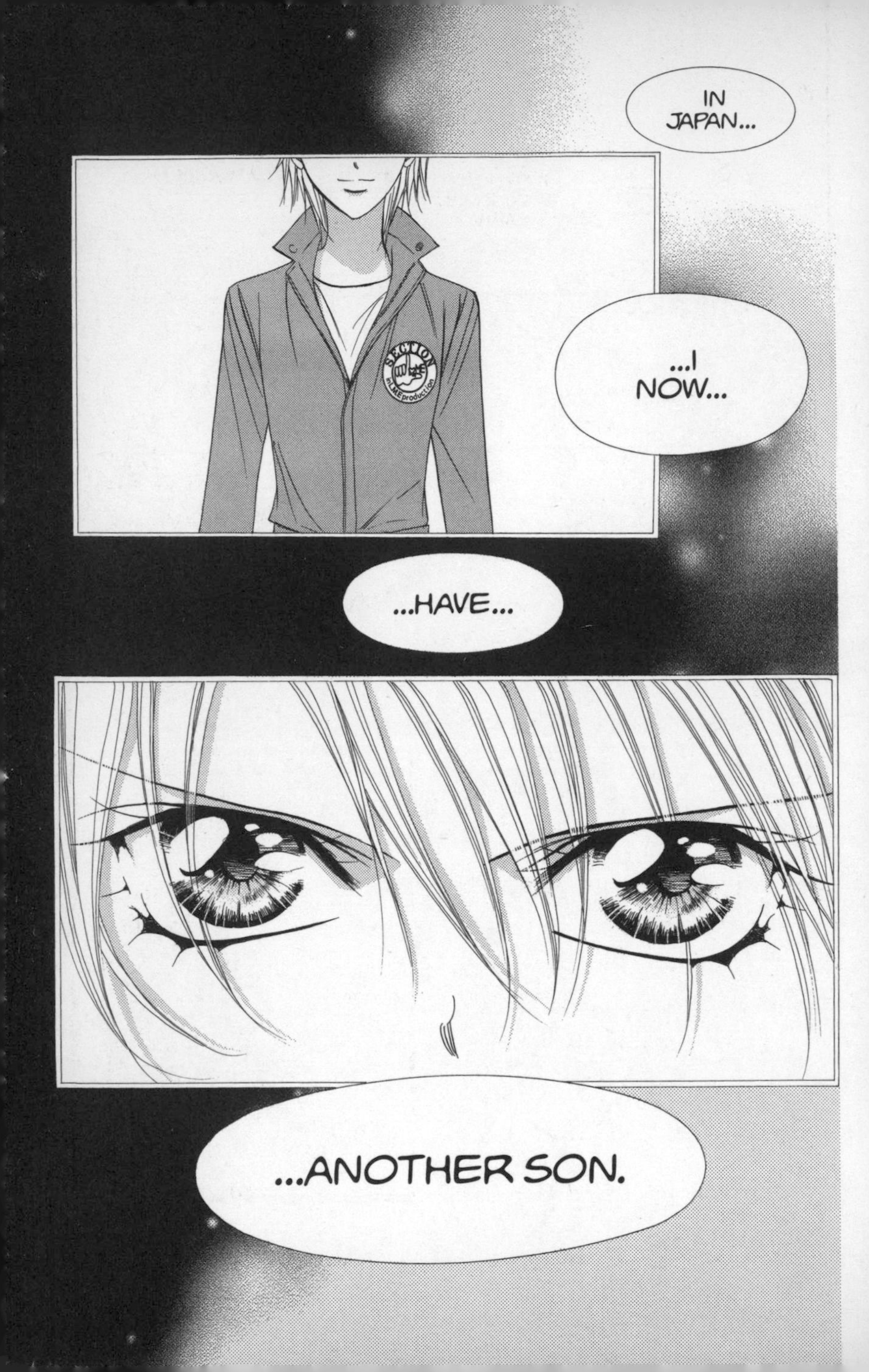
IN JAPAN...
...I NOW...
...HAVE...
...ANOTHER SON.

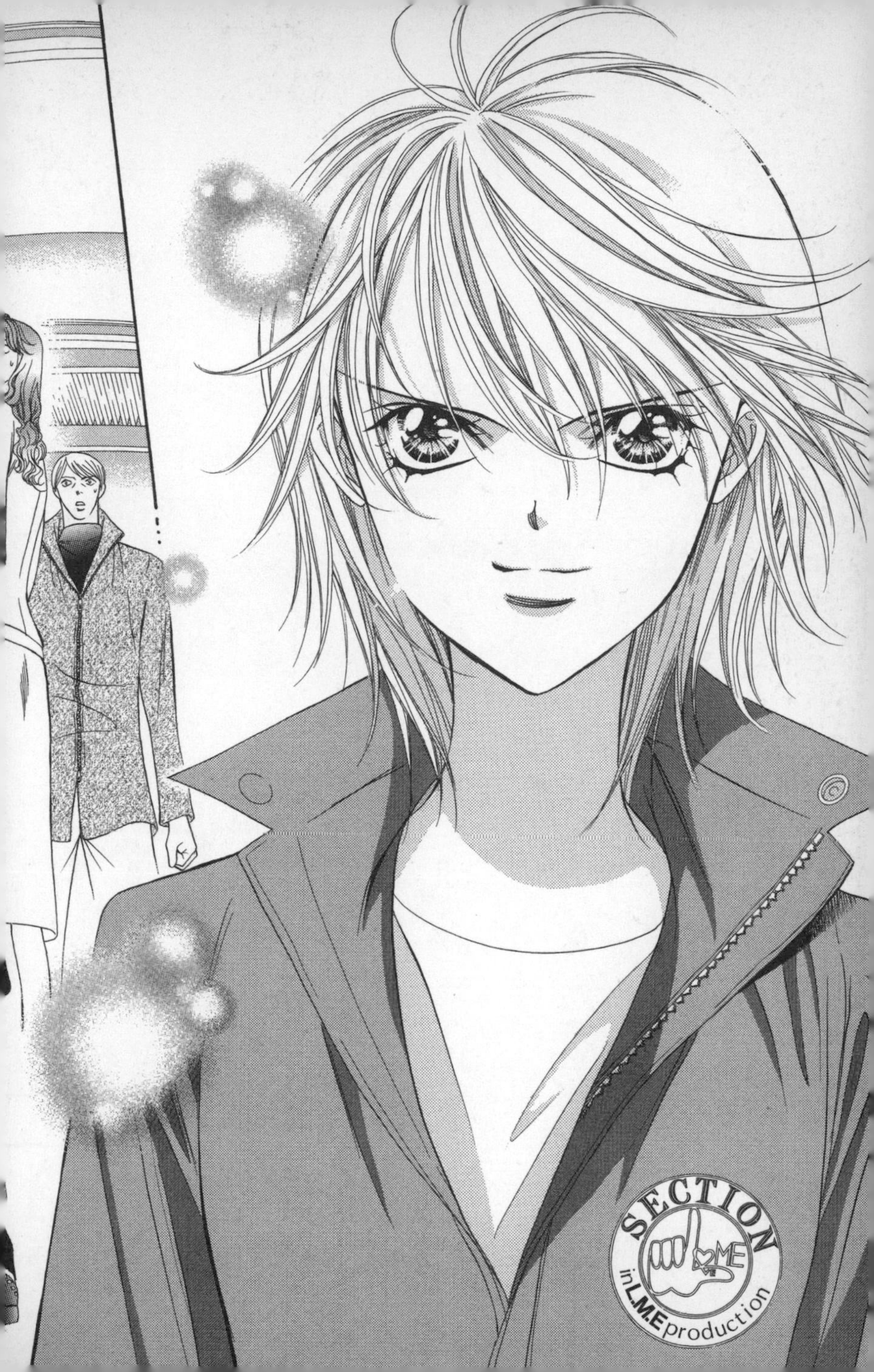
...
SECTION
LME
in L.M.E production

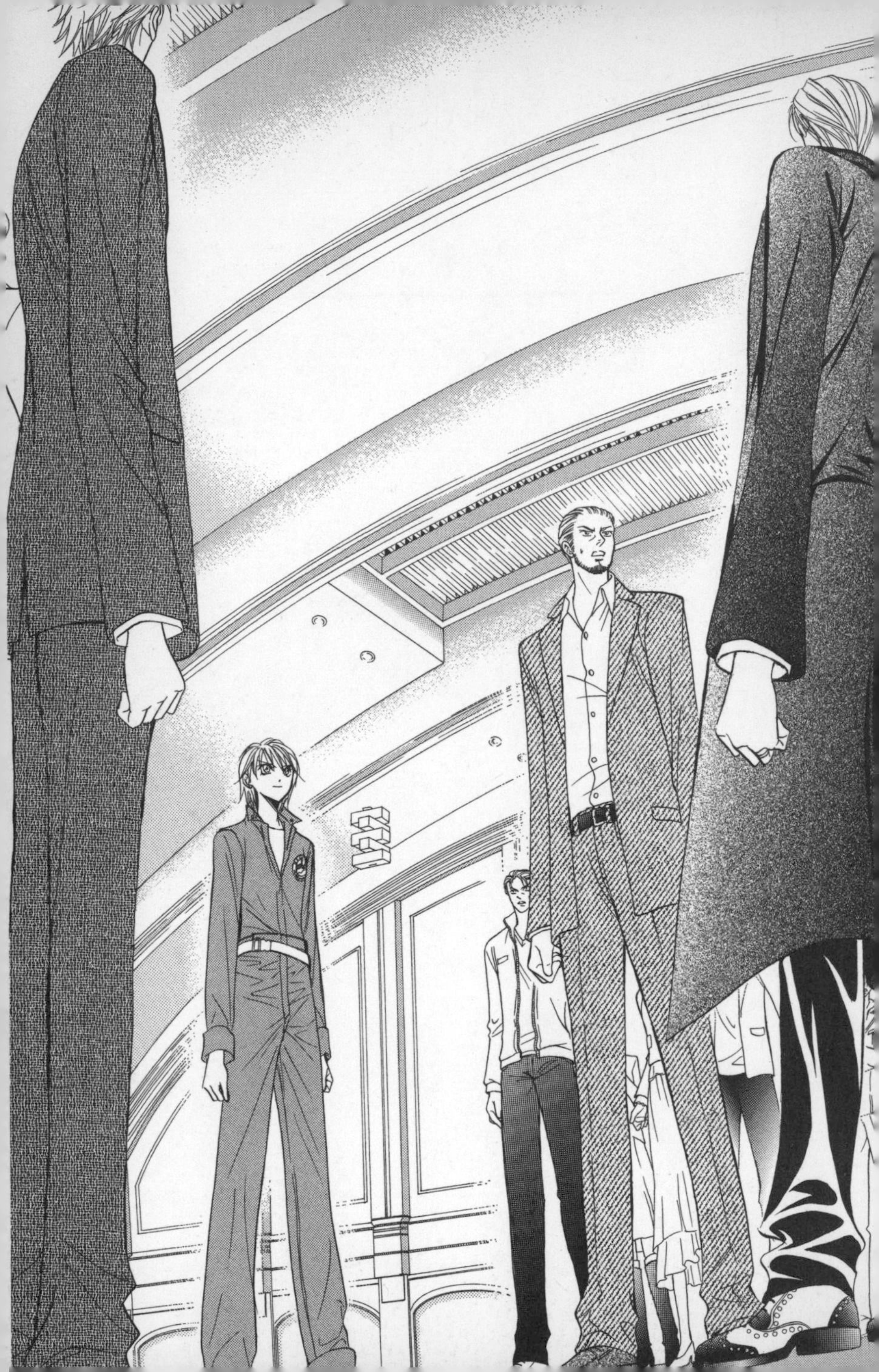

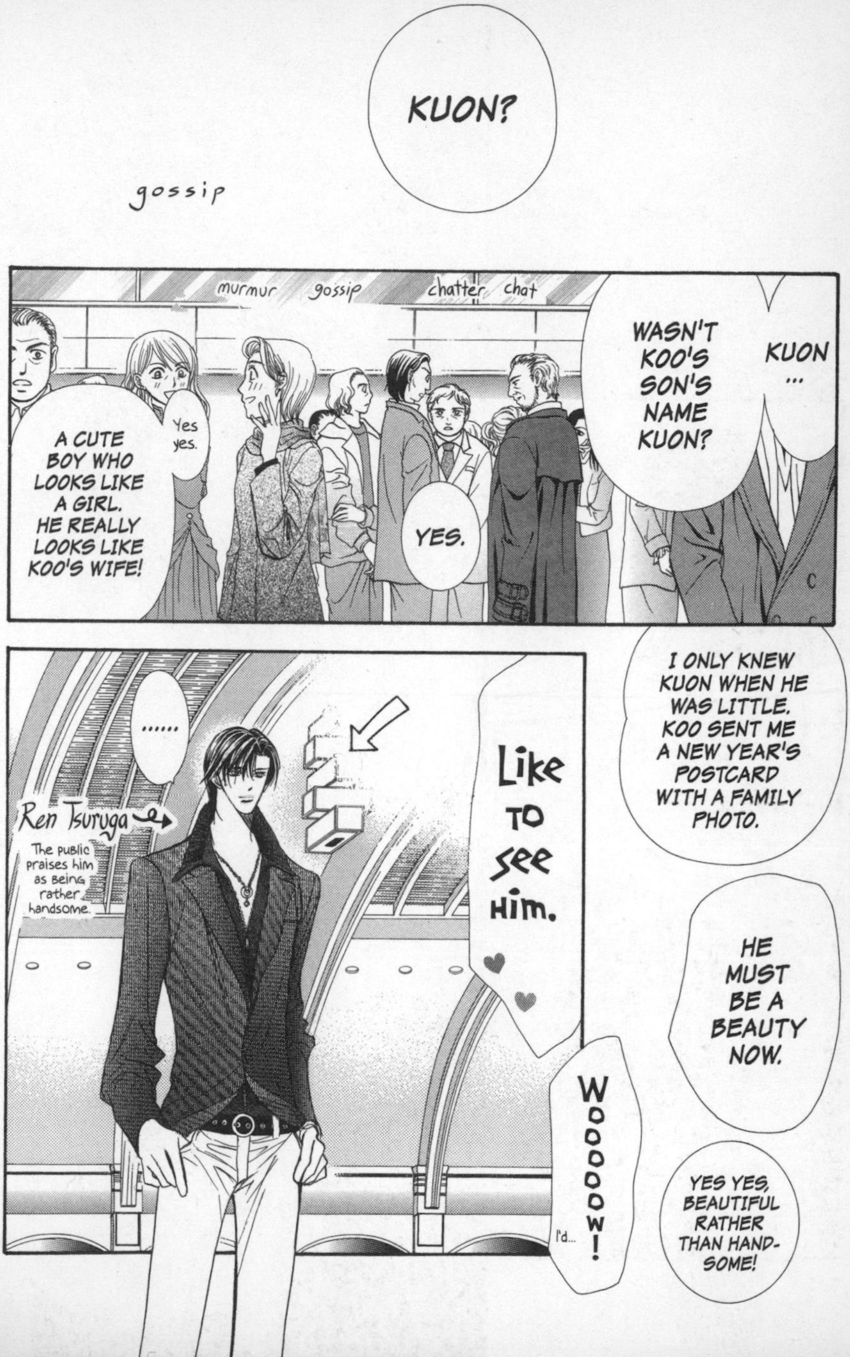
KUON?
gossip
KUON ...
WASN'T KOO'S SON'S NAME KUON?
chatter chat
murmur gossip
YES.
Yes yes.
A CUTE BOY WHO LOOKS LIKE A GIRL. HE REALLY LOOKS LIKE KOO'S WIFE!
I ONLY KNEW KUON WHEN HE WAS LITTLE. KOO SENT ME A NEW YEAR'S POSTCARD WITH A FAMILY PHOTO.
HE MUST BE A BEAUTY NOW.
YES YES, BEAUTIFUL RATHER THAN HAND-SOME!
Like to see him.
WOOOOOOW!
I'd...
......
Ren Tsuruga
The public praises him as being rather handsome.

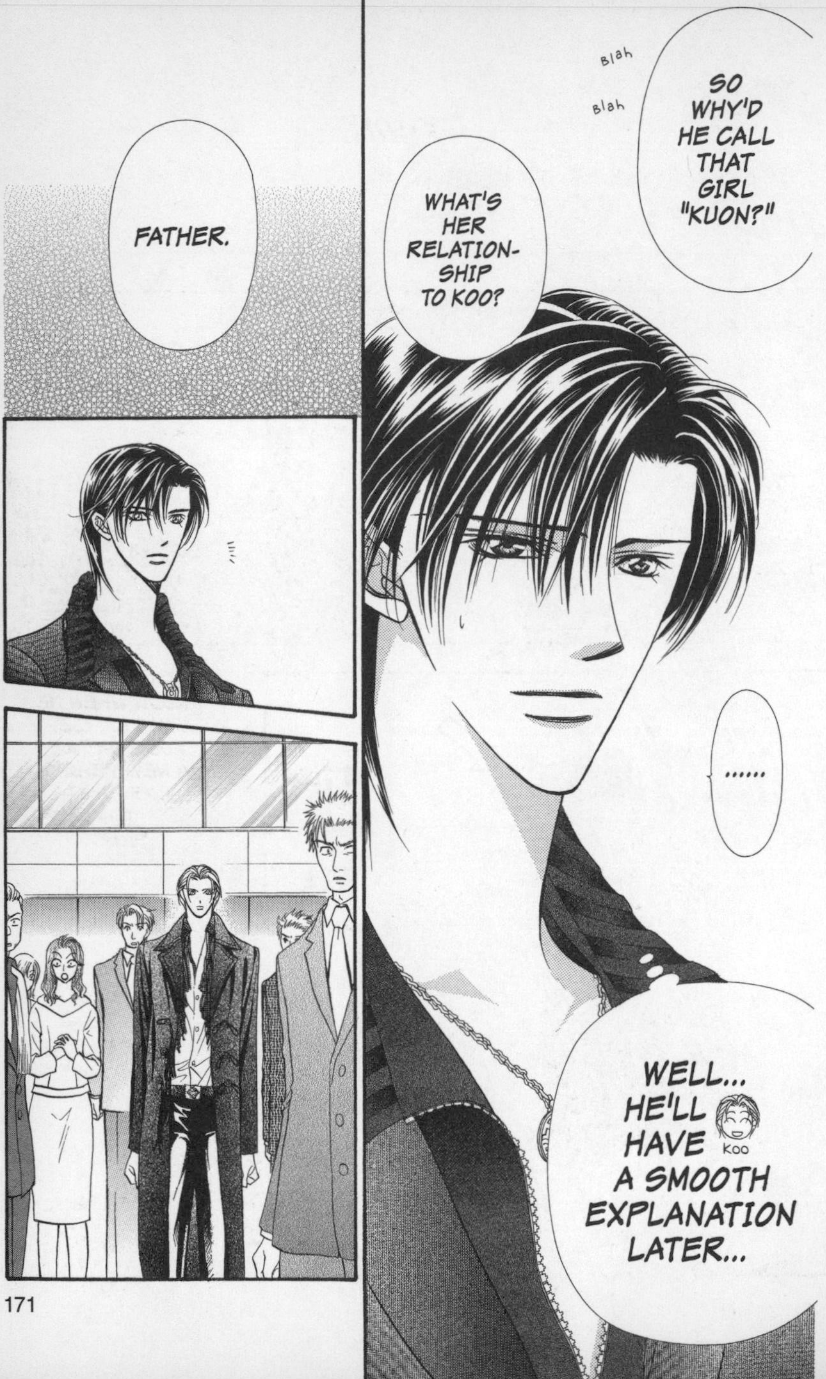
Blah
Blah
SO WHY'D HE CALL THAT GIRL "KUON?"
WHAT'S HER RELATION-SHIP TO KOO?
......
WELL... HE'LL HAVE A SMOOTH EXPLANATION LATER...
KOO
FATHER.

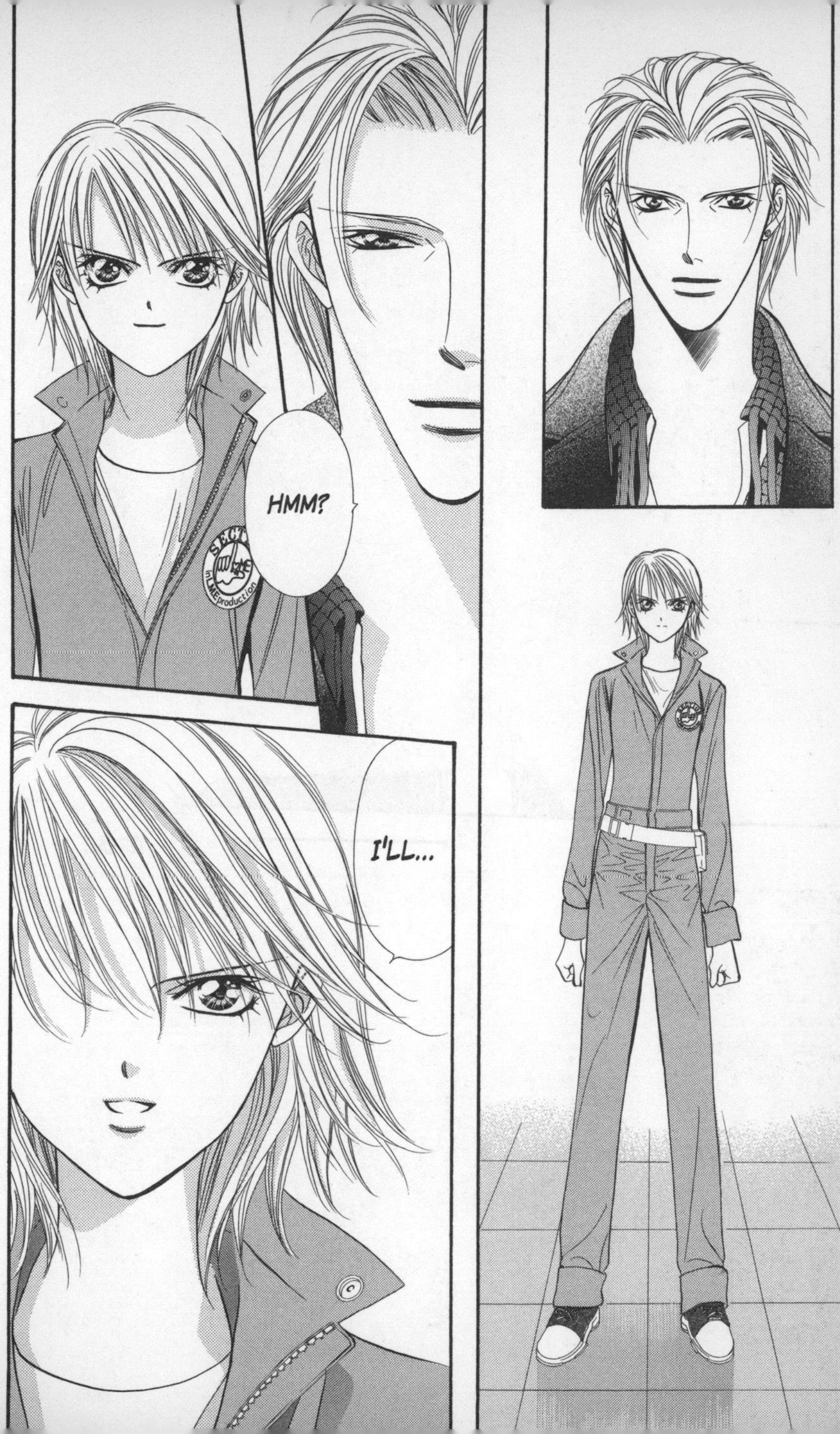
HMM?
I'LL...

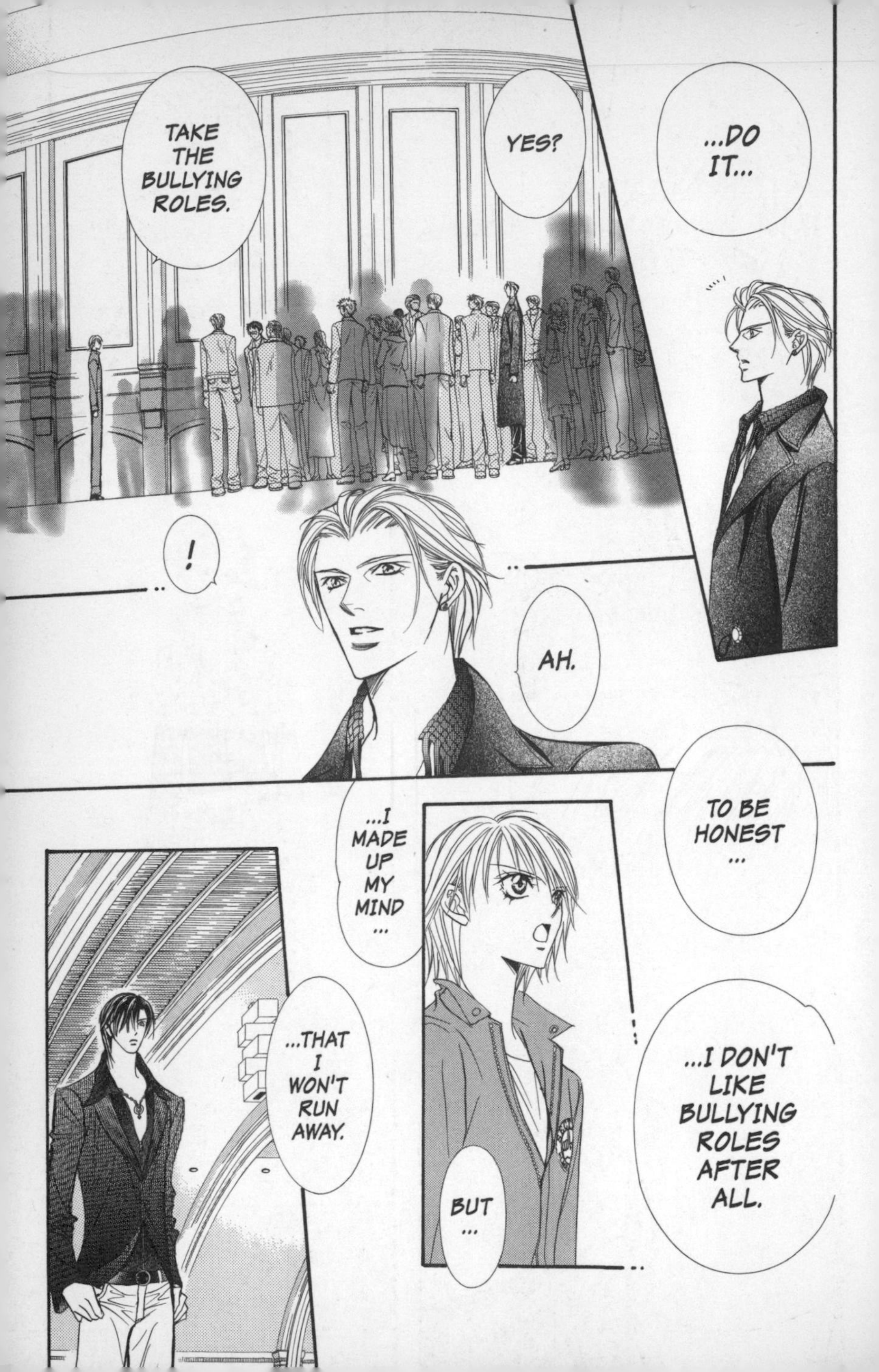
...DO IT...
YES?
TAKE THE BULLYING ROLES.
!
AH.
TO BE HONEST ...
...I DON'T LIKE BULLYING ROLES AFTER ALL.
BUT ...
...I MADE UP MY MIND ...
...THAT I WON'T RUN AWAY.

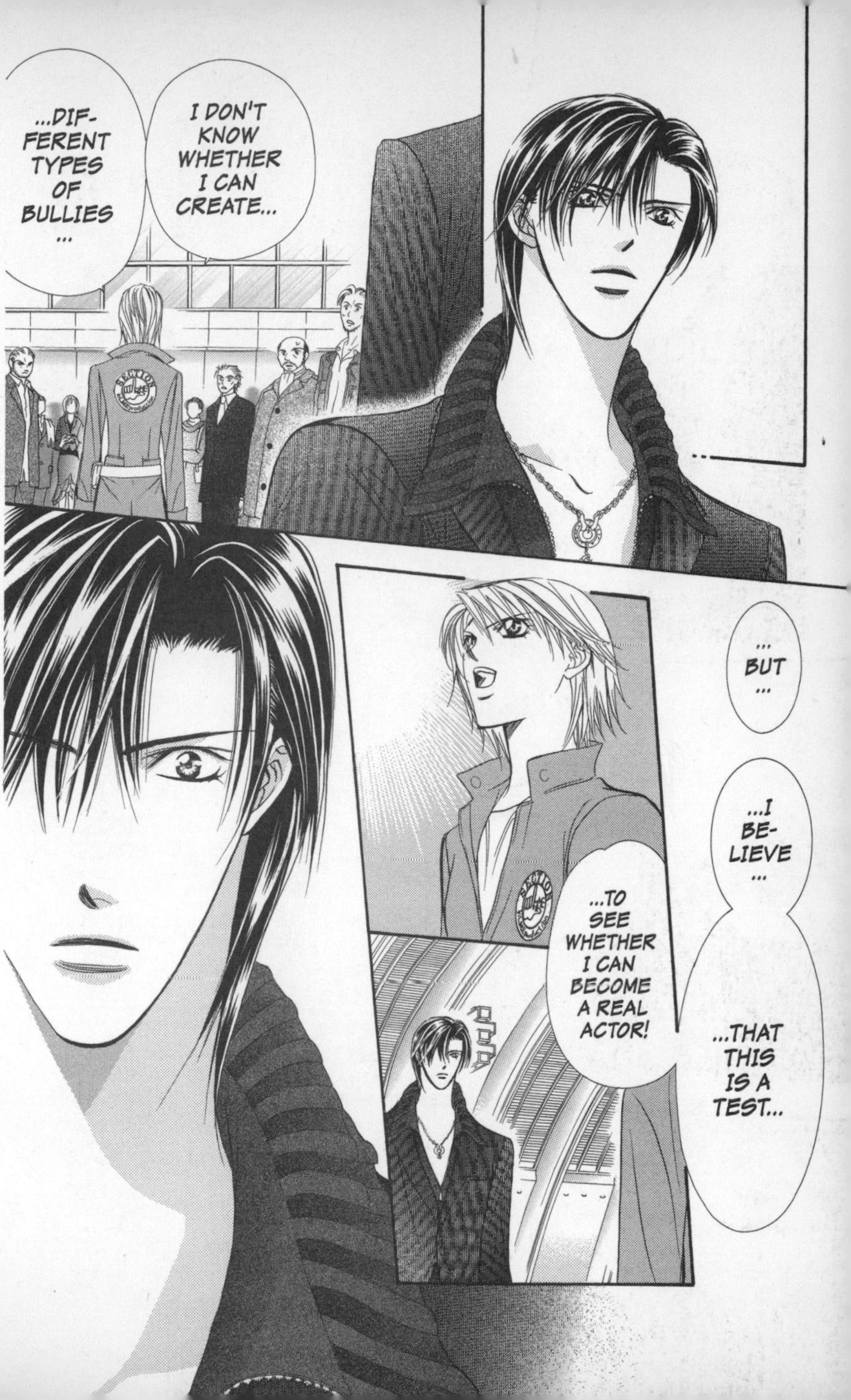
I DON'T KNOW WHETHER I CAN CREATE...
...DIF- FERENT TYPES OF BULLIES ...
... BUT ...
...I BE- LIEVE ...
...THAT THIS IS A TEST...
...TO SEE WHETHER I CAN BECOME A REAL ACTOR!

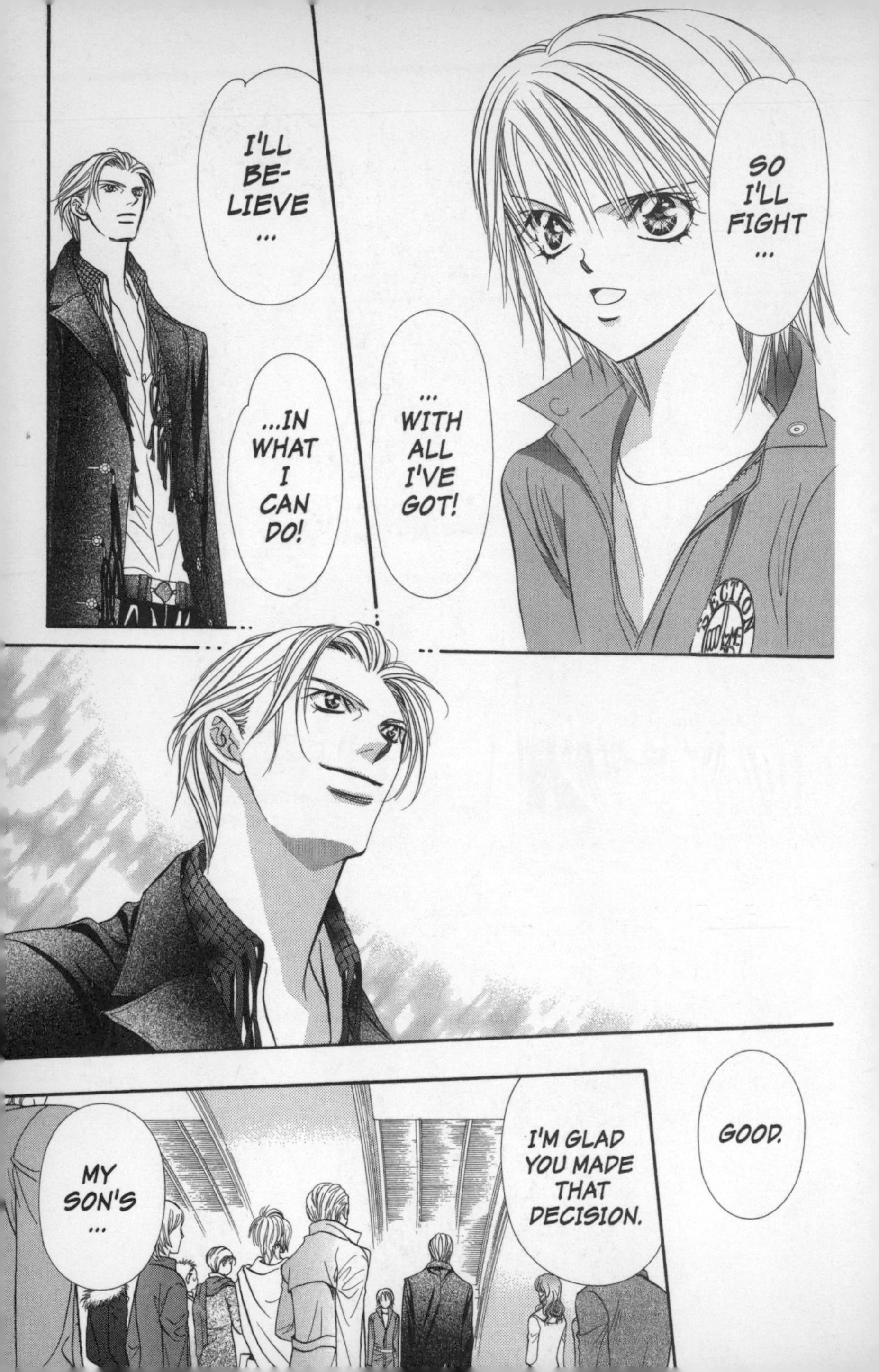
SO I'LL FIGHT ...
... WITH ALL I'VE GOT!
I'LL BE-LIEVE ...
...IN WHAT I CAN DO!
GOOD.
I'M GLAD YOU MADE THAT DECISION.
MY SON'S ...

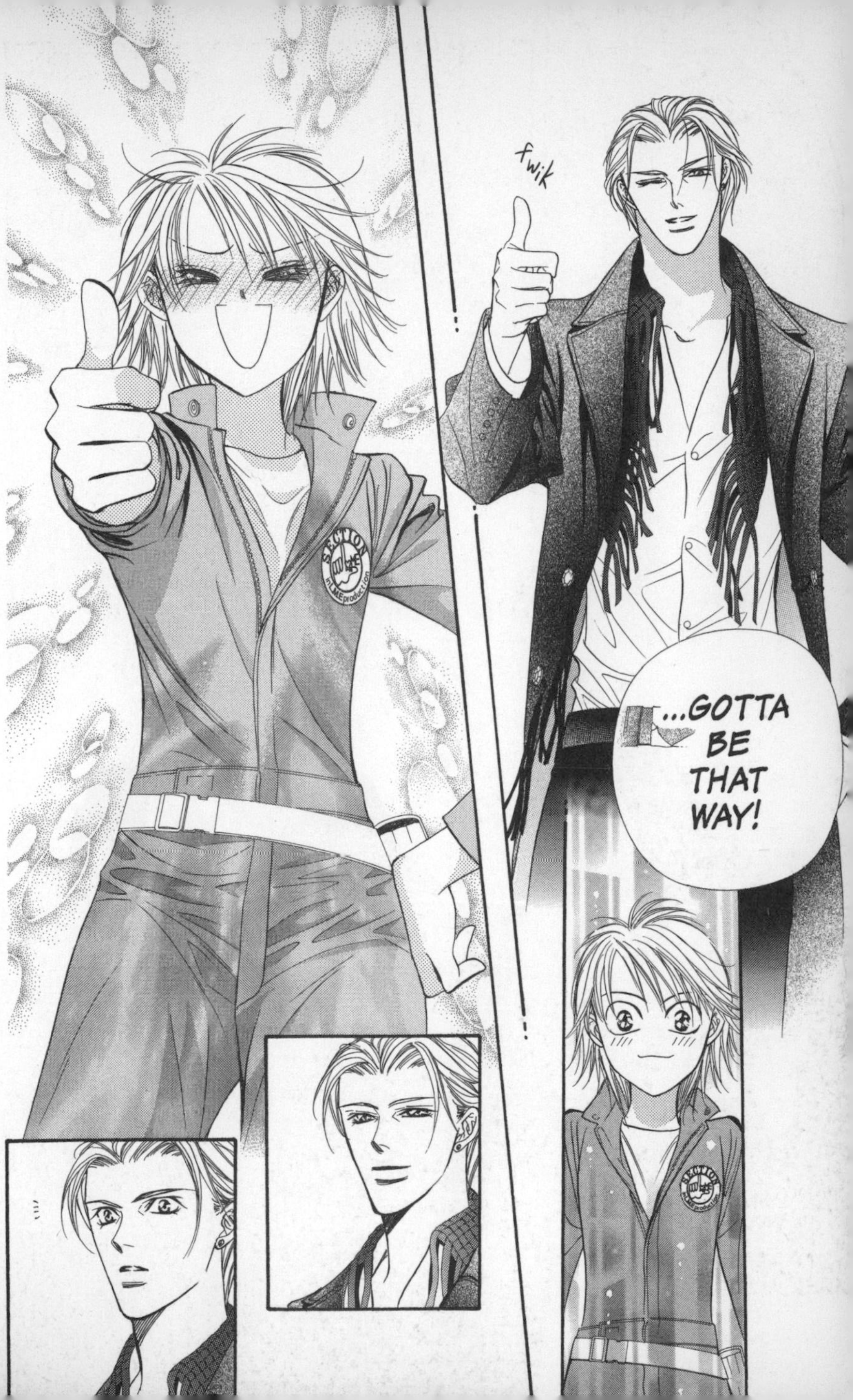
fwik
...GOTTA BE THAT WAY!

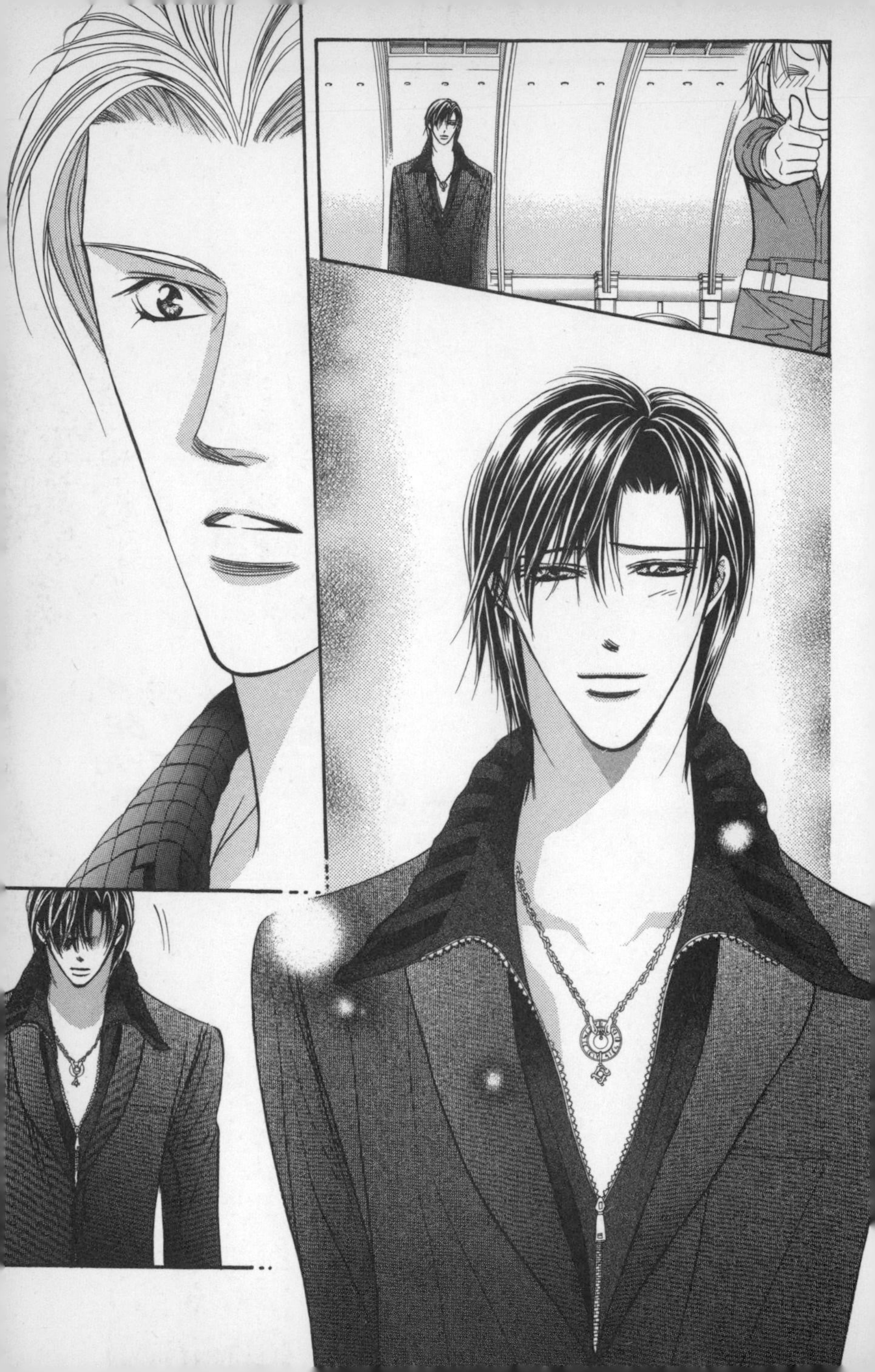

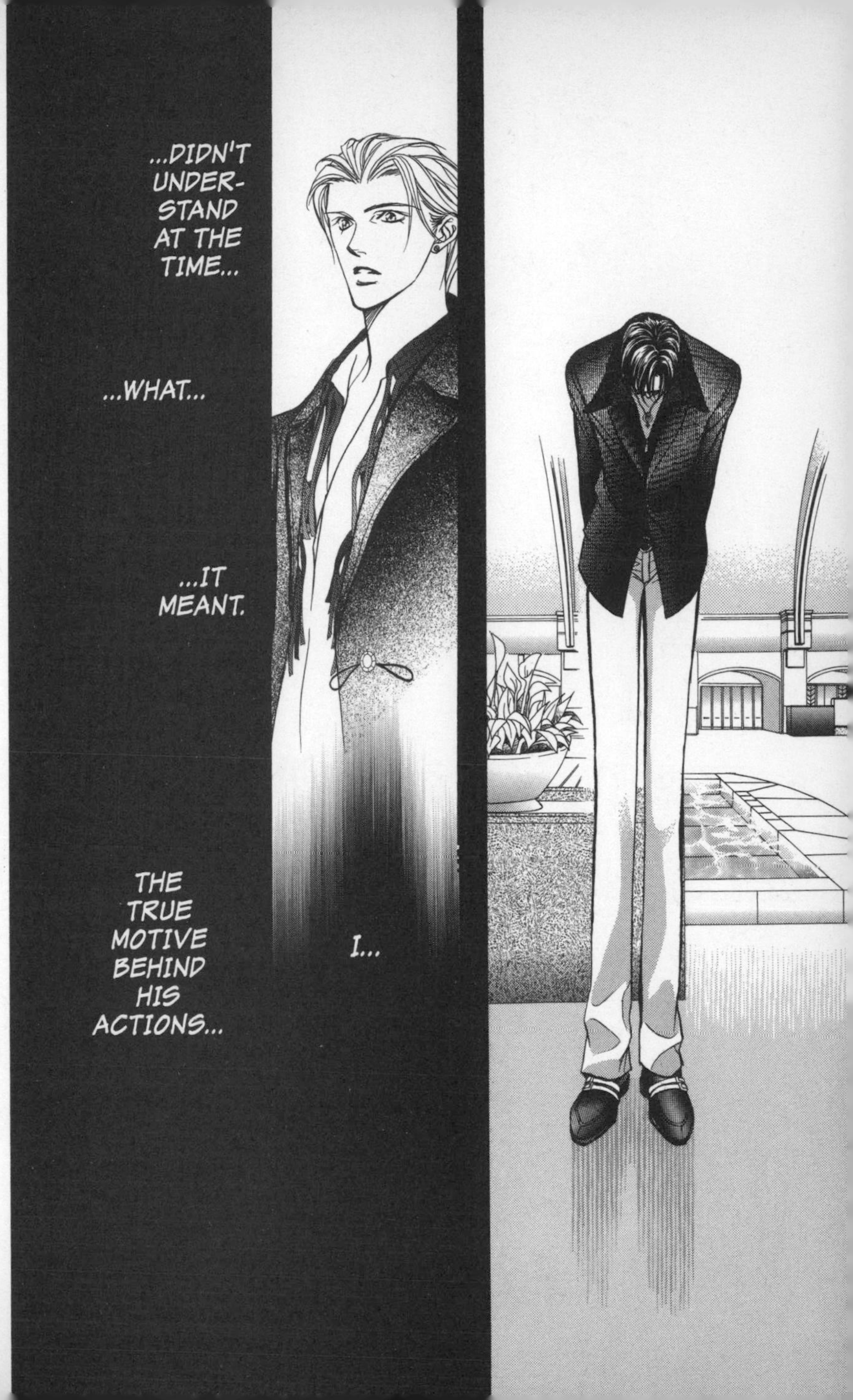
THE TRUE MOTIVE BEHIND HIS ACTIONS...
I...
...DIDN'T UNDERSTAND AT THE TIME...
...WHAT...
...IT MEANT.

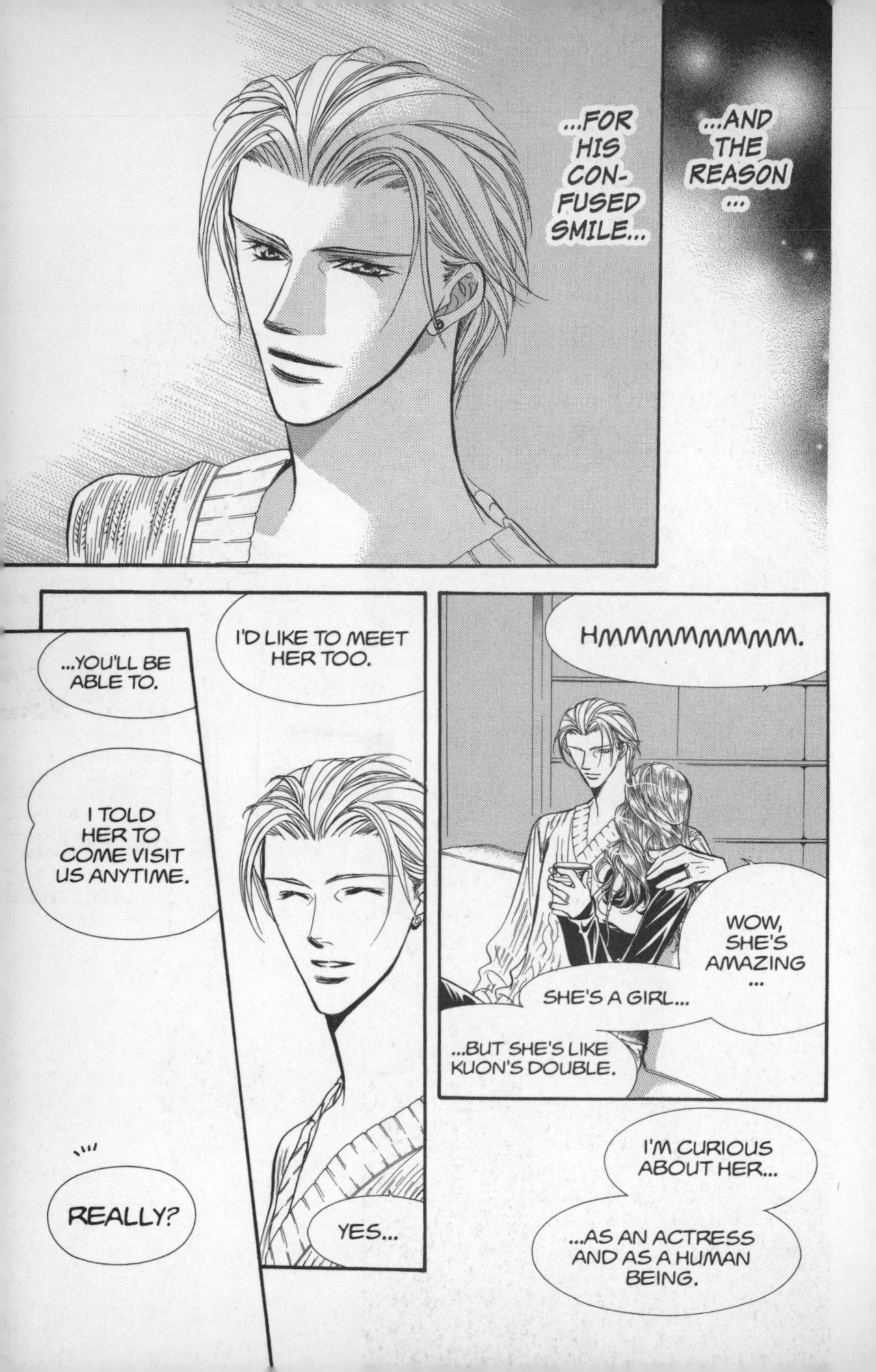
...AND THE REASON ...
...FOR HIS CON-FUSED SMILE...
HMMMMMMMM.
WOW, SHE'S AMAZING ...
SHE'S A GIRL...
...BUT SHE'S LIKE KUON'S DOUBLE.
I'D LIKE TO MEET HER TOO.
...YOU'LL BE ABLE TO.
I TOLD HER TO COME VISIT US ANYTIME.
I'M CURIOUS ABOUT HER...
...AS AN ACTRESS AND AS A HUMAN BEING.
YES...
REALLY?

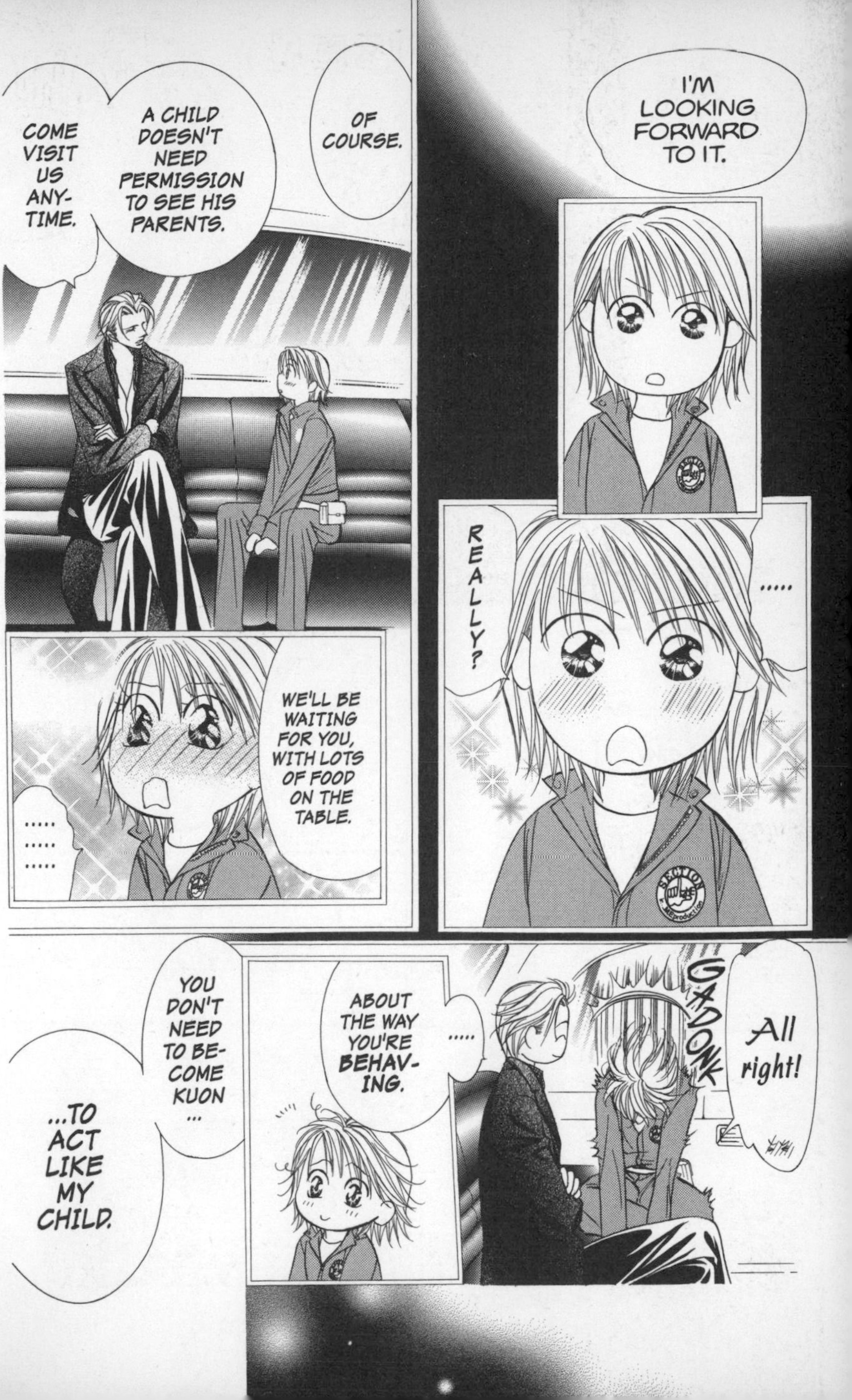
I'M LOOKING FORWARD TO IT.
REALLY?
.....
OF COURSE.
A CHILD DOESN'T NEED PERMISSION TO SEE HIS PARENTS.
COME VISIT US ANY-TIME.
WE'LL BE WAITING FOR YOU, WITH LOTS OF FOOD ON THE TABLE.
..... ..... .....
All right!
GADONK
.....
ABOUT THE WAY YOU'RE BEHAV-ING.
YOU DON'T NEED TO BE-COME KUON ...
...TO ACT LIKE MY CHILD.

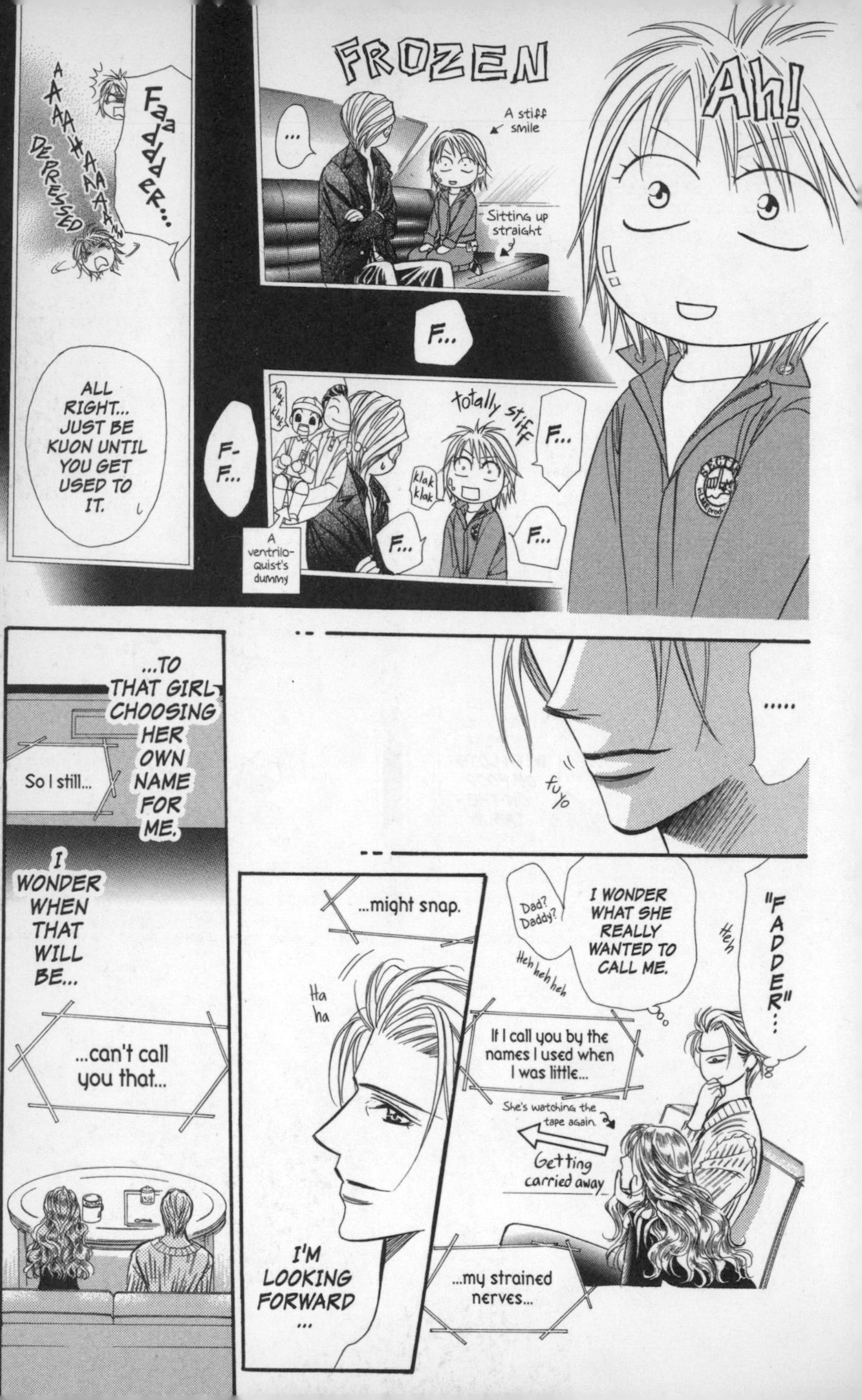
Ah!
F...
FROZEN
...
A stiff smile
Sitting up straight
totally stiff
F...
F...
klak klak
F...
F-F...
klak klak
A ventriloquist's dummy
Faaadder...
AAAAHAAAAAAnn
DEPRESSED
ALL RIGHT... JUST BE KUON UNTIL YOU GET USED TO IT.
.....
fuyo
"FADDER"...
Heh
I WONDER WHAT SHE REALLY WANTED TO CALL ME.
Dad? Daddy?
Heh heh heh heh
If I call you by the names I used when I was little...
She's watching the tape again.
Getting carried away
...my strained nerves...
...might snap.
Ha ha
I'M LOOKING FORWARD...
...TO THAT GIRL CHOOSING HER OWN NAME FOR ME.
So I still...
I WONDER WHEN THAT WILL BE...
...can't call you that...

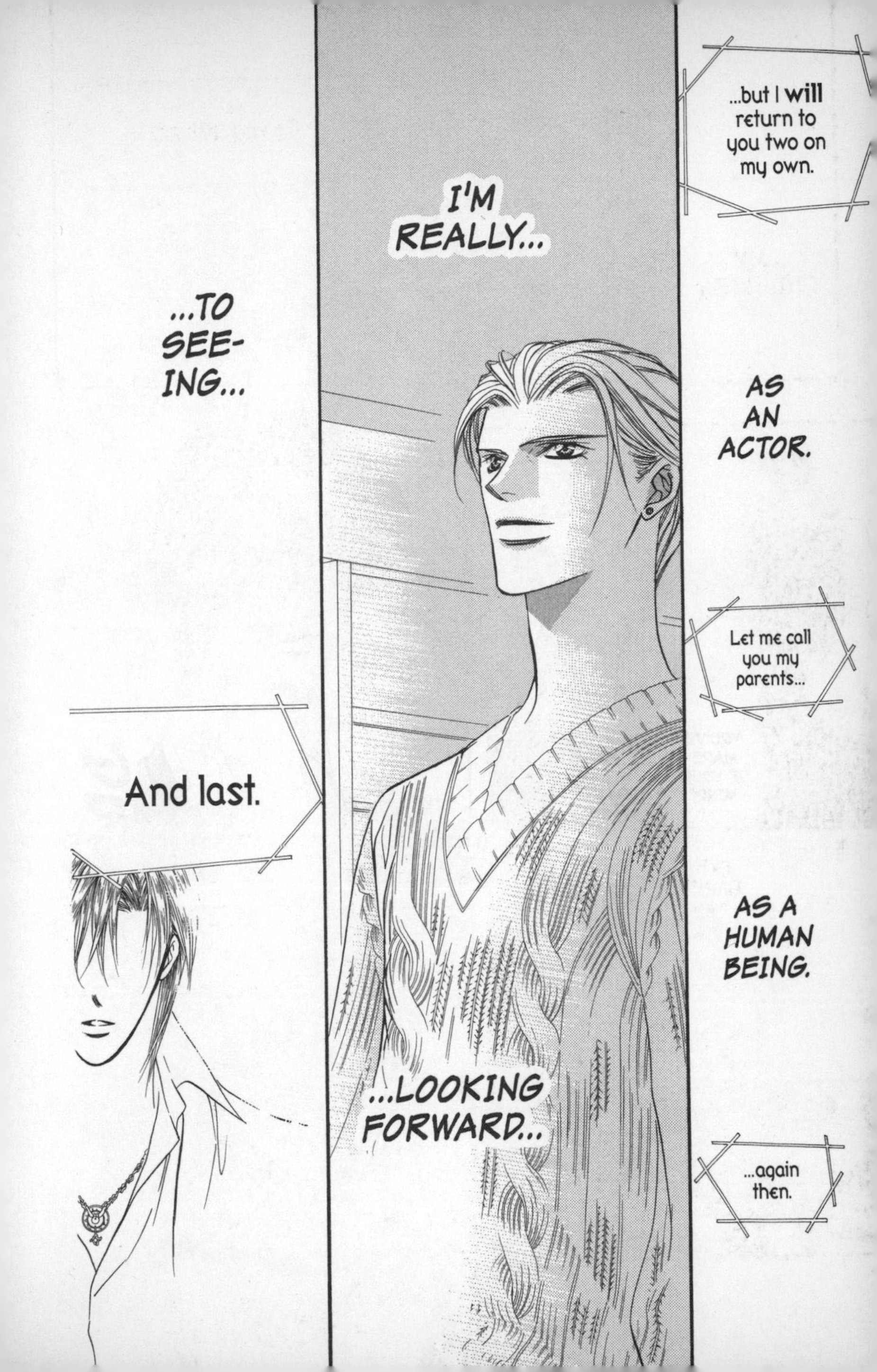
...but I **will** return to you two on my own.
AS AN ACTOR.
Let me call you my parents...
AS A HUMAN BEING.
...again then.
I'M REALLY...
...LOOKING FORWARD...
...TO SEE- ING...
And last.

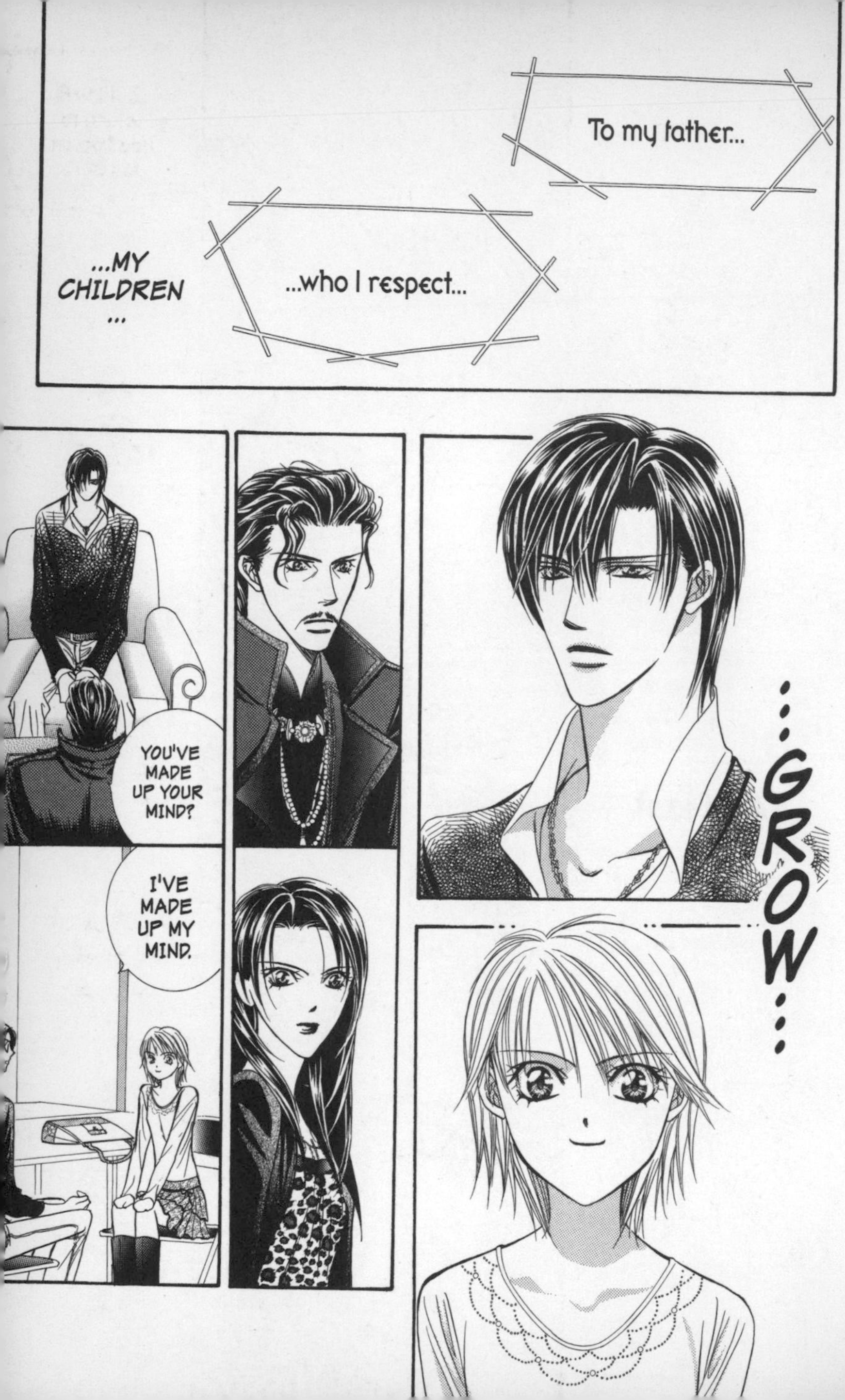
To my father...
...who I respect...
...MY CHILDREN ...
...GROW...
YOU'VE MADE UP YOUR MIND?
I'VE MADE UP MY MIND.

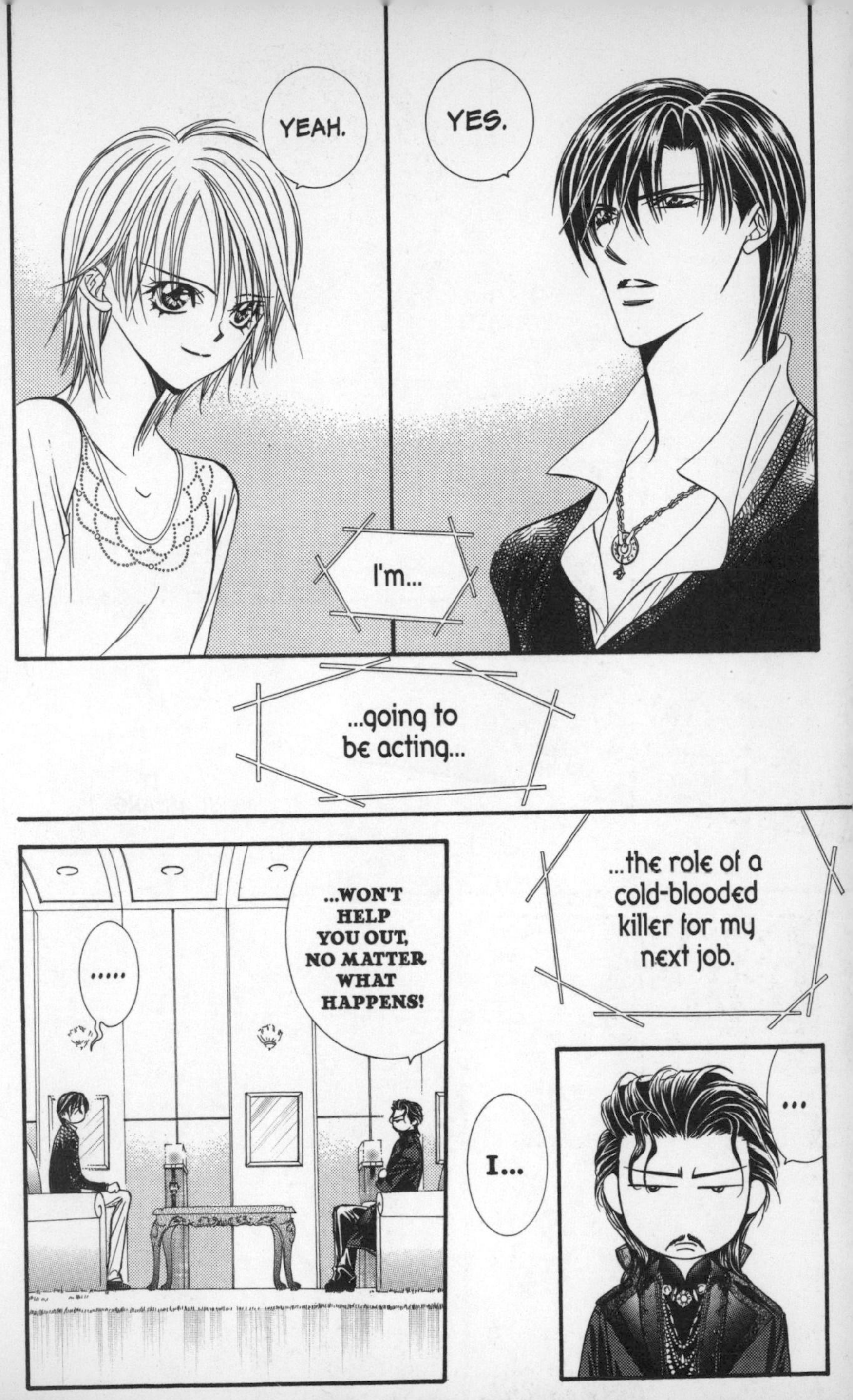
YES.
YEAH.
I'm...
...going to be acting...
...the role of a cold-blooded killer for my next job.
...
I...
...WON'T HELP YOU OUT, NO MATTER WHAT HAPPENS!
......

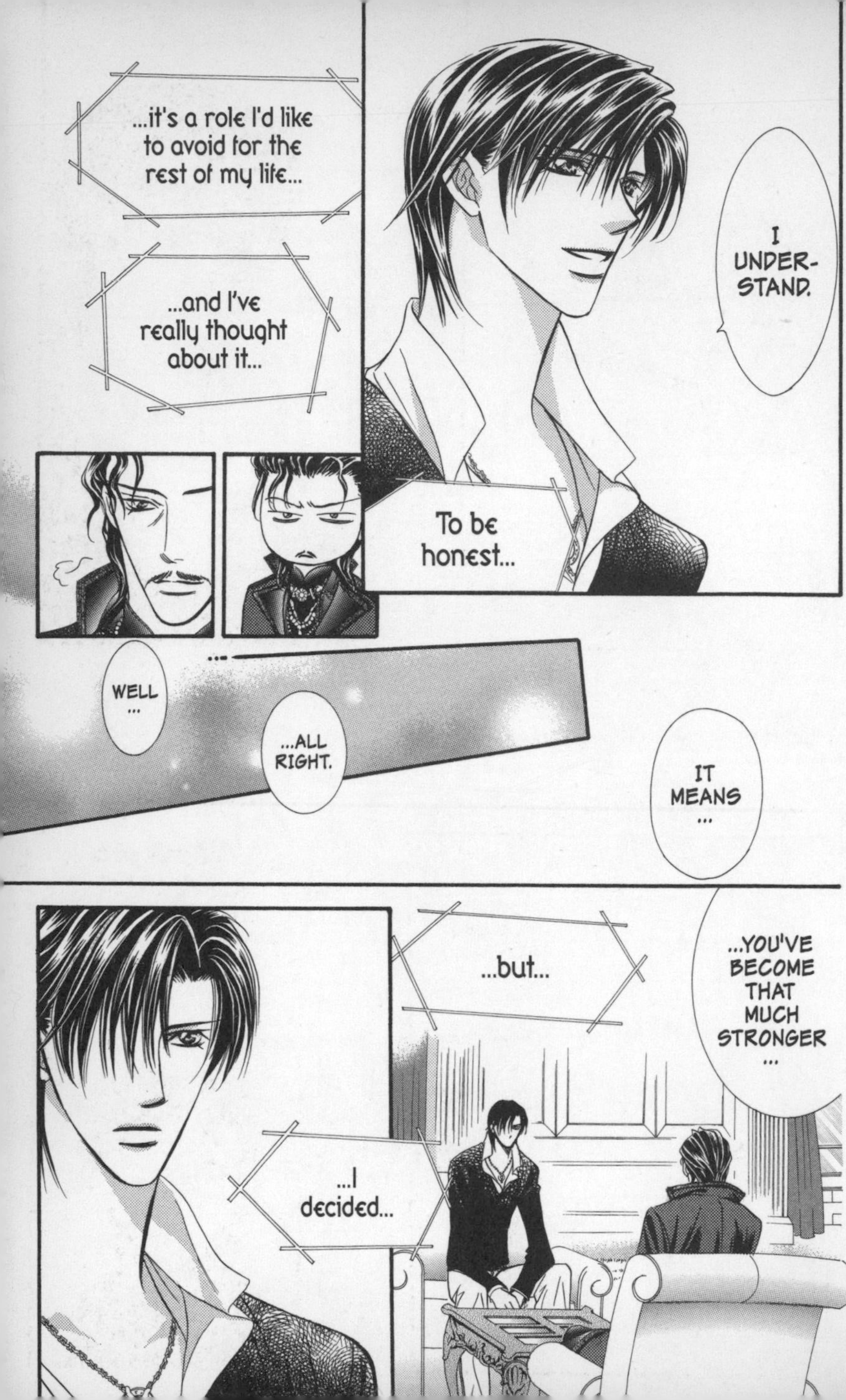
I UNDERSTAND.
To be honest...
...it's a role I'd like to avoid for the rest of my life...
...and I've really thought about it...
...
WELL...
...ALL RIGHT.
IT MEANS...
...YOU'VE BECOME THAT MUCH STRONGER...
...but...
...I decided...

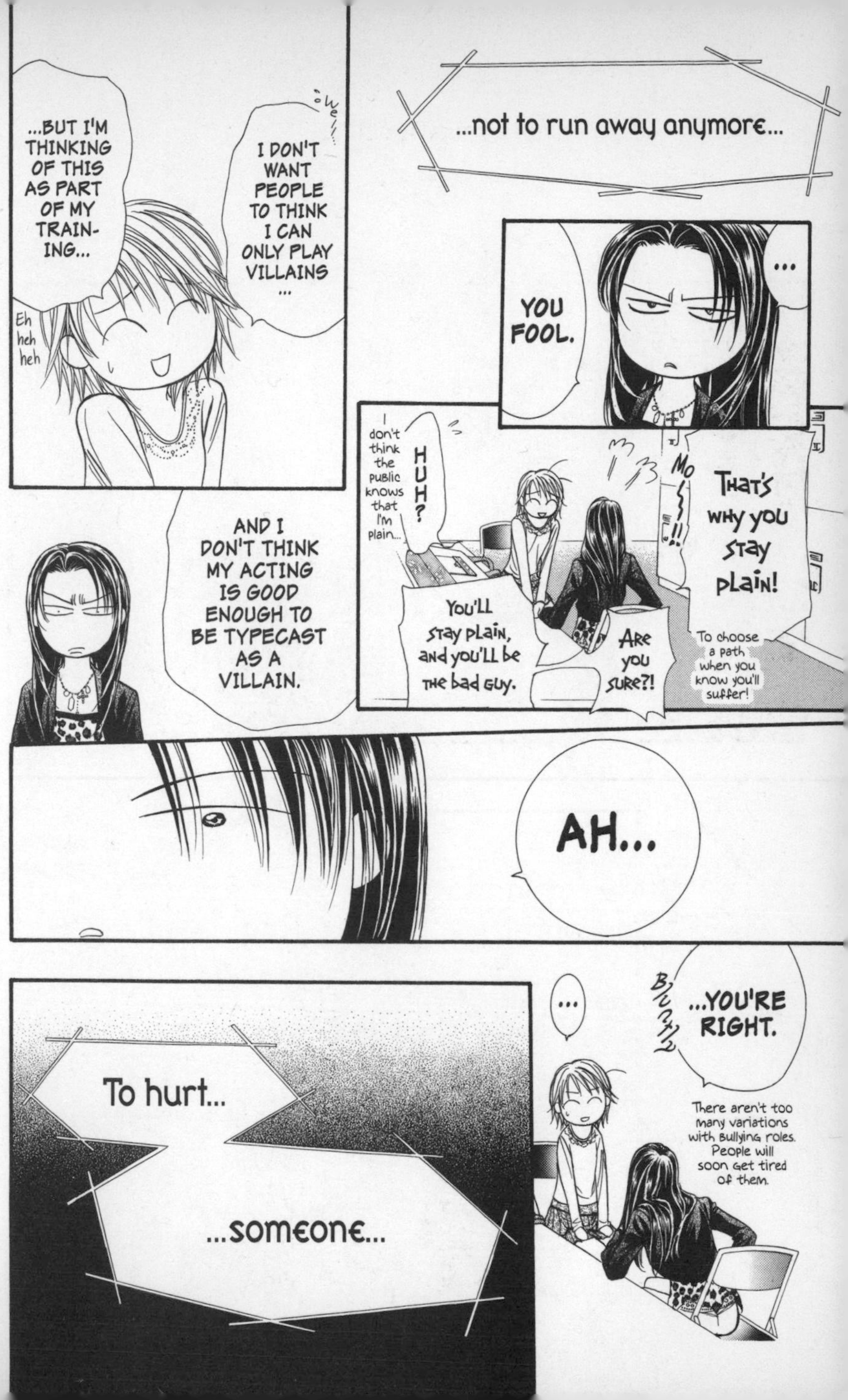
...not to run away anymore...
Well...
I DON'T WANT PEOPLE TO THINK I CAN ONLY PLAY VILLAINS...
...BUT I'M THINKING OF THIS AS PART OF MY TRAINING...
Eh heh heh
...
YOU FOOL.
THAT'S WHY YOU STAY PLAIN!
MO!!
HUH?
I don't think the public knows that I'm plain...
To choose a path when you know you'll suffer!
Are you sure?!
You'll stay plain, and you'll be the bad guy.
AND I DON'T THINK MY ACTING IS GOOD ENOUGH TO BE TYPECAST AS A VILLAIN.
AH...
...YOU'RE RIGHT.
...
There aren't too many variations with bullying roles. People will soon get tired of them.
To hurt...
...someone...

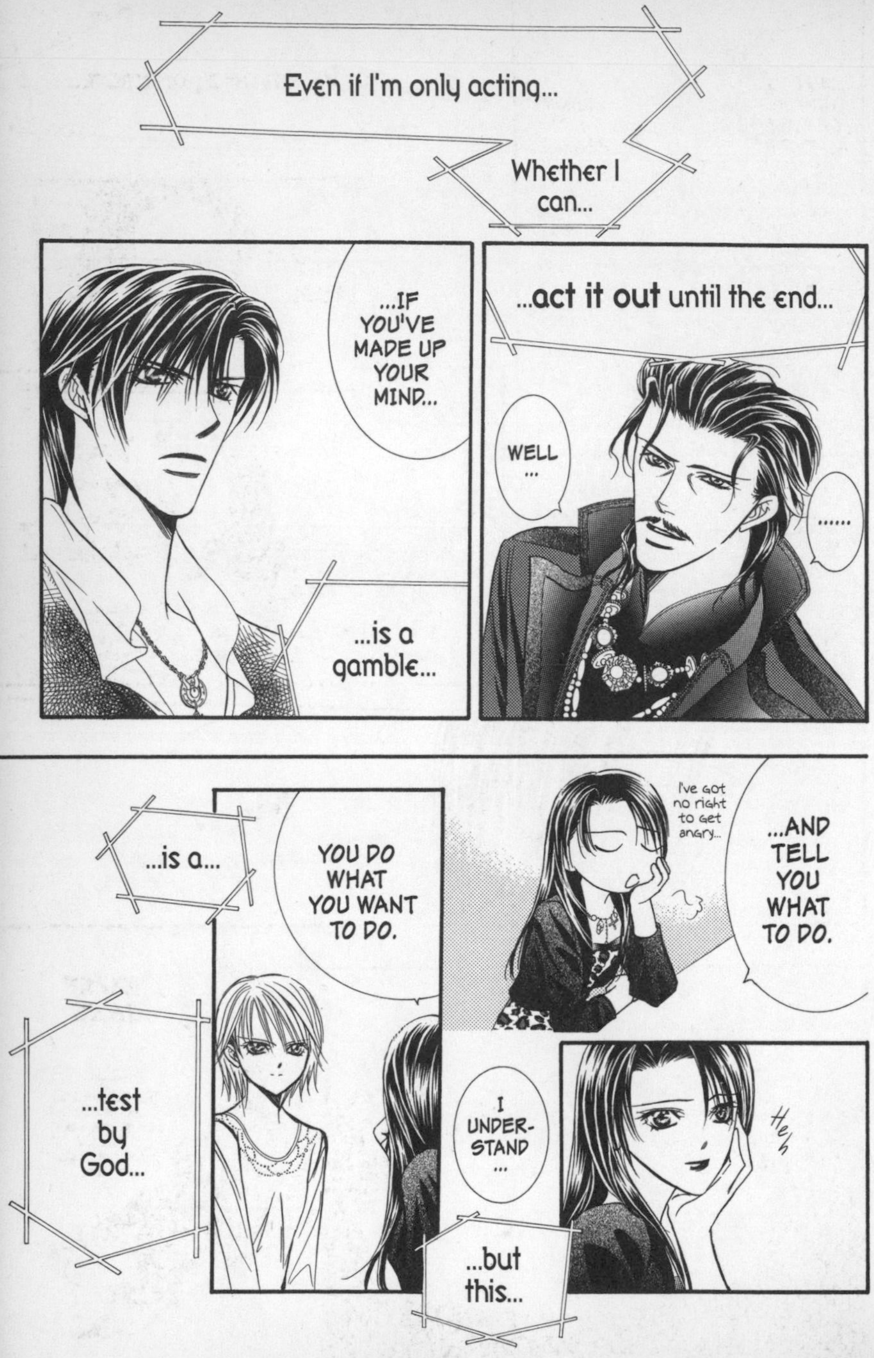
Even if I'm only acting...
Whether I can...
...act it out until the end...
WELL...
......
...IF YOU'VE MADE UP YOUR MIND...
...is a gamble...
I've got no right to get angry...
...AND TELL YOU WHAT TO DO.
I UNDER-STAND...
Heh
...but this...
...is a...
YOU DO WHAT YOU WANT TO DO.
...test by God...

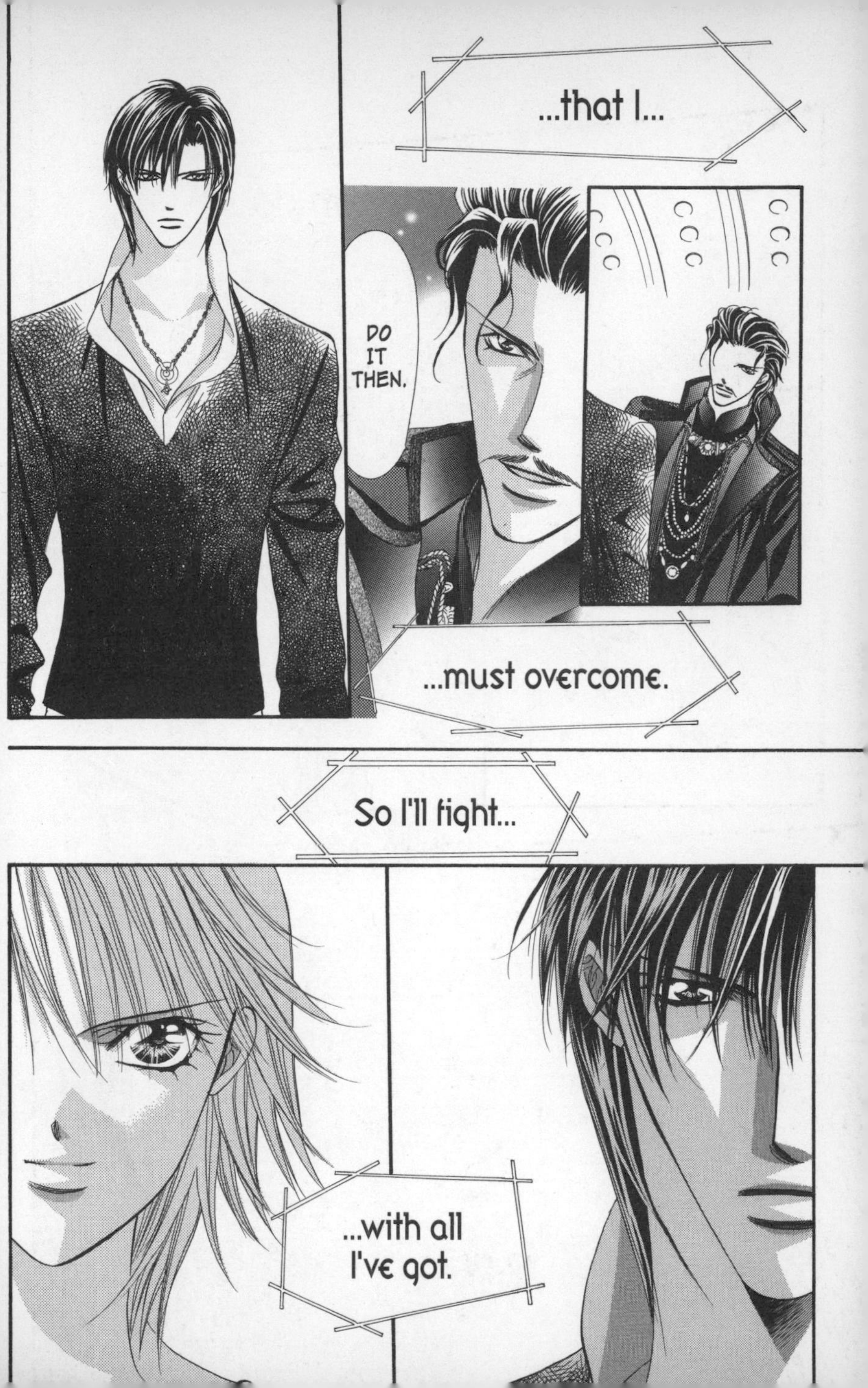
...that I...
DO IT THEN.
...must overcome.
So I'll fight...
...with all I've got.

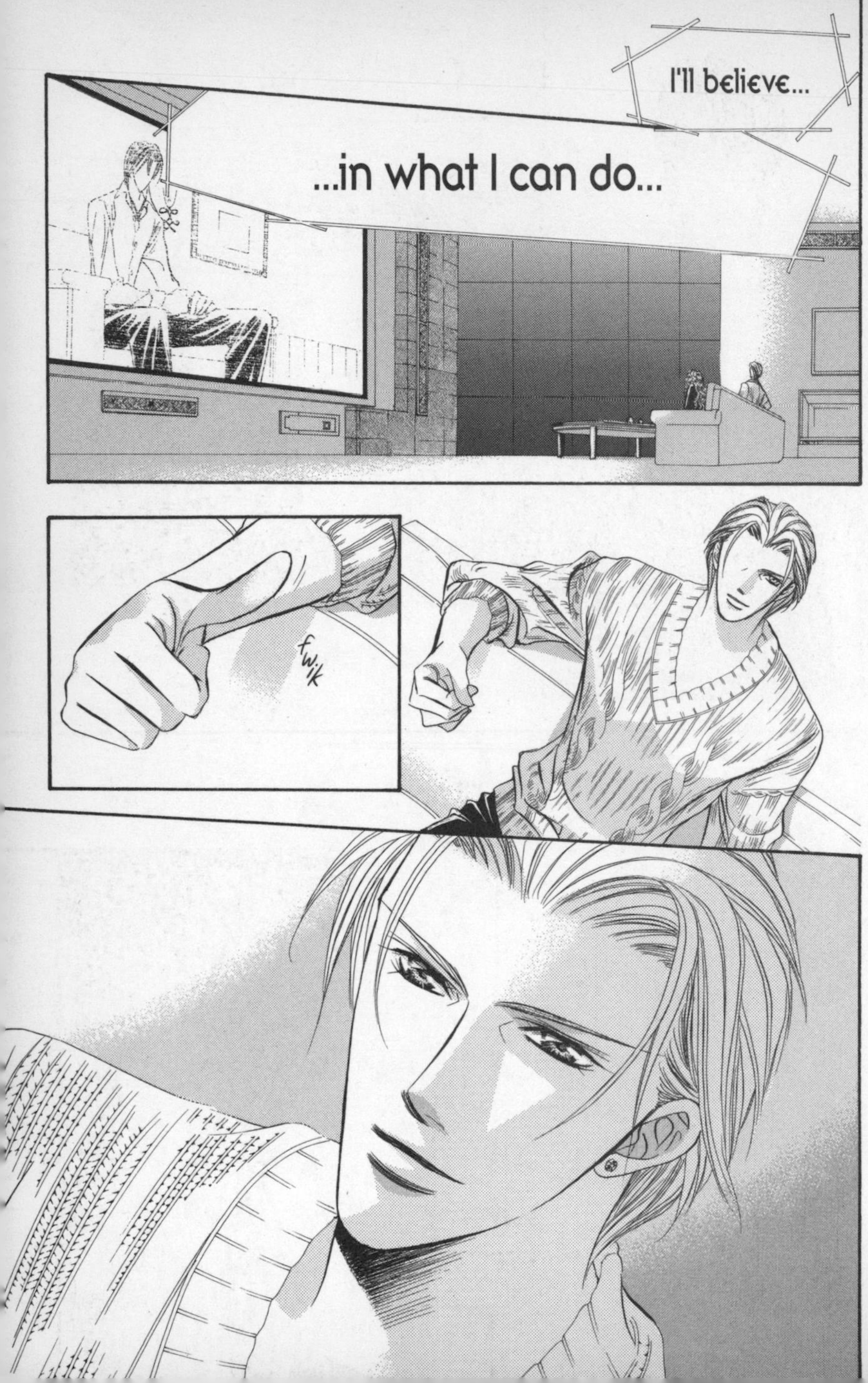
I'll believe...
...in what I can do...
fwik

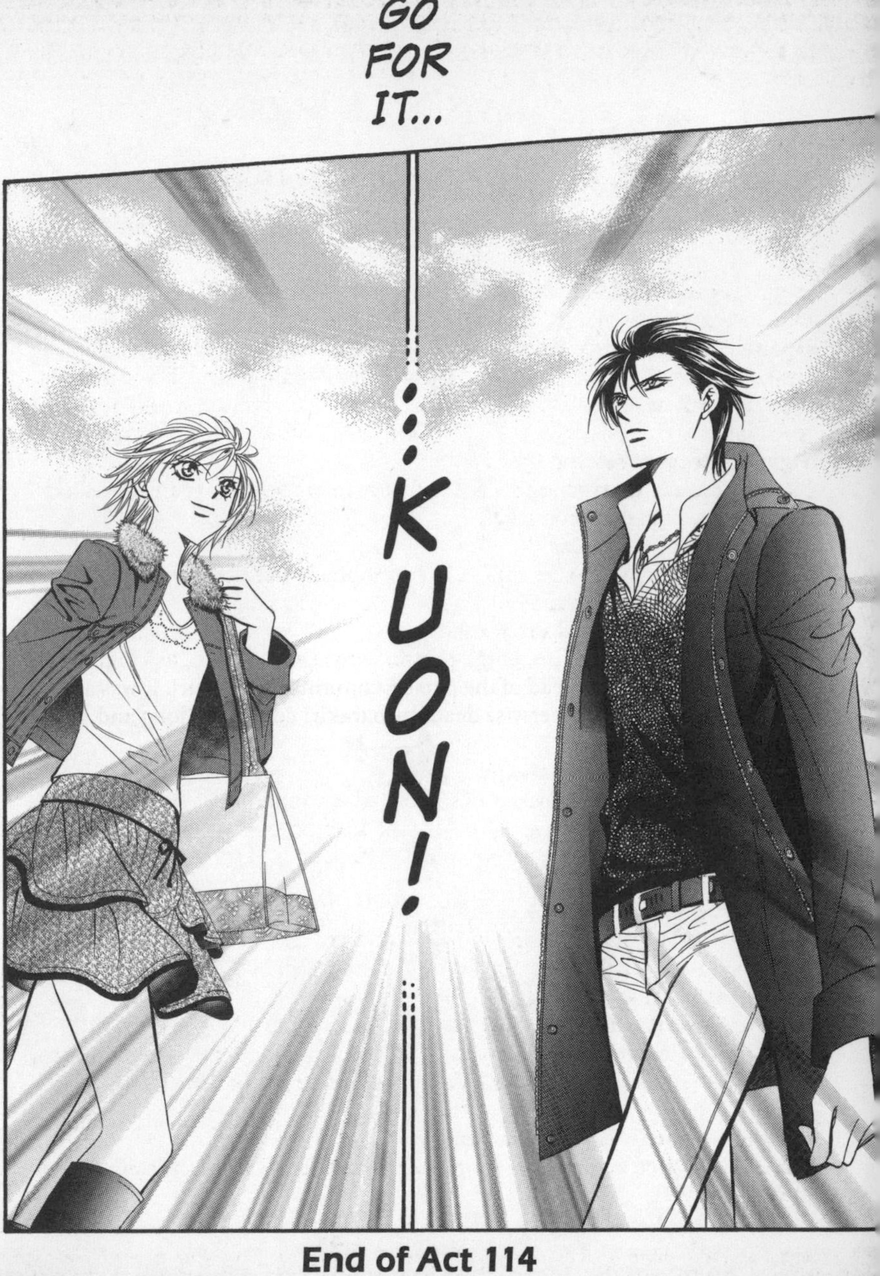
GO FOR IT...
...KUON!

End of Act 114

# Skip·Beat! End Notes

Everyone knows how to be a fan, but sometimes cool things
from other cultures need a little help crossing the language barrier.

**Page 21, panel 3: Daikon actor**
One meaning is similar to that of the phrase "ham actor" in English. In
Japanese, the word used for an actor's success and the way bad food affects
your system is the same—*ataru* or "shock." But daikon is considered a safe
food that will never make you sick, and likewise a daikon actor will never
gain success.

**Page 74, panel 3: Kaki no tane**
Literally means "persimmon seeds," and here refers to spicy orange crackers
in the shape of persimmon seeds.

**Page 93, panel 4: Harakiri**
Ritual suicide by slitting the stomach. Traditionally used by samurai to regain
honor in the face of defeat or after some disgrace. It is also known as *seppuku*.

**Page 93, panel 4: Second for harakiri**
The Japanese is *kaishakunin*, or the person who administered the coup d'
grace by cutting off the head of the person committing harakiri. It was a
trusted position, since otherwise death by harakiri could be a long and
painful affair.

**Page 104, panel 4: Teppanyaki**
Teppanyaki is a type of Japanese cuisine in which ingredients such as meat,
seafood or vegetables are cooked on an iron griddle, and was introduced
sometime around 1945. The word comes from *teppan* (iron plate) and *yaki*
(grilled).

**Page 121, panel 4: Chirashi-zushi**
Sushi rice served with thin strips of egg, pieces of raw fish, vegetables and
other things arranged on top. In the U.S., chirashi-zushi is usually served as a
bowl of rice with sashimi on top.

**Page 153, panel 2: Faddy**
Here Kyoko slips and says *oton*, which is a much more casual way of saying
father. The Kansai dialect is considered more informal than Standard
Japanese.

**Page 153, panel 3: Takoyaki maker**
*Takoyaki* are fried octopus balls, a popular street food that originated
in Osaka.

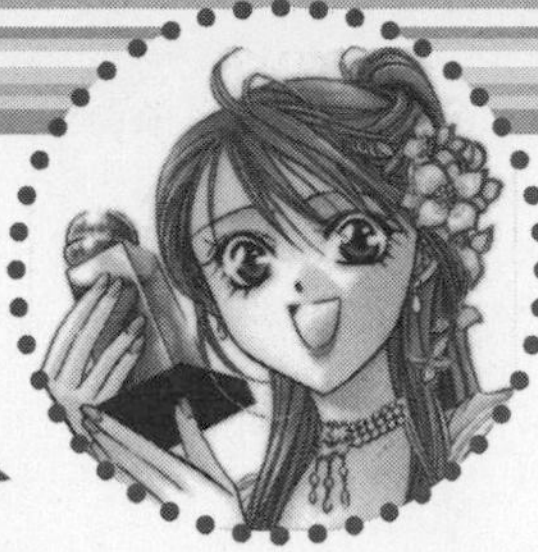

Yoshiki Nakamura is originally from Tokushima prefecture. She started drawing manga in elementary school, which eventually led to her 1993 debut of *Yume de Au yori Suteki* (Better than Seeing in a Dream) in *Hana to Yume* magazine. Her other works include the basketball series *Saint Love, MVP wa Yuzurenai* (Can't Give Up MVP), *Blue Wars* and *Tokyo Crazy Paradise*, a series about a female bodyguard in 2020 Tokyo.

# SKIP·BEAT!
## Vol. 19
### Shojo Beat Manga Edition

## STORY AND ART BY YOSHIKI NAKAMURA

English Translation & Adaptation/Tomo Kimura
Touch-up Art & Lettering/Sabrina Heep
Design/Ronnie Casson
Editor/Pancha Diaz

VP, Production/Alvin Lu
VP, Publishing Licensing/Rika Inouye
VP, Sales & Product Marketing/Gonzalo Ferreyra
VP, Creative/Linda Espinosa
Publisher/Hyoe Narita

Printed in Canada

Published by VIZ Media, LLC.
P.O. Box 77010
San Francisco, CA 94107

10 9 8 7 6 5 4 3 2 1
First printing, October 2009

www.viz.com   www.shojobeat.com

**PARENTAL ADVISORY**
SKIP·BEAT! is rated T for Teen and is
recommended for ages 13 and up. This
volume contains a grudge.
ratings.viz.com

RATED **T** FOR TEEN

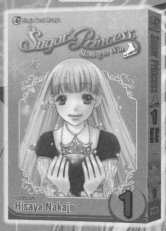
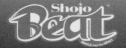

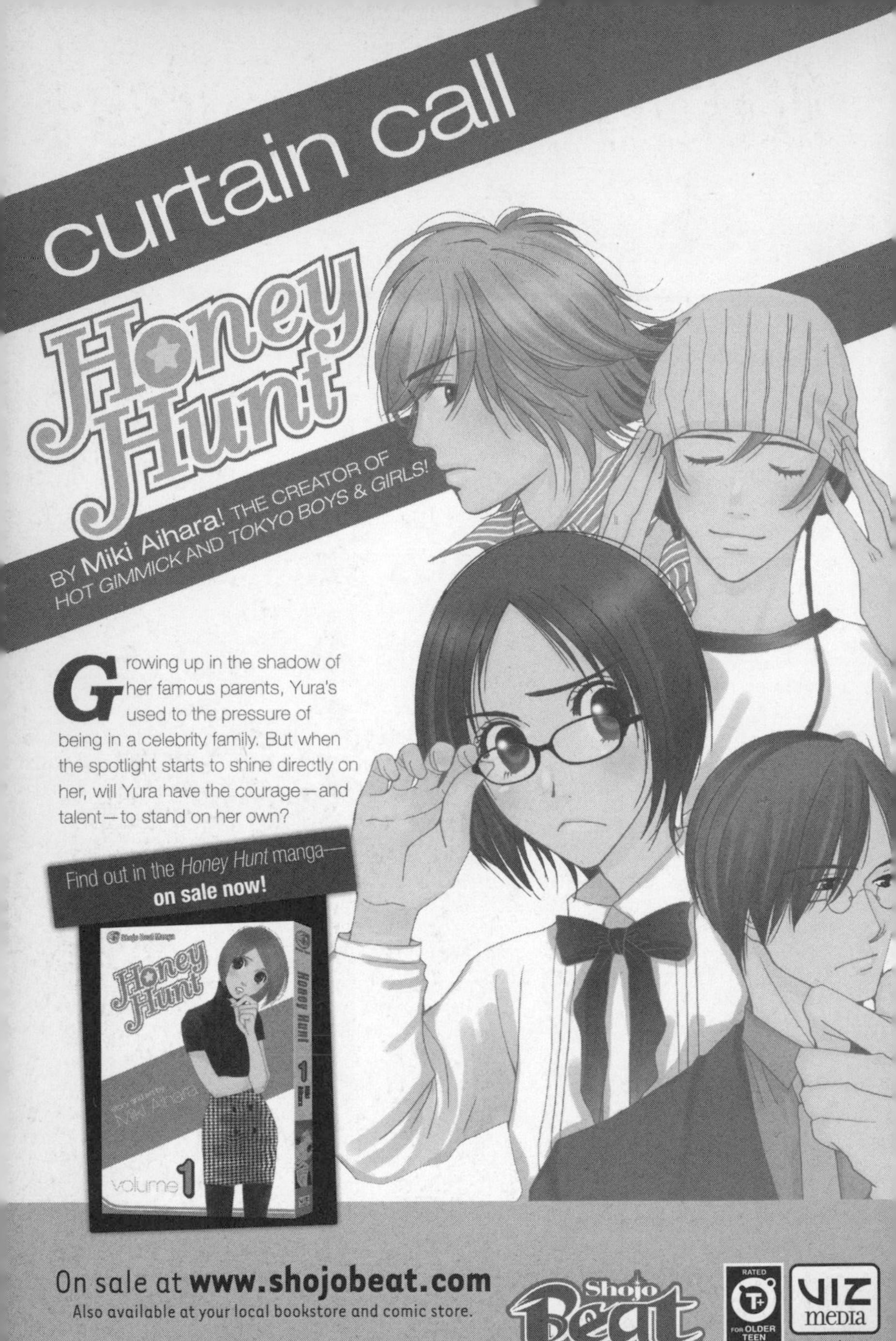

curtain call
Honey Hunt
BY Miki Aihara! THE CREATOR OF HOT GIMMICK AND TOKYO BOYS & GIRLS!
Growing up in the shadow of her famous parents, Yura's used to the pressure of being in a celebrity family. But when the spotlight starts to shine directly on her, will Yura have the courage—and talent—to stand on her own?
Find out in the *Honey Hunt* manga—
**on sale now!**
Honey Hunt
Honey Hunt
volume 1
On sale at **www.shojobeat.com**
Also available at your local bookstore and comic store.
HONEY HUNT © Miki AIHARA/Shogakukan Inc.
Shojo Beat
RATED T+ FOR OLDER TEEN
ratings.viz.com
VIZ media
www.viz.com

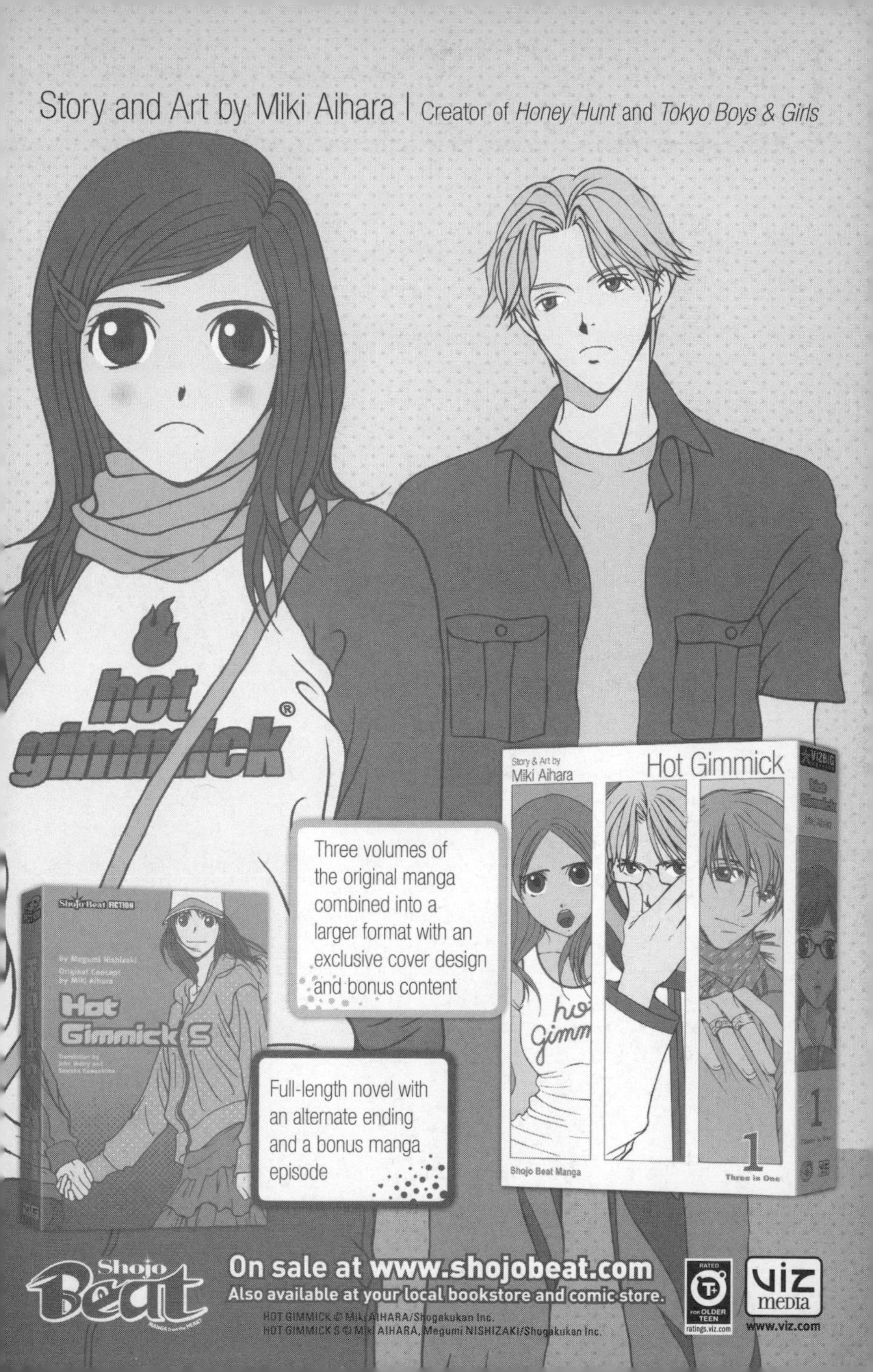
Story and Art by Miki Aihara | Creator of Honey Hunt and Tokyo Boys & Girls
hot gimmick®
Story & Art by
Miki Aihara
Hot Gimmick
1
Shojo Beat Manga
Three is One
Three volumes of the original manga combined into a larger format with an exclusive cover design and bonus content
Shojo Beat FICTION
by Megumi Nishizaki
Original Concept by Miki Aihara
Hot Gimmick S
Full-length novel with an alternate ending and a bonus manga episode
Shojo Beat
On sale at www.shojobeat.com
Also available at your local bookstore and comic store.
HOT GIMMICK © Miki AIHARA/Shogakukan Inc.
HOT GIMMICK S © Miki AIHARA, Megumi NISHIZAKI/Shogakukan Inc.
RATED T+ FOR OLDER TEEN
ratings.viz.com
VIZ MEDIA
www.viz.com

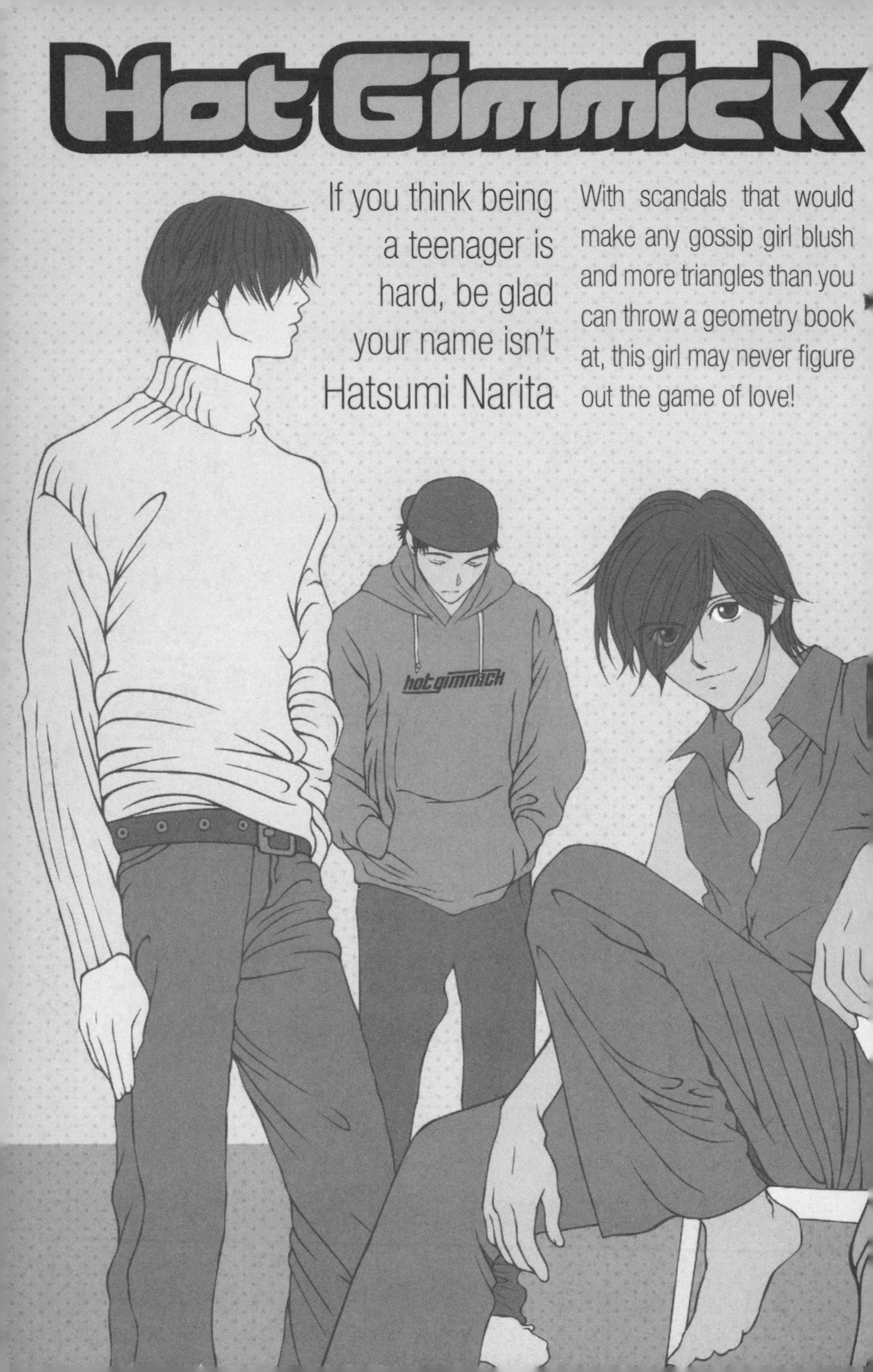
Hot Gimmick
If you think being a teenager is hard, be glad your name isn't Hatsumi Narita
With scandals that would make any gossip girl blush and more triangles than you can throw a geometry book at, this girl may never figure out the game of love!
hotgimmick

# LAND OF *Fantasy*

MIAKA YŪKI IS AN ORDINARY JUNIOR-HIGH STUDENT WHO IS SUDDENLY WHISKED AWAY INTO THE WORLD OF A BOOK, *THE UNIVERSE OF THE FOUR GODS*. WILL THE BEAUTIFUL CELESTIAL BEINGS SHE ENCOUNTERS AND THE CHANCE TO BECOME A PRIESTESS DIVERT MIAKA FROM EVER RETURNING HOME?

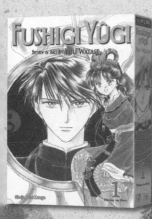

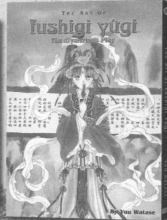

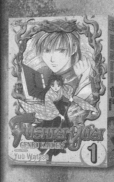

THREE VOLUMES OF THE ORIGINAL *FUSHIGI YŪGI* SERIES COMBINED INTO A LARGER FORMAT WITH AN EXCLUSIVE COVER DESIGN AND BONUS CONTENT

EXPERIENCE THE BEAUTY OF *FUSHIGI YŪGI* WITH THE HARDCOVER ART BOOK

ALSO AVAILABLE: THE *FUSHIGI YŪGI: GENBU KAIDEN* MANGA, THE EIGHT VOLUME PREQUEL TO THIS BEST-SELLING FANTASY SERIES

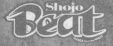

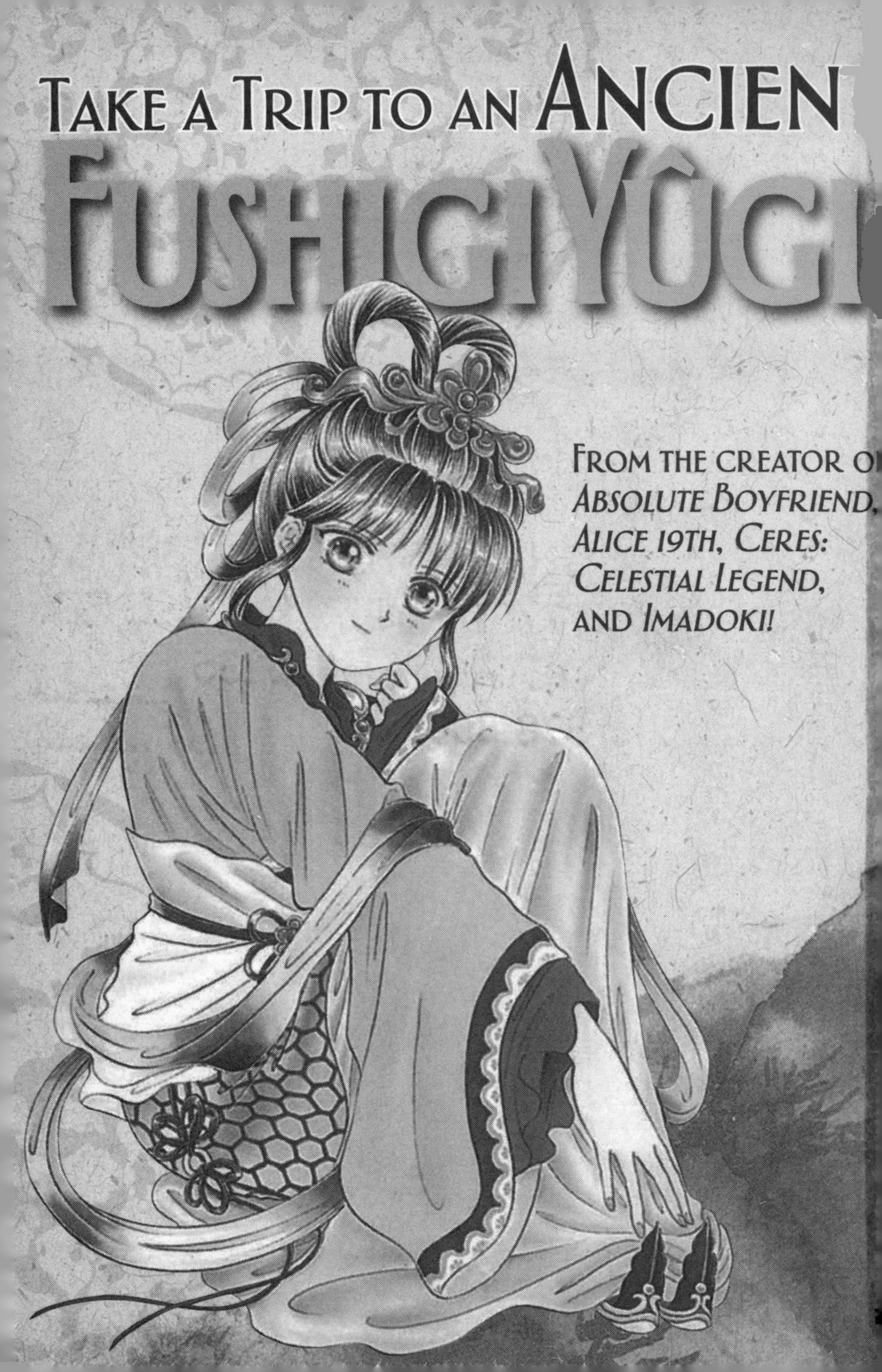
TAKE A TRIP TO AN ANCIEN
FUSHIGI YÛGI
FROM THE CREATOR O
*ABSOLUTE BOYFRIEND*, *ALICE 19TH*, *CERES: CELESTIAL LEGEND*, AND *IMADOKI*!

# Tell us wh
# about Shojo Beat Manga!

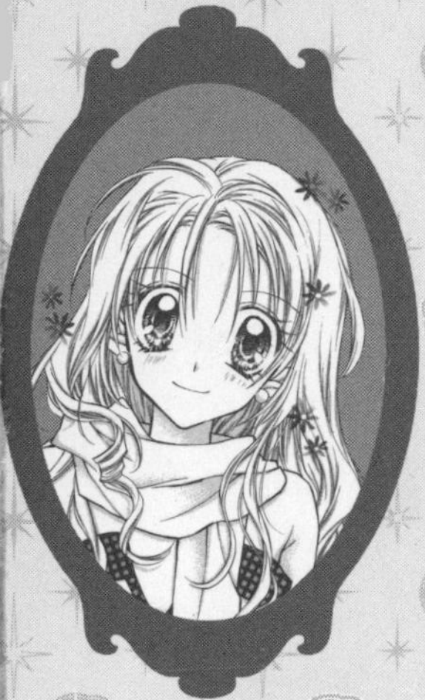

Our survey is now available online. Go to:

***shojobeat.com/mangasurvey***

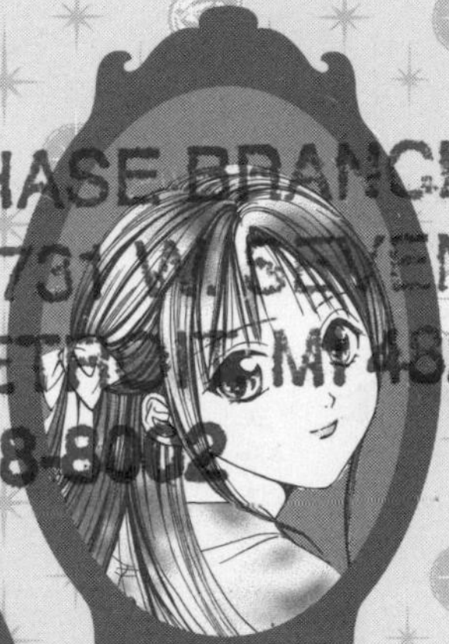



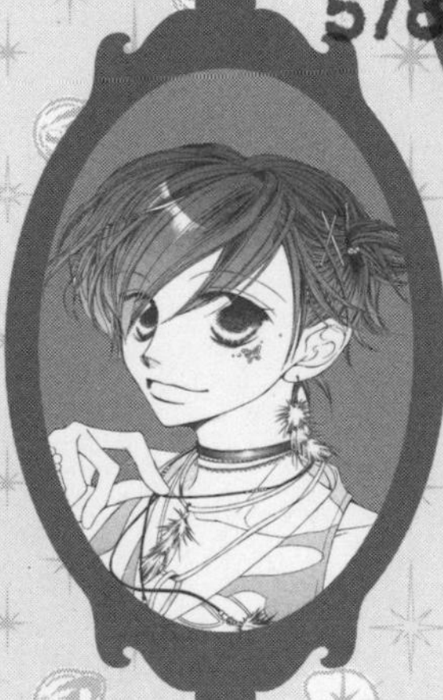

## Help us make our product offerings better!

VIZ media

Shojo Beat — THE REAL DRAMA BEGINS IN... — MANGA from the HEART